D1570458

The Presidential Election of 1896

The Presidential
Election of 1896

STANLEY L. JONES

The University of Wisconsin Press

MADISON, 1964

PUBLISHED BY THE UNIVERSITY OF WISCONSIN PRESS
430 Sterling Court, Madison 6, Wisconsin

Copyright © 1964 by the Regents of the University of Wisconsin

*Printed in the United States of America by
Vail-Ballou Press, Inc., Binghamton, New York*

Library of Congress Catalog Card Number 64-12715

For Adele

Acknowledgments

It would not have been possible to write this book without the courteous and informed cooperation of the men and women who administer the research collections in the libraries which I have visited. My greatest indebtedness is to the Newberry Library in Chicago, which, during the years the book was in preparation, provided for me a hospitable center for research and study. Also in Chicago, the research facilities of the University of Chicago, the Chicago Public Library, and the Chicago Historical Society have been extended to me with the utmost courtesy. The library of the Chicago Undergraduate Division of the University of Illinois has been helpful in providing reference services and in obtaining materials through interlibrary loan.

I list below the other libraries where I have collected materials for this book. I regret that this can be no more than a list which will not suggest the extent to which the men and women in charge of these collections, far beyond the call of duty, helped to locate the materials significant to my research. Such was the cooperation given me at the Library of Congress, Columbia University, the Connecticut State Library, the Indiana State Library, the Illinois State Historical Society, the Iowa State Department of History and Archives, the Maryland Historical Society, the Minnesota Historical Society, the New Hampshire Historical Society, the New York Public Library, the Southern Historical Collection of the University of North Carolina, Northwestern University, the Ohio Historical Society, the Historical and Philosophical Society of Ohio, the West Virginia Collection of West Virginia University, the Wisconsin Historical Society, and the University of Wisconsin. I also wish to thank the State Historical Society of Colorado for permission to quote from the Henry Moore Teller papers and the Nevada State Historical Society for permission to quote from the William M. Stewart papers.

The University of Illinois has, in many ways, helped me to move forward with the research and writing of *The Presidential Election of 1896*. An appointment as Fellow in History in the summer of 1958 and the grant of sabbatical leave during the second semester of the school year, 1959–1960, made it possible to concentrate on research and writing for long periods without the interruptions of classroom teaching. In addition, grants from the University of Illinois Research Board for travel and photo-reproduction of research materials enabled me to visit and use with maximum effect historical collections in many parts of the United States.

The encouragement and advice of my friends, Mr. and Mrs. Donald W. Riddle, have sustained me during the years the book was in progress. As it goes to press I know that they do not agree with all of this book, and they are certainly not to be held responsible for any of it. Yet they have contributed beyond measure to the making of it.

Two friends, Thomas E. Felt of the College of Wooster and H. Wayne Morgan of the University of Texas, have provided copies of manuscripts, given me leads to manuscript collections, and discussed with me ideas and interpretations regarding late-nineteenth-century politics. I am very much in their debt and am grateful for their sympathetic interest.

I find words pathetically inadequate as I try to express my gratitude to my family for their understanding and help. This book is a product of their love and labor.

S.L.J.

Chicago, Illinois
April, 1963

Contents

List of Illustrations

The Presidential Election of 1896

1

A Standard of Battle

It was 1896 and once again a presidential election was at hand. Men commenting on the approaching election, long before the calendar was turned to 1896, had predicted that it would be unusually contentious and divisive. For this was a period of great turbulence in the political life of the United States, when economic and social change— almost revolutionary in character—seemed to demand adjustment and reform at a faster pace than those who dominated the ordinary channels of government and politics were prepared to sanction. The economic depression of these years created harsh conditions in the lives of a people who already felt imposed upon by the unaccustomed demands of a centralized industrial society. In this setting violent currents of social and political criticism welled up to threaten the programs and the power of the established political organizations.

There was, certainly, abundant evidence that the two old parties, the Republican and the Democratic, were faced by a stern challenge to their leadership from the newly established People's party (more generally referred to as the Populist party), which campaigned on a platform calling for extensive economic, social, and political reform. Though their formal organization dated only from 1891, the Populists had made a strong showing in the presidential election of 1892; and it appeared likely that the heightened unrest which followed the Panic of 1893 would stimulate the party's growth. As depression continued, its leaders became optimistic over the possibilities of making a major gain, perhaps of winning, in the election of 1896.[1]

The Populists were not the only third party men who anticipated

3

that they might win advantages for themselves from the troubles experienced by the old parties. Others, such as the Socialists and the Prohibitionists, maintained a steady fire of criticism against the Republicans and Democrats in the hope that these parties would disintegrate under the attack. What reformers generally expected now was a climactic political disintegration, to be followed by reorganization, and finally the emergence of a great national reform party. The old parties would suffer. If they did not dissolve wholly, they would be seriously divided, their ranks depleted. Therefore, a third party, if it managed to establish a reputation for reform leadership, might emerge as dominant in a new party structure based on a distinct separation of conservative and reform elements.

Month after month the newspapers reported developments which reflected the instability of existing political alignments. In October 1893, for example, the St. Louis *Globe-Democrat* reported that in Iowa a life-long Democrat, who had served that party for twenty-four years in the state legislature, had left the Democratic party and had gone to the Populists. In a letter to the chairman of his county Democratic organization he had said: "We have come to a parting of the ways, a political revolution is upon us, the lines are rapidly forming...; the day for separating the sheep from the goats, or rather, from the wolves, draws nigh." [2]

In the months that followed, sentiments of this type were repeated so frequently that men in many quarters had begun to look to 1896 as the decisive year when the new political alignments which seemed to be taking shape would be sharply defined. Labor leader Eugene V. Debs, writing in his newspaper, *The Railway Times,* in September 1895, saw the Populist party as the answer: "The old parties cannot be reformed. There is an imperative demand for a new party and the People's party is that party. Let them (the workers) strip themselves of old party tags which symbolize their servility to corporation rule and uniting with their fellow workers in all the states of the union, march to the polls together and vote their way from slavery to emancipation. [3]

Early in 1896 a Nebraska Populist saw a new reform party of such scope emerging that the Populist party would make up only one part of it: "There is now forming a typical American political party, which will be composed of the farmers, laborers, and legitimate business men of the country, as opposed to the giant corporations and monopolists, and I think . . . that this party will sweep the country at the coming presidential election." [4]

Under these conditions the years from 1893 to 1896 saw a large number of individuals and groups jockeying for a position which would be advantageous to themselves when the anticipated political regrouping occurred. It was not only third party men and reformers who were affected by this excitement. The rifts in the old parties to which the third party men pointed with such glee did exist, and the old party men reacted to this situation in various ways. While some worked to close the gaps, others chipped and pried to widen them; and others, giving up their old allegiances, drifted off to the Populists or to another third party attachment.

Postmaster General William L. Wilson, a devoted Democrat from West Virginia, reflected the turmoil in his own party as he recorded in his diary a visit to Jefferson's Virginia home in the spring of 1896. Democrats gathered at Monticello on April 13 at the invitation of Jefferson Levy, owner of the estate. The meeting was sponsored by the National League of Democratic Clubs to promote party unity in the celebration of Jefferson's birthday. The Postmaster General, arriving late, found the platform occupied by Senator John A. Daniel of Virginia. Daniel was delivering a speech in which he defended heatedly the virtues of the free coinage of silver at sixteen to one, and he was receiving spirited encouragement from a highly partisan crowd. Wilson, who deplored free silver as contrary to Democratic party principles and as dangerously unsound economic doctrine, recorded his disappointment: "It seems sad indeed, that, after planning for several years this pilgrimage to the home and tomb of Jefferson, we have met there simply to show to the world how deep and, at present, irreconcilable is the division among Democrats on this issue." [5]

In this same month, Senator Henry M. Teller, a life-long Republican from Colorado, said in a speech in the Senate that if the Republican party in its convention in June adopted a platform advocating a gold monetary standard, he would leave his party. It was apparent that he was deeply moved as he concluded his speech with these words: "As I speak . . . so shall I vote, in the interest I believe of the great masses of men in this country; and in the interest, as I believe, of the great masses of men throughout Christendom." [6]

The chief characteristics of American political life in these months sometimes appeared to be sheer sound and motion. American politicians were speaking out on the issues and building organizations to promote themselves and their ideas with an intensity that was unusual, even in immediate pre-election campaigning. One of the most striking characteristics of this activity was the way in which it centered on issues rather than men. In the end no leader emerged to head up the reform agitation until, at the last hour, William Jennings Bryan came out of the Democratic convention. But long before Bryan became the leader one issue had assumed a dominant position in the agitation. That issue was the free coinage of silver at sixteen to one. It was that issue on which Postmaster General Wilson found Democrats divided at Monticello; it was that issue which was driving Senator Teller out of the Republican party; it was that issue which caused Populists to hope that they might become one of the nation's major parties in 1896. It was evident that free silver could divide men and parties; but if it could divide, it might also unite. Many men caught up in the agitation of these months came to view free silver as the essential rallying point for reformers who were breaking with old allegiances at this time of crisis.

The truth was that many Americans in these years were searching for a panacea to remove their hardships and allay their feelings of disappointment and inadequacy. If the free silver propagandists had not succeeded in making their cause the central issue in the campaign of 1896, it was likely that the Republicans would have succeeded in giving that position to the tariff issue. In retrospect the Republican argument that permanent well-being would flow from protective tariffs revealed no greater sophistication in the field of economic statesmanship than the free silver man's conviction that all would be well if the country would adopt his ideas about money.

What, in fact, did men intend when they advocated the free and unlimited coinage of silver at sixteen to one? They were proposing simply that the United States return to the bimetallic gold and silver standard of the Coinage Act of 1837 under which silver and gold were to be coined in unlimited amounts as they were brought to the United States mints. Under the Act of 1837 the coinage ratio between the two metals had been fixed at the market prices then prevailing. This ratio was 15.9884 units of silver to one of gold (or roughly 16 to 1), and the dollar of the 1837 Act contained 371.25 grains of silver or 23.22 grains of gold.

Shortly after the passage of the Act of 1837 increased production of gold caused its market value to decline in relation to silver. As a result, the official coinage ratio undervalued silver, and no silver was delivered to the government mints for coinage. This condition had persisted through the Civil War and continued into the post-war years. In 1873 Congress, in passing a new coinage law, took cognizance of the fact that silver was not being minted and included in the law no provision for the coinage of silver. Little publicity was given to this fact; and when, a short time later, increased production of silver brought prices down, making it advantageous to coin silver under the Act of 1837, silver producers expressed strong indignation when their product was turned away from the government mints with the explanation that the new coinage law made no provision for silver coinage.

The Panic of 1873 and the ensuing depression inevitably turned public attention to the nation's currency and banking structure. Soon pundits, in and out of politics, were relating the nation's depressed economy to monetary shortages growing out of the Coinage Act of 1873. Continuing controversy on this subject resulted in the development of a political doctrine which held that economic prosperity could be achieved only by the full use of silver under the terms prescribed in the Coinage Act of 1837. The Bland-Allison Act of 1878 and the Sherman Silver Purchase Act of 1890 were adopted in response to pressure from the adherents of this doctrine. The first of these authorized the Secretary of the Treasury to purchase not less than $2,000,000 and not more than $4,000,000 of silver each month. The Secretary then had the option of coining the silver or issuing silver certificates based upon it. The second Act instructed the Secretary of the Treasury to buy 4,500,000 ounces of silver every month and to issue treasury notes to cover the cost of the purchase. The silver thus acquired was to be stored. Of course, men who supported free coinage viewed these Acts as temporary expedients to be replaced as quickly as possible with free and unlimited use of silver as money under the terms of the Coinage Act of 1837. In the 1890's, then, as free silver protagonists carried on the propaganda campaign for their cause, they found little need to improvise an argument to support their position. There was already in existence a well articulated body of doctrine upon which they could draw.

The first principle accepted by those who advocated the free coinage of silver at 16 to 1 was the quantity theory of money: that the amount of money in circulation determined not only the general level of prices but also the level of activity within the economy. According to this theory prices and economic activity were at low ebb during the 1890's because the amount of money in circulation was not sufficient to sustain normal price levels and general prosperity.[7] It was argued further that, when money was in short supply, it drifted to the financial centers; and outlying regions suffered accordingly. John Peter Altgeld expressed the problem metaphorically: "Money in the business world and blood in the body perform the same functions and seem to be governed by similar laws. When the quantity of either is reduced the patient becomes weak and what blood or money is left rushes to the heart, or center, while the extremities grow cold." [8]

The quantity theory seemed to be borne out by the available statistics on monetary circulation and prices. That prices for farm products had suffered a sharp decline scarcely needed demonstration. The actual statistics of the price decline were shocking. Wheat which had sold at $1.19 a bushel in 1881 was sold at an average of 49.1 cents in 1894, while the price of corn declined from 63 cents a bushel in 1881 to 28 cents in 1890.[9] These were the prices paid at large commercial centers, not the prices paid at the farm markets. In June 1896, under the heading, "Farm Prices Ridiculous," the Chicago *Tribune* quoted prices at some of the farm markets. On the track at Onawa, Iowa, the price of number two corn was 15½ cents per bushel and of number two mixed oats was 9½ cents, while the railroad rate per hundredweight was 20 cents. At one point in South Dakota corn was selling at the railhead at 11⅛ cents per bushel and oats at 7 cents, while the rail rate per hundred pounds was 28 cents. As the *Tribune* observed, these prices for "coarse grains do not represent cost of production." [10] In the South the drop in cotton prices had been even greater than that of western grain prices. One student has concluded that "a majority of the cotton farmers in the late eighties and through most of the nineties were actually operating at a loss." [11]

Those who adopted the quantity theory of money to explain these low prices found that the statistics of per capita monetary circulation bore out their contentions. These statistics revealed that the amount of money in circulation had declined from a high of $31.18 per capita in 1865 to a low of $18.97 in 1875. Between 1875 and 1896 the amount of money in circulation remained at about $20.00 per person.[12] To the man who advocated the free coinage of silver at 16 to 1 the juxtaposition of low prices and a declining monetary circulation was more than accidental.[13]

During the 1880's a new spirit of inquiry appeared in American economic thought as younger economists challenged orthodox laissez faire analyses. These men, sometimes referring to themselves as "the new school" of economics, established the American Economic Association in 1885.[14] The records of the Association show that its members avidly discussed and debated the quantity theory as it related both to economics and politics in the 1890's. The record also shows that there was no general agreement on the subject among them. At the eighth annual meeting of the Association in December 1895, several papers were presented on the relationship of the volume of currency to prosperity and prices. On the one hand, Francis A. Walker, president of the Massachusetts Institute of Technology, and General Adoniram J. Warner, president of the American Bimetallic League, agreed that there was a direct relationship between low prices, depression, and the decreasing volume of currency in circulation and that something must be done to get silver in circulation to relieve the situation. On the other hand, Professor Frank W. Taussig, of Harvard University, stated that, "The only sound policy for the civilized countries of the West now is to adopt and maintain the gold standard." [15]

The chief argument used by economists to combat the quantity theory as an explanation for declining agricultural prices was that the fall in prices had occurred because of improvements in production techniques and reduced costs of transportation and distribution. This argument was advanced by a number of reputable economists, including David A. Wells, Edward A. Atkinson, and J. Laurence Laughlin, and was widely adopted by influential business and political leaders.[16] In April 1895, Atkinson wrote in *Forum* magazine: "Since 1860 the causes for a reduction in price of animal food are the extension of railways, the establishment of great packing-houses, the inventions in canning provisions, the application of freezing processes and cold-storage chambers, and the change from sail to steam on the ocean. In production, the rediscovery and use of ensilage and many other improvements in feeding stock of all kinds." [17] During the campaign of 1896 Atkinson wrote to the New York *Journal of Commerce:* "I affirm that there is not a single commodity which has been subject to a considerable fall in price since 1873 or 1865, of which that change or decline in price cannot be traced to specific applications of science or invention, subject to identification, either to the production or distribution of that specific article without any reference whatever to the change in the ratio of gold to silver or silver to gold." [18]

Carl Schurz, in his major speech of the 1896 campaign, stated that lower agricultural prices were due to improvements in production and transportation and that if such improvements had not been followed by lower prices then "modern civilization would, in one of its most important and beneficent functions be a flat failure." He stated further that the progressive farmers who adjusted their production to the use of the new techniques were prosperous and uncomplaining. It was, he said, the backward farmers who had become "the political farmers who wait for free silver to raise prices." [19]

Free silver publicists replied to this argument by analyzing the statistics of agricultural production to show that on a per capita basis there had been no increase in production in the United States during the latter part of the nineteenth century. One such analysis, developed by Herman Taubeneck, chairman of the Populist party between 1892 and 1896, showed that in 1880 when 9.9 bushels of wheat per person had been produced the price of wheat per bushel was ninety-five cents, while in 1895 when only 6.7 bushels of wheat per person had been produced, the price of wheat had been sixty cents. Taubeneck found the statistics on corn production and prices more convincing because, though it could be argued that the price of wheat was fixed on an international market and that therefore factors other than domestic production entered into the determination of wheat prices, the United States was the only major producer and user of corn. Corn production in 1880 had been 34.2 bushels per capita and the price forty cents per bushel, while in 1895 production had been 30.7 bushels per capita and the price per bushel twenty-six cents.[20]

Acceptance of the quantity theory was implicit in the popular free silver explanation for the demonetization of silver. The passage of the Coinage Act of 1873 was seen as an extraordinary departure from the usual process of legislation. It was, the free silver men believed, the product of a secret international conspiracy. Only a few men, including John Sherman who introduced the bill into Congress and John Jay Knox, Comptroller of the Treasury, had known that the bill demonetized silver. President Grant was seen as an innocent dupe, who for a long time after he signed the bill was ignorant of the fact that it had destroyed the coinage of silver.[21]

In recounting the details of this conspiracy the free silver men sometimes differed, but in the general outline of their story they agreed. English capitalists and Wall Street bankers (along with allied inter-

ests in Europe) were at the center of the plot. They had become aware
of the likelihood that increased production of silver would cause an
inflationary rise in prices. Since they were capitalists with large investments, they realized that a rise in prices would cheapen the value
of their investments. Therefore, they had conspired to reduce the
United States, and the rest of the world, to the single gold standard.

According to this conspiracy theory, the principal act by which the
capitalists who desired a universal single gold standard had achieved
their objective in the United States was the Coinage Act of 1873,
which the free silver men, who accepted the conspiracy story, referred
to as the "Crime of '73." The most commonly accepted story in regard
to the passage of this act centered on a shadowy figure by the name of
Ernest Seyd. It was claimed that he had come to the United States with
$500,000 in gold furnished by the Bank of England. Later, at his re-
quest, the Bank of England sent him another $500,000 to continue the
campaign to bring the United States Congress to pass a coinage act
demonetizing silver. Seyd supposedly managed to keep for his own
purposes much of the money furnished him, but in 1873 his efforts
produced the result desired when the Coinage Act passed by Congress
in that year made no provision for the coinage of silver. English bimetallist, Moreton Frewen, in a speech in 1889, said that the demonetization of silver had started in Europe but had reached its culmination in America: "Still, it is only when we pass on to the deed done
at Washington that the silver question fairly emerges as the biggest
and best planned financial coup of the century. The whole affair was
a vast 'job' and I believe that any jury would find a true bill on the
evidence that comes to us from America." [22]

Free silver men saw the Coinage Act of 1873 as essentially wrong
for reasons beyond the circumstances which appeared to them to explain its passage. They argued that the first coinage law passed by
Congress had provided for bimetallism, that it had been enacted in
the spirit of the Constitutional Convention, and that, therefore, silver
as well as gold was the "money of the Constitution" and the bimetallic
dollar "the dollar of the daddies." In addition they argued that, from
the adoption of the first coinage act in 1790 up to 1873, the United
States had been on a bimetallic standard in which silver had in fact
been the standard metal in relation to which the gold content of
the dollar had been changed whenever an adjustment was indicated.[23]

What free silver men saw as the most painfully wrong aspect of the whole affair, however, was the effect which the appreciation of gold had on the ordinary debtor. Up and down the land was heard the complaining cry of the debt-ridden farmer. He had borrowed when wheat was dear and money cheap. He now had to repay when wheat was cheap and money dear. Nebraska Congressman William Jennings Bryan, speaking in September 1893, on the floor of the Merchants' Exchange in St. Louis, said that he did not favor "making a man pay a debt with a dollar larger than the one he borrowed. That is what the monometallists want," he continued. "They loaned money, and now they want more than they loaned. If this robbery is permitted, the farmer will be ruined, and then the cities will suffer." [24] Bryan expressed an idea which found a ready response among farmers.

The situation in which the debtor farmer in the West and South found himself was bad enough in itself; but when he became persuaded that his condition was the result of a foreign conspiracy in which Wall Street had connived at the behest of English financiers, it became unbearable. It was not strange that in the gathering places of agrarian debtors, in the southern country store and in the western school house, words threatening violent and revolutionary action were commonly heard.

Those opposed to the free coinage of silver protested that since 1837 the market value of silver had declined by almost one-half and that in reality the market value between the two metals was about 32 to 1. They claimed, therefore, that the free silverites in demanding the coinage of silver at 16 to 1 were asking a privilege for their metal. If free coinage at 16 to 1 were adopted, the action of Gresham's Law would drive the dear money, gold, out of circulation; and the United States, reduced to the exclusive use of silver, would be on a cheap inflationary standard.[25] The free silver men replied that the value of silver had declined sharply only because of the Coinage Act of 1873, which had deprived silver of one of its major markets. They believed that when the United States government restored the bimetallic standard of the Coinage Act of 1837, the value of silver would rise until the market ratio of silver to gold would be approximately 16 to 1.

The men who were in total opposition to renewed coinage of silver were advocates of the monometallic gold standard, which had been established by the Coinage Act of 1873. At the beginning of the debate they won a tactical victory when newspapers and public speakers adopted the practice of referring to them as "the sound money men."

They rejected the quantity theory as it was developed by the free silver men, but then, curiously, they turned it about and used it to their own purposes. The argument which they most angrily and consistently advanced to oppose free silver pointed to the inflationary effect such a policy would have. It would, they said, raise prices. Thereby, it would cheat the creditor. Thereby, too, it would harm the worker whose wages would not rise so fast as prices. It would also be harmful to men and women living on fixed incomes. Bimetallist Francis A. Walker pointed to the inconsistency of their argument: "Apparently these gentlemen think that while an increasing money-supply raises prices, a diminishing money-supply has no necessary relation to prices." [26]

Intermediate between the advocates of gold monometallism and free silver bimetallism was a group of men who advocated international bimetallism. They believed in the restoration of bimetallism by reestablishing the use of silver; but felt that the United States could not hope to succeed alone and so should not even attempt to do this unilaterally. It could be done only if the major powers of the world acted in concert to reestablish silver, and they could do this only by the simultaneous restoration of the silver standard through international agreement.

During the last two decades of the century the United States participated officially in several international bimetallic conferences. Advocates of the free coinage of silver had not opposed the intentions of these conferences and had watched their proceedings in eager anticipation that they would lead to the reestablishment of silver as a standard currency, but as each conference ended in failure they had become disillusioned about the prospects of a successful international action in favor of silver.

Most exponents of international bimetallism believed that free coinage of silver unilaterally by the United States was impossible, but free silver men reached the conclusion that the adoption of free coinage of silver at 16 to 1 by the United States alone was the only lever that would pry the rest of the world to acceptance of silver as a standard metal. They believed that the United States had sufficient financial stability to adopt free coinage without suffering harmful effects and, further, that the international financial power of the United States would bring the other nations of the world to the use of silver once we had restored it domestically.[27]

As free silver men watched the failure of successive attempts to establish bimetallism by international agreement, they concluded that England, her policy dictated by overseas investors, would never voluntarily consent to the restoration of silver. They saw England playing the same game in her empire that she played in the United States. The miseries of the Irish farmer were blamed upon England's gold policy, which, since it caused the appreciation of the value of gold, made the rentals paid by Irish tenants increasingly burdensome.[28] In 1893 India abandoned the coinage of silver. This destroyed an important market for American silver, but it was also viewed as a blow by those who did not have an interest in silver mines. Richard P. Bland of Missouri saw the action in India as a conspiracy between English and American bankers to "bulldoze" the Congress of the United States into a policy which would perpetuate the gold standard.[29]

One of the major contentions of the free silver people was that maintenance of the gold standard gave a special advantage in United States markets to cheaply produced products of the Orient. Japan, it was argued, had been driven to manufacture for itself because goods produced in the United States had become too expensive. On the other hand, goods produced in China and Japan could be sold cheaply in American markets, not only because wages were low in those countries, but also because United States gold dollars were so highly valued in silver standard countries.[30] Senator Teller explained, for example, that Chinese wool was about to drive American wool off the market because wool produced in China at a cost of nine cents in Chinese silver currency could be purchased for five cents in American gold currency. Imported at the deflated price in gold currency wool from China gave stiff competition to the American product.[31] Frequently quoted by silverites was a statement by Moreton Frewen to the effect "that the yellow man using the white metal, holds at his mercy the white man using the yellow money." [32]

Frewen also believed that cheapening silver automatically cheapened wheat. He argued that the price of an ounce of silver and the price of a bushel of wheat on the London market remained approximately the same. Thus, the price of wheat at any other market in the world would be the price of an ounce of silver less the cost of delivery to London.[33] If Frewen's analysis was sound (and free silver men in the United States accepted it as such), then clearly the only way to raise the price of wheat was to raise the price of silver by restoring its use as money.

Free coinage of silver was not the only proposal for increasing the monetary supply advanced at this time. The treasury notes known as Greenbacks had several years earlier been placed on a gold redemption basis, but the advocates of monetary inflation had opposed the gold redemption policy and had demanded that the government issue un-redeemable Greenbacks in sufficient quantities to restore prices and good times.

Briefly in the 1870's and 80's a Greenback-Labor party had existed. Though not agrarian in origin, it was largely a farmer's party; and it achieved its greatest political success in farm regions.[34] The Green-back elements in the West and South figured prominently in the development of the state and regional Farmers' Alliances and the Populist party. Greenback monetary ideas had an important position in the Populist platform; and in 1892 the Populist candidate for President was James B. Weaver, who in 1880 had been the presidential candidate of the Greenback-Labor party.

Actually the Populists failed to develop a consistent and co-ordinated monetary program. On this question they never advanced substantially beyond the platform of 1892 in which they declared themselves sympathetic to the free coinage of silver, to Greenbacks, and also to a monetary panacea which had developed within the Alliance movement, the sub-treasury scheme. Under this scheme it was proposed that the United States government establish depositories, or sub-treasuries, in the States. These sub-treasuries would lend money to the people at a rate of interest not higher than 2 per cent per year on non-perishable farm products (e.g., grain, tobacco, wool, and sugar) and on real estate.

Another major proposal for increasing the amount of money in circulation was to increase the use of currency issued by banks. There were several ideas about how this might be done. There was some hope that the basis for issuing national bank notes might be broadened, so as to increase the circulation of this type of money. More popular, however, was the idea that the 10 per cent tax on state bank notes imposed during the Civil War be repealed as an encouragement to state governments to set up banking systems which would provide for a nationally circulating state bank currency. This had been a policy associated with the Whig party before the Civil War, and it was a curious perversity of history that the major proponents of this policy in the 1890's should have been conservative Democrats of the East, who judged that such a currency might be attractive to those southern Democrats who found the free silver, Greenback, and sub-treasury proposals so appealing. The Democratic platform of 1892 had contained a plank promising the repeal of the law which imposed a 10 per cent tax on state bank notes, and it was anticipated that the Cleveland administration would move in that direction.

There was no evidence that the radical agrarians West or South ever found merit in the various proposals for increased bank currency. Basic to all of their thinking was the traditional Jeffersonian-Jacksonian hostility to banks and to government use of banks in any way, and most particularly as banks of issue. It became evident as the monetary debate developed that the concepts of the pre-Civil War ideological battle over money and currency were still a major force in shaping the economic thought of the American people. Free silver emerged as the most favored monetary panacea in the West and South because it could be related to Jacksonian hard money principles more readily than Greenbacks or sub-treasury notes. This was true not only because free silver could be related to the hard money arguments of Jackson, but also because the putative authors of the "Crime of '73" corresponded so closely to the evil-doers whom Jackson had supposedly thwarted.[35]

None of the men who advocated free coinage of silver as a return to the policies of Jefferson and Jackson appeared to see that the earlier bank and monetary policies had been deflationary, while the free silver proposals were intentionally inflationary. Changing times and the need to face up to new problems had resulted, not in the development of basically new ideas, but in an attempt to apply old formulas to serve new demands and new motives.

Since Jackson's time, however, a major transformation had occurred in the class structure of the nation. Now the urban laborer was a much larger part of the population, and the backgrounds and traditions of the urban laborers of the 1890's were quite different from what they had been in the 1830's. Jackson's urban laborers were mostly American-born and thoroughly familiar with Anglo-American political traditions. Among the urban laborers of the 1890's there was a very large percentage of foreign-born, who had little or no knowledge of American political ideologies. The presence of this new class posed many important questions in American politics. How would the urban laborer react to the free silver controversy? Would he discover anything meaningful in the proposals of the free silver men?

Even more important, of course, was the reaction of the urban laborer to American politics in general. It was clear that Americans traditionally were political men, who turned to government to solve all kinds of problems, including problems involving personal morals and private economics. The American farmer had proved himself to be thoroughly devoted to this tradition. Would the urban laborer act within that tradition and turn to political action to solve his problems or would he try to find his solutions elsewhere?

2

Rallying Around the Silver Standard

The money question traditionally had a prominent place in American politics. Before the Civil War the major parties had taken well defined positions on the question. In the years after the war, money had remained as an issue in politics; but the Republican and Democratic parties had avoided, as far as possible, a clear definition of their attitudes toward it. Those who held definite points of view about the monetary question found little that was satisfying in the platforms of either of the major parties.

Equally unsatisfactory from the standpoint of those who held extreme views on money was the action which the established parties had accomplished in the field of legislation. Gold monometallists were satisfied, of course, with the Coinage Act of 1873; but they viewed with dismay the concessions which Congress had made to silver coinage in the Bland-Allison Act and the Sherman Silver Purchase Act. On the other side, free silver men saw the Act of 1873 as a "crime" and described the concessions of the Bland-Allison and Sherman Acts as completely inadequate to meet their demand that silver be treated as an equal with gold.

As the debate over the money question gathered momentum in the Nineties, the powerful eastern and middle western leaders of both parties tried desperately to avoid taking a clear stand for a single gold standard or for free silver. Each party contained members representing all shades of opinion on this question and customarily party compromises had been arranged satisfactory to the great majority. Such compromises were achieved in 1892, but against a background of protest in both Republican and Democratic ranks.

Very shortly it became evident, too, that the money question had reached a position in the Congress which militated against compromise. Legislators dedicated to the free coinage of silver, often holding a balance of power in the Senate, seemed determined to permit the passage of no legislation on any subject until Congress bowed to their demands on the money issue. In the chaotic legislative situation that resulted, only Grover Cleveland was able to achieve a victory in the repeal of the Sherman Silver Purchase Act, but he won this victory at the expense of positive accomplishment in other fields of legislation.

To men looking for a party organization to take up the campaign for free silver it did not seem likely that either the Republican or Democratic party could ever be brought beyond compromise to an outright declaration for free coinage of the white metal. Yet, there was always the tantalizing possibility that one of the parties could be converted to free coinage. During the 1890's such action by the Republicans appeared less and less likely, but large numbers of Democrats in the West and South became converted to free silver and loudly voiced their support for it. Nevertheless, eastern conservatives who followed the lead of Cleveland on the money question had traditionally dominated the party, and free silver sceptics believed it likely they would continue to do so.

Free silver men looking to the Populist party for political action to win silver coinage found a situation little more to their satisfaction than that existing in the major parties. There was no hesitancy on the part of the Populists to accept the free coinage of silver as a part of their platform. The difficulty was in bringing them to the "one idea" that silver was *the* solution. There were powerful factions among the Populists dedicated to the Greenback and the sub-treasury panaceas. Many of them believed that free coinage of silver was much too conservative an action, which would fall short of producing the additional quantities of currency needed in the economy.

Actually an independent silver organization came into existence before the Populist party was established. Though, in the American tradition, it was dedicated to political action, through most of its history it acted as a pressure group rather than as an organized party. This organization, which was named the American Bimetallic League, was established in a meeting held in St. Louis in November 1889. This meeting came about as the result of suggestions published by the mining editor of the St. Louis *Post Dispatch*, who was supported by the members of the St. Louis Mining Exchange and the silver miners of the Rocky Mountain states and territories.

When the formal call for the meeting was issued in July 1889, it was intended to bring together representatives of the silver mining industry for the purpose of shaping a coordinated policy to present to the Congress which was to convene in December.[1] By the time the conference met in November a significant change in strategy had occurred. No longer was it merely a conference of silver miners. Now it had become a general conference of all men who believed that the monetary use of silver must be increased. Delegations came to the conference from nearly every state in the Union, many of them officially appointed by the governors of their states. As the conference organized formally, as the speeches were delivered, and as the conference leaders gave interviews to the press, it became evident that the purpose now was to link the silver miners of the West with the farmers of the South, Great Plains, and Middle West in a national movement to win the free coinage of silver at 16 to 1.[2]

In line with this policy, leadership in the convention and in the national silver organization which developed from it was given to delegates from the southern and middle western states. Richard P. Bland of Missouri was made chairman of the resolutions committee, and General Adoniram J. Warner of Ohio became permanent chairman of the convention. When it was decided to set up a permanent national silver committee, General Warner was appointed to be its chairman. He thereby assumed a position which became of great strategic importance in the free silver movement, a position which he was to retain through the years into the 1896 campaign.[3]

The attention of the conference was directed first to the action to be taken on silver coinage in the approaching session of Congress. St. Louis had been chosen as a meeting place because many Congressmen coming from the West would go through St. Louis en route to Washington. Others from the South and Middle West could, without great inconvenience, arrange to attend the conference. Many did so. The resolutions adopted by the conference emphasized the desirability of congressional action to effect free coinage at 16 to 1; but until that was done, Congress should require the Secretary of the Treasury to coin every month the maximum amount of silver provided for by the Bland-Allison Act.[4]

The executive committee authorized by the convention and appointed by Warner contained several Congressmen and Senators from the West and South. Shortly after Christmas a meeting of the executive committee was held in Washington, where Warner had set up a silver lobby.[5] Thus was created in 1890 a silver committee or lobby, which, by coordinating the actions of representatives from the western mining states and from the agrarian regions of the South and West, without regard to party, was a major factor in exerting the political pressure which brought about the passage of the Sherman Silver Purchase Act.

These first steps in the direction of the organization of free silver sentiment set a pattern which persisted until the adoption of the Democratic platform at Chicago in 1896 brought the silver movement within one of the major parties. First emphasis was always on the development of political pressure on the Congress to bring about remedial silver legislation. This meant that those connected with the independent silver organization concentrated their efforts on influencing the judgments and actions of men who were already affiliated with established parties. Within the movement there was always some speculation as to the possibility or desirability of establishing a silver party as an independent force in politics; few people in the silver movement, however, valued such talk of independent political action for any other than the effect it would have upon already established parties.

Between 1889 and 1893 there was an increasingly active discussion of the silver question. In the Rocky Mountain and Great Plains states particularly, state and regional conferences on the silver issue were convened. The National Executive Silver Committee headed by General Warner remained in existence and was active.[6] It was not, however, until February 1893, that Warner and his committee issued a call for "the first annual meeting" of the American Bimetallic League.

When the American Bimetallic League convened at Washington, D.C., on February 22, 1893, the country was on the eve of the transition from the Harrison to the Cleveland administration. The Democratic capture of the presidential office was, however, not the only development of interest to independent silver men in the election of 1892. In that election the Populist party had emerged as a force in national politics. The Populist party from the first had backed the free coinage of silver at 16 to 1; and as the delegates to the American Bimetallic Convention gathered in Washington, members of the Populist party were very much in evidence in the convention hall. Among them were James B. Weaver of Iowa and General James G. Field of Virginia, respectively the presidential and vice-presidential candidates of the Populist party in 1892. Present also were Mary Elizabeth Lease, Populist orator from Kansas; H. L. Loucks, president of the Farmers' Alliance; Lafe Pence of Colorado; Benjamin O. Flower, editor of the Boston *Arena;* and many other Populists from all sections of the country, but particularly from the party's strongholds in the agrarian South and West.[7]

Of course, the usual strong contingent of representatives from the silver mining states was at the convention; but even more than in 1889 they were content to remain comparatively inconspicuous, while General Warner took charge of the general meetings and Weaver acted as chairman of the resolutions committee. More in evidence than in 1889, too, were prominent Democrats from the South; and when a new executive committee was constituted, it included (with General Warner continuing as chairman) United States Senators John W. Daniel of Virginia and Alfred H. Colquitt of Georgia.[8]

It was evident then that there was still strong emphasis in 1893 as in 1889 on uniting mining interests with western and southern agrarians; but it was also evident that new developments seemed to demand shifts in emphasis and strategy. Not only had the Populist party emerged as a new political factor, not only were southern and western Democrats showing strong interest in the free coinage of silver, but reformers outside of politics were also showing sympathetic interest in the silver movement. In addition the nation's labor organizations were being urged to enter more actively into political reform activity and were showing some interest in the silver question. It was therefore fitting that, as the conference prepared to adjourn after adopting resolutions calling for the free coinage of silver at 16 to 1, a delegate from Kansas, speaking from the floor, presented a resolution which the conference adopted. It provided for the appointment of a committee of five to draw up and and circulate an invitation to every labor and industrial organization in the United States, and possibly throughout the "civilized World," to send delegates to future meetings of the American Bimetallic League.[9]

When, midway in 1893, Grover Cleveland called a special session of Congress with the object of having the Sherman Silver Purchase Act repealed, the machinery of the American Bimetallic League began immediately to function. It was announced that the League was setting up headquarters, in charge of General Warner and Congressman-elect Francis G. Newlands of Nevada, at the national capitol. The first announcements issued by this headquarters indicated that the League was looking beyond the legislative session to the fall elections. It announced that it planned to send free silver literature and to assign speakers to states that were holding elections. The announcement stated that, since the middle and eastern states were hopelessly opposed to free silver, the League would concentrate its activities in the South and West.[10]

A few days after the headquarters office was established in Washington, General Warner called the American Bimetallic League into convention at Chicago on August 1. In his message announcing the Chicago convention, General Warner called attention to the fact that the special session of Congress summoned by President Cleveland to repeal the Sherman Act was scheduled to meet on August 7. He said that it was the intention of the Bimetallic League to stir public opinion through the meeting at Chicago and at the same time to reshape the organization's executive committee so as to enhance its effectiveness for the forthcoming struggle in Washington.[11]

From the standpoint of attendance, enthusiasm, and organization, the meeting in Chicago, which extended over three days, was an exceptional success. Nearly every state in the Union was represented. There were delegations from the eastern states; the western states, like Colorado, and the prairie states, like Kansas and Iowa, sent delegations numbering as many as two hundred individuals. The South sent large, determined delegations. There were farmers, laboring men, business men, and miners. There were Democrats, Republicans, Populists, Prohibitionists, Socialists, and reformers of all persuasions. A special delegation of labor union representatives was sent from Colorado, and an evening meeting for Chicago laboring men was organized on the shores of Lake Michigan. Terence V. Powderly of the Knights of Labor was made an honorary vice president of the convention. The American Federation of Labor sent representatives. Financiers and business men who favored free coinage of silver were conspicuous in the delegation from New York.[12]

The central figure in making the local arrangements for the Chicago meeting was William H. Harvey. Though not yet a well known personage in the organized silver movement, Harvey, who had recently moved to Chicago, had quickly captured the attention of the local press. The *Tribune,* which spoke of him as a "side-partner" of Senator William M. Stewart of Nevada, said that he had come to Chicago from the West to engage in educational work to promote the cause of silver. The *Tribune* quoted him as saying: "I look for some man like old Abe Lincoln to turn up or be the result of the new conditions now forming. The country is now staggering along like a man depleted of half his blood, and will continue to do so until silver is added to our metallic money as it existed prior to 1873." [13] Harvey believed that the free silver cause had the relevance to his own time which the slavery issue appeared to many to bear to the Civil War. In a few months he would publish his little book, *Coin's Financial School,* which would become the *Uncle Tom's Cabin* of free silver.[14]

"Coin" Harvey, with his colorful idiosyncrasies and fixed idea, was not an exceptional figure among the delegates in Chicago. Most of the country's outspoken reformers and their political allies were there. Like Harvey, many of these men were committed to one idea; but, unlike him, they were not necessarily convinced that the free coinage of silver was the essential solution. Most of them had established their reputations through their speeches. Most of them had several speeches on their favorite idea committed to memory. Nearly every one of them somehow maneuvered himself upon the convention's stage. Hotel lobbies reverberated with the voices of men and women in heated and earnest discussion. One newspaper reporter found shifting crowds of two to three hundred gathered around the debaters in the Palmer House lobby: "The Greenbacker took an inning and then the railroad reformer came to the front. The Populist free silverite was on deck most of the time." [15]

In the convention hall it was difficult for the leaders to carry out their intention of concentrating on the silver question. In the first session one of the leading free silver organizers, Thomas M. Patterson of Colorado, touched one of the exposed nerves of many at the convention when he introduced a resolution providing that the committee on resolutions be composed of one man from each political party in each state delegation. At once the convention was thrown into confusion as voices shouted, "We want no party lines!" This set off a debate in which Patterson explained that his intention had been to remove all appearances of partisanship. Others protested that what they wanted was a completely new silver party which would ignore other parties. To this the Populists replied that, if it was a silver party which was wanted, it already existed in their own organization.[16]

In the end the Chicago meeting represented a victory for silver. The largest delegation at the convention came from Colorado, and the most influential men guiding the convention behind the scenes were the men from Colorado and the other silver mining states. For the first time in the organized silver movement, western Republican leaders such as Henry M. Teller, Senator from Colorado, were at the convention. Though the resolutions committee was headed by Ignatius Donnelly, the author of the comprehensive reform program of the Populist platform of 1892, the resolutions which he presented at Chicago concentrated upon free silver. There was bitter opposition from Greenbackers, led by Populists from Kansas; but their objections were voted down.[17]

In the formal organization great care was taken to keep agrarian southerners and westerners to the front. Allen W. Thurman, Jr., able son of a distinguished Ohio Democratic leader, was elected as permanent chairman of the convention. When the convention appointed a committee to proceed to Washington to act as a silver lobby during the impending session of Congress, General Warner was appointed as its chairman while George F. Washburn, Boston Populist, was made secretary; and Herman Taubeneck, chairman of the Populist party, was made a member. Ignatius Donnelly and the Alabama Populist, Reuben F. Kolb, were made members of a sub-committee on propaganda; and the permanent committees appointed to carry on the work of the American Bimetallic League were staffed almost exclusively with men associated with the independent silver movement and the Populist party.[18]

The western silver interests, having established a closer link with agrarian and labor leaders of the West and South through the American Bimetallic League, attempted through another organization, the Pan-American Bimetallic League, to draw the business men of these sections into the free silver movement. Originally this organization drew its membership only from the mountain and Pacific Coast states and was almost entirely a miners' organization. President of the group was Colonel A. C. Fiske of Colorado, who was also on the executive committee of the American Bimetallic League. Fiske called a convention of the Pan-American Bimetallic League to meet in St. Louis early in October 1893.

At the opening of the convention Fiske and the secretary of the Pan-American League tried to set the tone of its sessions by stating that the convention was not a free silver affair but a commercial congress intended to draw together the business men of the West and South against the East. St. Louis, they said, would become a great commercial city linking these two regions in their mutual business interests.[19] As it turned out, few if any business men attended the convention.

The political leaders inevitably filled the vacuum left by the failure of business men to respond to Fiske's invitation; and the meeting became frankly a free silver and a political gathering, the most significant and avowedly political gathering which the free silver movement had yet produced. The conference was more successful in drawing southern delegates than earlier silver meetings had been. Among the southern delegates was Governor "Pitchfork Ben" Tillman of South Carolina, who was elected to serve as temporary chairman of the convention and as chairman of the committee on resolutions. A large crowd of western Populists, including Governor Waite of Colorado, Lewelling and Lease of Kansas, and Weaver of Iowa, was on hand.[20]

The politicians did prove eager to discuss one of the themes on Colonel Fiske's agenda, for they agreed with him that the times demanded an alliance between the South and West against the East. Mary Elizabeth Lease coined an expression to the effect that the western-southern alliance which was now emerging would turn the Mason-Dixon line on its axis at right angles to its former position.[21] Tillman bluntly forecast such an alliance in his keynote address: "We of the South have been crushed between the mill-stones of sectionalism, and have felt the steel of Northern hate, and the West, in its mean, contemptible, cowardly adhesion to the Northeast is getting some of the same experience." [22] Before the convention adjourned many of the delegates had seriously proposed a new political organization based on a sectional alliance of the West and South and achieved through their common desire to establish the free coinage of silver.[23]

The Pan-American Bimetallic League, in its name and in the discussions at St. Louis, revealed another approach to the money question and to sectionalism. On one hand, Colonel Fiske hoped that Latin America could be drawn into the commercial relationship which was expected to develop between the West and South; and Colorado's Governor Waite, looking at another aspect of the situation, passionately favored monetary action by the states which would cement such a commercial relationship. He advocated that the states make the silver coins of certain Latin American nations legal tender within their jurisdiction.[24] More specifically, he proposed that Colorado ship silver to Mexico, where it would be minted into Mexican coins and then returned to Colorado for circulation. In an article published in January 1894, he recommended that each state "enact that the silver dollars of the United States and of our sister Republics in North and South America, containing not less than 371¼ grains fine silver, shall be legal tender by tale, or at 100 cents each for all debts, public and private, collectable within that State." [25]

The resolutions committee refused to report Waite's proposal for circulating Latin American coins. When its report was submitted to the delegates for discussion and action, Waite presented from the floor a resolution recommending that the state legislatures act to make foreign silver legal tender. However, another proposal, which the resolutions committee had also rejected, acted as a counter to Waite's program. This was a recommendation that the United States issue legal tender currency based on land values. After a brief but violent discussion both these proposals were withdrawn, and the convention adopted a straight-out recommendation for free silver.[26]

By now the basic elements in the free silver agitation had become clearly visible. Only two groups were persuaded that the free coinage of silver would be of sufficient service to their interests to justify enthusiastic and sustained devotion: the silver miners of the West and the farmers of the West and South. These men were originally attached to various political organizations and derived predominantly from no political party. Their recent experience with depression had loosened them from their attachments to established political organizations. Already many of them had left the Democratic or Republican parties for the Populists, but this new attachment was not necessarily permanent. Their conversion was not to Populism as much as it was to free silver; and they were committed to whatever maneuvers, political or otherwise, were essential to the achievement of their objective.

In 1893 few people outside the silver movement saw the free coinage of silver as an independent political force. Republicans, Democrats, and Populists who attended the silver conventions usually saw free silver as only one part of a complex of reforms. However, some of the silver people viewed the conventions which were held that year in St. Louis as merely the prelude to a series of similar meetings "which will act as the escape valves to an agitation, counted upon to result in the formation throughout the West and South of a new political organization—partly Democratic, partly Populist—but above and before anything else a free silver party." [27]

As a result of effective organization and the success of its educational activities, the American Bimetallic League acquired a dominating position in free silver politics. The established parties, with their traditions of standing on a comprehensive platform containing many issues, undoubtedly would have considered putting some concession to silver in their platforms but would, in ordinary circumstances, have been unwilling to emphasize the silver question to such a degree as to dwarf other issues. The persistent activity of the American Bimetallic League created a situation in which the silver issue was always before the public and the politicians. When, for example, Congress finally acceded to Cleveland's wishes and repealed the Sherman Silver Purchase Act, it was announced that the American Bimetallic League would carry the fight for the free coinage of silver into the next presidential election, if, before then, Congress had not passed and the President signed a free coinage act.[28] In July 1894, General Warner, the president of the League, stated that the best men of both the Republican and Democratic parties were becoming convinced of the significance of the silver issue. That issue alone, he said, would determine the result of the next presidential election.[29]

Warner's mid-summer claims that the silver issue had taken command of the minds of many men in the regular parties seemed amply justified by the developments of the autumn congressional campaign. The American Bimetallic League entered the campaign early by holding a conference on campaign strategy in Washington on August 16 and 17. In 1893 Populists had been the most conspicuous figures at the League's conferences. Now it was Republican and Democratic leaders upon whom attention centered. Papers were read by Republican Senator John P. Jones of Nevada and by two Democratic silver congressmen, William Jennings Bryan and Richard P. Bland.

In a special, printed report of the conference, signed by the president and the secretary of the American Bimetallic League, it was stated that enough time had elapsed since the repeal of the Sherman Act to show that the repeal action was no solution to the depression.

The passage of the Wilson-Gorman Tariff had removed the tariff issue from politics. Therefore, the way had been cleared to make the monetary issue paramount in both 1894 and 1896. The report recommended to the voters that they send no representatives to Congress who would not guarantee to make "party considerations subsidiary to the cause of bimetallism, vote for no candidate for President who is not pledged to sign a free silver bill, and send none but free silver men as delegates to national conventions." Regional silver conferences in the mining and agricultural states were recommended to draw up plans which would bind those sections to these objectives.[30] A month later General Warner was writing privately: "It is the determination of silver men to force the silver question to the front as the paramount issue, and if neither of the principal parties will take this question up and in good faith to restore the bimetallic standard, then a new party must be formed to do this work." [31]

The elections of 1894 produced no clear-cut free silver victories; but, by enhancing the feeling of instability in the established parties, they served the free silver cause well. In all sections of the country the Democratic party was badly shaken. This was true even in the South, where the Populists, allied with Republicans, greatly increased their strength. In North Carolina such an alliance gave the Populists control of the state administration and made possible the election of a Populist and a Republican to the United States Senate. In the West and Middle West Democrats were beaten under circumstances that led them to believe that, if they had campaigned on a distinct and uncompromising party stand for free silver, they would have won.

The Populist party increased its national vote and registered decisive advances in the South and Middle West; but in the old strongholds in the mountain and prairie states of the West, where it had marked up its more striking gains in earlier elections, it suffered defeat. The returns made it evident that western Populists had not established themselves in their section as an independent party capable of winning elections without cooperation from the Democrats. The silver issue was now flaunted before the Populists as the one issue upon which they could rally a majority and, in the agrarian West and South, displace the Democratic party.

The Republican party won strong victories in the East and Middle West, but the deterioration of party strength in the Rocky Mountain and Great Plains states, signalled in the 1892 elections, was still in evidence. This development, which found Republicans in the area east of the Mississippi winning an election on issues that meant defeat to Republicans west of that river, foreshadowed serious difficulties within the party.

Though the 1894 election campaign and its results assured continued interest among the politicians of the regular parties in the silver issue, the propagandists and organizers for free silver did not pause in their campaign to bring that issue to the fore. Two weeks after the election General Warner issued a call to the members of the American Bimetallic League and all "friends of bimetallism" to meet in conference at St. Louis beginning November 27.[32] This conference was to be held at the same time that a Trans-Mississippi Commercial Congress was meeting in St. Louis, and it was hoped that delegates to the Trans-Mississippi Congress would attend the silver meetings. It was also hoped that congressmen en route to Washington from points South and West would find it convenient to attend both these meetings.[33] As it turned out, this arrangement was very convenient for at least one congressman, William Jennings Bryan, who was a conspicuous figure in both conventions.

This was the sixth annual convention of the Trans-Mississippi Commercial Congress, which had long since proved itself to be a staunchly sectional but not necessarily a free silver organization. It was a purely western organization devoted to promoting the growth and prosperity of western agriculture and commerce. Scheduled for discussion at St. Louis were such topics as irrigation, the Indian and the public lands, a proposal for a bounty by the United States government on agricultural exports, and, inevitably, the remonetization of silver. There was opposition to the free coinage of silver in the Congress, but the die was cast when William Jennings Bryan was made chairman of the resolutions committee. The resolutions adopted by the Congress and the public reports of its discussions concentrated on the silver issue.[34]

Meanwhile a great deal of mystery surrounded the meetings of the American Bimetallic League. The meetings were closed to newspaper men; but the reporters disclosed that, as they hung about the doorway of the room in which the sessions were being held, they overheard all established parties, including the Populist, being "cussed." Rumors were soon circulating that the conference was getting set to issue a call for a new, independent silver party. These rumors persisted after the conference adjourned, even though the resolutions which General

Warner slipped to the reporters mentioned nothing of a new political organization but spoke only of the need for the supporters of free silver to subordinate everything to the cause of the white metal. The resolutions did promise more effective non-partisan organization at the grass-roots level by providing for the appointment of a committee of five to take charge of the formation of silver leagues in every city and town in the United States.[35]

It was clear that Warner and the others in the American Bimetallic League were investigating the possibility of organizing an independent silver party. The organization of such a party appeared as a serious threat to many western Populists, particularly those who concluded that the election returns of 1894 revealed that the Populist party must turn to free silver to win future elections. In late December 1894, in response to a call from the party chairman, leaders of the Populist party held a policy meeting in St. Louis. After a spirited discussion a majority of the conferees rejected a resolution calling for abandonment of the broad program of the Omaha platform of 1892. The movers of the defeated resolution had proposed that the party concentrate on the single issue of free silver. This action did not end the debate within the Populist party. General Weaver and other western leaders continued to work to bring the party to a concentration on the silver issue, and the rapidly growing public interest in free silver worked in their favor.

The silver organizers of the American Bimetallic League did not wait for the policy fight within the Populist party to be resolved, but at an unpublicized conference in Washington, between February 22 and March 5, 1895, decided to launch a new independent silver party. In the address which the League published announcing this decision the Populist party was not mentioned. It was explained, however, that the Republican and Democratic parties had declared for gold and that the silver men within those parties showed little inclination to break with their party on the currency issue. The movement for silver, then, must come from the people; and the new party they were establishing was the necessary vehicle for that purpose.

In this conference the Bimetallic League established a tentative political organization for the states and territories and set up a plan for the appointment of a provisional national committee. An executive committee, headed by General Warner and composed exclusively of men associated with the American Bimetallic League, was to be created.

As if to announce their total independence of established parties, they also stated in their address that if they had the authority to announce their candidate for the president of the United States, their choice would be Joseph C. Sibley of Pennsylvania.[36]

The decision of the silver forces to launch an independent political movement came at the very moment that their attempts to educate the public to accept free coinage arguments were bearing fruit. From the free silver standpoint the happiest event in the history of their agitation occurred in June 1894, when William H. Harvey published *Coin's Financial School.*[37]

In this little book Harvey used the device of placing an adolescent by the name of Coin upon the platform of the lecture hall of the Chicago Art Institute. Eventually the cogency of his arguments for free silver drew Chicago's most distinguished bankers, business men, and scholars to the Art Institute. Here they brought out their arguments against free silver. Repeatedly Coin forced them to admit errors in fact and logic, until all had agreed that his exposition of free silver doctrine was correct. These lectures had never occurred, of course; but they were described so graphically in Harvey's book that many people believed they had. Some of the men named in *Coin* wrote letters for publication denying that they had participated in the public meetings which Harvey described.[38]

By the beginning of 1895 *Coin's School* had become a national bestseller. Train "butchers" did a brisk business with the book; and the silver organizations distributed it over the country, selling it where they could and giving it away elsewhere.[39] Copies of the book rapidly passed from hand to hand, for it was eagerly read. Where it was read, discussion groups were formed because the book stimulated study of the arguments which it set forth.

The extent of *Coin's* influence was reflected in the interviews and letters by congressmen from their home districts in April 1895, after the adjournment of Congress. From Tennessee Josiah Patterson wrote: "The anonymous book called 'Coins School' has been very extensively circulated. It is cleverly written and well calculated to mislead the people. It has done and is doing much harm and yet it is extremely fallacious."[40] From Mississippi Congressman T. C. Catchings wrote that even in Vicksburg free silver was making headway, because "A little free silver book called 'Coin's financial school' is being sold on every railroad train by the newsboys and at every cigar stand and it is being read by almost everybody." [41] In Wisconsin the chairman of the Democratic State Central Committee wrote that in his state "A pamphlet entitled 'Coins Financial School' has attracted a great deal of attention and has done some harm to the cause of sound money." [42] A plainly worded warning came from Missouri: " 'Coins Financial School' is raising h— in this neck of the woods. If those in favor of honest money don't do something to offset its influence the country is going to the dogs." [43] A Minnesota correspondent wrote to *Outlook* magazine: "Dozens of men in this representative community can quote chapters and chapters of the book, while my high school boys are about equally divided between silver and baseball, with a decided leaning toward the former." [44]

Harvey's book became a best-seller in a highly competitive field, for the country was now being deluged with literature of all kinds on the subject of money. Apparently the demand was equal to the supply, for *Coin* was not the only publication which recorded phenomenal sales. Several months earlier Seymour F. Norton had published a pamphlet, *Ten Men of Money Island,* which argued the virtues of Greenback currency.[45] This booklet sold more than 100,000 copies. Ignatius Donnelly, imitating the format of *Coin,* including the use of cleverly devised cartoons, published a book with the title, *The American People's Money.* In his book a farmer and a banker met casually in a railroad car and became involved in a debate on the money question. The farmer coolly demolished the banker's arguments for the gold standard.[46] Donnelly's book had a wide sale.

Also widely distributed was a book published by the American Bimetallic League, titled *Facts About Silver.* It enjoyed an extensive sale because it was a handy reference book for use in the silver discussions and debates which were becoming a standard feature of life in communities urban and rural west of the Alleghenies and south of Maryland.[47] Harvey continued to add to the flood by issuing new volumes in *Coin's Financial Series,* including in 1895 a new book describing a new series of imaginary debates in the Chicago Art Institute under the title, *Coin's School Up to Date.*[48]

Published replies to the pro-silver books and pamphlets were, for the most part, heavy handed and humorless. For example, Horace White replied to Harvey in a pamphlet titled, *Coin's Financial Fool.* The main points made in White's book were these: the entire story of the book was a lie, because a boy twelve years old could not lecture upon such an abstruse subject; there was no such person as the "young Medill" who appeared in the book; and Gage and Laughlin, on their own affidavits, had not participated as the book described; the economic and financial arguments of the book were wrong; the statistics were falsified; the analysis of England's interest in our currency was "either broad farce or blatant demagogism"; the book's popularity was due to its cartoons. "Without them," wrote White, "not five hundred copies of such a senseless book could have been sold or given away." [49]

By mid-1895 the flood was at full crest. Pamphlets and books by the hundreds and thousands streamed from the presses. Special newspapers and periodicals were established to propagandize the people on the money question, and the columns of established publications were heavily burdened with silver articles. Everywhere speeches, debates, discussions, and study groups found a ready public audience.

It was evident that the American Bimetallic League had succeeded in its original objective of bringing men of all sections and all interests to support of the free coinage of silver. Success in this direction had, indeed, been so great that much of the initiative in the organization lay with men from the agrarian West and South; and a man from Pennsylvania was being promoted as the silver candidate for the presidency.

Nevertheless, by establishing a new party, however tentative the organization might be, the League had, from some points of view, exceeded its original intent to engage solely in educational work for free silver. There was criticism in the western states of the selection of Sibley as the silver presidential candidate, and some westerners felt that a new organization devoted solely to propaganda work was desirable.[50]

On May 15, 1895, on the call of the governor of Montana, delegates from ten western states and territories convened at Salt Lake City. After extended discussions they announced that they had established the National Bimetallic Union. This organization was to be dedicated exclusively to educational work for the free coinage of silver at 16 to 1. One of its major projects was the establishment of a weekly news magazine, *The National Bimetallist,* which began publication in Chicago in October 1895. It was intended that the organization be national in scope with a committee composed of one member from each state and territory in the Union. Central headquarters was established in Chicago because of the belief that the great battle ground for silver was in the Middle West. In origin, however, this organization was strictly western. Its executive committee was made up of western representatives, and throughout its existence its funds derived almost entirely from western sources.[51]

3

The Democrats:
Divided and Defeated

The Democratic party had won a notable victory in 1892. Cleveland's popular majority was not massive, but the Democrats had made significant inroads in traditional areas of Republican power. This was particularly in evidence in the Middle West. Illinois and Wisconsin, which had not given their electoral votes to the Democrats since the Civil War, had presented the ticket of Cleveland and Stevenson with small majorities. Further, the electoral victory did not stand alone. Congressional districts which had been represented by Republicans since 1860 elected Democrats in 1892. The Cleveland administration came to power with a Congress in which both houses were controlled by the President's party. The election of Democratic state administrations in Illinois and Wisconsin also bore striking evidence of the general surge in Democratic strength.[1]

From the point of view of eastern and southern Democrats, it was true, certain features of the election were not altogether gratifying. In most southern states Democratic votes had declined, in most instances quite decidedly (in the case of Mississippi and Florida by more than one-half, but this was due, in part, to the adoption of new voting laws intended to disfranchise Negroes). Republican votes had not increased proportionately in the southern states. It was instead into the Populist party that Democratic votes in the South had been deflected. The appeal of the Populist party to Democratic voters in the South was disquieting to eastern Democrats. Since the Civil War the easterners had depended for national victory on their alliance with the southern Democrats, who usually had followed unquestioningly the conservative leadership of the East.

There were other developments to disturb eastern Democrats. Probably most troubling was the fact that they did not have absolute control of the Senate, for the balance of power was held by a silver bloc, Democratic, Republican, and Populist in composition. The desire of this silver bloc for a policy of monetary inflation through increased governmental use of silver was anathema to the conservative eastern Democrats. Events soon revealed, too, that eastern Democrats were unhappy over the fact that for the election in certain Prairie and Rocky Mountain states Democrats had fused with Populists on the Populist ticket,[2] with the result that the electoral votes of those states were cast for General Weaver, the Populist candidate.

It was Democrats from the Middle West, the Great Plains, and the Far West who found a new enthusiasm and confidence in the victories of 1892. Long accustomed to local defeat and a position of minor influence in the councils of their party, they saw in their triumph new power and importance for themselves not only in local politics but also within their national party organization. After March 1893, when the Cleveland administration formally took power, Democrats from the West and Middle West, coming to Washington on party business, expressed their confidence in future Democratic victories in their sections, if tariff reform was achieved and the Cleveland administration was successful. Senator-elect W. N. Roach from North Dakota, a Democrat elected by a Populist-Democratic fusion ticket, said that the tariff issue was the great issue in the rural districts of the West and Northwest. He promised that the Democrats, if the administration followed party principles and used its patronage power wisely, would carry the state in the next election. Nine-tenths of the Populists in North Dakota, he said, were Republicans dissatisfied with their party's leadership and policies. They already had one leg in the Democratic party, and in the next four years they could be pulled all the way in on the tariff issue.[3]

A newspaper editor from Kansas believed that his state was becoming a Democratic stronghold. He said that such a development was "within the bounds of near future possibility" if the Cleveland administration lived up to its promises on tariff reform.[4]

John G. Shanklin, influential Democratic leader from Indiana, expressed his belief that "pretty much the entire west and northwest will be democratic at the next national election, if things go all right under this administration." He believed that Wisconsin and Illinois would remain Democratic and that surrounding states like Ohio and Michigan would join them. According to Shanklin these changes would have an important bearing on developments within the party: "All this will deprive New York state of her imperial power. National results and politics can no longer be dictated by politicians in New York city and in the next national election the east will look to the west instead of the west looking to the east." [5]

Spokesmen from Illinois reflected similar ideas. A reporter from the Washington *Star*, on hand in February 1893, to witness the ceremonies conducted at Bloomington on the departure of Vice-President-elect Stevenson from his home town, found Stevenson spoken of as a likely presidential candidate in 1896. His candidacy was analyzed as an aspect of the shift in power which had taken place in 1892 from the East to the Middle West. New York, Democrats were saying in Bloomington, had dominated the party's nominations too long.[6] William H. Hinrichsen, elected Secretary of State in the new administration of John Peter Altgeld and Altgeld's closest political confidante, boasted in a Washington interview that Illinois was safely Democratic on the basis of the party's large Democratic majority in Chicago and the careful organization developed by the party throughout the state.[7]

From Minnesota came Daniel W. Lawlor, defeated as gubernatorial candidate in 1892, but stating that Minnesota was a low tariff state and that the Democratic party would benefit accordingly.[8] A party spokesman from Iowa said that through close organization and the interest of the farmers in the tariff issue the Democratic party was rapidly growing.[9] A prominent Ohio Democrat believed that the Democrats were educating the citizens of that state on the tariff and that Governor McKinley would be defeated in his campaign for re-election.[10] Leaders from Wisconsin spoke with similar confidence of the future of the Democratic party in their state.[11]

Not all who came to Washington claiming Democratic allegiance and victory found a ready welcome in the offices in which Democrats were now taking control. Patronage difficulties emerged in western and southern states, particularly in those places where Democrats had adopted a free silver platform or where Democrats had cooperated with third party groups. Soon the newspaper columns at the capitol were reflecting the dissatisfaction of visitors who had come to claim the rewards of victory and had been turned away empty handed.

Kansas had cast its electoral votes for Weaver in 1892. On the approval of the Democratic national campaign committee Kansas Democrats had cooperated with Populists to achieve this result.[12] In March 1893, two Kansas delegations came to Washington to talk with Cleveland. One was composed of "regular" Democrats, the conservative and orthodox leaders of the very small minority of Kansas Democratic voters who had refused to vote for Weaver (Cleveland's name was not on the ballot in Kansas). The other delegation was composed of the leaders of the Populist-Democratic fusion which had won a solid majority of the votes of that state.

By March there was no doubt about Cleveland's decision as to which of the Kansas committees would receive the administration's recognition on patronage questions. Before his inauguration representatives of the Kansas fusion group had visited Cleveland to urge him to appoint a Kansan as secretary of agriculture. Cleveland had told them that he was thinking of appointing Sterling Morton of Nebraska to that post. The committee reported that when they expressed surprise at this since they believed that Morton, by refusing to withdraw in favor of fusion with the Populists, had been responsible for the Republican victory in Nebraska, Cleveland had answered, "The republican ticket ought to have been elected if the democratic ticket could not be. In no event should the populist ticket have been elected." [13]

The chairman of the regular group which came from Kansas to Washington to protest the Populist-Democratic attempt to obtain Cleveland's patronage support adopted the same argument as the President—that Democrats would much rather be defeated by Republicans than join with Populists. As if replying to the question that William Allen White would ask three years later, he said: "There is nothing the matter with Kansas, except her politics. The people are prosperous, well housed and fed, have a fine soil and are capable of producing the greatest crops in the world—if the populists will only let them alone." [14]

White, however, recalled in his *Autobiography* what he saw when he came to Emporia, Kansas in 1895:

Unemployment had beaten down the price of corn, wheat, hay, hogs and livestock until farming was unprofitable. The protest of Populism was the political phase of the unpainted farm house and barns one saw all over the midwestern country, the run-down fences, the fallow, weedy fields; and in towns, the vacant stores and bankruptcy sales. . . .

Yet in the big houses . . . people lived well. The bankers and some of the doctors and lawyers drove spanking teams to carriages that cost as much as three hundred dollars. . . . People who had money were living well in Emporia; others, hanging on by their eyebrows. And Populism was raging across the state, across the Missouri Valley, and through the South.[15]

White related these conditions to the Panic of 1893; but the truth was that long before the financial panic occurred in the spring of 1893 Kansas farmers, along with the farmers of the entire nation, North and South, had been suffering the hardships of depression. There had been no basic recovery in farm prices in the years since the Panic of 1873; and in the late 1880's, after a brief swing upward, a further decline in agricultural prices had occurred.[16] Drought in the western farm states in the early 1890's had caused great suffering in that region, but had not produced an improvement in the prices of farm commodities to benefit farmers in sections not affected by drought. Populism, to borrow White's phraseology, had raged across Kansas and nearby states in the early '90's long before the Panic of 1893.

Democrats in Kansas and nearby states were customarily the minority party. These states had been as much one-party Republican states as the southern states had been one-party Democratic. From the point of view of many Democrats in these states nothing was to be lost through the rise of Populism; only the Republicans could lose. Democrats, if only in the opportunity to destroy Republican power, saw promise in the rise of Populism. In reality the changes in western politics attending the rise of Populism appeared to hold much promise for the Democratic party itself. Democrats often worked closely with Populists and sometimes (as in the case of Bryan's candidacy for a congressional seat in Nebraska in 1892), campaigning as Democrats, managed to win valuable Populist support.

It was not difficult for western Democrats to reconcile themselves to such cooperation, for it seemed to them that the Populist program was strongly within the Democratic traditions as established by Jefferson and Jackson. Therefore, it was a program to which Democrats could, in large part, subscribe. It was a program which many Democrats believed would ultimately draw the Populists into the Democratic party. Many western Democrats considered it a program which they might follow out of their party, if their party betrayed them by adopting an alien gold platform.

When Cleveland repudiated western fusion with Populists and attacked Populist platforms as inimical to Democratic policies, western Democrats found themselves in an exceedingly difficult position. Now, as they gave interviews during visits to Washington or when they spoke in the West upon return from visits or periods of service at Washington, they gave vent to their irritation and frustration with the Cleveland policy. Speaking in St. Louis of Cleveland's drive to repeal the Sherman Silver Purchase Act, the young Nebraska congressman, William Jennings Bryan, said that, since the party had always favored bimetallism, repeal of the Sherman Act without any other legislation providing for the use of silver would be a departure from party policy. The effect would be to "injure the party in the South and West." [17] Cleveland retaliated by refusing to recognize Bryan's patronage claims.[18] Bryan fought back, directing the full force of his oratorical powers against Cleveland.[19] In 1894 Bryan issued a stern warning to his party when, at the Nebraska State Democratic Convention, he said that "duty to country is above duty to party" and "if the Democratic party, after you go home, endorses your action [backing the Cleveland administration] and makes your position its permanent policy, I promise you that I will go out and serve my country and my God under some other name, even if I must go alone." [20]

In the mountain West where the development of the silver movement and the rise of the Populist party had offered even more promise to the Democratic minority Cleveland's policy was extremely unpopular. In late October 1893, a Democrat from Montana, interviewed in Washington, expressed his belief that it would be very difficult indeed to find a Cleveland Democrat in Montana or, for that matter, in any of the surrounding western states.[21]

While Democrats from the West and Middle West had rejoiced in the promises of the victories of 1892, southern Democrats saw warnings of future difficulties in their reduced majorities. There was little doubt about the direction in which southern Democratic voters were drifting. The Populist party in many a southern state had received a surprisingly large vote; and in the South the Republican party, as the permanent minority party, found the possibilities of defeating the Democrats through fusion with the Populists very attractive. In only a few southern states was it true that the Populists held the balance of power in that their votes in 1892, coupled with Republican votes, would produce an anti-Democratic majority. But in many states this was so close to being a possibility as to constitute a disturbing threat to the Democrats.

To most southern Democrats it appeared that the drift from their party was caused by Cleveland's failure to produce programs to solve the problems of agricultural depression. They believed that their future depended upon his actions. If the administration could produce agricultural prosperity, then, of course, all would be well. Realistic southern Democrats did not, however, expect miracles. If the Cleveland administration could not produce immediate prosperity, it could reasonably be looked to for an aggressive reform of the tariff, a constructively partisan patronage policy, and a monetary and banking policy which would produce the larger amounts of currency and credit which most southerners believed essential to the improvement of their economy.

Therefore, keen were the chagrin and disappointment of southern Democrats when, within weeks after the Cleveland administration came to office, a savage panic threw the South into depression. The drift toward Populism perceptibly quickened. From the point of view of beleaguered southern Democrats, the policy of the Cleveland administration became a policy of defeatism and betrayal. The move to repeal the Sherman Act, the failure of tariff reform, and the gold bond sales became symbols of an administration that had betrayed the majority of its party in the South.

Even more maddening for southern Democrats, though, was the fact that the Cleveland administration applied in the South, as in the West, the rule that free silver Democrats were to be cut off from administration patronage. Before taking office President Cleveland had fixed a policy of punishing uncooperative Democrats in Congress. In January 1893, he wrote to his future Secretary of the Treasury, John G. Carlisle: "One thing may as well be distinctly understood by democrats in Congress, who are heedless of the burdens and responsibilities of the incoming administration and of the duty our party owes to the people. They must not expect us to 'turn the other cheek' by rewarding their conduct with patronage." [22]

In South Carolina Benjamin Tillman had performed a major service for Cleveland by preventing his own followers and the South Carolina Alliance from supporting the Populists. But when he wrote to Cleveland shortly after the inauguration, offering his help in distributing the patronage in South Carolina, Cleveland published the letter and proceeded to give appointments in that state to persons unfriendly to Tillman.[23] By October 1893, it had become clear to Congressman Joe Bailey of Texas "That whenever an opportunity presents itself, the Administration intends to discriminate against Democrats [who are] in favor of free and unlimited coinage of silver. . . ." [24]

As never since the Civil War western and southern Democrats found themselves drawn together by common problems, common policies, and, perhaps more compelling than anything else, common hatred of Grover Cleveland. They had come to dislike Cleveland not only because of his policies but because they saw him as a symbol of eastern domination of their party.

In these months President Cleveland was experiencing an ordeal of personality and party which increasingly made him a lonely, bitter, and pessimistic man, writing in this vein to his friend, Ambassador Thomas F. Bayard, in London: "Think of it! Not a man in the Senate with whom I can be on terms of absolute confidence. . . . Not one of them comes to me on public business unless sent for and then full of rumination and doubts. We are very far apart in feeling, and, it seems to me, in purposes." [25]

Speech livid with hatred of the President was heard everywhere in the West and South and from the representatives of those sections in Washington. In the summer of 1894 rumors circulated that the President was planning a fishing trip to Colorado, and a warning was forwarded to him that he would place his life in danger if he traveled into the West:

Those Colorado people are in a desperate and frenzied state of excitement and contain the most lawless element in the world and the mutterings against the president are heard on every hand. They have a governor in Colorado whom many people at least believe would pardon the man who would kill the president of the United States, because he won't destroy the financial standing of the nation to benefit their local industries.[26]

What was the nature of the developments which had so reduced the prestige of the President of the United States?

First in both time and importance was the financial panic which occurred in the spring of 1893 only a few weeks after Cleveland had taken office. Though it was international in scope and had very little, if any, causal relationship to the vicissitudes of politics in the United States, unavoidably Cleveland's administration was saddled with much of the blame for this economic collapse. When financial panic was followed by a prolonged depression, naturally the attacks on Cleveland became bitter and angry.

Though the tariff had been the foremost issue in the campaign of 1892, Cleveland found after he took office in 1893 that he had to give priority to the crisis precipitated by the alarming decline in the gold reserves of the United States Treasury. The Treasury tried to keep its gold reserve, established chiefly to maintain redemption in gold of the greenbacks and the treasury notes issued under the Sherman Act of 1890, at a minimum of $100,000,000. When Cleveland took office this reserve was threatened by heavy withdrawals; and on June 30, 1893, he called for a special session of Congress to convene in early August. His object in this special session was repeal of the Sherman Silver Purchase Act, which he believed to be the major cause for the drain on the Treasury's gold reserves.

Cleveland believed that repeal of the Sherman Act was more than a solution to the Treasury's problem, that in addition it was an alternative to the Republican explanation that the depression was due to the threat of tariff reduction. Cleveland argued that it was the Sherman Silver Purchase Act, a Republican measure, which was chiefly responsible for the depression. Hence its repeal was essential to economic recovery. Events, of course, disproved Cleveland's thesis before the election of 1896; for, though he did achieve repeal of the Sherman Act early in 1894, the repeal produced no visible improvement in the economy. Worse yet it appeared not to have eased the crisis resulting from the drain of gold from the treasury, for in the months that followed repeal the administration was faced with succeeding crises as the government's gold reserve sank below the $100,000,000 figure which was considered the level of safety.

When the gold reserve was reduced to $69,000,000 in January 1894, the Treasury initiated the policy of selling bonds for gold. Repeated sales of bonds in 1894 and 1895 proved no more than temporary expedients as the gold accumulated in the Treasury by this method was drained away as rapidly, or more rapidly, than it was acquired. By January 1895, the reserve was reduced to $45,000,000. In this crisis the Cleveland administration made an arrangement with the New York bankers, J. Pierpont Morgan and August Belmont, for the delivery of approximately $62,000,000 in gold to the Treasury in exchange for four-per-cent bonds. Altogether during Cleveland's administration the public debt was increased by $263,000,000 in this futile attempt to maintain the gold reserve.[27]

Cleveland's decision to deal with the problem of the declining gold reserve by selling bonds angered the public and the politicians of the agrarian sections. More disastrous to Cleveland, however, was the fact that in pressing for repeal of the Sherman Act he had alienated much of his party. He used the patronage stick ruthlessly against those who would not swing into line, not realizing that men like Bryan in Nebraska and Tillman in South Carolina knew that, in their constituencies, the appeal of Populist reforms was more powerful than a few appointments to minor federal offices.

Cleveland dealt as ruthlessly with eastern Democrats who advocated a compromise solution rather than outright repeal of the Sherman Act. Senator Arthur P. Gorman of Maryland introduced a compromise proposal, because he recognized that the debate over repeal was splitting the Democratic party. Gorman's efforts angered the President, who turned Maryland's patronage over to Gorman's opponents. Privately Cleveland stated that he believed Gorman to be a traitor to the Democratic party.[28]

Western and southern Democrats found Cleveland's attempt to blame the Sherman Act for the depression doubly troublesome. First, it placed the Democratic party at odds with the free silver sentiment which was sweeping their sections. Second, it contradicted their explanation of the depression, which they believed to be the only rejoinder the Democratic party could use to counter the Republican claim that the depression was due to the Democratic tariff policy. For southern and western Democrats, in direct opposition to Cleveland, argued that it was the abandonment of free coinage of silver which had caused the depression. This policy, they argued, dated back to the "Crime of '73" and was peculiarly Republican policy; therefore, the Republicans were at fault for the Panic of 1893. The Democratic party, they pointed out, had always advocated bimetallism, even in the platform on which Cleveland had campaigned in 1892. As they viewed the situation, Cleveland was violating party promises, betraying his fellow partisans, and denying them their one chance for victory in 1896 and, probably, for many elections to follow. Thus, western Democrats, who saw their gains of 1892 dissipating, and southern Democrats, sorely pressed by the growing popularity of the Populist party in their districts, saw little but doom in the Cleveland policy to repeal the Sherman Silver Purchase Act.

The factional and sectional bitterness which pervaded the Democratic party after the repeal of the Sherman Act was increased by each succeeding development in the months which followed. The tariff battle which resulted in the passage of the Wilson-Gorman Bill revealed the lack of party discipline, created new factions in the President's party, and heightened the dissatisfactions which western and southern Democrats found with Cleveland's leadership.

Before the tariff issue was settled by Cleveland's decision in August to permit the bill to become law without his signature, the Pullman strike had driven another wedge into the Democratic party. The winning of the governorship of Illinois by John Peter Altgeld in 1892 promised much for the Democratic party in the Middle West and in the nation. The importance of Democratic control of the state of Illinois could scarcely be exaggerated because of the central position which the state possessed geographically, politically, and psychologically.

Of even more importance potentially was the nature of the man who had won control of Illinois for the Democrats. John Peter Altgeld possessed an understanding of the new forces at work in American society. He knew well the poverty and insecurity of the industrial worker. He was equally conversant with the problems and the psychology of the debt-ridden farmer. He was an able politician and under his direction the Democrats had organized Illinois thoroughly. He was an adroit politician, capable of compromise; and he recognized that the Democratic party had able leaders from all ranks of life. He himself had achieved a large degree of business success in Chicago, and he enjoyed being entertained by the rich and liked moving in their social circles. During the campaign in 1892 he had accepted aid from all directions; and when he won, he was prepared to render the political services he knew would be expected of him. He and ultra-conservative Senator John M. Palmer did not always see eye-to-eye, but Palmer had supported Altgeld in 1892. Shortly after the campaign Altgeld wrote to Palmer: "Thank you for your grand efforts during the late campaign to wheel the state into the democratic column. I will feel under obligation to you for any suggestions that you may be good enough to make at any time and if there is anything you feel a personal interest in, I hope you will feel free to communicate with me fully in regard to it." [29]

After Altgeld's pardon of the Haymarket convicts and his fight with Cleveland on the Pullman strike, he found himself cut off from most Democrats like Palmer; but wherever possible he clung to his friendships with conservative Democrats, though they ceased to sympathize or cooperate with him in politics.[30] Unlike Cleveland, he did not expect acceptance by his friends of all his own political ideas and ideals. Unlike Bryan, he never spoke of the possibility that he might leave the Democratic party. He was, without qualification, a Democrat.

Every aspect of Altgeld's approach to politics suggested that up to the time of the Pullman strike he expected to cooperate with the Cleveland administration, even though economic reversals and Cleveland's errors were embarrassing to the party in Illinois. When the Illinois Democratic convention met in 1894, the keynote was union and conciliation. Dissidents from southern Illinois appeared at the convention asking the adoption of resolutions condemning Cleveland and advocating the free coinage of silver at 16 to 1, but Altgeld exercised firm control and routed them. The platform adopted by the convention endorsed both Cleveland and Altgeld and on the money issue contained a plank which was an innocuous compromise.[31] Two weeks later Cleveland and Altgeld quarreled bitterly over federal intervention in the Pullman strike. Once the break had occurred neither man seriously attempted a reconciliation. Altgeld, who had earlier accepted bimetallism and the quantitative theory but had not paraded his convictions, now joined those members of his party who were attacking Cleveland on the silver coinage issue.

Altgeld realized that Cleveland had enemies among Democrats in the conservative East, and he now made overtures toward an alliance with them. In autumn 1894, the most powerful of the eastern Democratic bosses, David B. Hill, was campaigning for the New York governorship. At stake was not only the governor's office but also control of the powerful Democratic machine in New York. Cleveland Democrats knifed Hill's campaign in every possible way.[32] Cleveland himself wrote about the New York contest: "I am dreadfully depressed about the political situation and want to keep as far away from it as possible. I am undoubtedly wrong as usual but I dont see how anybody who knows what democratic principles are or cares to see them prevail can support the man the democratic organization of New York State has defiantly and impudently attempted to cram down Democratic throats." [33]

It was, therefore, with deliberate intent that Altgeld in late October sent George Schilling, the secretary of the Illinois Board of Labor Statistics, to New York to work with the leaders of organized labor in that state to secure the election of Hill.[34] As events developed Hill lost the race for the governorship, and no alliance of permanent significance was made between Hill and Altgeld. More important, however, was the fact that Cleveland by the middle of his administration was isolated from the two most powerful Democratic state leaders in the country.

The pattern of the Illinois Democratic campaign in 1894—endorsement of Cleveland and at the same time a vaguely worded endorsement of free silver—had been generally adopted in the Middle West and Great Plains states.[35] In the South and Far West Democratic platforms were less compromising, which meant that they were more hostile to Cleveland and more explicit in their endorsement of free silver. Cleveland and the members of his administration, however, made no attempt to discriminate between differences on the silver question. They opposed proponents of free silver of whatever degree, with the result that in the campaign of 1894 Democrats often fought each other more bitterly than they fought Republicans or Populists.

The election returns in 1894 were universally disturbing to Democrats. In eastern Democratic strongholds such as New York the Republicans surged to victory. In the Middle West, where the results of 1892 had raised Democratic hopes, the Republicans regained lost ground and developed new areas of strength. In the Great Plains and Far West Populist votes increased, largely at the expense of Democrats. In most states in this region Republican candidates won the offices, the Populist party became the second party, and the Democrats became a minor third party. The only exception to this generalization was found in Nebraska, where the Democrats had fused with the Populists and could make some claim to success. In the South, Populists, often working in fusion with Republicans, made disturbing inroads into Democratic majorities.

As the election campaign progressed in 1894, disunity among Democrats increased. When the returns spelled out the unpopularity of the party, all restraint upon intra-party bickering was removed. Inevitably

President Cleveland became his party's scapegoat. On election night a Washington reporter watching the reactions of Democrats as election returns came into campaign headquarters at the Wormley Hotel observed that "as the returns became worse and worse the remarks took on a tone very uncomplimentary to the administration. . . ." [36] On the other side, the administration, in its inner councils, found satisfaction in the defeat of Democratic leaders whom it had come to look upon as enemies. A comment from North Carolina, where the Democrats had been badly beaten, pretty well summed up the situation nationally: "Nine-tenths of them [Democrats] are angry with Cleveland, angry with Congress, . . . and angry because cotton is 5 cents a pound. The party is torn to pieces by dissensions." [37]

It was particularly to southern and western Democrats that the election returns of 1894 became a sign and a portent. They had long chafed at eastern domination of the party. Now the hostility of Cleveland and his associates and the thorough defeat suffered by the eastern Democrats had destroyed much of the influence which they had once possessed in the party. It was doubtful, of course, that western and southern Democrats would have remained loyal to the Cleveland leadership, even if the Cleveland group had won a strong victory in the East; for the election returns in the South and West threatened total destruction of the Democratic party in those sections if that party adhered to the Cleveland policy on money and banking.

To embattled Democrats in the South and West the issue of the free coinage of silver at 16 to 1 appeared to be their only hope for victory in 1896. Their path to acceptance of that policy was eased by the fact that they generally had little difficulty in relating the free silver policy to Democratic party traditions. That it was popular at the polls every recent election development proved. That failure of the Democratic party to give free silver a prominent place in their platform would cause Democrats in the West and South to flee to the Populist party every recent development indicated. That Democrats would hold to their party and that Populists and Republicans would move into it if it boldly backed free silver seemed probable. With these considerations in mind Democrats in the West and South, and also increasingly in the Middle West, immediately after the 1894 election proceeded to organize to bring their party to free silver.

4

The Democrats
Debate the Currency Issue

In the minds of many Democrats the necessity for a direct fight with the Cleveland administration on the silver issue had been evident long before November 1894. After the repeal of the Sherman Silver Purchase Act had been accomplished, Congressman Richard P. Bland, who had become a symbol for Democratic support of free silver in the South and West, had introduced a seigniorage bill, through which the treasury would issue money based on reserves of silver which had been accumulated in seigniorage charges. Bland believed this to be a moderate concession to the silver cause which Cleveland, without greatly stretching his conscience, could sign.

Many conservatives in the Middle West saw the seigniorage bill much as Bland did, a compromise which would reconcile free silver Democrats to their party; and they advised Cleveland to sign it. Cleveland, however, sternly followed the dictates of conscience (which, his papers reveal, were sharpened by strong letters from eastern bankers) and vetoed Bland's bill. Shortly after this, in May 1894, an article by Bland was published in the *North American Review*. In this article Bland spoke of the coming "battle of the standards." As Bland saw it, "On the one side will be arrayed the rich and powerful banks of the Old World and of the New; on the other, the mass of our party, especially those west of the Allegheny Mountains, loaded down as they are with debts and mortgages, with a vast country yet to be touched by the hand of industry and enterprise, demanding money without limit, except as to its supply from nature." [1]

Bland was defeated in his congressional campaign in 1894 in a bitter race in which the machinery of the Cleveland administration was turned in all its force against him. After his defeat it was rumored that Bland had said that he was ready to break with his party. Bland quickly denied this rumor.[2] He and those like him were not ready to break with their party until they had tested their ability to control it. If they lost that struggle, and Cleveland and his men retained control, then and then only would they address themselves to the possibility that for them their party held no future.

As was to occur so frequently in these months it was William Jennings Bryan who brought the debate sharply into focus. On February 14, 1895, he spoke in the House of Representatives in opposition to an administration bill authorizing the issue of over $65,000,000 of three-per-cent gold bonds. Of Cleveland he said:

The President of the United States is only a man. We intrust the administration of the government to men, and when we do so, we know that they are liable to err. When men are in public office we expect them to make mistakes. And if the President does make a mistake, what should Congress do? Ought it to blindly approve his mistake, or do we owe it to the people of the United States, and even to the President himself, to correct the mistake so that it will not be made again? But some gentlemen say that the Democratic party should stand by the President. What has he done for the party since the last election to earn its gratitude? I want to suggest to my Democratic friends that the party owes no great debt of gratitude to its President. What gratitude should we feel? The gratitude which a passenger feels toward the trainman who has opened a switch and precipitated a wreck. What has he done for the party? He has attempted to inoculate it with Republican virus, and blood poisoning has set in.[3]

Of the silver issue and national politics, he spoke these words:

But, Mr. Speaker, I desire, in conclusion to call the attention of our Eastern brethren to the fact that this controversy can be no longer delayed. The issue has come and it must be met. On these financial questions we find that the Democrats of the East and the Republicans of the East lock arms and proceed to carry out their policies, regardless of the interests and wishes of the rest of the country. If they form this union, offensive and defensive, they must expect the rest of the people of the country will drop party lines, if necessary, and unite to preserve their homes and their welfare.

If this is sectionalism, the East has set the example. The demand of our Eastern brethren, both Republicans and Democrats, is for a steadily appreciating monetary standard. They are creditors; they hold our bonds, and our mortgages, and as the dollars increase in purchasing power, our debts increase and the holders of our bonds and mortgages gather in an unearned increment. . . . The necessary result of their policy is the building up of a plutocracy which will make servants of the rest of the people.

.   .   .   .

The time will come when the unjust demands and the oppressive exactions of our Eastern brethren will compel the South and West to unite in the restoration of an honest dollar. . . .[4]

Bryan not only used his position in the House to make himself an important spokesman for the free silver Democrats but he also took the lead in initiating action through which the free silverites would gain control of the party. As the congressional session neared its end, he originated and circulated among the Democrats in the House an address urging all Democrats and Democratic newspapers to organize and agitate for the purpose of making the Democratic party a free silver party. Ultimately thirty-one members of the House of Representatives, including Richard P. Bland, signed the address. Two Democrats, Evan P. Howell and J. Floyd King, who were not then members of the House of Representatives, also signed the document. This action represented the first attempt of any significance to organize the silver Democrats to control their own party.[5]

At the time that Democrats in the House of Representatives issued their address, Illinois Democrats, under the leadership of their state chairman, William H. Hinrichsen, were preparing a call for a special silver convention in Illinois. Hinrichsen early in 1895 made an extensive investigation to discover the causes of the defeat of the Illinois Democrats in the November elections. From correspondence with Democratic party leaders he learned that they blamed their party's defeat locally and nationally on the failure to adopt a free silver policy. They reported that thousands of Democrats in Illinois had voted Republican in the election in November 1894, that other thousands had voted Populist, while others had refused to vote. Hinrichsen concluded that the Democratic party, which had won control of the state in 1892, now held the loyalties of none but a few old Bourbons and federal office holders.

Hinrichsen made no secret of his wish that the Democratic silver convention in Illinois would initiate a movement leading to the commitment, at its 1896 convention, of the national Democratic party to the financial policy of the free coinage of silver at 16 to 1.[6] In a newspaper interview granted immediately after the call for the Illinois convention had been released, Hinrichsen said: "This movement will be in effect a reorganization of the Democratic party. It will be built from the township up, and the men nominated for office will not dare to deviate one iota from the instructions given them in such plain language by their constituents. We expect to carry every state west of the Alleghenies and south of the Ohio river, and it is more than possible that we will carry every state in the Union." [7] However, when the Illinois convention met early in June, discussion of the silver issue had become so extensive that the convention's recommendations for a Democratic silver policy received comparatively little attention.

In March and April, 1895, it was evident that a major battle was underway within the Democratic party. The Cleveland administration finally had taken the initiative on several fronts. The President himself overcame his reluctance to speak out publicly on issues which divided his party. In mid-April he sent a letter to Chicago business men who had invited him to address them. In this letter he attempted chiefly to demonstrate that urban workers would be harmed by a cheap money policy such as the free coinage of silver at 16 to 1.[8] Cleveland was as ready as Bland to recognize the battle of the standards, for he wrote, "Disguise it as we may, the line of battle is drawn between the forces of safe currency and those of silver monometallism." Conservative sound money Democrats cheered the President on, telling him that the crisis demanded "bold and aggressive leadership." [9]

William Jennings Bryan seized the opportunity occasioned by Cleveland's letter to the Chicago business men to publish a letter in reply. In his letter Cleveland had written that "What is now needed more than anything else is a plain and simple presentation of the argument in favor of sound money." In his reply Bryan stated that a "vast number of people" found *Coin's Financial School* a convincing "presentation of the argument in favor of sound money." Bryan questioned Cleveland's monopolization of the phrases "sound money" and "safe Currency" to describe his own financial policy and called attention to the fact that at no place in his letter did Cleveland define what he meant by these terms. Bryan then, in a paragraph, succinctly defined what the free silver people intended when they demanded the free and unlimited coinage of both gold and silver. There were many sharp thrusts at Cleveland in Bryan's letter and throughout the tone was harsh and unconciliatory. The final sentence was typical: "If 'the proprieties' of your 'official place oblige' you 'to forego the enjoyment' which you would derive from the writing of another letter explaining your last letter and defining your position on the financial question, please designate some one who has authority to speak for you so that the people may be 'afforded an intelligent opportunity,' as you suggest, to study and decide this now paramount public question." [10]

Both sides in the contest saw that Illinois was a pivotal state. The free silver people of all parties believed that on the monetary issue it would be possible to unite the electoral votes of all the states south of the Ohio and west of the Mississippi rivers. If to these votes could be added those of one or two of the middle western states east of the Mississippi, free silver could win the election. Cleveland's Chicago letter was an overt recognition of the Administration's concern over Illinois.[11]

Elsewhere in the Middle West the Cleveland administration exerted whatever pressure was available to swing Democrats against free silver. Earlier, in Indiana, Cleveland had achieved one of his few successes in the use of patronage when he persuaded Senator Daniel W. Voorhees to play a leading role in the fight for the repeal of the Sherman Silver Purchase Act. This relationship between Cleveland and Voorhees continued into 1895, but progressively Voorhees found himself isolated, because the propaganda of free silver proved to be as potent in Indiana as elsewhere.[12] Though Voorhees stayed with Cleveland and a gold policy, the Democrats of Indiana did not. Soon influential leaders among the Democrats, such as Voorhees' Senate colleague, David Turpie, had adopted free silver.

The Cleveland campaign against free silver failed to catch fire in the Middle West. Partly, as in Indiana, it was because the winds were already blowing too strongly for free silver. The free silver cause was palpably popular, and it was the only issue available to Democrats which might cause the people to forget to associate their party with economic panic and depression.

Another cause for the failure of the Cleveland movement was the ineptitude and lassitude of the men to whom he looked to defend his policies. In Illinois, for example, the men who took up the fight for Cleveland's policies were accurately described as "not the men who go to Conventions but rather those who put on dress suits and talk at banquets on great subjects." [13] Such a man was Lambert Tree, whose letters show an excessive inconclusiveness and hesitancy.[14] In Wisconsin Senator William F. Vilas, informed by the state Democratic chairman of the alarming growth of free silver sentiment in that state and pressed to adopt a program to counteract this development, had counseled instead "inaction with patience." [15] Secretary of Agriculture Morton, in whose home state of Nebraska the free silver fires were burning very brightly indeed, was following a policy of inaction with impatience. He, like Cleveland, demonstrated in this period an astounding ability to anger western constituencies without, at the same time, developing his own policy with any forcefulness.[16]

Certainly a major cause for Cleveland's failure to develop a counter force to free silver in the Middle West was his own stubbornness and ineptitude. His patronage policy was a failure; his friends were not drawn to him by an intimate exposition of his policies; he permitted his own anger and frustration to intervene between himself and his friends. Increasingly he and his administration were isolated from the leaders of their party and from the people of the nation.

The most strenuous efforts of the Cleveland administration to fight the free coinage of silver were mounted in 1895 in the South. Two members of Cleveland's cabinet were from the lower South, Secretary of the Interior Hoke Smith from Georgia, and Secretary of the Navy Hilary A. Herbert from Alabama. In addition, Secretary of the Treasury John G. Carlisle was from Kentucky, considered a key state in the Upper South; and Postmaster General William L. Wilson was from West Virginia. All of these men spoke in their home states and in other areas in the South in the spring and summer of 1895. Their efforts proved unpopular, and the public response was generally unsatisfactory. The practice begun by the New York *World* of printing Smith's name as "Hoax Myth" was widely copied in the South. In 1894 Georgia had given a surprisingly large vote to the Populist party. Georgia was a free silver state; and Smith's efforts there had little, if any, impact on public opinion.[17]

The most vigorous and effective cabinet supporter of the Cleveland gold policy was Carlisle. His department had more patronage resources than the others, and Carlisle's efforts to build an anti-free silver policy were conducted on a national scale. It was expected, however, that he would be particularly effective in the South and in his home state of Kentucky.[18] Again expectations failed, even in Kentucky, where the appeal of free silver sentiment among the people proved stronger than Carlisle's patronage offers or his monetary strictures. Carlisle was embarrassed in these months by the use on the part of his opponents of a statement which he had made in 1878 supporting bimetallism. Bryan frequently referred to it, and the *National Bimetallist* quoted the following section of it on the first page of every issue which it published in 1895 and 1896: "According to my view of the subject, the conspiracy which seems to have been formed here and in Europe to destroy by legislation and otherwise from three-sevenths to one-half the metallic money of the world is the most gigantic crime of this or any other age." [19]

Postmaster General Wilson's efforts had particularly unhappy results for him personally. His name was associated with the unpopular Wilson-Gorman tariff. He had further compounded his guilt in the summer of 1894 by making a speech in London defending his policy in relation to the tariff, and the London speech had been widely blamed for the party's defeat in the election of 1894. Since his midterm appointment to the Cabinet he had been an intimate associate of Cleveland. None of these developments had increased Wilson's popularity in West Virginia; and when he returned home, where once he had been an object of hero-worship, he found former friends cold and distant and the general populace warmly hostile.[20]

Southern conservatives believed that if Cleveland visited the South and made a number of speeches there, he would contribute immeasurably to the fight against free silver. Cleveland, however, avoided such a demonstration of his beliefs and again went no further than writing a letter for publication. In April 1895, the President received a letter from Governor John M. Stone of Mississippi. This letter stated that in spite of the fact that Stone believed the people of Mississippi to be for Cleveland all but one of the United States congressmen and senators from that state were opposed to him. Governor Stone said that he personally had no ax to grind, but it was discouraging to see the patronage in Mississippi being given to those who opposed the President.[21]

In replying to Stone, Cleveland defended his monetary policy, saying that he could not believe that bimetallism could have any appeal to the people of the South. He pointed out that they exported much of their produce in exchange for gold and argued that silver monometallism would mean monetary losses for them on their exports. Further, he declared, silver monometallism was Republican policy; and, "If we should be forced away from our traditional doctrine of sound and safe money our old antagonist will take the field on the platform which we abandon, and neither the votes of reckless democrats nor reckless republicans will avail to stay their easy march to power." He referred in harsh terms to the "officials who devote themselves so industriously to villification and abuse of those under whom they hold office." On this point he concluded, "In the interest of good government such office holders must not be surprised if they are summarily dealt with." [22]

This bluntly worded letter achieved no success in wooing southern Democrats to Cleveland's monetary policy, for it neither conciliated nor persuaded. The threat of loss of patronage as punishment for opposing Cleveland carried no sting, for the nation's Democrats had long since learned that this was the practice of the administration. In October, Cleveland, with Vice-President Stevenson, Secretary Carlisle, and five other members of his Cabinet, traveled to Atlanta, Georgia, to speak to the Cotton States Exposition. This was a ceremonial occasion, and he did not speak on the currency or on any other controversial question in the address he delivered there.[23]

Few of the hard-pressed southern congressmen remained loyal to Cleveland. One of the exceptions, Josiah Patterson of Tennessee, carried out the most vigorous of all Democratic campaigns to educate the South to support Cleveland's monetary policies. After Congress adjourned in 1895 Patterson campaigned through the South, speaking everywhere for Cleveland's program. The culmination of his efforts came in June when a convention of conservative, pro-administration Democrats was held in Patterson's home town, Memphis, Tennessee. The chief feature of this convention was a speech by Carlisle, who was at this time on a tour of the Upper South.[24]

The Memphis sound money convention was well attended, particularly by southern bankers and business men who had received letters from the New York Chamber of Commerce, urging them to come to the meeting; and it did inspire some confidence among northern conservatives that southern opinion was rejecting free silver. However, it also had the effect of stimulating the free silver Democrats in the South to further activity.[25]

The Cleveland administration was closely associated with one other effort to win public opinion to support of Cleveland's monetary policies. This was the campaign developed by the Reform Club of New York, an organization controlled by Democratic business men and headed by a friend of Cleveland, John DeWitt Warner. One of the activities of the club was organized around a Sound Currency Committee; and, between May and August, 1895, this committee was at work in all parts of the United States, distributing literature, sponsoring speakers, providing broadside materials and plates for newspapers, particularly the small country newspapers, and carrying on a multitude of other activities to spread the gospel of Grover Cleveland's financial policies.[26] This Sound Currency Committee was particularly active in Indiana, where cooperation with William D. Bynum enabled them to accomplish much at small expense. They distributed thousands of copies of the speeches of Hoke Smith and John Carlisle and participated actively in the campaigns in Kentucky, Georgia, Indiana, and Ohio.[27]

Eastern bankers influential in the Cleveland administration believed that the popularity of free silver in the South could be countered with a plan for the use of state and national bank notes as the basis for an increased monetary circulation. The first step was to be the repeal of the Civil War law placing a 10 per cent tax on the circulation of state bank notes. The next step would be the enactment by Congress of a law expediting the issue and circulation of notes by state and national banks. The Sound Currency Committee of the New York Reform Club had a prominent role in the campaign of propaganda for these proposals.

In a curious way this program did admit the argument that there was a need to get more money into circulation. There was little evidence that it had any appeal to free silver men North or South. Nevertheless, proposals of various kinds for such currency appeared in the Democratic national platform in 1892, in many Democratic state platforms, and in legislation sponsored by Democrats in the United States Congress. Democrats argued that the popular memory of pre-Civil War state bank issues as "wild cat" currency was not wholly correct, that rather there had been in New York, Massachusetts, and Indiana state banking systems which had permitted banks to issue paper notes on a sound basis.

In 1894, the American Bankers Association, meeting in Baltimore, proposed a plan by which banks, both state and national, would be permitted, under federal supervision, to issue currency in amounts up to 50 per cent of their paid-up, unimpaired capital, the average yearly circulation to be subject to a tax of one-half of one per cent. An additional note issue equal to 25 per cent of the capital was also to be authorized. In order to insure the retirement of such issues when there was no economic need for them, they were to be subject to a heavy annual tax. The proposed plan provided for double indemnity of stockholders, with the notes being a first lien on the assets of any bank issuing them. In addition special guarantee and redemption funds were to be set up.[28]

Bradford Rhodes, editor of *Rhodes Journal of Banking*, advocated another plan by which the nation's currency would be made up chiefly of bank notes. In his annual message in December 1894, Cleveland threw his support to a plan for bank currency which had been developed by Secretary of the Treasury Carlisle; and, in the weeks which followed, a bill based on Carlisle's plan and other bills providing for state bank currency were introduced and debated in Congress.[29]

Again it was Nebraska's Congressman, William Jennings Bryan, now a lame-duck, who articulated the opposition of western and southern free silver Democrats to this "heresy" from the East. In a magazine article commenting on Cleveland's message Bryan presented a Democratic argument against bank currency. Quoting extensively on the subject from the writings of Thomas Jefferson, he argued that traditionally the Democratic party had opposed bank paper. The use of bank note currency, he stated, was an act of governmental favoritism to bankers, not any more justified than permitting the farmer to issue currency against his farm or the professional man against his library. Bryan further objected that reliance upon bank note issues gave private individuals control of the volume of currency. When bankers gained such a privilege, he wrote, they meddled in politics to prevent the enactment of legislation which would interfere with their business. In conclusion, Bryan condemned Cleveland for failing to propose "a substantial remedy for our financial ills." He said: "We suffer from a disease which is world-wide in its extent, namely the appreciation of gold. There is but one remedy, the restoration of silver; and the longer we delay, the greater will be the difficulty of applying it." [30]

By late summer 1895, observers began to express the belief that the efforts of the Cleveland administration to convince the public of the wisdom of Cleveland's financial policies had been rewarded by success. Comments to this effect were made not only by administration supporters but by bimetallists as well.[31] Thus encouraged, the Cleveland administration slackened its efforts in August; and at the same time the Sound Currency Committee of the New York Reform Club abandoned most of its work. Josiah Patterson and other grass roots politicians protested that the battle was far from won, that, in fact, sound money men ought to redouble rather than reduce their efforts.[32]

When the elections in November 1895, brought further disastrous losses for the Democrats in Illinois, Kentucky, and Ohio, the tragic division within the party was revealed in the disparate analyses of the causes for defeat. Altgeld, for example, analyzing the losses in Ohio and Kentucky, concluded that it was the endorsement there of the financial policy of the Cleveland administration which explained Democratic defeat.[33] On the other hand, a spokesman for Cleveland returning to Washington from voting in Kentucky said: "I think it would have been an easy thing for Mr. Blackburn to have secured enough delegates to have insured his re-election to the United States Senate if he had refrained from heaping personal abuse on the President and other members of the administration, had not pressed the silver issue and had run on his personal popularity." [34]

One of the leaders of the movement to commit the Democratic party to free silver. Senator Isham Harris of Tennessee, spoke on the long-range, national significance of the Democratic defeats in the election of 1895: "In the light of recent election results there is, in my opinion, no hope of Democratic success in 1896 unless we can succeed in so organizing the bimetallic Democrats as to secure in the National Convention a plain, distinct and unmistakable declaration in favor of the free and unlimited coinage of both silver and gold, without regard to the financial policies of any country, and, therefore, it appears to me that we should redouble our efforts to secure such organization." [35]

In December 1895, Cleveland made his last major attempt to stop the national drift to free silver, when he devoted most of his annual message to Congress to an analysis of the currency situation and a defense of his policies. He blamed the shrinkage in the gold reserves on the McKinley tariff, the Sherman Silver Purchase Act, and the agitation for the free and unlimited coinage of silver. He defended his sale of bonds to the Morgan syndicate, saying, "I have never had the slightest misgiving concerning the wisdom or propriety of this arrangement." He proposed that the Greenbacks and the treasury notes issued by the government under the Sherman Silver Purchase Act be retired and that the deficiency in currency thus created be made up by an increase in the circulation of national bank notes.[36] From Denver, Colorado, by telegraph came this reaction: "You have this day declared for dear money and cheap humanity." [37]

5

Mobilization
of the Silver Democrats

During the weeks that administration Democrats, under the half-hearted leadership of Cleveland, were making gestures toward the organization of a campaign to oppose free silver, the free silver Democrats proceeded energetically to establish a national organization to win control of their party. In 1895 three particular circumstances appeared to make such activity desirable. First, conservative Democrats were organizing, though ineptly, to shape the party's opinion and to control its machinery. Second, the free silver movement was being organized outside of regular political lines, on both the state and national levels; and the popularity of free silver ideas in the West, Middle West, and South created a real threat that Democrats would be attracted to an independent free silver party. Third, free silver had always been a plank in the Populist party's platform. Now some Populist leaders advocated that the party give this issue a central, if not exclusive, position in their platform, with the object of winning to the party those voters who were unhappy with the monetary policies of the old parties. In the West and South the possibility of such action by the Populist party was a clear threat to the Democrats.

It was the conference which Josiah Patterson had organized in June which gave silver Democrats an occasion to begin the organization of a national movement to commit their party to silver. Concerned about the possibility that Patterson's efforts at Memphis might strengthen conservative resistance to free silver in their party, silver Democrats called a meeting to convene in Memphis in mid-June, shortly after the meeting inspired by Patterson's efforts had adjourned. Patterson's meeting had been a gathering of southerners and partisanly Democratic. The Memphis silver meeting was national in scope and nominally non-partisan. Actually most of the delegates to this meeting were from the South, and most of them were Democrats. There were a number of westerners and middle westerners in attendance, though, as well as several Populists and independent silver party men; but no silver Republicans made an appearance.[1] William Jennings Bryan was there as one of the principal speakers, and he managed to capture more than his share of newspaper publicity by dramatizing the way in which he and the other silver Democrats were searching their souls for an answer as to whether to fight for silver within the Democratic party or outside it. Before the convention adjourned, however, Bryan made it clear that he was committed to the fight to make the Democratic party clearly and distinctly a free silver party and that he would not leave his party until that fight was lost.[2]

The most significant outcome of this meeting was the organization at Memphis shortly after the convention had adjourned of a National Democratic Bimetallic Committee. It was this Committee which organized silver Democrats to control their national convention in 1896 and which organized and controlled the convention formally to commit the Democratic party to the free coinage of silver. The action at Memphis took the form of a letter signed by Senators Isham G. Harris of Tennessee, James K. Jones of Arkansas, and David Turpie of Indiana. It was addressed to prominent silver Democrats throughout the country. In their letter the senators explained the necessity of a "thorough organization" of free silver Democrats, if they were to succeed in "controlling the action of the National Democratic Convention of 1896, upon this vitally important question." To complete an organization of silver Democrats for this purpose they called a conference in the District of Columbia on August 14, 1895.[3]

When prominent silver Democrats from the West, Middle West, and South streamed into Washington in mid-August, Cleveland was at his summer retreat in New Jersey. It was perhaps best that Cleveland was not in the vicinity of this convention in which so many men so thoroughly hated him. At one point this exchange occurred as ex-Congressman Fithian from Illinois said: "I was defeated at the last election because I, with other gentlemen, had to bear the odium of an administration that did not voice democratic principles." "Cleveland beat you," shouted another delegate, as Fithian sat down; and the convention gave way to a turmoil of shouting.

When quiet returned, a delegate said: "Grover Cleveland and John G. Carlisle will go down the ages, hand in hand, amid the execrations of mankind, as two of the most stupendous frauds of the century." [4]

This gathering was exclusively Democratic in membership. It was national in scope. It included office holders and ex-office holders as well as Democrats who had never aspired to office. Those who came were acting in their individual capacities and not as the representatives of machine organizations or party clubs. In the first session Senator Harris presided temporarily, yielding the chair when Senator Jones was elected permanent chairman of the convention. Next a committee on resolutions, composed of a delegate from each state and headed by Senator John W. Daniel of Virginia, and a committee on organization, headed by ex-Senator Jarvis of North Carolina, were established.

As the delegates expressed their sentiments informally and as their ideas were formally presented in an address adopted by the convention, it could be seen that certain notions had become fixed in their minds. They were, first of all, convinced that the free coinage of silver was traditional Democratic doctrine. The formal address adopted by the convention stated that the purpose for which they met was to "rescue the old party founded by Thomas Jefferson from plutocratic domination." The address then gave a history of coinage in the United States and concluded that, from the beginning of government, following policies formulated by Jefferson and firmly established by Jackson, the Democratic party had been the party of bimetallism. The Republican party had struck the first blow at bimetallism by passing "surreptitiously" the Coinage Act of 1873; and now, through their policies of recent years, the Cleveland Democrats had joined the Republicans on this issue.[5]

On another aspect of the problem—that Democrats might be enticed into other parties on the silver question—they were also clear. "We do not want democrats to have to go into the third party in order to show their allegiance to silver . . . ," said a Tennessee delegate. Other delegates were reported as expressing the feeling that a declaration for free silver by the Democratic party, even if it did not lead to victory in 1896, would help the party because it would bring free silver Democrats trooping back from the Populists.[6]

The committee on organization provided the lasting achievement of the convention in submitting a plan for a permanent organization of free silver Democrats. This plan established a national committee composed of one Democrat from each state, territory, and the District of Columbia. Also there was to be an executive committee, for the time being composed of Senators Harris, Jones, and Turpie, Secretary of State Hinrichsen of Illinois, and ex-Congressman Casey Young of Tennessee. The members of the national committee were to be appointed by the free silver Democrats of each state by whatever methods they judged expedient in their own states. The state representative so delegated was to have broad responsibility for organizing the silver Democrats county by county, setting up silver clubs to recruit non-Democratic silverites into the Democratic silver movement, and to conduct any other activity which might be helpful to the cause.[7]

Without delay the executive committee began to organize the western and southern states for "the control of the next National Convention."[8] Free silver, the orphan of American politics, had found a home within a faction of the Democratic party. Could it be made a permanent party adoption?

Within recent months there had been emerging another force for free silver within the Democratic party, a strikingly independent, self-propelled, one-man committee—William Jennings Bryan of Nebraska. Bryan possessed a quick and well disciplined intelligence; and he had the aid of a devoted wife, whose intellectual qualities complemented his own. His major asset undoubtedly was an unusually beautiful speaking voice, which he could project with ease to the furthest corners of a large and crowded public hall. Working with his wife he composed and rehearsed his speeches carefully and committed them to memory. But he could think on his feet; he could improvise readily for any occasion. He was a virtually faultless public speaker.

Bryan's effectiveness in politics was not confined exclusively to the public lecture hall, however. He possessed a magnetism which readily inspired confidence and affection. He cultivated and mastered the arts of personal politics. Friendships established as Bryan traveled and spoke over the country were not neglected. From his office issued a steady flow of letters, newspaper clippings, autographed photographs, and reprints of speeches. He was a tireless hand shaker; he had a large file of names and addresses; he and his wife maintained an extensive correspondence. It is probable that few men in the history of American politics have had so many friends so passionately devoted to him as did Bryan.

William Jennings Bryan's career was a dedication to the nineteenth-century, middle-class belief that conscientious application to the duty at hand could result in the highest recognition, including election to the Presidency of the United States. When the presidential lightning struck Bryan is not known. Probably Bryan himself could not have named the moment. But the manner in which Bryan from an early age cultivated his talents and watched for his opportunities made him, in this respect, a model to aspiring Americans of all classes.

It was of little moment that Bryan achieved slight success as a lawyer. He exercised his talents with eminent success in another field—the field of public inspiration and enlightenment. In one sense his career was a failure, for he was defeated in three attempts to win the Presidency. Viewed, however, from the standards of his own generation Bryan was a great success. He became to the multitudes who venerated him the great crusader for political truth and social justice. No one used the prevailing media of public information with such success as he did. And Bryan lived to believe that he had seen his crusade become a success. Before his death he was able to point (and he frequently did) to a long list of significant reforms for which he had campaigned and which had become law.

Though Bryan lived through one quarter of the twentieth century, in his thinking, his ideals, and in his political techniques he was always of the nineteenth century. When other talented youngsters from the Middle Border and the Middle West turned East, toward the glittering opportunities of urban America, Bryan, after studying law in Chicago, turned his back on the metropolis. After a brief trial at law in downstate Illinois, he deliberately pulled up stakes and went west to Nebraska. Here among the fast disappearing vestiges of America's last frontier he found his proper home, as one of the last among nineteenth-century men to give shape and voice to the agrarian political ideologies of Jefferson and Jackson.

Contemporaries of Bryan from the prairies would also make their voices heard in the land, for the origins of Willa Cather, Hamlin Garland, Vachel Lindsay, and Edgar Lee Masters were much like Bryan's. These voices, like Bryan's, came out of the frontier; and they always showed its influence. But they turned eastward to the cities, became a part of the twentieth century, making a transition which Bryan never achieved. Nevertheless, the reactions of Cather, Lindsay, Garland, and Masters to Bryan show that they sympathized with his crusades in the 1890's. In those years they deeply admired him. Each when he wrote of Bryan saw him in his truest role—that of the crusader for popular democracy. This appreciation is found in the analytic approval of an essay in praise of Bryan written by Willa Cather early in her career, in the enthusiasm of Garland's campaign support in 1896, in the lyric ecstasy of Lindsay's poem, "Bryan," and it is insistent in the prose of Edgar Lee Master's little book, *The New Star Chamber:*

> The period of American political history between 1896 and 1900 belongs distinctively to Mr. Bryan. When a retrospect shall be taken of it a long time hence he will stand out as the greatest figure of all men then living in the United States. . . . The chilling shock to the ideals of liberty administered by his second defeat can never be fully expressed. Succeeding generations must mature and suffer before they can gather from the words which embodied the people's hope of him, and the words which recorded his loss of the election their deep and painful significance.[9]

The economic depression of the 1890's provided the ideal stage upon which William Jennings Bryan would rise to prominence. Bryan did not create the popular opinion that the nation's economic ills were due to the abandonment of the free coinage of silver, but the argument that this was so was well suited to Bryan's temperament and purposes. It was an argument that economic disaster had struck because Democratic principles found to be good and true in former years had been betrayed.

It was only an accident of time and place that the great crusade of Bryan's life should have been conducted on the issue of free silver. Beyond this very little was accidental in Bryan's career with free silver through 1896. Once he recognized the importance of the issue in politics he set out to master it, and no one of his generation mastered it so well in its political implications as he. He read all the books on the subject which came to his attention, he took notes, he asked questions of those better informed on free silver than himself. He wrote speeches, polished them, delivered them, rewrote them, gave them again, and again, and again. His wife helped him in all the stages, down to the last, when she sat in his audience and watched for mistakes in gesture, intonation, and expression which he must not repeat the next time.

The extent of his mastery was evident in August 1893, when, in the special session of Congress which Cleveland had called to repeal the

Sherman Silver Purchase Act, Bryan, speaking against repeal, delivered an extraordinary speech on the money question. It was the high point, at least for advocates of free silver, of that session of the Congress. To multitudes who believed that the free coinage of silver would ease their burdens Bryan became a hero. Already the people were coining heroic sobriquets—"Nebraska Cyclone," "Knight of the West," "The Silver-tongued Orator." The silver cause had never lacked heroes, men like Bland, Teller, and Stewart; but none of these had the eloquence or the personal magnetism of William Jennings Bryan.

Bryan's speech against repeal of the Sherman Act was a good example of his intellect and rhetoric. It began with an allusion to a great moment in the historical past, when, as in 1893, the fate of mankind seemed to hang in the balance: "Historians tell us that the victory of Charles Martel at Tours determined the history of all Europe for centuries. It was a contest 'between the Cresent and the Cross,' and when, on that fateful day, the Frankish prince drove the followers of Abderrahman he rescued the West from the 'all-destroying power of Islam,' and saved to Europe its Christian civilization. A greater than Tours is here!" [10]

Having set his subject upon a large stage, Bryan next proceeded to a thorough analysis of it, leaning heavily upon quotations from the authorities, and especially the authorities who favored the gold standard. Thus he quoted from J. Laurence Laughlin and William Stanley Jevons to demonstrate that the price of gold was unstable and that a dollar under gold monometallism would suffer from instability. To prove that there was not enough gold in the world to sustain normal business operations and that the exclusive use of gold would have a numbing effect on business prosperity he quoted again from Jevons and others. [11]

Bryan demonstrated his learning and his technical mastery of the subject, but he also provided ample proof that he knew the world of the common man. For example, in arguing that the appreciation of the value of gold increased the real mortgaged indebtedness of the farmer, he said:

The mortgage remains nominally the same, though the debt has actually become twice as great. Will he [the farmer] be deceived by the cry of 'honest dollar?' If he should loan a Nebraska neighbor a hog weighing 100 pounds and the next spring demand in return a hog weighing 200 pounds he would be called dishonest, even though he contended that he was only demanding one hog—just the number he loaned. Society has become accustomed to some very nice distinctions. The poor man is called a socialist if he believes that the wealth of the rich should be divided among the poor, but the rich man is called a financier if he devises a plan by which the pittance of the poor can be converted to his use.

The poor man who takes property by force is called a thief, but the creditor who can by legislation make a debtor pay a dollar twice as large as he borrowed is lauded as the friend of sound currency. The man who wants the people to destroy the Government is an anarchist, but the man who wants the Government to destroy the people is a patriot.[12]

Here are the apt metaphors, the comparisons based on everyday things, and the twisted logic of the "Cross of Gold" speech. Later in the speech appeared something else, which Bryan used with telling effect. He linked his immediate subject to a larger cause, that of civilization and mankind, which he reminded his listeners, was linked to the past and the future of the Democratic party. As in the "Cross of Gold" speech, this feature emerged most distinctly in the peroration with which he concluded:

He was called a demagogue and his followers a mob, but the immortal Jefferson dared to follow the best promptings of his heart. He placed man above matter, humanity above property, and spurning the bribes of wealth and power, pleaded the cause of the common people. It was this devotion to their interests which made his party invincible while he lived and will make his name revered while history endures. And what message comes to us from the Hermitage? When a crisis like the present arose and the national bank of his day sought to control the politics of the nation, God raised up an Andrew Jackson, who had the courage to grapple with the great enemy, and by overthrowing it, he made himself the idol of the people and reinstated the Democratic party in public confidence. What will the decision be today. The Democratic party has won the greatest success in its history. Standing upon this victory-crowned summit, will it turn its face to the rising or the setting sun? Will it choose blessings or cursings—life or death—which? which? [13]

Now Bryan was a national figure. Invitations for speaking engagements poured in from all sections of the nation, and Bryan traveled by rail in all directions to speak for the "cause." He arranged for special printings of his speeches, had a portrait photograph made of himself, and distributed his speeches and his photograph widely, particularly in the rabidly free silver areas of the agrarian West and South.[14] He appeared at many silver conferences where typically, even if he were not scheduled to speak, the cry would go up, "Bryan! Bryan!" On such occasions he always spoke, and spoke effectively, stirring his listeners to enthusiastic shouts of approval. On his tours he made hosts of friends, who were added to his list of correspondents. Before long their letters to Bryan contained phrases such as these:

The re-formation of parties has got to come & you are the right man in the right place.[15]

When the great west and the south join hands and touch elbows politically as they ought have done long ago we are for you for President.[16]

I have begun to talk you for President—and I mean it. No gift in the hands of the people is too high for you in my Judgement—, and you can rest assured that I am for you all of the time.[17]

Soon newspapers were publishing comments of similar character. Among them were these: "Congressman Bryan is, to use the street vernacular, a 'hot thing'. . . . It is not unlikely that Mr. Bryan will shine as a presidential possibility next year." [18] And, "Mr. Bryan for president is not a possibility but a strong probability." [19]

Bryan did not run for Congress in 1894, but in 1893 and 1894 he was one of Nebraska's leading candidates for election to the United States Senate. In 1893, in a legislature in which the Democrats held the balance of power between the Republicans and the Populists, Bryan, seeing that he could not command enough votes to win the post for himself, threw his support to the Populist candidate, William V. Allen.[20] The following year Bryan campaigned for election to the Senate, but in that election the Republican party won undisputed control of the Nebraska legislature.

In 1894 Bryan accepted an appointment as editor of the Omaha *World-Herald*, an important western propaganda organ supporting free silver. This position was given to him under an agreement that was not severely demanding on his time or energies. He was required only to furnish several editorials a week. Thus, he found another opportunity to bring his name and his ideas before the public. Of course, most of his editorials were on the subject of the free coinage of silver.[21]

As the intensity of the financial debate mounted in 1895 Bryan remained a central figure in the free silver agitation in the Democratic party. No one individual was as active or ubiquitous. Yet, as the Democratic National Bimetallic Committee emerged as the formal organization to fight for free silver within the party, Bryan praised it and cooperated with it; but he did not join it. He was not a member of the executive committee; he was not the Nebraska member of the national committee.

Bryan did not work in the Democratic National Bimetallic Committee because he had already assigned himself a larger role in the silver cause and in the Democratic party. The task which he undertook was to unite all those who believed in free silver—independents, Populists, Republicans, and Democrats—with the object of bringing them together under one banner and that, if at all possible, the banner of the Democratic party. What he was undertaking was to carry out on a national scale the kind of campaign which he had waged successfully in Nebraska. When Bryan was elected to the House of Representatives in Nebraska, no Democrat could win in his district without independent, Populist, and Republican votes. It now appeared that rehabilitation of the Democratic party and ultimate electoral victory nationally depended upon similar tactics throughout the Nation, even in the traditionally Democratic South. Therefore, while the Democratic National Bimetallic Committee shouldered the burden of reorganizing the party internally, Bryan individually took on the larger task of rallying the great multitude of free silver voters, who were not traditionally Democrats, into a silver Democratic party.

Bryan never tried to dissociate himself from the Democratic party. Though he did talk of leaving the party, he made it clear that this would happen only after the party had in effect abandoned him by adopting policies in conflict with its traditions. Conservatives in his own party spoke of Bryan as a Populist, but Bryan never agreed with this. He never admitted that he had anything more than free silver in common with the Populist party. Their platform contained, he said, many principles with which he did not agree. True, he wrote to a correspondent in October 1893, that the Populist party at its worst was not as dangerous as the conservative wings of the two old parties; but this declaration must be considered in the context of the entire letter in which Bryan also wrote: "I have not left the Democratic party, but I am ready to do so as soon as I am satisfied that it is wedded to the gold standard." [22]

Of course, such demonstrations of independence on Bryan's part made him attractive to the Populists. They believed that the logic of events would be such that men like Bryan would be forced out of the Democratic party and into the Populist party. Bryan hoped and believed that events could be shaped to create a somewhat different logic which would cause Populists to abandon their party and become Democrats.

In the South "Pitchfork" Ben Tillman went further in the direction of cooperation with the Populist party and edged closer to repudiation of the Democratic party than Bryan. Indeed, Tillman became so closely identified verbally with Populism that in the press there was a great deal of confusion as to which party he belonged. Actually Tillman, like Bryan, remained consistently a Democrat and was never close to breaking with his party, though his capacity for speaking with violence often made it appear that he was on the verge of so doing.

Bryan and Tillman were playing much the same game in their respective sections, and much about Bryan's motives and tactics was revealed when Charles M. Rosser of Texas attempted to establish a Bryan-Tillman axis in which the two would cooperate as the leaders of a national silver ticket in 1896. In February 1896, Rosser wrote Bryan proposing a ticket headed by Bryan with Tillman as his running mate. Such a ticket, said Rosser, would rally many Populists and Democrats, "who might be on the eve of deserting us." He proposed that Bryan inform the Populists that he planned to stay with the Democratic party until it became clear that it was controlled by the "gold-bugs." The next step, Rosser continued, would be to persuade the Populists to hold their convention after the Democratic convention, "so that in [the] event a Reform party was a necessity they might fuse with us." [23]

Rosser had outlined a program which Bryan had already had in operation for several weeks, with the exception that Bryan did not view Tillman as a suitable running mate.[24] On January 1, 1896, Bryan had mailed to the Populist leaders, James B. Weaver, Ignatius Donnelly, Marion Butler, James Kyle, William V. Allen, and Clarence Darrow, a letter in which he said that those who believed in free silver could succeed in the campaign of 1896 only if they were united on the same ticket. He could not, he wrote, undertake to predict exactly how this could be done; but he believed that there was one line of strategy which the Populists must adopt: "I think it is of vital importance that the populist convention shall not be held until after the democratic and republican conventions. It can then take advantage of the errors of the old parties. Wise action will be much more probable if the convention meets at such a time as to be able to take a survey of the whole field and understand all the conditions." [25]

If, during 1896, the Cleveland forces controlled the Democratic party, in the revolution which would follow in the West and South

Bryan would readily find a home in the Populist party. On the other hand, if the silver Democrats controlled their party in 1896, Bryan's friendships with the Populists and the other independent silver elements would make him an important personality in his party because of his ability to draw these elements into it. Meanwhile, all silver elements recognized that he was doing yeoman service for the cause, and that recognition carried its own rewards.[26]

Increasingly Bryan was asserting leadership in his own right within the Democratic party itself. With what must have appeared to some as a considerable degree of presumption, Bryan wrote to Democratic leaders throughout the nation asking from them reports on the organization of their party for silver within their states and districts. He was setting himself up as a clearing-house for information on silver and as a conscience to the Democratic party.[27]

On February 26, 1896, he spoke to troubled free silver Democrats who were worrying over their course of action, if the Democratic convention should be controlled by Cleveland "gold-bugs." He pointed out that eastern Democrats would not support a free silver candidate, and he demanded for western Democrats the same freedom not to support a "gold-bug." More important, however, was another argument he advanced to justify a break from a gold standard candidate and platform:

> If to continue Mr. Cleveland's financial policy is to declare war against the common people, what friend of the common people would be willing to enlist in such a warfare, even at the command of his party? . . .
> If the question was an unimportant one it might be settled within the party and the decision acquiesced in; but it is a question that touches every man, woman and child in the nation, a question of right or wrong, a question of justice or injustice, a question of freedom or slavery.[28]

Western Democrats who faced in their localities similar problems to those experienced by Bryan in Nebraska were enthusiastic about the position which Bryan had taken.[29] Southern Democrats, who viewed the Democratic machine in their section as an instrument essential to white supremacy, sympathized with Bryan's arguments but were reluctant to announce for publication that they would bolt a gold standard nomination.[30]

Bryan, consciously or unconsciously, was also providing for free silver Democrats another element essential to the victory of their cause in his emergence as a leader, who, unscarred by long service on the battle fields of politics, was now building a national following on the issue which seemed fated to dominate the coming election campaign. In preparation was the leader who would stand before the Democratic convention in 1896 and, through his ability to relate free silver to social justice and Democratic traditions, take the final step which would give him control of the party.

6

The Populists Outflanked

The Populist party was the result of a native American and basically agrarian movement. It grew from the discontent of the farmer with the refusal of the Democratic and Republican parties to develop programs which showed any concern for the economic and financial problems which pressed upon the farmers in the decades following the Civil War.

The Populist party did not emerge until the 1890's, but in every decade since the Civil War agrarian leaders had found it necessary to build third party political organizations to fight for objectives which farmers keenly desired but which the regular party organizations ignored. Building upon Jacksonian traditions, the Granger movement, though an organized political movement only on the state level, had taught the farmer to suspect railroads as monopolistic corporations and had accustomed farmers to believe in government regulation of corporations. The Greenback-Labor movement had introduced the farmer to the arguments of monetary inflation and had led him also to see the advantages of wooing industrial labor to the support of popular movements. By the time the Farm Alliances began to emerge in the agricultural states of the West and the South in the 1880's the farmer had developed a lengthy roster of reforms which seemed important to him, but which the regular parties faithfully ignored.

It has been shown that most of the leaders of the Populist party and most of the men elected to office as Populists were not farmers but were instead lawyers, editors, business men, and professional reformers.[1] This should not, however, obscure the fact that the ideas with which they worked derived from the agrarian traditions of the pre-Civil War period. There was not a foreign-born personality among the Populist leaders. Most were born before or during the Civil War and grew up in an environment strongly permeated with the agrarian philosophies of Jefferson and Jackson. This was also true of the great body of labor and independent reform leaders, like Debs, Sovereign, George, and Bellamy, who cooperated with the Populist party in the '90's and who supported Bryan in 1896.

The constituency with which the Populists worked most effectively was the rural, native American of English or Irish descent. Populism did not thrive in those communities where recent German, Scandinavian, or other European immigrants were concentrated. This was first of all true because Populism belonged to a tradition of agrarian radicalism so distinctively an outgrowth of American political belief and experience that recent immigrants found in it little that was congenial or identifiable. It was also true because most of these immigrants were reared in traditions of political thought which caused them to view Populistic monetary proposals as either dangerously radical and experimental or absurdly conservative and wholly innocent of the reforms fundamental to the reconstruction of society. As a result, German and Scandinavian immigrants in the rural West, when confronted with the financial heresies of the Populists, hastened into the folds of the Republican or Democratic parties, where they found the assurance of orthodox financial policies.[2] On the other hand, German Socialist immigrants tended to find Populism hopelessly naive. They agreed with Daniel DeLeon, leader of the Socialist Labor party, that it was not a revolutionary but rather a reactionary movement. DeLeon said that Populism's "object is to perpetuate a class that modern progress has doomed, and its only result can be to prolong the agony of the poor people who belong to it by deferring the day of their complete emancipation."[3]

The Populist leadership was aware of the potential significance of the labor vote, and they made overtures in various ways to organized and unorganized labor. They did succeed before 1896 in persuading James R. Sovereign, head of the Knights of Labor, to join their executive committee; but Terence V. Powderly, whom Sovereign had recently displaced as president of the Knights, joined the Republicans. The value of the support given by the Knights of Labor is doubtful, because that organization was rapidly deteriorating.

Another labor leader sympathetic to the Populist movement was Eugene V. Debs of the American Railway Union, but prior to 1896 Debs was in a transitional phase in his conversion to political action, and his services to Populism were minor. As for his union, the Populists gave it no aid in its crisis during the Pullman strike in 1894; and after that the American Railway Union declined rapidly and had little claim to recognition in either unionism or politics.

On the rise was the American Federation of Labor. The leaders of this organization, however, after careful study of the American industrial community and the American working man, had concluded to build a conservative, job-conscious union which would avoid any but pressure politics. Unlike the radical, politically oriented Knights of Labor, American Railway Union, and the later Industrial Workers of the World, all of which had predominantly native American leadership, the American Federation of Labor was conceived and led in its early years by immigrants who had little or no experience with the agrarian traditions of American political action. These were the formative years of the Federation; it was far from wielding the power it later possessed. The Federation would not have added measurably to Populist success had it been fully cooperative; but it was significant that at the moment the Populists were trying to attract labor votes, the organization which in later decades would dominate organized labor was developing a tradition hostile to the political radicalism of the Populist movement.[4]

The first principle in the tradition in which the Populists labored was a belief in political action, which included a strong tendency to look to the national or the state capital for remedies to oppressing ills. The program of the party can be broken down into two broad categories: (1) Proposals to use political power to effect economic or social regulation in the public interest; and (2) proposals for political reforms which would restore control of government to the people that they might have the power to use government to establish regulations for public purposes. In the first category were the declarations for currency and banking reform, government regulation or ownership of railroads and telegraph, destruction or public control of monopolistic corporations, and the development of legislation and administrative policies to protect labor. In the second category were direct election of United States Senators, a limitation of service in the Presidency to one term, direct legislation such as initiative and referendum, and the recall of public officials.

The first Populist successes in the West in 1891 and 1892 were spectacular for a political movement so recently established. In 1892, through fusion with the Democrats, the Populists took control of the state government of Kansas, excepting the lower house of the legislature, which the Republicans controlled by a small margin. In many of the western states the Populists easily outdistanced the traditionally weak Democratic party and were well on the way to establishing themselves as the second party in that section. In the presidential election of 1892 in many western states the Populists managed to put up fusion electoral tickets with the Democrats by which the Democratic ticket did not appear on the ballot and the Populist candidate, James B. Weaver, with the combined support of the Democrats and Populists, received the electoral vote. The confidence of the western Populists was now at its peak. As they saw the situation, they had developed an independent position so persuasive to the average voter that by absorbing both Democrats and Republicans they had become the majority party in their section. Southern Populists had not achieved such striking success, but they were no less energetic and enthusiastic.

The election of 1894 brought a reversal of the western and southern Populist successes. In the West, the Populists, confident of their ascendance, spurned the fusion with the Democrats which they had welcomed two years earlier. As a result, though they gained votes, they lost control of the offices which they had won in 1891 and 1892. Only in Nebraska, where some fusion with Democrats had been arranged, could they claim any victories. The hard lesson of the election returns in the West seemed to be that the western Populists had not yet established an independent movement which could win a majority vote without Democratic fusion aid.[5] In the South, on the other hand, Populists succeeded in establishing fusion with Republicans; and in North Carolina, Populists and Republicans won a stunning victory through which they captured control of the state legislature and elected a Populist and a Republican to the United States Senate.[6] In other southern states Populists did not gain victories as they did in North Carolina, but in several states of the lower South the Populist vote doubled.[7]

Another heartening feature of the election for the southern Populist was the readiness shown by southern Republicans to make fusion arrangements. There was little, if any, meeting of minds between Populists and Republicans on the basic planks of their respective platforms, but both groups had the common problem of getting a fair ballot and a fair count in the one-party South. In mid-term election years, at least, they could unite in their common hatred of the Democrats and unfair Democratic election practices.[8] It was not clear that fusion would be so attractive to either party in the South in a presidential election year.

In the Middle West, the election of 1894 also saw a significant gain in Populist votes. In Illinois, Indiana, Ohio, Wisconsin, and Minnesota the Populist vote in 1894 was significantly larger than in 1892. But in this section the fact that both the Democratic and Republican organizations were strong in their own right discouraged fusion by either with the Populists.

As Populist leaders in the various sections analyzed the results of the 1894 election and considered their strategy for the future, it became apparent that there were in the party sharply divergent points of view, based in part on sectional alignments. One group, which had its strongest support in the West and Middle West, advocated narrowing the emphasis for the immediate future upon a few key issues of the Omaha platform. The subjects usually singled out for such emphasis were government regulation and ownership of railroads, initiative and referendum, and the free coinage of silver.

Those who advocated simplification of the program in this fashion left little doubt that they anticipated that the major emphasis should be placed on the latter issue—the free coinage of silver. Herman Taubeneck, chairman of the National Executive Committee of the party, in an interview published a few days after the election, expressed enthusiasm about the results in both the South and the West and concluded that these two sections must unite politically under the leadership of the Populist party. He believed that the silver issue would be the instrument of such an union. Promising that the party would begin to organize immediately for the 1896 campaign, he said, "We shall, more than likely, confine ourselves to the money question in the future, and make that the test of party fealty." [9]

The Populist failure to win control of Kansas in its own right without Democratic fusion caused the Populists of that state to conclude that they must find an issue which would give them majority control.

This statement by Senator William A. Peffer indicated the direction in which most of them were moving: "Speaking for myself, and I think, for the populists generally, I am perfectly willing to unite in such an organisation and make free silver the single issue of the campaign." [10]

There was another powerful faction in the party which opposed narrowing the program to free silver. This group had its supporters in all sections: in the West in Davis H. Waite, the Populist governor of Colorado; [11] in the Middle West in Ignatius Donnelly, who was the author of the Omaha Platform; and in New England in George F. Washburn. But the section in which it found its most articulate and universal support was the South. To some extent, the southern attitude was due to Populist election successes in that section in 1894; mainly, though, it was caused by Populist fear of the Democratic party, from which most of its members had been recruited.

In the one-party South, where the issue of race supremacy was an omnipresent factor in politics, Populists lived with the threat of ballot-box cheating and physical violence in their struggle to overcome traditional Democratic control. By November of 1894 southern Democratic leaders were trying to disassociate themselves from Cleveland's defense of the single gold standard and were beginning to advocate the free coinage of silver as Democratic doctrine. Southern Populists saw little chance to compete with the powerful Democratic organization if the election campaign should be narrowed to the single issue of silver. Southern Populists, therefore, argued that their party must stay "in the middle-of-the-road," adhering faithfully to the comprehensive program of the Omaha platform. The fear of southern Populists that they would be absorbed by the Democrats if they concentrated on the silver issue was well expressed by a Missouri Populist: "They [the Democrats] simply run with the stampeding cattle until they circle them back into camp. That is what they will do in the coinage matter." [12]

Populist opposition to a narrow free silver platform was based in certain quarters on a reluctance to abandon other financial reforms which the party had proposed. Some Populists saw in the issuance of Greenbacks or similar paper currency a solution to the money problem more fundamental than free silver, while others believed that the sub-treasury system would provide the essential financial action. B. O. Flower, editor of the *Arena*, advocated "a return to the money of our Fathers," with gold, silver, and paper used interchangeably.[13] Marion

Butler, in a Washington interview, said that what the Populists "really want is a change involving the entire overthrow of the present financial policy." [14] James Baird Weaver advocated that the Populists go to the people on the money question alone. "Not," he wrote, "on the silver issue alone, but distinctly favoring unrestricted coinage at the ratio of 16 to 1, and legal tender government paper, with neither bonds nor banks of issue." [15]

A socialist faction comprised the third group within the Populist party. They had no major argument with the planks of the Omaha platform, and in party debates they supported the "middle-of-the-roaders" against the "one-ideaed" silverites. There were never many active socialists in the Populist party; for the organized socialist movement, the Socialist Labor party, never viewed the Populist party as an organization which they might permeate. Mostly it was unaffiliated socialists, influenced more strongly by English than by continental socialism, who were intrigued by the possibility that the Populist party might be used as the basis for an American socialist movement.

A major effort in this direction was made in Chicago, where a group of men and women strongly drawn to the ideas and methods of English socialists, tried to persuade the Chicago and Illinois Populist organizations to declare their support for the nationalization of the means of production. The leaders of this movement, Henry Demarest Lloyd and Thomas J. Morgan, devised a program declaring for "collective ownership by the people of all means of production and distribution." But attempts in 1894 and 1895 to get Illinois Populists to declare their support for such a platform were bitterly opposed and were defeated.[16] In Milwaukee Victor Berger, a leader of the Socialist Labor party, was sympathetic to Populism and believed that his organization and the Populists could find some basis for cooperation.[17] Berger's disciple, Eugene Debs, was also sympathetic to Populism; but he never made a major effort to convert the party to socialism.[18]

The broad scope of the Omaha platform and the sympathy shown by men like Waite, Donnelly, and Weaver to reform ideas of all kinds encouraged other reformers to believe that they and the Populists might arrange a mutually beneficial combination. Prohibitionists, for example, appreciated that their program for government control or ownership of the manufacture and sale of alcoholic liquors had features similar to Populist programs for government control of banking and transportation. Also many Prohibitionists were inspired with sympathy for the laboring classes; and, like the socialists, believed that they might realize worthy social objectives through cooperation with the Populists. For the same reason, single-tax enthusiasts tried to persuade the Populists that their program, linked with the social reform features of the Omaha platform, would lead the way to winning public support for a major transformation of society. Political reformers, such as those who advocated direct legislation through initiative and referendum, also hoped to find acceptance and sympathetic cooperation in the Populist movement. In Ohio Jacob Coxey advanced his theories about government issues of money, bonds, and public works projects within the Populist party. In 1894 as a Populist candidate for the United States House of Representatives he ran a close second to the Republican victor while polling more votes than his Democratic opponent.[19]

The encouraging and yet disquieting results of the 1894 elections, the deepening financial depression and the accompanying social unrest, the apparent success of the free silver agitation, and the increasing pressure from socialist and other reform organizations caused many Populists to feel, after the November elections, the need for a party conference to consider reshaping the Omaha platform. As a result Chairman Taubeneck, on December 10, issued a call for a conference in St. Louis on December 28 and 29, 1894. The call, sent to labor leaders and reformers, as well as Populists, was described by Taubeneck as "broad enough to include all who work and vote with the Populist party." [20] The conference had been initiated by western Populists, who believed that events had conspired to make the money issue the chief issue in politics. The silver Populists did not, however, succeed in controlling the St. Louis conference, which concluded in a strongly supported action to reaffirm the Omaha platform.

The action of the St. Louis conference did not settle the policy debate within the Populist party. It was, in fact, only the first engagement in a struggle that was to last for more than a year. Western Populists did not accept the St. Louis action as the final word. Within two weeks after the adjournment of the conference, General Weaver wrote Ignatius Donnelly that he was not satisfied with the results of the meeting, that the silver question had become the "great contention of the age," and if in the next year the Populist party did not seize the issue and carry it to the people, the party would have failed to seize its opportunity to grow to greatness. He said that it was a "universal law in the science of conflict" to fight one battle at a time, and the Populist party was unrealistic in assuming it could fight successfully for the entire Omaha platform at one time. He proposed a meeting of sympathetic Populist leaders who, acting as individuals, could issue a statement on the money issue which would serve to keep the Populist party in step with events.[21]

Though nothing came of Weaver's efforts to bring about such a conference, the major argument of his letter, that silver was becoming the central issue in a great agitation, seemed compellingly evident to many Populists, even those who advocated adhering to the Omaha platform. Marion Butler in Washington in his first term of service in the United States Senate found the Democratic and Republican parties breaking up on the financial question in a way that would produce "large accessions to the People's party from both of the old parties." Moreover, he believed that the various silver organizations were likely to endorse the Populist nominee for the presidency. As a result of his discoveries at the capitol he had reached a most optimistic conclusion: "Before arriving here I had not hoped that we could elect a People's Party President before 1900, but the situation grows more encouraging each day and if the demoralization in the two old parties continues as it is going on now we will have a chance to elect our candidate for President in the next contest." [22]

Thus, as the silver propaganda increased and the silver movement grew, the pressure became very great within the Populist party to respond to it. When the American Bimetallic League announced its intention in March 1895, to organize an independent silver party, the silver agitation had produced another factor which threatened Populist success. After that the growth of the silver movement in the Democratic party was too much to be borne quietly by silver Populists. When the Illinois Democrats called at Springfield a state silver convention of their party with the intention of adopting a platform and initiating a movement by which their party would be committed to silver, Taubeneck went to Springfield to protest that "the Democrats are trying to steal our platform, and I am here to object. The People's party is the only simon-pure silver party." [23]

Unavoidably silver Populists were drawn into close association with the independent silver leaders and with the silver men in the Democratic and Republican parties. They cooperated in the congressional struggles over silver and acted together within the conferences of the

American Bimetallic League. The Populists had come out of the old parties, and they had much in common with the men who had stayed in the old parties. Now on the silver question the possibilities of inter-party cooperation seemed very promising, indeed.

Hence, the situation produced two disparate reactions among silver Populists: first, hostility to the independent silver movement and the silver Democrats both of whom threatened to rob the Populist party of what it considered to be one of the original features in its platform; second, a feeling that since the silver issue had become paramount to all others, men of all parties who believed in silver must cooperate within or without the Populist party to make that cause victorious at the polls. To effect such cooperation, it was felt, the Populist party might very well for the time being abandon some of the principles of the Omaha platform and concentrate on free silver—or, at least, the broader subject of banking and currency.

What had actually happened by the close of 1895 was that the silver question had become a force with such power over public opinion that the Populists could no longer ignore it and (to their disaster) could not control it. Like the other parties, they had no recourse but to try to keep afloat in the raging storm of public debate. A year earlier, when at St. Louis they had decided to stick with the Omaha platform, they were still free to make that decision with some expectation of surviving and growing, though they did not give special recognition to silver.

Now, as 1895 was played out and the nation moved into 1896 with the presidential election only a few months away, the Populists discovered that, without any particular organized aid from them, interest in the silver question as a major reform had grown until it appeared to have overshadowed all other issues. This was a triumph not for Populism but for the American Bimetallic League. Therefore, the initiative in the reform movement, at least for the moment, lay with that organization. Even more threatening to the Populists was the possibility that in the future that initiative might be seized by the silver Democrats, who in the past year had developed a forceful campaign to convert their own party to the service of silver as a basic popular reform. It was possible that the silver agitation had created a cul-de-sac from which the Populists had no escape; but when early in 1896 the Populist Executive Committee, in an opportunistic move, agreed to coordinate its political activities in the election campaign with the

American Bimetallic League, it had chosen the path which would lead to its destruction.

The first step toward self-destruction was taken when the Populist party decided to hold its nominating convention in mid-summer after the other parties had met. On this subject, two poles of thought existed. One group argued that the party ought to take independent action in a convention held early in the year, as early as February or March, at which time they could adopt a reform platform with strong emphasis on silver and offer their party to the people as the aggressive, leading reform party of the nation.[24]

Another group, made up principally of those who believed in narrowing the reform fight to the silver question, advocated a late convention which would be in a position to assume leadership of the reform movement by taking advantage of the divisions which the silver fight would create in the conventions of the regular parties. They believed that both the Republican and Democratic parties were firmly in the control of gold standard men and that when their conventions declared for gold these parties would be seriously split. The silver men from both parties would then flock to the Populist party as the central party of silver reform.[25]

The silver Populists who advocated a late convention were urged to this policy by the silver men outside their party, by men like Teller in the Republican party, Bryan and like-minded Democrats, and the entire directorate of the non-partisan silver movement. They were persuaded to become part of a silver cabal drawn from all parties and dedicated to making the campaign a fight for silver within the framework of one of the established parties if possible, or, if necessary, from within an entirely new party. They were led to believe that inevitably the Populist party would be the only existing party to adopt a platform supporting the free coinage of silver without reservations and that all the recent converts to silver would be brought into their party.[26]

It appeared that in November and December, 1895, both Populists and independent silver men at different places in the country arrived at the idea that the two groups ought to attempt to organize a coordinated campaign for silver. In the Middle West Ignatius Donnelly published in his newspaper, *The Representative*, a suggestion that the two groups arrange to hold their nominating conventions in the same city at the same time, with the object of arriving at parallel decisions in the interest of silver. At the same time Bimetallic League members and Populists working in California had arrived at a decision to publish a similar suggestion in Senator Stewart's paper, the *Silver Knight*.[27] Chairman Taubeneck wrote to Donnelly that he liked his suggestion "that we must get together," that he would talk with the silver leaders and see what could be done. He believed that "all will come out all right when our conventions meet." [28] In Indiana, M. C. Rankin developed and published a detailed proposal for Populist and independent silver cooperation.[29]

To men such as Donnelly, Taubeneck, and Weaver the emergence of the silver movement as an independent political force was a serious threat to the Populist party. Taubeneck believed that Republicans and Democrats who left their party on the silver issue would go to the National Silver party rather than to the Populists.[30] They rushed into a rather subservient cooperation with the independent silver movement in the vain and desperate hope that they could direct its forces into their own organization. Taubeneck and the executive committee arranged to hold their meeting to decide on the date and place of their nominating convention after the Democrats and Republicans had announced their convention plans. When the Populist National Committee met in St. Louis on January 17, their most definite action was to set up a coordinating committee to attend the conference of the Bimetallic League in Washington, D.C., on January 22. The Populists at St. Louis did not name the date or place of their convention but left this question to be decided in Washington in conference between their coordinating committee and the Bimetallic League.[31]

At the same time the silver Democrats were urging the Populists to take action which would unite all the silver forces.[32] In reply to such prodding from Bryan, General Weaver wrote: "Our National Committee will meet at St. Louis Jany 17th and if possible we intend to see to it that no convention is called until opportunity is given for consultation with kindred bodies and interests. We have had quite enough middle of the road nonsense, and some of us at least think it about time for the exhibition of a little synthetic force if we would accomplish any good purpose—The elements are now at hand out of which we certainly can construct an enduring and formidable force for the defense of popular rights." [33]

A few days later Weaver again wrote Bryan saying that Bryan's plans accorded with those of Taubeneck and himself and that they not only planned to set a convention date to follow the Democrats and Republicans, but that they did not intend to set the date until they had consulted with other men outside the Populist party, as Bryan had recommended in his letter.[34]

The Bimetallic League was now in the driver's seat. Populists might claim that they were the original free silver party; but free silver sentiment had become a force in itself, conceivably capable of producing its own political organization. In fact, the Bimetallic League had already taken steps in that direction. Moreover, though the Bimetallic League welcomed and cultivated cooperation with the Populists, it also encouraged the efforts of the silver Democrats to control their party. In November 1895, General Warner, returning to his Washington office from observing the autumn elections, said that in Ohio the Democrats had been defeated because they ran a silver candidate on a gold platform and that the only chance the party had for success in 1896 was to nominate a silver candidate on a silver platform. General Warner said that the Republican party was a hopeless "gold-bug-affair" and could not be counted on in the calculations of the silver forces. Even the silver Democrats were handicapped because of their continued association with Cleveland. For these reasons Warner stated that he favored a silver movement independent of previously established parties.[35]

The American Bimetallic League had but one issue to put before the people. The established parties, including the Populists, had traditions by which they had strong commitments to other issues, and it was evident that they were reluctant to abandon their traditional positions to stand before the country on free silver alone. It was for this reason that the independent silver men decided early in 1896 to establish a distinctive free silver party, to hold their own convention, and if necessary to make their own nominations.

Though the American Bimetallic League had announced early in March 1895, its intention to establish an independent silver party, it was not until January 1896, that such a party was in reality launched. Late in 1895 the American Bimetallic League, the National Bimetallic Union, and the National Executive Silver Committee initiated a series of discussions which were completed in Washington, D.C., on January 22 and 23, 1896. At that time they agreed to set up two organizations: a non-political educational organization to be known as the American Bimetallic Union; and a political party, officially titled, "The American

Silver Organization," but known to most people through its brief history as the National Silver party.

The new American Bimetallic Union was to sponsor non-political silver clubs in all the states of the Union, with decentralized organization from state to state, and central offices in Washington, D.C., Chicago, and San Francisco. It was also to continue publication of the *National Bimetallist* from Chicago. The chairman of the Bimetallic Union was General A. J. Warner. The National Silver party was to be organized in every state of the Union, was to have its headquarters in Washington, D.C., and was to have at the beginning a provisional executive committee headed by J. J. Mott of North Carolina. The conference which set up the new party issued the call for its first presidential nominating convention to meet at St. Louis on July 22, 1896.[36]

The conference which created the American Bimetallic Union and the National Silver party also carried out the first significant concrete arrangement for inter-party cooperation within the free silver movement. The liaison committee appointed by the Populists in their conference in St. Louis on January 17 was in Washington to observe the silver conference. The Populists had been assured that the independent silver men, when they launched their new party, would welcome an opportunity to hold their nominating convention at the same time and place as the Populist convention. The National Silver party's decision to meet in St. Louis on July 22 was approved by the Populist committee, which immediately announced that their party would meet in the same city on the same date.

Populist party chairman Herman Taubeneck described how he envisaged the cooperation that would take place between the two organizations in their conventions at St. Louis: "Each convention will be officially notified of the presence of the other in order to give an opportunity for conference committees to be appointed. After this has been done some common ground will be found upon which the two bodies can come together. When this is done they can proceed to the nomination of candidates ... and the formulation of a platform." [37]

The Populist party was now in the position that ardent silver men inside the party and out had recommended, with a convention date following both the Republican and Democratic conventions, and arranged apparently in such a way as to consolidate all the strength of the free silver movement within the Populist party.[38] The Populist leaders who had maneuvered their party into acceptance of a late convention date remained confident for some time that they had assessed the situation correctly and that neither the Democratic or Republican parties would declare for the free coinage of silver. Yet they received no important accretions through defections from the other parties; for the silver men in each of the old organizations were determined to carry the fight into their conventions, the Republicans chiefly to dramatize that it was hopeless to stay in their own party because of its intransigent opposition to silver, the Democrats because they believed they had a very good chance of controlling their convention.

Silver men, whatever their party, were convinced of the necessity for united action to support free coinage; but first they had their obligations to their own parties. They felt that they must play the game out before they could take the plunge and bolt their old party affiliations. They were all guilty of the opportunism of politicians; and the Populists were as opportunistic as any of the others, waiting as they did, to take in the debris from the anticipated wreckage of the old parties, rather than assuming bold leadership of the new popular cause.

From the first the campaign of the Populists and the National Silver party for common action had a major weakness—it failed to discover or develop a strong, popular presidential candidate. No man of national stature had developed within the Populist party. The older leaders like Weaver and Donnelly had stature of a kind as agrarian reform leaders, but they had little appeal as the leaders of a great national silver fusion. Populists who had come more recently to national attention had, like Marion Butler of North Carolina, appeared too late to be well known or, like Davis Waite of Colorado, had been unsuccessful office-holders and had already been retired by the voters.

The National Silver party was never more than on the periphery of American politics as far as actual campaigning went; and the only active and prominent politicians associated with it were western senators, like Jones and Stewart of Nevada, who never figured seriously in presidential calculations. There were three men from Pennsylvania who were discussed by the National Silver party as acceptable presidential candidates, Joseph Sibley, Don Cameron, and Wharton Barker; but the campaigns for these men never got beyond the discussion stage. They were appealing to the National Silver party only because they were symbolic of the fact that there was some support in the East for the free silver movement and because they were not associated in the public mind with violent political partisanship.

As the nominating conventions approached and it became an established fact that, under the leadership of Senator Henry M. Teller, a number of delegates from far western and middle western states would walk out of the Republican convention once it adopted a platform declaring for gold, the Populist-Silver party men took up Senator Teller as their candidate. From many points of view he was an attractive coalition man. His devotion to the cause of silver was beyond doubt, but he was much more than a free silver reformer. He related the free silver campaign to the broader objectives of the agrarian reform movement and advocated free silver as the first step toward restoring economic, social, and political well-being.[39]

Teller would not be objectionable to southern Populists, for he had not been associated with any of the unpleasant episodes of the Civil War and Reconstruction. In fact, his Republican background made him attractive to southern Populists as a fusion candidate. Southern Democrats remembered that in 1891 he had, in the interest of southern and western coalition on the silver question, voted against a Republican-sponsored Force Bill intended to protect Negro voters. Richard Bland stated that it was the vote against this bill by Teller and his western colleagues that had made possible the western-southern coalition on economic questions, because it was a demonstration that the eastern-western coalition against the South on the Negro question had been broken.[40]

Democrats also had concrete evidence of Teller's willingness to abandon protective tariffs in order to press for the free coinage of silver. Teller would be most appealing to Democrats and Populists, however, because he took no narrow view of the silver issue but believed, as they did, that it was the cause of the people against the plutocrats. For them his pronouncements on the subject had a solid Jacksonian ring.

Unperceived by most, even those with great influence in the silver movement, a silver coalition leader was emerging in these months within the Democratic party—a youthful and energetic man who possessed a subtle understanding of the other men brought forward as leaders of the silver movement and who understood the need within the movement for a leader having the qualities which he possessed.

Through all the agitation, through the organization, re-organization, and counter-organization of the silver coalitions, William Jennings Bryan continued his one-man campaign for the cause and for leadership of the cause. With increasing boldness he advocated that silverites break with any party which failed to adopt their platform. He appealed to silver men of all parties, through editorials and personal letters, to work for silver union on a non-partisan basis.[41]

So it was that the national political stage was set for a silver campaign. Through great expanses of the agrarian West and South and in the Middle West the people were debating the free coinage of silver and were being converted to it as a social gospel. There were signs that the contagion was spreading into the East, even into New England. In every party its influence was felt. In no party could it be ignored. In each party it had produced deep, perhaps irreconcilable divisions. In the end it would be an issue fought between parties on sharper alignments than the country had known since the Civil War; but early in 1896, before the campaign got underway, it was an issue fought within parties.

7

The Silver Wedge
in the Republican Party

As they studied the shifting alignments in the other parties, Republicans uneasily pondered the decisions being forced upon them by changing times and unforeseen events. To many Republicans it was frightening to see the people in so many sections concluding that there was one economic cause and one economic solution for their problems, respectively, the demonetization of silver and the free coinage of silver at 16 to 1. Many Republicans were distressed by the apparent economic radicalism of the free silverites. Many, too, feared that the silverites, through the success of their propaganda were displacing Republican explanation for the nation's prosperity or lack of it—protective tariffs.

On the tariff issue the Republicans were united; on this issue they had a traditional position and well developed arguments. When depression came in 1893, even though the Wilson tariff had not yet been passed, it was convenient for the Republicans to claim that the mere threat of lower Democratic tariffs had been sufficient to frighten business into the cutbacks which led to depression. When the depression continued, following the passage of the Wilson bill, it was argued further that Democratic tariff policies blocked the road to recovery. Another appealing feature of a tariff campaign to Republicans was the fact that most of the prominent leaders of the party, possible candidates for the party's nomination, had established their reputations and their political following on the tariff issue. On other issues, and most particularly on the silver question, their positions were vaguely defined, often contradictory, and certainly seemed to give them slight claim to any popular following.

Another feature of the silver agitation which caused uneasiness in the Grand Old Party was the serious policy debate which it had created within the party, a debate so bitter that it threatened to divide the party on sectional lines. Traditionally the newer states in the Far West had been Republican, and their admission to the Union had brought important new strength to the Republican party in the electoral college and in the Congress. Republicans from these areas had been staunch supporters of protective tariffs and other Republican policies. They were, however, from the great silver producing states of the Union. They also had important agricultural constituencies. Silver prices had slumped to the point where they made production of silver unprofitable except in the most efficient mines.[1] In addition the farmers of this section had suffered more than the farmers of other sections from the agricultural depression of the '80's and '90's. Thus, every part of the population—the mine operators, the miners, and the farmers—was desperately close to financial disaster. Under these circumstances free silver propaganda had met little resistance in this section, where it became the prime doctrine of every party, including the Republican.

By the 1890's it seemed abundantly evident to far western Republicans that they could not survive politically if they did not subscribe to free silver doctrine. The result was that every Republican congressman from the Far West was an advocate of free silver. He knew personally that he must be to survive, so that his own position on the question was not a problem. His problem was: how successfully could he continue to control politics in his own section if his party failed nationally to back his own free silver doctrines? The growth of Populist and free silver Democratic strength in the Far West seemed to supply the answer to that question. The election of 1892, which resulted in a Populist victory in Colorado and Weaver electoral victories in many western states demonstrated to western Republicans that if they continued to campaign under the traditional policies of their party they were headed toward political oblivion.

Another cause for Republican concern was that the party at this moment lacked a leader who could speak authoritatively to the party or for it. Benjamin Harrison, the nominal leader of the party, had virtually abdicated his leadership. In any case, he lacked the following and recognition which would have enabled him to speak with authority, had he chosen to do so. During this period the chairman of the National Committee was Thomas Carter, a silverite from Montana. He campaigned actively to persuade his party to adopt a platform favoring bimetallism and to nominate a free silver candidate. But he was forced to recognize that he represented, at least for the time being, a minority Republican point of view. No one seriously viewed his pronouncements as party doctrine.

As the depression worsened during the months in which preparations were being made for the approaching presidential election and the likelihood of a Republican victory grew, the number of voices which sought to speak authoritatively for Republicanism increased. Republican ranks were filled with presidential aspirants and would-be president-makers. All the leaders in the presidential race had defined their positions on the tariff issue with the result that the tariff offered little opportunity for maneuver; but the silver issue, on which most of them had taken only the vaguest and most peripheral stand, invited individual and opportunistic interpretation.

The platform on which the party had taken its stand in 1892 was uncompromisingly clear on the tariff issue, but the silver plank was the result of a convention compromise. Its vague and comprehensive phraseology committed the party to no definite monetary policy. In this respect it was consistent with party tradition, however; for in the history of contention and legislation in the years since the passage of the Coinage Act of 1873 the Republican record on the money question was consistent only with a policy of political opportunism. The truth was that the party had accustomed itself to make vague promises, entangled in such phrases as "equal use of gold and silver" and "bimetallism by international agreement." No wonder that many Republicans grew uneasy as a large public insisted upon a sharper definition of the party's stand on the financial question and a segment of the party itself joined the public in that demand.

One of the solutions advanced for the silver question was the proposal that an international bimetallic standard be established by international agreement. This proposal was popular among certain Republican leaders. Several international bimetallic conferences were called by European powers during the '80's and '90's, and the United States participated officially in all of them. At first western Republicans had believed that these conferences offered a genuine promise of the re-monetization of silver. When the early conferences adjourned without reaching agreement and the difficulties of persuading European governments to adopt bimetallism became evident, the westerners became disillusioned with the conferences and were unwilling to make international agreement the chief objective of a bimetallic campaign. In fact, they used the failures of these conferences to substantiate one of the major elements in the free silver argument—that English financiers controlled their government and would use that control to press the rest of the world into financial slavery to their creditor interests.

An influential group of New England and New York Republicans was persuaded that international bimetallism was sound policy financially and an essential policy politically, because it could be used to keep dissatisfied western Republicans in the party. Their friendships with European intellectuals who advocated international bimetallism convinced them of the intellectual respectability of the idea. In February 1894, New England bimetallists organized in Boston a committee to promote international bimetallism in cooperation with similar groups in Europe. They restricted the membership of their committee to inhabitants of the Boston area, for the purpose, as they explained it, of avoiding any possible confusion between their organization and the American Bimetallic League.[2] As a result of the correspondence among the bimetallic organizations of several countries, coupled with frustration over the failure of the English Liberal government to call an international bimetallic conference, the British Bimetallic League sponsored an unofficial meeting of bimetallists beginning on May 2, 1894, in London. Two United States delegates attended; and though nothing material came of it, the conference stimulated discussion of international bimetallism in the United States.

The efforts of the Boston bimetallic committee included an attempt to bring Thomas Brackett Reed forward as a presidential candidate sympathetic to international bimetallism. At the time the London conference convened, Henry Cabot Lodge, who supported Reed's candidacy, published a proposal that Congress amend the Wilson tariff to provide discriminatory rates against England until she agreed to cooperate to establish international bimetallism.[3] A short time later Reed suggested an improvement upon Lodge's proposal. In an interview first published in the London *Fortnightly Review,* he advocated that as many nations as were so disposed should join with the United States in an agreement to use silver currency and then force countries which did not join them in that policy to the use of silver by imposing discriminatory tariffs against their goods.[4]

There was no doubt of the sincerity of Reed and Lodge in their interest in international bimetallism nor in their impatience with England at refusing cooperation, but they were also aware that the posture adopted by Reed might have a beneficial reaction in national Republican politics. Democratic silverite Richard Bland immediately stamped such a policy as Republican doctrine and said that in his opinion the farmers of the United States would never sanction a tariff war which would close European markets to American agricultural products.[5]

The truth was that most Republican leaders preferred to stand off from the monetary issue in the hopes that they could straddle it in the immediate future as they had in 1892. The more positive alternatives appeared already to have been seized by others in any case, since the Democrats under Cleveland's leadership had placed the country on a monometallic gold standard and had committed their party to that policy, while the Populists had taken a bold stand for free coinage of silver at sixteen to one. If small segments of the party in mining and agricultural regions were in difficulty because of the party's timidity on this issue, this was unavoidable, and certainly much preferable to the bitterness certain to develop within the party if it defined a position clearly on either side of the debate.

During the 1890's, as events proved, such a temporizing policy had its limitations, however. Many questions rose up to disturb the complacency of Republicans who sought the middle way of compromise. Would the growth of public sentiment for free silver make it inescapably the chief issue in 1896? Would western Republicans find it expedient to remain in a party so thoroughly compromised on an issue of such importance to them? Would the silver propaganda spread into the agricultural regions of the Middle West and make silver the deciding issue there? Would urban laborers be persuaded that silver coinage was advantageous to them? Would silver Democrats gain control of their party, make silver the major issue of their campaign, and thereby steal from the Republicans the advantage of a campaign centered on the tariff issue?

Unfortunately for the party, in one traditional Republican stronghold, the Far West, there was slight promise of future success. After the election of 1892 some western Republicans found it impossible to stave off a complete break with their party.[6] The most dramatic break prior to the convention of 1896 came in September, 1894, shortly after the fall elections, when Senator John P. Jones of Nevada formally renounced his allegiance to the Republican party and joined the Populists. In a letter explaining his action he said that he still believed in a protective tariff and had broken with his party on the silver question alone.[7]

Other western Republicans approached an open break with their party more cautiously than Senator Jones. For many it was the party of their first allegiance, and their emotional bond with it was very strong. Then there was the problem of where they would carry their political allegiance. To many silver Republicans the gap between Populism and Republicanism seemed too great to be bridged through agreement on silver alone. In Colorado, for example, where the Populists had controlled the state under Davis H. Waite, the Republicans had bitterly opposed Populist policies and had concluded, as Senator Teller said, that the Populists "must go." [8]

The alternative to cooperation with the Populists, to work with the Democratic party, seemed equally distasteful. It was the party of their traditional opposition; it was a low tariff party and they were protectionists. A further hindrance to cooperation with either Populists or Democrats was the fact that these two parties were already cooperating with each other in many of the western states. Both the Populist and Democratic parties had their established leaders and principles. It was evident that most western Republicans who left their own party for the other parties must sacrifice the political eminence and very many of the political principles which they had known as Republicans.

Between 1892 and 1896, therefore, the western Republicans, faced by unpleasant alternatives if their party failed to back silver bimetallism, attempted to maneuver their party to a compromise on candidates and platform which would enable them to remain Republican without committing themselves to political oblivion. Their first gambit was to develop a campaign for Don Cameron of Pennsylvania as Republican presidential candidate. He was a silver man, yet he was an easterner; and thus, through a combination of principle and geography, his candidacy might serve to keep western and eastern Republicans united.[9] Through the period from the election campaign of 1894 into the early months of 1896 the western Republicans succeeded in keeping Cameron's name before the public as a presidential possibility. Rumors that Cameron's campaign for the nomination would have the support of Matthew Quay, Pennsylvania's powerful boss, caused the movement to be discussed seriously among Republican leaders.[10]

Western Republican hopes for a platform compromise on principles rested chiefly on a combination of eastern tariff interests with free silver. This was implied in the candidacy of Cameron; and it was stated boldly as a threat by Senator Teller in the Republican congressional caucus early in 1896, when he said that he would vote for no tariff bill which did not carry a free silver amendment.[11] A few weeks later the threat was carried out when western senators voted against a tariff bill. In March 1896, the western hope for a tariff-free silver combination between East and West was dramatized strikingly, when a large delegation of Pennsylvania manufacturers visited Washington for the purpose of consulting with the silver Republican congressmen and were closeted with them for several hours in a private conference.

In their discussions with the eastern manufacturers the silver Republicans emphasized the argument that demonetization of silver placed American producers at a competitive disadvantage with Asiatic producers. A Philadelphia manufacturer was quoted as saying at the Washington conference that tariff duties could not be made high enough to give adequate protection to American manufacturers as long as the single gold standard was maintained.[12] Yet the western Republicans were generally persuaded that hopes of such cooperation between eastern manufacturers and free silver westerners were false. They accepted philosophically the action of the Manufacturers Club of Philadelphia in formally disavowing the participation by its president in the Washington conference.[13]

In the early months of 1896 it was apparent to the western Republicans that time had run out for them, that they must make their choice. They could remain in their party, which was the equivalent of choosing political retirement; or they could leave their party and make a union with silver men in one of the established parties or in a new party. For a long time western Republicans had been cooperating in various ways with the silver leaders of other parties and with the American Bimetallic Union. They were recognized widely outside their own party as sincere advocates of free silver and as leaders of ability.

Senator Teller was the ablest and the least partisanly Republican of the western Republicans, and he was their spokesman and leader. He was the most radical among them, and he early came to the decision that the western silver Republicans could not stay in their own party. It was not easy for his western colleagues to arrive so directly at the decision that Teller had reached. Even Senator Edward O. Wolcott reported that he was "much embarrassed" because he could not agree with Teller that the outlook was hopeless for Republicanism in Colorado.[14]

At the end of April 1896, Teller openly took the position toward which for several months he had been moving, when he declared in the Senate that if the Republican party adopted a single gold standard platform at its next convention he would leave the party.[15] Developments in the weeks that followed made it evident that many of Teller's Republican colleagues from the West reluctantly were persuaded that they too must leave their party. Republicans in the northern tier of the middle western states, finding their constituents infected with the free silver virus, were also drawn into cooperation with the far western group. As far east as Minnesota, Republican leaders, such as Congressman Charles A. Towne and John Lind, prepared to cooperate with Teller and the westerners if they decided to bolt their party.

Thus free silver had pried some members of the Republican party from their traditional moorings. Would these erstwhile Republicans drift into the Populist party to swell the ranks of that organization and help it to become an established party on the American political scene? Would they end up in the Democratic party, if the free silver men won control there, and so bring a reversal in the traditional alignment of western politics? Would they cooperate with men from other parties to establish an entirely new party devoted exclusively to a victory for the free coinage of silver at 16 to 1? The decisions which would give the answers to these questions lay immediately ahead in the campaign of 1896.

8

McKinley Early in the Field

Republican leaders in the East and Middle West, the men who formed the central core of the party's policy makers, at first paid but slight attention to the debate over the silver question. In their judgment the major lines of the party's policy had been laid down, and they assumed that the meaningless straddle which they had been accustomed to adopt on the money question would serve for the approaching campaign. The Panic of 1893 had brought a collapse of Democratic prestige, had punctured Cleveland's popularity, and had caused the defeat in the elections of 1894 and 1895 of many Democratic leaders who might otherwise have been attractive to the voters. It appeared with every passing week more likely that the man who won the Republican nomination would win the presidential election. The attention of most Republican leaders, therefore, was drawn to the contest to win the party's presidential nomination. They were impatient with any suggestion that mounting public interest in silver might change the nature of the terrain over which they must fight their battle for power.

There was no dearth of candidates for the Republican nomination. Several men were openly aspiring to wear the mantle of Republican leadership; and several others, whose candidacies were not avowed, were sufficiently available to be mentioned in the public discussion of potential candidates. Always of primary consideration was the attitude of Benjamin Harrison, the most recent Republican president and the party's candidate in 1892. He had no intention of running again; but he had not so stated, even to his most intimate political advisers, in such a fashion as to persuade them that he could not be prevailed upon once more to seek the nation's highest office. His following was loyal, and influential. Intimations that he was a candidate, though they never came from Harrison himself, were an important factor in the race for the nomination.

Harrison was the strongest candidate of his age group and generation; but there were three older men who did figure with some importance in the campaign for the nomination—Governor Levi P. Morton of New York and Senators Shelby Cullom of Illinois and William B. Allison of Iowa. Two younger aspirants were William McKinley of Ohio and Thomas B. Reed of Maine.[1]

The list of lesser figures (usually referred to euphemistically as "favorite sons" rather than "dark horses") who tried to place themselves before the public and their party in such a way that the presidential lightning might strike them became very long. There were two major reasons why such a large field of candidates materialized. First, the fact that there were several well known candidates invited a convention stalemate in which, when it developed that none of the front runners could get the nomination, the convention would nominate a dark horse. Second, the stirring events of the Cleveland administration and the Republican victories of 1894 and 1895 brought Republicans prominently to public attention for the first time. Thus, in the discussion of Republican candidates the names of such men as Senators Cushman K. Davis of Minnesota, Stephen B. Elkins of West Virginia, and John C. Spooner of Wisconsin appeared.[2] Also in consideration were Governors William O. Bradley of Kentucky and Henry Clay Evans of Tennessee.[3]

It was generally believed that a major influence in determining the Republican nomination would be exercised by the men who controlled the party machinery in Pennsylvania and New York. There had been a sharp contest for control of the party in these states, but by the beginning of 1896 Matthew Quay was in effective command of Pennsylvania and Thomas C. Platt was in control in New York. Prior to 1896 these bosses had not definitely aligned themselves with a presidential aspirant, and there was considerable speculation as to how they would use their power in this matter. It was assumed in many quarters that on this question Quay and Platt would support the same candidate. Astute observers also assumed that the final action of these men would be determined by their desire to consolidate their control over their state machines rather than by any concern for the national interest of the party.

On January 1, 1896, the leading contenders for the Republican nomination were Reed, McKinley, and Allison. Harrison had given no indication that he was a candidate; but if he should make any overt move in that direction, he would immediately enter the ranks of the front runners. Each of these candidates had already set up an organization to develop his campaign. Allison and Reed had chosen as their campaign managers two well known Republican professionals, James S. Clarkson and Joseph H. Manley. McKinley's manager was Marcus A. Hanna.

Only in the retrospect of McKinley's victory was it seen that Clarkson and Manley were ill fitted to run a campaign in competition with Hanna. They were established political leaders who knew the right bosses, the right business men, and all the tricks of their craft. They conferred with the powerful bosses, with the influential business men, and set up the traditional campaign machinery only to discover that in the year 1896 none of the familiar tactics worked.

In January 1894, Manley's value tactically was enhanced when he was elected chairman of the Republican Executive Committee. At this time he was already campaigning for Reed's nomination in 1896; but the worth of his services elsewhere was recognized early in 1894 when Elkins and Davis and their West Virginia coal group employed him to watch out for their interests in the congressional tariff debate and also in arranging for sales of coal to New England railroads. In a letter recommending to his father-in-law that Manley be employed for these purposes, Elkins made this evaluation of him: "Since matters have taken such a turn at Wash. & after talking with J. H. Manley I think he could do great good with the Republicans in Congress from now out. He has a strong position. Chmn of the Ex.Com. & can & is always heard by the leaders about political matters." [4]

Allison's manager, James S. Clarkson, was an almost exact counterpart of Manley, except that the axes of his political and business interests were in New York and Iowa. He was the Iowa representative on the Republican National Committee, though for several years his business interests had caused him to spend most of his time in New York. He was for a period during the '90's president of the National League of Republican Clubs. He was on the board of directors of the

Standard Telephone Company of New York and had for several years been deeply involved in the affairs of that organization. Clarkson was a political intimate of Quay and Platt, was in constant touch with them in this period, and was often a member of their strategy sessions.

It was to be expected, therefore, that the Reed and Allison campaigns would have similar features. Both Manley and Clarkson assumed that the major strength of their candidates would stem from the loyal support which they would receive from their own sections. In the early stages of the campaign Manley repeated so often that Reed would have the solid support of New England that this seemed to be the sole theme of the Reed campaign.[5] Clarkson, in his first letter to Allison, which recommended that they begin the campaign for the nomination right after the 1894 elections, said that Allison would have his strongest appeal as a western candidate, and that McKinley and Reed would both appear as easterners in Allison's section.[6] They also both assumed that outside of their own sections the major centers of their power would be in New York and Chicago. In New York both depended upon their association with Platt to swing his influence ultimately to their campaigns, even after Platt initiated Morton's candidacy; for they believed that Morton was mainly a stalking-horse for Platt's ambitions.[7]

In Chicago both managers looked toward John Tanner for potential support, recognizing him as one of them in the desperate game he was playing to gain control of Illinois Republican politics; but both of them also arranged to have Chicago agents work directly for them. Reed and Manley used Representative James Franklin Aldrich, a Chicago congressman, as an agent in their campaign; and Aldrich, who had close relations with many Chicago business leaders, succeeded initially in winning strong support for Reed in Chicago and elsewhere.[8] Medill and Patterson of the Chicago *Tribune* were also in the Reed camp at the beginning of the fight, giving to Reed an advantage which Allison never possessed, for he did not win the backing of any of the Chicago papers.[9] Clarkson and Allison believed that their major strength in Chicago would be based upon the support of the railroads. They looked to James E. Blythe of the Burlington Road to head up this part of Allison's campaign, which they visualized as spreading out from Chicago across the West.[10]

It was assumed in both camps, of course, that they would have the support of certain business groups because of the business connections of their managers and because of the way the candidates had served various business groups during their legislative careers. Reed assumed that eastern manufacturers would be an element in support of his campaign because he had watched their interests in tariff legislation, while at the same time he looked to the support of Medill and Patterson and the Chicago people because they thought him not such a rabid protectionist as McKinley.[11] When Allison's campaign began actively late in 1895, General Dodge working from New York, C. E. Perkins working from Boston, and James E. Blythe working from Chicago concentrated on lining up railroad support for Allison.[12]

Another feature common to the Reed and Allison campaigns was their failure to make headway against the tide which was running toward McKinley. In fact, both campaigns from the moment they were launched were in retreat. The calm confidence with which each candidate claimed the support of his own section, soon gave way to desperate assertions that each must retain control of his own section, and ended with bitter accusations that Hanna by winning support for McKinley in their sections had violated the rules of the game.

Though Mark Hanna lacked the long-term experience in upper-echelon Republican politics possessed by Clarkson and Manley, he was far from being a novice in politics. He had never held office (nor had Manley or Clarkson held elective office), but he had attended Republican conventions and had long been active in Ohio politics, in itself experience sufficient to give him a keen insight into the workings of American politics.

Prior to 1888 Hanna had been a close friend of Joseph Benson Foraker, and in 1888 he had been the convention manager in the nomination campaign of John Sherman. Since then he had become disillusioned of Foraker's probity; and, judging that Sherman's moment had passed, he threw his support to McKinley as Ohio's candidate for the Presidency. In the months which followed Hanna found no reason to regret his decision.[13]

A kind of political mythology soon accumulated around the friendship of McKinley and Hanna. The first element in this myth was the public image of Hanna himself. Actually there were two sharply contrasting images. To his enemies he appeared as a clever and ruthless manipulator of men, a greedy and self-centered business man, crudely exploiting his inferiors. In this perspective he was most aptly characterized in Homer Davenport's cartoons in the New York *Journal* during the 1896 campaign. These cartoons revealed a bloated, crafty, and cruel face surmounting a gross figure clad in a suit covered with dollar signs. In his hand was a bull-snake whip resting on a skull entitled "Labor." As a final touch, a dwarfed William McKinley was tucked under his belt or stuffed in his vest pocket.

To his friends Mark Hanna appeared as a superb manager of men and money, an honest and dependable associate, a man who reached his decisions on the basis of careful calculation and logic, who, within their experience, gave way to his emotions on one ground alone—in his devotion to William McKinley. For the central figure in the McKinley-Hanna myth was undoubtedly William McKinley, and the men who had done most to create the McKinley myth and who believed most fervently in it were business men like Mark Hanna. To such men McKinley epitomized the highest in intellectual and moral achievement.

These two men accepted the myth of which they were a part before it became public property, for they saw in each other the ultimate achievement in a civilization in which they unreservedly believed. The union of their efforts in the McKinley campaign, for the politicians and business men who viewed the world of the 1890's as they did, was the best of all possible developments. Even before the campaign ended they came to view the McKinley-Hanna relationship with an almost mystical reverence. In retrospect, it seemed aptly symbolical of the relationship between business and politics which existed within the Republican party at the end of the century.

It was easy for those who viewed the world of the 1890's through other lenses to find much that seemed sordid and suspect in the relationship which existed between McKinley and Hanna. To most hostile political imaginations the fact that Hanna was rich and McKinley poor and that the McKinley campaign was lavishly financed suggested evil. When it was known (and McKinley made no effort to conceal it) that Hanna and other rich business backers of McKinley had saved him from bankruptcy by assuming a debt of over $100,000 for which he had unwittingly become liable, McKinley's enemies concluded that he could be no more than a pawn to Hanna. In Davenport's cartoons the belt by which McKinley was bound to Hanna always carried the label, "Those $118,000 notes."

McKinley's opponents, both Republican and Democratic, had a repertory of stories reciting how Hanna used his money in dishonest ways to aid the McKinley cause, but none of these was ever corroborated. There was no denying that Hanna used very large sums of money of his own to finance the McKinley campaign, and he also persuaded like-minded business men to contribute generously to funds largely under his exclusive control, but the accusations that this money was used for wholesale bribery or in other dishonest practices were never proved.

In actuality, during the period that the pre-nomination campaign was developing, the relationship between Hanna and McKinley and the established Republican bosses made it appear that McKinley was on the side of the angels. This was an aspect of the McKinley myth contemporary with the campaign which was soon forgotten. Its major content was summed up in the slogans, "McKinley against the bossess" and "The people against the bosses." It was one of the factors which caused men like young Robert La Follette to take a leading part in the campaign for McKinley's nomination and liberal Democratic papers like the St. Louis *Post Dispatch* to write editorial comments which made McKinley appear as a heroic knight in shining armor tilting his lance against the corrupt and entrenched bosses of his party.

Myron Herrick, in reminiscing about the campaign, described how Hanna and McKinley at one of the early strategy sessions arrived at the decision to use the phrase, "The people against the bosses." Herrick said (and Kohlsaat in his reminiscences recounted a similar story) that Hanna in 1895 had met secretly with the eastern bosses and had made patronage arrangements with them by which they would throw their support to McKinley, but that when he told McKinley of these arrangements McKinley "solemnly refused" to accept their support, because he did not want the Presidency with his hands tied. In the discussion that followed McKinley said, "How would this do for a slogan: 'The Bosses against the People?'" When Hanna agreed, the slogan, altered to read, "The People against the Bosses" became the motto of the McKinley pre-nomination campaign.[14] The McKinley group did not yet consider Hanna to be a political boss, and in relationship to McKinley they never believed that he played such a role. Their reminiscences of the relationship between these two men always placed McKinley in the role of maker of the important strategy decisions.

William McKinley had devoted his career to tariff protection with a singular concentration. It was literally true that he knew nothing else, that the issues of money and banking, foreign policy, and so on, were largely mysteries to him. His speeches, besides the repetitious discussion of tariff problems, were decorated with references to patriotism and Americanism, which he correlated with the tariff and the care of the Civil War veterans. He directed his tariff arguments to all the interests, the farmers, the laborers, manufacturers of all kinds, and was never at a loss for statistics and arguments to illustrate the need of any group for extreme protection. His intellectual interests were narrow and provincial. He did not read books; he did not travel except when politics required it; he did not correspond with or make any special attempts to meet personally the intelligent or creative minds of his day. He was self consciously of the Middle West and did not like the East or its politicians.

In all his prejudices and attitudes McKinley found a parallel in Hanna. Hanna had devoted much of his life to business success with the single-mindedness that McKinley had given to political success. In their relationship, therefore, it remained true that while Hanna developed a unique mastery of politics, he always bowed to McKinley's judgment in that field as superior to his own, while McKinley viewed Hanna as a prince-like prototype of the successful business man, the figure who stood in his opinion at the apogee of civilization, the finest product of man's historical development.

By 1896 the McKinley campaign was of considerable age, having been in existence at least since 1888. At first it was nursed along by McKinley and a few political friends; and while McKinley did not permit it to starve to death, he did not encourage it to be precocious, lest by too early a struggle with established and experienced giants it be prematurely destroyed. Thus, though it was in evidence and considerably popular in 1892, McKinley did not permit it to become a serious challenge to the nomination of Harrison on the first ballot. The McKinley people themselves believed that McKinley had much greater support in popular opinion and in the convention in 1892 than his actual convention vote showed and that they had been fortunate in keeping the McKinley vote as low as it was. It did little harm to McKinley to let the impression develop that there had been a groundswell for McKinley which he had suppressed. By this time Hanna had become a prominent member of the McKinley group and his comment to McKinley quoted by one of that group, "My God, William, that was a damned close squeak," reflected the relief of the McKinleyites that their candidate had not got any closer to the nomination.[15] For one thing, they did not believe that 1892 was a Republican year, and they did not want to expose their candidate to defeat in a race with the Democrats; but second, they did not want to involve McKinley in 1892 in the bitter convention battle necessary to secure his nomination.

It was in the mid-continent in a triangle with its bisecting points at Columbus (later Canton), Cleveland, and Chicago that Hanna and McKinley concentrated their campaign to make McKinley president. An important step in this campaign was the election of McKinley as governor of Ohio in 1891. This, as far as personal preference was concerned, was a less congenial post to McKinley than that of congressman; for McKinley had grown to love the give and take of congressional debate and the political atmosphere of Washington. He had been defeated in the race for Congress, however, in 1890; and there was no strong likelihood that he could regain his post in the election of 1892. The Ohio gubernatorial elections came in odd-numbered years and provided an early opportunity to recoup his loss of 1890. Furthermore, the Ohio constitution made the governor's position one of few duties and but little power or responsibility. It would provide McKinley a position of prestige from which he could conduct his presidential campaign with slight chance of local embarrassment. There was one gamble which had to be taken and that was that the course of politics in Ohio and the nation would be such that McKinley could be reelected by a handsome majority in 1893. If he failed of reelection or won by a narrow margin, his prestige would be crippled perhaps irremediably. When the presidential election of 1892 resulted in a Democrat sweep, the hopes for McKinley's reelection dimmed.

In February 1893, McKinley's career seemed for a moment to have been wholly killed when his impending bankruptcy because of the Walker notes was first announced. Kohlsaat, one of his important Chicago backers, was reported as saying, "The governor will retire from politics, since he cannot hold office and again get up financially." [16] Kohlsaat, if correctly quoted, expressed a mood that was only temporary; for, once he, Hanna, Herrick, and the others had acted to restore McKinley to financial solvency, it was rumored that McKinley was willing to run for governor again if his party and the public desired him.[17] It was reported that letters of sympathy and contributions were pouring in from all over the country, that the trustees set up to handle McKinley's indebtedness had tried at first to return the contributions coming by mail but had retreated because of the persistence of the contributors.

McKinley, asked by the reporter of a local Ohio newspaper to read from some of the letters he was receiving, was reported as saying, "No, I cannot do it; they are too tender and too touching to me to give them to the public. You may say that they come from all classes and conditions of men and are full of expressions of sympathy." [18] It was concluded that the incident in its development had served to strengthen rather than weaken McKinley. For his intimate campaign supporters and for the general public it was a demonstration that there was a dimension to his personality and character which they had previously believed existed but which he had not proved.

Only a little more than a month after the episode first became public it was evident that McKinley was again traveling the road to his ultimate destiny when it was publicized that at the protective tariff banquet of the Republican club of Canton, attended by prominent Republicans from all over the nation, McKinley, standing before a banner with the slogan, "American wages for American workmen, American markets for American people, and protection for American homes," had spoken on the subject, "The Republican President." [19]

The McKinley campaign for reelection in the summer and autumn of 1893 was thorough; and the Panic of 1893, combined with the ineptitude of the Cleveland administration, created a groundswell for Republicanism. Before the election McKinley's friends predicted that an election plurality of 50,000 votes would give him the inside track in the presidential nomination race. When his plurality in November 1893 exceeded 80,000, McKinley became more than ever a leading contender for the Republican nomination.[20] One commentator saw him already standing in the ranks of the Republican immortals: "We are a nation of hero worshippers, and each of our great parties has to have its demigod. McKinley is the demigod of the republican party. He fills the niche where stood Garfield and Blaine, and his worshippers hope to elevate him to the White House." [21]

Though William McKinley was well on his way to becoming the demigod of Republican politics, among a faction of Ohio Republicans led by Joseph Benson Foraker he had long been unpopular. The memories upon which this factionalism fed in Ohio carried back to the Republican presidential nominating convention of 1888, when it had appeared to the McKinley-Hanna group that Foraker had betrayed Sherman, Ohio's candidate.[22] Foraker claimed that such a reading of his actions in the 1888 convention was inaccurate. He was not believed by the other side; and, over the years, the hostility was sustained as the two factions fought each other for the plums of Ohio politics. That the McKinley-Hanna-Sherman faction had won the recent rounds was indicated by the fact that McKinley was governor and Sherman United States Senator. Nevertheless, the Foraker faction remained a power to be reckoned with in Ohio politics. In 1895 they captured control of the state convention and nominated Foraker's friend, Asa Bushnell, as the Republican gubernatorial candidate to succeed McKinley.[23]

Hanna and McKinley were forced to recognize early the impracticality of trying to destroy Foraker and his group, but they understood equally as well that it would be a constant embarrassment to McKinley to have, during the campaign, a faction within his home state aggressively hostile to him. McKinley, therefore, sought a pragmatic alliance with Foraker in 1895, by which he would be guaranteed the support of the Foraker faction in his presidential race. Fortunately for McKinley's purposes the United States Senate seat held by Democrat Calvin Brice was to be filled early in 1896. The fact that the Ohio legislature was Republican assured the election of a Republican, and Foraker more than anything else wanted to be elected to Brice's place. It was evident prior to Foraker's election to the Senate in January 1896, that Foraker and McKinley were no longer opposing each other in their accustomed fashion; but not until the day of Foraker's election did they reach a definite understanding.[24] On that day McKinley visited Foraker in his hotel room, and they worked out an agreement by which they ended factional competition, at least until after the election in November.[25] It was also agreed between McKinley and Foraker that Foraker would travel to New York to see Tom Platt and there try to develop through himself a liaison between McKinley and Platt.[26]

Of course, in local Republican politics in Ohio politics went on as usual as the minor political leaders worried about and fought over the delegates to be chosen to the national convention and the nominees for Congress and other offices; and the press was as full as ever with speculation about the McKinley-Foraker rivalry. Members of the McKinley camp in interviews tried to quiet newspaper discussion of the rivalry and to reassure lesser politicians throughout Ohio that since the McKinley people had not opposed Foraker's election to the Senate, Foraker in good faith would help McKinley to get the united support of the Ohio delegation at the presidential nominating convention. Foraker made a major contribution to unity in March 1896, when he delivered a widely publicized address at the Ohio State Republican convention advocating united state support of McKinley.[27]

McKinley, however, wanted Foraker to undertake another responsibility which would symbolize even more dramatically that Ohio Republicans were behind him as a unit. He wanted Foraker to attend the national nominating convention and make the speech placing McKinley's name before the convention.[28] Foraker hesitated long before agreeing to be a delegate to the convention, because he feared that somehow McKinley might be defeated and that then he would be accused of betraying McKinley in the same way he had been accused of betraying Sherman in 1888.[29] A few weeks before the St. Louis convention and after much prodding from McKinley, Foraker did consent to go to the convention and to place McKinley in nomination.[30] Foraker kept faith with McKinley. As he himself reminded McKinley shortly after the November election: "Whatever of factional differences there may have been in Ohio in past years, there have not been any, as I think you well know, so far as you and I are concerned, since our talk in my room at the Neil House in January last."[31] The unity of the Ohio Republicans was a major asset to McKinley as he carried his campaign to the rest of the nation.

At Columbus McKinley was developing a corps of trusted and able Ohio Republicans to aid him in his campaign. One of his first moves was to have a friend, Charles Dick, appointed chairman of the Ohio State Central Committee. His appointee as State Insurance Commissioner, William M. Hahn, was elected to the Republican National Committee. Hahn often sat in with McKinley in conferences with visiting politicians, who trooped to Columbus in large numbers.[32] Joseph P. Smith, to whom McKinley gave the sinecure of State Librarian, became a valuable political secretary. He proved useful as a liaison agent between McKinley and influential friends throughout the nation.

The McKinley staff at Columbus was later transferred to Canton when McKinley early in 1896, after retiring from the governor's post, moved back to the small industrial city which he considered to be his home town. Canton was not far from Hanna's home, Cleveland; and there were convenient rail connections. Soon Joe Smith, forced by an unsympathetic legislature to resign his post as State Librarian, was transferred to Cleveland where he took up the task of handling Hanna's political liaison with McKinley and Republican politicians the country over. Both Cleveland and Canton were also conveniently reached by train from Chicago; and when in 1894 the young Nebraskan, Charles G. Dawes, who had recently moved to Chicago to establish a business career, was given charge of the McKinley campaign in Illinois, the essential mid-continental link was forged. Both at Cleveland and Chicago Hana and Dawes could call upon the aid and support of influential and well-to-do men, who were devoted to McKinley and had long been interested in his election. In Cleveland Myron Herrick and in Chicago Herman H. Kohlsaat were but outstanding examples of a large group of business men who thought it an honor to be asked to contribute their talents and their fortunes to his campaign.

Though McKinley and Hanna early recognized the Middle West as the central battle ground they by no means ignored the rest of the country. They did not set up an elaborate organization in the East; but in Boston McKinley's cousin, William M. Osborne, had a strategic position which he used to work for McKinley in Reed's home territory. Osborne, personable and widely acquainted, traveled in the East, the South and the Far West cultivating, with unusual success, support for McKinley's nomination. McKinley and Hanna also arranged to set up an organization among the Ohio congressmen at Washington to work in the interest of McKinley. These Congressional efforts were under the direction of Congressman Charles Grosvenor.[33] Grosvenor proved to be an effective part of the McKinley staff in Washington, in Ohio, and traveling in various areas of the country in McKinley's interest. In the states other than Ohio and Illinois, the McKinley group set up no separate campaign organization but depended instead on the support of leaders and groups within each state; and they cultivated this support by various maneuvers and devices.

Among McKinley's major sources of strength were the enduring friendships which he had made during the years he had served in the Congress at Washington. He was a politician's politician; and generally he had the respect, though seldom the warm friendship, of his peers. Another major source of strength was his willingness to travel and to campaign to aid the cause of Republicanism in other districts. He was an effective campaigner, and he had many friends who believed that his campaign speeches in their districts had saved their political skins. During the campaigns of 1894 he was ideally situated to add further to his reputation as a campaigner and to serve Republicans the nation over in a way which would make them feel personally obligated to him. There was no gubernatorial campaign in Ohio, and he had no intention of running for reelection in 1895. The Republican machine in Ohio was functioning efficiently, and it was not necessary for McKinley to pay close heed to the local situation. McKinley barnstormed up and down and across the country—north to St. Paul, Minnesota; at a special call, a hurried trip south to New Orleans; deep into the prairies to Kansas; and then east to Maine. His biographer, Olcott, claimed that overall in 1894 he traveled 12,000 miles and addressed around 2,000,000 people. On one day, beginning at six in the morning at Des Moines and ending at ten in the evening at St. Paul, he made twenty-three speeches.[34]

McKinley was not a spell-binder, but he had a ready platform wit and was particularly effective in that type of political speech-making in which the speaker engages in repartee with his audience. In this campaign one of his favorite devices was to ask whether there was a man in the audience who was working now who had not been working in 1892 and then to ask whether there was a man in the audience who had worked in 1892 who was not working at all this year. With such pointed satire McKinley put his audience in a temper to listen sympathetically to his arguments correlating prosperity and protective tariffs.[35] Not that McKinley's tariff arguments were usually based on careful economic analysis; more typically they were emotionally slanted appeals that implied by indirection that a Republican victory would lead to new protective tariffs which, in turn, would lead to prosperity. In 1894 he conducted a "give 'em Hell" campaign as he told the people they were "tired of this tariff-tinkering, bond-issuing, debt-increasing, treasury-depleting, business-paralyzing, wage-reducing, queen-restoring administration." [36] When victory came to the Republicans in 1894, though he had campaigned for no office for himself, William McKinley of Ohio was one of the chief beneficiaries of that victory.

Hanna and McKinley established another axis in their campaign at Thomasville, Georgia. Here, deep in southern Georgia, Hanna acquired a comfortable winter home at which he entertained hordes of southern politicians of both races. Here, also, in the early months of 1895 he entertained Governor and Mrs. William McKinley. McKinley traveled southward as inconspicuously as possible, interviewing along the way a number of southern politicians. Once he was established at Thomasville great numbers of men came, as quietly as possible, to visit McKinley, while members of McKinley's staff traveled through the South talking to politicians who would or could not visit Hanna's home and, if circumstances indicated, trying to persuade them to travel to Georgia to talk with McKinley.[37] Every effort was made to avoid publicizing these political activities, to make McKinley's visit with Hanna seem no more than a pleasant social occasion. McKinley in traveling south, at Thomasville, and in a brief visit in Florida studiously avoided public occasions which might be used to promote his campaign. As he wrote to one southern correspondent who proposed an overt demonstration: "I cannot get the consent of my mind to do anything that places me in the position of seeming to seek an office and anything I might say or do would be at once interpreted as an effort in that direction." [38] Hanna writing to an Ohio friend wryly described McKinley's visit as, doubtless, he wished the public to view it: "The Gov. is here having a pleasant time and a much needed rest. The newspapers are trying to make it out that there is any amount of political significance in his visit to the South. It certainly is successful in developing the fact that he is a very popular 'American Citizen' and welcomed by everyone regardless of political affiliation." [39]

9

McKinley Ascendant
in the Middle West

In the Middle West and Great Plains states McKinley was a popular figure. He had campaigned extensively and successfully in that region; and he, Dawes, Hanna, and others of his campaign staff had friends there whom they used to develop McKinley support. Iowa alone the McKinley men, at the candidate's request, made no attempt to invade in recognition of McKinley's belief that Allison's campaign was a serious and valid effort in its own right.[1] Midwest states other than Iowa produced their favorite sons, but McKinley claimed that these candidates were merely stalking-horses for the eastern bosses and made no effort to halt attempts to organize these states for him.

Thus, the Davis campaign in Minnesota from the first faced strong McKinley opposition. Senator Cushman K. Davis was a scholarly man, who won the attention of Theodore Roosevelt for his knowledge of history and his ability to quote classical literature.[2] Davis had received little public attention until the summer of 1894, when, during the Pullman strike, he sharply reprimanded Minnesota labor leaders who had asked him to support a resolution condemning Cleveland's policy. The politicians working for him hoped that similar labor difficulties might occur in 1895 and 1896 to provide Davis with more opportunities to come before the public.[3] Davis' pronouncements on our Hawaiian and Caribbean policies had also received considerable notice. With this in mind some observers concluded that the interest taken by his supporters in nominating him for the presidency was merely intended to prepare the way for his appointment as secretary of state.[4]

The framework of Davis' campaign structure was developed early in 1895. It was composed of Congressman James A. Tawney of Winona, Minnesota, working in Washington and Minnesota; Samuel R. Thayer of Washington, D.C., working in the East; Captain Henry A. Castle, of St. Paul and a life-long friend of Davis, heading up the campaign in Minnesota; and senatorial colleagues of Davis from states adjoining Minnesota, notably Richard Pettigrew of South Dakota and Elisha Keyes of Wisconsin. Castle, Tawney, and Thayer put in some hard work for Davis, but they did not have a Clarkson, Manley, or Hanna to provide the leadership for a nationally coordinated campaign. Davis was not well known, even in the states adjoining Minnesota, a handicap recognized by Tawney: "One of the principal obstacles in our way is the fact that he is not as well known as he might and should be in order to do effective work outside of our state."[5]

The greatest handicap of all to the Davis campaign, however, was that he could not claim the loyal support of all Minnesota Republicans. Allison had some support in the state of which the Davis people were inordinately jealous; but it was the McKinley forces, led by Davis' enemy, William R. Merriam, who delivered the *coup de grace* to Davis' ambitions by taking the state away from him. By the twelfth of March, with the Minnesota state Republican convention less than two weeks off, it was clear to Davis that he had lost Minnesota to McKinley. A few hours before the convention met he withdrew from the race, and the convention adopted a resolution declaring its full support for the nomination of McKinley. Davis was left to reflect on his betrayal by friends who had drifted off to "that stupid harloting with Merriam that has recently made us so much trouble."[6]

The emergence of the Manderson campaign in Nebraska was from the first interpreted as a move to keep the convention votes of that state out of the McKinley column. Dawes had lived at Lincoln, Nebraska, for several years, and a group of his Nebraska friends had become the nucleus of an extremely effective organization which was working tirelessly with funds furnished by Hanna to bring the state under McKinley's control. One of the major objectives in the strategy of the McKinleyites in Nebraska was to win Senator John M. Thurston to their side, an objective they seemed almost to have attained when, late in January 1896, Charles F. Manderson began to emerge as a candidate. What the McKinleyites hoped to achieve in Nebraska was the adoption of resolutions by the Republican state convention instructing Nebraska's delegates to vote for McKinley. They had already found Thurston reluctant to join them in working for such an objective, and his reluctance to do so increased when Manderson's campaign emerged.[7]

If Manderson succeeded in winning control of the Nebraska delegation, his control would ultimately be used in the Republican national convention to aid Allison or Reed, perhaps both. Manderson, formerly United States Senator from Nebraska, had virtually no claim to national or local recognition. Like Allison he was closely associated with western railroad interests, and observers believed that his campaign may have been initiated by the same Burlington interests that were backing Allison, and that, therefore, whatever Nebraska strength he garnered would ultimately be thrown to Allison.[8]

Events soon proved that Manderson had no chance to succeed. The McKinley forces were too active and too well organized. They had been on the ground too early. Above all they were working with a candidate who was widely known and truly popular in Nebraska. Add to these elements the important fact that the McKinley men always had money, money in increasing quantities as the campaign struggle tightened. The Nebraska State Republican convention adopted resolutions instructing its delegates to cast their ballots for McKinley; and through the remainder of the year, at the convention and during the election campaign, Senator Thurston was a conspicuous member of the McKinley advisory group.

Through the period of the preliminary campaign maneuvers into the first weeks of 1896 the shadow of one Republican personality loomed ominously over the preparations of every candidate. Was or was not ex-president Harrison a candidate for renomination? Harrison himself knew with more certainty than most men in his position that he was not. Inevitably he was hounded by rumors that he or his friends were jostling and maneuvering to put him in line for nomination in 1896, and he realized that any public denial he made of these rumors would be interpreted as invitations for support. In fact, the private denials made to his most intimate friends were not taken by them as his final answer; and they continued to work quietly to keep the way open to his nomination, believing that he would not be able to reject it if it were delivered to him.

In February Harrison made public a letter to the chairman of the

Republican state committee of Indiana saying that he did not wish to be a candidate for the nomination. The following words which he struck out of his copy before it was released to the press revealed his true feelings: "Indeed the thought [of returning to the White House] has been repellant rather than attractive. There could be nothing in the office for me but toil and weariness, and I have had enough of these." [9] He did permit these words to be published: "There has never been an hour since I left the White House that I have felt a wish to return to it." [10]

Until Harrison in this fashion definitively withdrew, the other candidates worked with strong suspicion that he would emerge ultimately to defeat them in his own cause or that he would throw his strength against them to another candidate. Clarkson, for example, viewed with jaundiced eye a Harrison trip to New York and Pennsylvania in May 1895; and in reports to Allison tried to assess how successful Harrison had been in winning support for his own campaign and in weakening Allison's.[11] In New England Reed's supporters watched Harrison's movements with similar distaste, believing that "Whatever strength he got would harm Reed more than anyone else." [12] Only one man appeared to have any chance for advancement through Harrison —Stephen B. Elkins of West Virginia. Elkins had been in Harrison's Cabinet; and he remained friendly with Harrison. During the months when Harrison's candidacy was rumored, his name was often linked with Elkins as his prospective running mate.

The one candidate to whom Harrison was unquestionably hostile was William McKinley. Even though McKinley was a much younger man and had not used his strength either in 1888 or 1892 to block Harrison's nomination, the relationship between the two had steadily been that of unfriendly rivals. McKinley was a very popular man in Indiana, and rumors persistently cropped up to the effect that the state was being organized for him. The Harrison men felt particularly uncertain of the attitude of the chairman of the Indiana Republican Executive Committee, John K. Gowdy. Their suspicions, though largely intuitive, were justified; and Gowdy, after Harrison declared his "sincere and final" decision not to be a candidate, lost little time in joining the McKinley movement. Immediately after Harrison's withdrawal letter was published, Hanna sent Charles Dick to Indiana to set up an organization to work for an Indiana delegation instructed for McKinley. Dick talked with William R. Holloway, Gowdy, Daniel Ramsdell, and others. Within a matter of hours after Harrison withdrew, the Hanna-McKinley organization working in Ohio and Indiana had seized the initiative for their candidate.[13] One Indiana observer described their activity thus: "Gov. McKinley's friends ... have jumped right into our State and have been working it day and night since Gen. Harrison's withdrawel [sic]. These McKinley fellows have almost taken our breath away by the enthusiasm they manifest for their candidate." [14]

Before this onslaught the disorganized anti-McKinley forces retreated to the futile negativism of opposition to convention instructions of any kind and wistful hopes that Harrison would change his mind and hold the Indiana delegation from the McKinleyites through his own candidacy. The rapid conquest of Indiana by McKinley left Harrison with a feeling that he had been betrayed, but he gave vent to his bitterness only in private communications to his most intimate associates.

Harrison's control of Indiana, though potentially a serious threat to McKinley's candidacy in that state, also proved to be beneficial to McKinley; for though Harrison was hostile to McKinley, he did not try to throw his power in the state for or against any candidate. Therefore, when Harrison definitively withdrew, McKinley entered the state with chances equal to those of any other candidate as far as Harrison was concerned.

Harrison was not friendly with any of the bosses who were managing the campaigns from the East. In fact, he was distinctly hostile to Platt and Quay. He did place some confidence in former associates, such as Stephen Elkins and Louis T. Michener, and through the campaign welcomed reports from them informing him of developments as they saw them. Michener (though he never abandoned hope that Harrison would emerge as a candidate) was disposed to favor Allison and so was Harrison, but the opportune moment to bring Harrison into an open declaration for the Iowa candidate never developed.[15]

New York's candidate, Levi Morton, had been Harrison's vice president, but in the Republican convention in 1892 he had been denied the right to be Harrison's running mate for a second term under conditions that made him unfriendly to Harrison. Still, during the years he had been in office with Harrison Morton had established some friendships in Indiana, and he assumed that these might be useful to him. Early in March a delegation of New Yorkers representing Morton traveled into Indiana and spent several days establishing contacts with men who might be persuaded to support Morton's candidacy. They reported to Morton from Indianapolis that they had found a "volcanic McKinley eruption" and that, though something might be done later to get Morton delegates and stop McKinley, to work actively now would serve only to increase the preponderant McKinley sentiment.[16]

Mark Hanna, fully informed of the New York invasion of Indiana, wrote one of his Indiana agents that he was glad they had come; for now the Indiana workers would be stirred to greater exertions for McKinley. That he was not deeply worried was indicated by this laconic comment by which he characterized the Morton campaign: "They seem to have but one idea in politics, and that is that money can do everything." [17]

In the end there was no evidence that anyone but Hanna put money into Indiana and that would appear to have been the result of an excessive zeal for perfect organization, for McKinley was popular in the Hoosier state. Though they had no elaborate organization like that in Illinois, McKinley, Hanna, Smith, and Grosvenor kept track of the details of the Indiana campaign, prodding their friends to remember that the ultimate goal was a delegation instructed to vote for the Ohio man. This objective was accomplished readily when the Indiana Republicans convened.

Early in 1896 attention in the Middle West rapidly settled on Illinois as the state in which the most dramatic and crucial fight was being waged. Here Hanna and McKinley gambled that the young and inexperienced Dawes would prove able to organize the state successfully for McKinley. In Illinois the base for McKinley support was a small group of business men in Chicago and a large crowd of politicians in the down-state area outside of Chicago. Opposition to him was centered among the professional politicians in the Chicago-Cook County area. McKinley had newspaper support in Chicago, chiefly through Herman Kohlsaat and his paper, the *Times-Herald;* but there was newspaper opposition to McKinley in the Chicago *Tribune,* controlled by Medill and Patterson. Medill and Patterson, however, were responsive to public opinion and hesitated to use their newspaper too aggressively against McKinley for fear that they might find themselves politically isolated if McKinley should win.

Dawes, though much younger, was similar to Hanna in the capacity for effective organization which he brought to the campaign and in the devotion which he felt for William McKinley. Both men achieved their greatest success in the selection and direction of the men who worked for them. They worked like commanding generals (within the organization Dawes was referred to as "The General"),[18] developing first the overall strategy of the campaign, next selecting their lieutenants for the field campaigns, and then as the battle developed, watching and guiding with infinite care each detail in the struggle. They rarely became immediately involved themselves but managed to maintain an upper echelon detachment from which they could supervise each particular battle in terms of the strategy of the national campaign. Also each of these men imbued his subordinates with some of the devotion and affection which he felt for McKinley, for this was an element of major importance in McKinley's ultimate success.[19]

Dawes was one of the most enthusiastic supporters of the McKinley campaign against the bosses. In the local situation in Illinois Dawes saw the Cook County bosses spearheading the attack on McKinley. He was willing to make compromises with them on advice from Hanna and McKinley or, if in his judgment the strategic situation warranted it, but he seemed happiest when there was no alternative to a clearcut fight with them.

Dawes organized the campaign in Illinois by selecting two men to travel in the state, General C. W. Pavey, who was assigned to the southern counties, and William G. Edens, who was given the responsibility of covering the northern counties.[20] He had a small corps of dependable and affluent workers in Chicago who cooperated loosely under the direction of General John McNulta, who also handled the distribution of literature throughout the state.[21] With the aid of these men Dawes covered the field thoroughly. They worked intensively in each district as its local convention approached, often bringing a number of men to travel over a particular district a week or so before the district convention. Throughout the campaign Dawes kept Hanna and McKinley informed of how his work was progressing and sought their advice at certain crucial stages. The key men in the national McKinley organization traveled to Chicago to confer with Dawes, and at various times in the campaign he was visited by McKinley, Hanna, Joe Smith, and Osborne. Hanna's office supplied him with large sums of money to finance the campaign in Illinois and elsewhere.[22]

No detail escaped Dawes' observation. It was customary among Illinois Republicans to have a dinner conference in January of every year, an occasion which had become known as a "love-feast." In 1896 this event was held on January 27. Dawes made special arrangements that McKinley's name should be mentioned at an opportune time and that when this occurred McKinley supporters among the diners should be alert to make appropriate noises expressing their enthusiasm. Senator Cullom journeyed to Springfield from Washington to attend the dinner and make it the occasion for launching his campaign for the nomination. Under these circumstances the event became a popularity contest between Cullom and McKinley in which Cullom came off second best. McKinley shouters found an opportunity to cheer for McKinley even before the time arranged by Dawes, when one of the diners speaking in praise of Cullom inadvertently mentioned McKinley's name. Cullom, however, used the demonstration which followed the mention of his name as justification for formally announcing that he was a candidate for the presidential nomination and that he "must have our delegation now, if possible." [23]

Two days after the Springfield "love-feast" Mark Hanna and "Will" Osborne were in Chicago conferring with Dawes and the other McKinley workers to learn their reactions to the event and to plan the next stages in the campaign. A few hours after Hanna returned to Cleveland McKinley went from Canton to Cleveland to confer with him. A few hours later Dawes was in Cleveland with Hanna and then traveled from Cleveland to Canton to see McKinley before returning to Chicago. Hanna and Osborne on their trip to Chicago had traveled up to Milwaukee where they conferred with Wisconsin leaders.[24] Such was the pace of the McKinley campaign.

Actually the McKinley-Hanna concern about Illinois at this moment was prompted by a development of much greater significance than the Springfield "love-feast." Hanna had recently received a telegram from the leaders of the Cook County Republican organization asking that Hanna confer with them in Chicago.[25] Exactly what the leaders of the Cook County machine had in mind Dawes and Hanna did not learn, for Cullom's appearance in Illinois caused them to change their plans, and the leaders who had asked for the conference with Hanna failed to keep their appointment.[26]

This was Dawes' first brush with a problem that was to hound him throughout his fight to gain instructions for McKinley in Illinois. This was the problem of the relationship which the McKinley workers should establish with the Republican organization in Cook County and with John Tanner, whose control of Illinois rested to a large degree on the support of the Cook County group. Cullom's unexpected visit to Illinois had thwarted Cook County organization efforts to make a deal with Hanna, and they now moved with speed to organize the area which they controlled and place it behind Cullom by calling for their conventions to meet on February 15.[27] Dawes received a telegram announcing this action by the Cook County machine when he was in Canton conferring with McKinley and recorded in his journal that this news "greatly disconcerted both the Governor and myself." [28]

When Dawes returned to Chicago, he was disposed to use the Chicago city machine backed by public opinion to fight the Cook County organization; but he ran into the opposition of Herman Kohlsaat, one of McKinley's most powerful friends. Kohlsaat refused to permit ex-Mayor Swift, leader of the Chicago machine, to make an open fight for the McKinley delegates, thus thwarting any opportunity for Dawes to challenge the hold of the regular organization in Cook County,[29] for the support of Kohlsaat's newspaper, the *Times-Herald*, was too valuable to be antagonized.[30]

Both sides in the Illinois struggle, having tested each other's lines and having discovered that there was no possibility of reaching a compromise by which they could agree on control of the state, now settled down to working the state over with a political fine-toothed comb. They studied and worked every district, the McKinley people attempting to win instructions for their candidate, the Cullom people fighting instructions on principle in those cases where it appeared that they could not win instructions for Cullom. The McKinley managers, however, possessed the initiative and they never relinquished it.

McKinley's campaign in Illinois was further advanced by an event carefully arranged to set the theme of the McKinley campaign on a national scope. The Marquette Club of Chicago had established the tradition of holding an annual Lincoln Birthday dinner at which they invited a prominent Republican leader to speak. In 1896 McKinley was invited to make the major speech of the evening on the subject, "President Abraham Lincoln." Several other speakers were placed on the program, all of them prominent figures in the McKinley campaign. This speech in Chicago was the only major political speech which McKinley delivered outside of his home town of Canton in 1896, and the arrangements made for the event and for the national distribution of the speech left no doubt of the significance attached to it by McKinley and his co-workers. McKinley partisans from all parts of the country were at the dinner, and special delegations of political workers traveled to Chicago from the West and South for private conferences with McKinley. The Chicago *Tribune* published a special small-sized edition, titled the "Marquette Club Edition," and the McKinley managers arranged to have many thousands of copies of the Chicago *Tribune* and *Times-Herald* containing the text of McKinley's speech distributed in bundles containing several hundred copies to key workers in the various states.[31]

The theme of the Marquette Club dinner was not Lincoln but McKinley and McKinleyism. Lincoln was not exactly forgotten; he was kept in the background and brought forward occasionally to join the others in applauding the greatness of McKinley. When Senator Thurston from Nebraska spoke of "that man whose name would be recognized as an American platform in itself" and said that the "Republican masses have one name enshrined in their hearts; one name ready to burst forth hallelujahs from their lips," it was not Lincoln but McKinley to whom he referred.[32] It remained only for McKinley now to walk out upon the stage which had been set for him and speak the lines which not man but destiny itself seemed to have written:

The whole world knew a year in advance of its utterance what the Republican platform of 1860 would be, and the whole world knows now, and has known for a year past what the Republican platform of 1896 will be.

Then the battle was to arrest the spread of slave labor in America; now it is to prevent the increase of illy-paid and degraded free labor in America. The platform of 1896, I say, is already written—written in the hearts and at the homes of the masses of our countrymen. It has been thought out around hundreds of American firesides,—literally wrought out, by the new conditions and harsh experiences of the past three years.

On great questions still unsettled, or in dispute, between the dominant parties, we stand now just as we did in 1860, for Republican principles are unalterable. On the subject of protection to American labor and American interests we can re-affirm, and will re-affirm, the Lincoln platform of 1860. . . .[33]

The Illinois State Republican convention was scheduled to meet on April 28. A month before it met the issue had been settled in Illinois. McKinley had control of it. This did not mean that the problems of the Illinois managers were ended. One phase of their work was completed, but they had immediately to look forward to the next phase: healing the rifts within the party caused by McKinley's invasion of the state in order that the party present a united front against the Democrats once McKinley was nominated. Of course, once McKinley had won control in Illinois and it was apparent that the Illinois victory was only part of a national pattern of victory, the McKinley managers had a strong lever to use upon their opponents. Shelby Cullom came around in late March, when through a Chicago friend, Judge Grosscup, he offered to withdraw and leave the field to McKinley in return for guarantees by McKinley that he would grant certain prerogatives to the regular Illinois Republican organization. Judge Grosscup's letter to McKinley caused a flurry of activity in the latter's camp, even causing Dawes and General McNulta to make a quick trip to Canton to talk with McKinley.[34] Cullom now found himself caught in a very uncomfortable position between the regular organization and McKinley. McKinley would not give Cullom the guarantees which he wanted, primarily to square himself with the regular organization so that they would not feel he had betrayed them, while the organization, under the control of John Tanner, recognizing where strength lay, proceeded to make its peace with McKinley.

When the Illinois convention met, Dawes had arranged with Tanner that after the convention had made the state nominations through that for attorney-general, the regular order of business would be suspended to permit the introduction of a resolution instructing the Illinois delegates to the national Republican convention to cast their votes for William McKinley.[35] Under this arrangement Tanner was given the support of the McKinley group for the gubernatorial nomination which he desired in exchange for his support of a maneuver by which the convention adopted resolutions of instruction for McKinley before choosing its delegates to the national convention.

As each development in Illinois increased the likelihood of a McKinley victory, Dawes stepped up the pressure and activity of his campaign. He allowed nothing to be lost by default. When the state Republican convention met in Springfield on April 28, Dawes marshalled his forces like a veritable Napoleon of politics and won a victory of which Ohio's Napoleon, waiting anxiously in Canton, was highly appreciative, more so because the battle ended with Republican lines in Illinois well organized for the assault upon the true enemy—the Democrats. Shelby Cullom looked somewhat silly and felt very outraged, but he was virtually alone now, and his impotence was evident to everyone.

Wisconsin could well have proved to be a thorny state for the Mc-Kinleyites, for in the words of Joe Smith, "the complications" there were as "delicate almost as the Foraker and anti-Foraker relations in Ohio."[36] La Follette supported McKinley from the first, but in the final result that support was of slight significance in 1896. La Follette proved unable to control the state in his own interest that year. Ultimately Wisconsin Republicans declared their support for McKinley at their state convention on March 17 because of McKinley's overwhelming popularity among the people.[37]

Long before the Wisconsin Republican convention met, it was evident that most of the state's leading politicians thought it would be advantageous to them to appear to be on intimate terms with Mc-Kinley.[38] As a result the various Republican factions flooded the state with rumors that one or another of their leaders was slated to be in McKinley's cabinet or in his post-convention campaign organization. A battle royal developed between La Follette and Elisha Keyes, both residents of Madison, to be elected in the primaries as the delegate from their district to the national convention. While Keyes appealed to party leaders like Philetus Sawyer for support, La Follette's backers appealed to the voters in letters expressing such sentiments as these: "You know La Follette and McKinley were not only great friends but worked together on the Ways and Means Committee in Congress. Our old friend Keyes want [sic] to go but he has been to many conventions & Bob never went to one."[39]

After La Follette beat Keyes in the primary elections Keyes tried to minimize La Follette's influence in the convention by defeating La Follette's attempt to persuade McKinley to assign him the task of giving one of the speeches seconding McKinley's nomination.[40]

Michigan, where the reformer Hazen Pingree, had established control of Republican politics and was preparing the way for his gubernatorial campaign, was a force unto itself in 1896. However, Pingree was not hostile to McKinley; and General Russell A. Alger, not now much of a power in Michigan politics but of some value as a confidante of Platt, Quay, and the other bosses, finally allied himself with McKinley. With little debate Michigan Republicans adopted instructions for McKinley at their state convention.

There was a clear pattern in the activity for McKinley throughout the Midwest. Wherever they found an opportunity, quietly and efficiently the McKinley managers organized and developed a state or district to secure instructions for McKinley at the Republican state convention. "General" Dawes, through his friends in Nebraska, was helpful in setting up McKinley organizations in Nebraska, Kansas, and the Dakotas, organizations which were stimulated and strengthened by monetary contributions from Hanna.[41] When necessary, western workers found it comparatively easy to travel to Chicago to confer with Dawes, Hanna, Osborne, or others at Dawes' headquarters. Sometimes, if particularly pressing circumstances required, they might be asked to travel to Canton to talk with McKinley.[42] They were in Chicago in great numbers at the time of McKinley's Marquette Club address. The McKinley campaign in this part of the country was eminently successful, with the result that in the spring of 1896 the Republican state convention in every middle western state but Iowa adopted resolutions instructing for McKinley.

Allison had failed almost totally to retain the support of his own section. At first he had welcomed the candidacies of Manderson and Davis, because he thought they would be able to hold their own states at least against McKinley and that eventually he would get their votes. Before long he and Davis were disputing control of the two Dakotas; and Allison, Senator Richard F. Pettigrew, and Davis became involved in a three-way argument over South Dakota. When both Davis and Manderson withdrew from the race on the eve of the Republican conventions in their own states, Allison believed that they had betrayed him in McKinley's interest.

In reality all three men failed in their combat with McKinley in the Middle West for the same reason—their failure to develop campaigns that possessed any popular appeal comparable to McKinley's. They could not hope and did not try to rival McKinley on the tariff issue. On the money issue none had spoken any more clearly or achieved any more distinction than McKinley. The men who managed Allison's and Davis' campaigns recognized that their candidates were handicapped because they had not distinguished themselves in the discussion of public issues and tried vainly to persuade them to speak out boldly in such a way as to capture the imagination of the people. It was on the issue of boss control that these men were hopelessly out-classed and out-maneuvered by McKinley. Allison and Manderson particularly were already reputed to be under the control of railroad or other business interests, mere ciphers in a grand game of "boodle"; so that the accusations of the McKinley workers that these men as candidates were merely pawns for the old-line eastern bosses appeared convincing. The people, disillusioned and desperate, sought a new type of leadership, dissociated from the old, discredited party machine; and the McKinley campaign of "The People against the Bosses" promised some realization of their aspirations.

10

McKinley's Mastery Challenged in the South and Far West

Traditionally in Republican conventions the votes of the southern delegates were hotly contested through shamelessly crude and corrupt methods. Since southern states rarely produced Republican electoral votes, it was at the nominating conventions that southern Republicans exerted their greatest power in the nation's political life. Only to a minor extent did presidential candidates competing for the votes of southern delegates find it advisable to speak out on national issues. Traditionally they found it necessary to affirm their belief in Negro rights and in honest elections. In the 1890's it was sometimes claimed that the industrialization occurring in the South made tariff protection attractive in that section; and in Louisiana and a few other specialized agricultural areas it was evident beyond argument that protection was desired.

The popularity of protection was debatable in the South; but it was clear here, as in the sections where its popularity was certain, that on the tariff issue McKinley was in a position to gain the advantage over the other candidates. Not only did he benefit from the association of his name with the tariff of 1890; but he had spoken frequently in the South on the tariff issue, including, during a crucial point in the 1894 campaign, a widely publicized trip to New Orleans. As a result, whatever high tariff influence did exist in the South had drifted into McKinley's camp early in the campaign. Since most of the southern protectionists were affluent white men, McKinley's opponents thought they might make some political capital by accusing McKinley of discriminating against Negro Republicans. McKinley, ever on guard, descried the most subtle attempts to discredit him on racial and religious questions; and he acted quickly to disprove such accusations.[1]

Though the McKinley-Hanna organization capitalized strongly on public opinion in other quarters of the nation, they recognized from the beginning that opinion would play a very small role in fixing the loyalties of southern delegates. Personal contact was of the essence in wooing the southerners; and through the Hanna and McKinley visits at Thomasville and with Osborne, Grosvenor, Smith, Dick, Herrick, and others traveling extensively and frequently in the South, the McKinley-Hanna organization had decisively won control of the delegations from that region before the other candidates opened their campaigns. The major exception to the McKinley sweep was Texas, where the McKinley-Hanna maneuvers revealed how thoroughly they knew and how readily they employed the crudest political techniques, when their use appeared to be necessary.

The McKinley organization failed initially to win Texas because Republican politics in that state were controlled by Nathaniel Wright Cuney, a well-to-do and influential Negro from Galveston, who was a power in Republican politics throughout the Lower South. Cuney owed his political prestige and influence mostly to Clarkson and Allison; and he remained loyal to them, though the McKinley-Hanna group made a strenuous effort to bring Cuney to their side. In March 1895, when McKinley was at Thomasville, Hanna and Joe Smith invited Cuney to visit McKinley there. Cuney's refusal of the invitation because of his wife's illness was followed by a request from Hanna that Cuney travel to New Orleans to talk with William M. Osborne. When Cuney again refused, pleading the illness of his wife, Hanna wrote him a letter saying that he had arranged to bring Jim Hill of Mississippi into the McKinley organization and that within the month both Hill and Joe Smith were likely to travel to Galveston, where they would attempt to see Cuney. Hill did visit Cuney but failed to sway him from his allegiance to Allison. Shortly after this Hanna wrote to Cuney:

I will say to you frankly that I am very anxious to have you take charge of Gov. McKinley's interests in Texas, which I feel should receive some attention. I appreciate that it is something of a task to fully perfect an organization and that there would be expenses, etc., which no one should be asked to bear alone. Then as to the proper men from whom to ask assistance in the several Dist's—I will gladly co-operate in all this and write personal letters to those whom you may suggest—where you think it will have influence. And in any other way do all I can to assist you, all contingent of course upon your willingness in the matter. I write you this in confidence because I have understood that you were friendly to Gov. McKinley. If you have seen Joe Smith he will have told you how favorable everything is for the Gov. and I assure you I can see no reason why all our hopes should not materialize.[2]

A year later, in March 1896, when the Republican state convention met at Austin, Texas, Cuney was still working for Allison and before the convention had combined with the Reed forces in such a way as to control the convention under normal conditions.[3] General Dodge reported to Senator Allison that "clever detailed work" with the help of the railroads had won Texas, claiming that Cuney had controlled the convention through the 250 delegates from northern Texas that the railroads had brought into Austin in Allison's interest.[4]

The McKinley-Hanna organization, when they failed to win Cuney to their side, had turned to John Grant, chairman of the Republican State Committee, had gained his backing, and provided him with the kind of aid they had promised Cuney.[5] During the convention Myron Herrick was in Austin, from where he maintained telegraphic communication with Hanna in Cleveland. When the doors to the convention hall were opened on the first morning, McKinley delegates who were contesting for the seats held by Allison and Reed men rushed into the hall and tried to take control by force. There was much pushing and shoving and a flourishing of guns, but Cuney had been forewarned and had a group of strong-arm men protecting his control of the platform. He retained control of the machinery of the convention, and the credentials committee brought in a report seating Cuney's slate of delegates. The convention then completed its work by selecting delegates to the national convention committed to vote for Allison and Reed. However, when the Cuney group abandoned the hall, the McKinley delegates took it over, held a convention of their own, and claimed that the slate of delegates which they elected were the legitimate representatives of Texas Republicanism. Thus, the McKinley-Hanna organization was in a position to carry the contest for Texas delegates into the national convention at St. Louis.[6]

Every candidate who attempted to win support among southern delegations was accused of using money and promises of future political rewards, and the evidence strongly indicated that the accusations were justified. The press reported that Morton was sending money into the South in unprecedented amounts. One McKinley leader wrote years later that Morton had used money in Florida but that he had been persuaded to work to win Florida for McKinley in 1896 by the promise that he would be consulted in the distribution of patronage in the state.[7] The Allison and Reed forces did not have much money to spend among the southern delegates, and the steady drift in the South to McKinley soon made it evident to his opponents that it was a matter of too little, too late. Still, contesting delegations were cheap in the South, and most of the 158 contesting delegates who appeared at the convention were from southern states. If the game could be played by McKinley in Texas, it could be played by Reed, Allison, and Morton elsewhere, and was. The correspondence of Tom Platt and James S. Clarkson at the end of May 1896, just prior to the Republican convention, revealed that they were raising money and organizing railroad transportation to make certain that contesting delegations were brought to St. Louis in full force, provided with the evidence necessary to prove their case and with "entertainment" calculated to whet their enthusiasm for their candidate.[8]

There were two states in the Lower South in which Republicans had since 1892 won victories by cooperating with the Populists. In North Carolina the Populist-Republican fusion victory had resulted in the election of Republican James C. Pritchard to the United States Senate. In Alabama the Populist Reuben Kolb, by combining Populist and Republican votes, had probably won a majority of the votes of the state but had been fraudulently counted out by the Democrats. During the period when the campaign for the nomination was underway Kolb was making a desperate but futile effort to force recognition of the election fraud and to be instated in the governor's office. He received considerable aid from Republican politicians, particularly those like Senator Chandler whose political careers extended back into the period of radical Reconstruction.[9]

Kolb was a Populist, however, and Governor Morton's correspondence from Alabama revealed that developments among the regular Republicans in that state were being guided in much the same channels as elsewhere in the South. Once he decided to be an active candidate, Morton wrote to an old Alabama friend, William Youngblood of Montgomery. Morton reminded Youngblood that the latter had written him several months earlier pledging his support to Morton who had replied indecisively because he had not decided to be a candidate.[10]

Youngblood replied that Morton had made his application too late, that he had joined McKinley's campaign. His letter described the circumstances under which he had made his decision: "It is his [Morton's] and Mr. Platt's fault that this state is not solid for him. I had to line up with whoever sought me to hold my own at home. I could not wait. Now that I am for McKinley I will be loyal hard as it goes to be against Mr. Morton." [11] That he had become emotionally involved in the McKinley campaign Youngblood revealed by the bitterness with which he denounced in his letter to Morton the use of money by Reed and Morton agents in Alabama and the combination of their forces to try to beat McKinley.[12]

McKinley-Hanna control in North Carolina was established with even greater ease. From the first McKinley had the support of Pritchard and the other Republican leaders responsible for the victory in North Carolina, and without a hitch they brought the delegation from their state to the McKinley column at the Republican National Convention.[13]

In Louisiana Republican politics proved to be so complicated that all factions despaired of understanding the situation, to say nothing of controlling it. One of the dominant elements in the situation in that state was the expectation of the Republicans that they might capitalize on discontent among the sugar planters with the bounty provided in the Wilson tariff. Early in 1895 the traditionally Democratic sugar planters expressed their unhappiness by setting up a separate political movement to gain control of the state. From the first this movement had the opportunistic cooperation of the Republicans and the Populists.[14] Both McKinley and Allison had supported high domestic sugar bounties in the congressional tariff debates, and McKinley had spoken forcefully on this issue in his speech at New Orleans in the 1894 campaign, with the result that both men had popular support in Louisiana. Organization support, however, was held largely by Reed and McKinley, through the leadership of clever and unprincipled agents, William Pitt Kellogg and Henry Clay Warmoth. Kellogg, who lived in Washington, D.C., from which he tried to maintain a kind of absentee-landlord control over Louisiana politics, had long been for Reed. Warmoth was originally a Harrison man, but he felt his power slipping from him and turned to support the popular McKinley to shore up his strength.

Warmoth made his first contribution to McKinley at the meeting of the Louisiana Republican State Committee in December 1895. The committee at first was under Kellogg's control, but Warmoth pressed for the admission of thirty additional men from his faction. William Osborne was on hand to help Warmoth and through private interviews persuaded several of the committee to withdraw their opposition to Warmoth's request, with the result that the Warmoth group was seated and gained a balance of power in the committee.[15] Warmoth, in writing to McKinley about these developments, expressed his continued loyalty to Harrison. McKinley replied that his interest in Louisiana was that of any other citizen "who desires to see the public sentiment of the state expressed through its delegates. I appreciate what you say about your devotion to General Harrison, and think your position is one of manliness." [16] As a result of this development the delegates at large from Louisiana, chosen by the State Central Committee, were equally divided between Reed and McKinley, while in virtually all the districts two separate conventions were held and two contending delegations were chosen, one for Reed and one for McKinley.[17] Thus, the disposition of most of the votes of the Louisiana delegation awaited the action of the national convention in St. Louis.

In Mississippi Republican affairs became as complicated as they were in Louisiana or Texas. As in most southern states two factions emerged, but in Mississippi there was considerable confusion about the loyalty of each of them. Apparently they played all the candidates for whatever they could get from them. As early as March of 1895 Hanna was using James Hill as a personal emissary in the South; but the anti-Hill faction, led by John R. Lynch, also claimed to be for McKinley. In April of 1896 James Clarkson wrote Allison that Lynch had visited Canton; and if the Lynch delegation was recognized by McKinley, Allison would have the Hill delegation "solid." [18] From Mississippi, therefore, two disputed delegations went to the national convention. The McKinley-Hanna organization had never had any serious doubts of the loyalty of the Hill group, and they were duly seated.

In the Border South since 1892 Republicans in their own right, without the aid of Populists, had scored impressive victories. McKinley more than any other national Republican figure was to profit from the growth of Republican strength in the area. During the campaign of 1894 he spoke in the major cities of all the Border States.

In 1894 the Republican party won control of West Virginia, electing

Albert B. White as governor and through control of the legislature sending Stephen B. Elkins to the United States Senate. White committed himself to the support of McKinley early in the campaign, and he proved useful to the McKinley-Hanna organization in shaping opinion and in lining up the local politicians. White and Elkins cooperated closely in the management of West Virginia politics, but Elkins was far too deeply involved with maneuvers to win for himself the most advantage possible from the power which he held in West Virginia to make an early commitment.

By experience and conviction Elkins was disposed to side with the old-line bosses. He was friendly with Harrison, had been in Harrison's Cabinet, and undoubtedly would have joined openly in a Harrison campaign had it been launched. He did not have the antagonism toward Platt and Quay which Harrison possessed, and like many of the old-line politicians he undoubtedly preferred their honest opportunism to the hypocrisy which he saw in the McKinley campaign. Like most of the old Harrison men he was attracted strongly to the Allison campaign but never found it expedient to make an open declaration.[19]

Elkins did not discourage talk of himself as a presidential candidate but never seriously hoped that this would bring him anything beyond the vice-presidential nomination. With great difficulty he managed for several weeks to maintain friendly relations with all camps. R. C. Kerens, Elkins' St. Louis business associate, acted as a liaison agent between McKinley and Elkins; and McKinley used Kerens' assurances that Elkins was friendly to him to open a correspondence in which he asked Elkins to support the adoption of resolutions of instruction for McKinley at the Republican State Convention.[20] Elkins replied that West Virginia Republicans had not "instructed" since 1880, and he thought this a good tradition to maintain.[21] In correspondence with West Virginia Republicans Elkins admitted that McKinley was the leading candidate in West Virginia, that any delegates chosen by the convention would be for McKinley, and that it might be well to adopt resolutions expressing a preference for McKinley, but that he opposed instructions.[22] At the same time McKinley was writing to West Virginia men asking them to bring resolutions for him into their state convention, if they thought such instructions likely to succeed.[23] Again the McKinley-Hanna organization achieved its objective because McKinley was popular and because it worked the state over more thoroughly than anyone else. At Clarksburg on May 14 West Virginia Republicans adopted resolutions instructing their delegates to the national nominating convention to vote for McKinley.[24]

Kentucky was, like West Virginia, a state in which the Republicans had achieved a notable victory in 1894. Governor Bradley, the chief beneficiary of that victory, was, like Elkins, an opportunist with great political ambitions locally and nationally. He, too, had no objections to having his name bandied about as a possibility on the Republican presidential ticket; and he seriously hoped that he might win the vice-presidential nomination. In part because McKinley's nomination would make his own candidacy for the vice-presidency virtually impossible, Bradley was not an enthusiastic McKinley supporter. The McKinley-Hanna organizers were not without resources in Kentucky, however. They relied heavily on Sam J. Roberts, a former resident of Canton, who in the early '90's had gone to Lexington. There he had established a newspaper, the Lexington *Leader*, which became one of the major centers of the McKinley campaign in Kentucky.[25] Before that campaign had ended Bradley found it expedient to link his fortunes with those of McKinley.

In Missouri, where the national convention was to be held, and where there were more convention delegates to be chosen, the stakes were higher and Republican politics were in a particularly muddled condition.[26] The fight for control of the Missouri Republican organization centered in St. Louis, where the control held by Chauncey Ives Filley was challenged by Richard C. Kerens. Both men hoped to use McKinley's popularity in Missouri to their own advantage, while McKinley welcomed pledges of support from each man and entertained each of them at his home in Canton.[27]

The intentions of Kerens were straightforward and easily discerned. He was a McKinley partisan from the first. Even the most experienced politicians, however, had difficulty fathoming the objectives of Filley. For a while Hanna and McKinley thought they might use Filley in negotiations with Platt. After Platt proved to be inaccessible, and rumors began to appear that Filley was in reality allied with the anti-McKinley combine, McKinley continued to correspond with Filley in a spirit of confidence and friendship.[28] The anti-McKinley group originally believed that Filley was one of them and that he could be depended upon to bring an anti-McKinley delegation into the convention, but eventually the intricacies of his maneuvers disillusioned them and they concluded that his "game" was "too deep to be safe." [29] Under the circumstances, with both Missouri bosses working at least ostensibly in his interest and with public opinion solidly behind him, McKinley had little to fear. In the end Kerens beat Filley out of control of the state, won the post of National Committeeman from Missouri, and brought the Missouri delegation into the national convention united in support of McKinley. Filley, isolated and embittered, became, after the convention and too late for any effective purpose, an avowed anti-McKinley partisan.

Maryland, Tennessee, and Arkansas were won for McKinley with comparatively few complications. Maryland and Arkansas were McKinley states from the first because McKinley and the members of his organization gained the friendship of the men who controlled Republican politics in them.[30] In Arkansas particularly the powerful support of Powell Clayton was valuable, not only in the state itself but in the nearby states and territories.[31] Other candidates did have a foothold in Tennessee, where the victory of Henry Clay Evans in the gubernatorial race in 1894 had placed the Republicans in power. Osborne traveled with good results in Tennessee; McKinley had campaigned there; and Evans' ambitions soon brought him to the McKinley bandwagon.[32]

In the western states and territories, along the Pacific Coast and in the Rocky Mountains, McKinley was undoubtedly more popular than any of the other Republican candidates; and his organization was as thorough and aggressive there as in other sections. Here, however, McKinley met another kind of adversary not so easily quelled as the Allisons, Reeds, and Mortons—the craze for free silver. In peripheral states, like California and Oregon, where mining was not the major industry, Republican state conventions, with little protest, declared for both silver and McKinley.[33] Wyoming Republicans took similar action.[34] Arizona, worked by winter-vacationing Whitelaw Reid, much as Hanna had worked Georgia, also declared for McKinley.[35] But the mountain states and territories were angry and irreconcilable. From their point of view McKinley's monetary policy was unacceptable.

The western silver Republicans never gave McKinley serious consideration as a candidate. They listened to the declarations of his western friends that he was favorable to silver and watched the adoption of resolutions for silver and McKinley in adjoining states with mounting impatience. Late in March Nevada's Senator John P. Jones, in an interview in New York, said that McKinley was "neither flesh, fish, nor fowl," that he was a "straddler, pure and simple," and that the western men preferred that the Republican convention nominate a "gold-bug" like Governor Morton so that the financial issue could be put squarely before the people.[36] A few weeks later Jones' Nevada colleague, Senator William Stewart, addressed a strongly worded letter to McKinley, asking that he declare his position on the financial question. Stewart pointed out that Senator Sherman in a recent letter to the Brooklyn Young Men's Republican Club had said that there was no doubt that McKinley was committed to maintaining "the present gold coin of the United States as the standard of value." Stewart concluded that if McKinley's views were accurately described by Sherman, then he was slandered in the West where,

> Your Republican friends . . . claim that you are in favor of the free and unlimited coinage of silver at the ratio of 16 to 1.
>
> Will you define your position or will you continue to hold out hopes to both sides one or the other of which you must disappoint after the election.[37]

Less than a month before the convention the *National Bimetallist* expressed the disgust of the silverites with the two-faced character of the McKinley campaign on the money issue by concluding that he had "no moral right to reach the goal of his lofty ambition by turning a silver-plated cheek to the West and one of solid gold to the East." [38]

The silverites had long since abandoned hope that McKinley or any of the other leading candidates for the Republican nomination would declare for the free coinage of silver. The only objective of their pre-convention attack on McKinley was to smoke him out and force him to make a clear declaration for a gold policy. The policy which the western silver Republicans would take themselves was more and more slipping into the hands of Senator Teller. The action that Teller would take at the convention was foreshadowed by the action of the Colorado State Republican Convention, meeting at Pueblo on May 15, 1896. Teller, held by his senatorial duties at Washington, could not attend; but he sent to the convention a letter which left no doubt about his position. He said that he could not go to the Republican National Convention as a delegate if the Colorado convention did not adopt a declaration stating that the silver issue was the paramount issue of the coming campaign. He continued:

The State convention should act with the full knowledge that I do not intend to support a candidate on a gold-standard platform or on a platform of doubtful construction.

If this course puts me out of sympathy with the Republican sentiment of the state, . . . I will accept that result with all its logical consequences. . . .[39]

The Colorado Republican convention acted so as to leave no doubt of its adherence to Teller's views by electing Teller as the head of the delegation to the national convention and adopting instructions that the other Colorado delegates should cast their votes as Teller decided.[40]

11

McKinley Battles the Bosses

McKinley was the man to beat. Scattered polls of public and political opinion for months had shown that he was strongly preferred at the home fireside, the workshop bench, and the ward office. The difficulty in this situation for the bosses was that they found it well nigh impossible to take him or Hanna seriously. McKinley had long been one of them, and they had taken his measure. They had evaluated him against Reed, or Harrison, or Allison, and they had been unimpressed. Of Hanna they appeared to take little thought. He was not one of them; they had not succeeded in carrying through any deals with him; they could not understand the simple devotion that he and men like him had for the weak and wooden personality which they found in William McKinley.

The early tactics of McKinley and Hanna seemed consistent with the impression the bosses had of a naive and inept leadership. From their perspective, to bring a candidate so early into the field was to invite everybody else to gang up on him and chop off his head. At first this appeared to be just what was happening. Certainly the bosses were working together, exchanging information and encouragement, and even coordinating the expenditure of campaign funds. At the appropriate times they trotted out their candidates; they corresponded with old friends; they traveled or sent their agents to visit strategically located individuals. They discovered that everywhere McKinley seemed to have preceded them and that very often he had taken their old friends into his camp. Everywhere he had become the people's choice, yes, but also alarmingly the choice of the local politicians.

139

By 1896 the McKinley group and many newspapers had begun to refer to the eastern bosses and their associates as "the combine," implying that the bosses had formed a conspiracy of the corrupt against the popular champion. The travels and the frequent conferences of the bosses were made to appear as furtive and sinister, but futile. Then shortly after the turn of the year they were discovered at the bottom of a new development, which again the McKinleyites described as political maneuvering of the meanest sort, the bringing forth of a whole new field of candidates, the "favorite sons." Suddenly in a field in which Allison, McKinley, and Reed had been the only serious candidates, campaigns were initiated for Cullom, Davis, Manderson, Quay, and Morton.

It was undoubtedly true that the old-line bosses, Platt, Quay, Clarkson, and Manley did stimulate the favorite-son movement as a rather desperate maneuver to stop the McKinley drive. They hoped that Cullom would win the support of Illinois and prevent that state from instructing its delegates to the national convention to vote for McKinley; and they expected that Quay, Davis, Manderson, and the others would succeed in the same objective in their states. They saw nothing sinister or unfair in what they were doing; it was an accepted gambit in the game of politics. They doubtless felt as Joseph B. Foraker did when he wrote to a New York correspondent in April 1896:

> We are for McKinley, and will do all we can to secure his nomination, but I do not support him in hostility to the men whom you term "bosses." The truth is I feel very friendly as a general thing to the men who are assailed under that name. I have had a good deal of the same kind of abuse poured upon my head. Nine times out of ten the man who is thus assailed has provoked the assault by faithful and distinguished service to his party. I do not like people who are reputed to be too good. I have never known one yet who was not a fraud.[1]

Nevertheless, the McKinley group resented these new developments and were persuaded, as was much of the press and public, that there was something particularly unfair about them. Chiefly the unfairness seemed to spring from the suspicion, soon accepted as a verity, that they had no logic or support in themselves, but were merely maneuvers to hold the candidate's home state and, if possible, surrounding states for the use of "the combine" in their struggle to defeat McKinley. The discussion of these campaigns in the newspapers and in the correspondence among the McKinley people, therefore, did not accept these new men as serious candidates but speculated rather on whether their support would eventually be given to Reed, Allison, or Harrison; for the latter continued to be a subject of political speculation in spite of his firm withdrawal.

Realization of the formidable character of the McKinley challenge led to meetings in New York and Washington in December 1895, and January 1896, among Manley, Clarkson, Platt, Quay, and others.[2] In reports to Allison on these conferences Clarkson said that it was understood between him and Platt, Quay, and the others that while Reed was to hold the East against McKinley, they expected Allison to hold the West in line,[3] that they expected to hold the South between Allison and Reed by not competing in those states where one of them had possession of the ground, and that in the critical state of Illinois they did not trust each other and were in more or less open competition.[4]

The first and major failure of the old guard bosses was their failure to concentrate their support upon one candidate. Unlike Hanna they had no master national plan. Also, unlike Hanna, they did not operate with the secure knowledge that they had firm control in their own states. In New York, for example, Platt's control had been challenged in a bitter and prolonged fight. He had managed to gain the upper hand in 1895, but not so securely as he wished; and a part of New York's delegation to the Republican nominating convention was pledged to vote for McKinley. Yet with Morton as New York's candidate and with Platt as Morton's manager, Platt was in a position to demand the loyalty of New York leaders who would otherwise oppose him.

In Pennsylvania Matthew Quay found himself caught in a factional fight much like that which Platt faced in New York, and not until late in 1895 was he able to establish firm control over the state Republican machine. Even then he was challenged by a faction centered in the Pittsburgh area which favored sending delegates to the national convention pledged to vote for McKinley. Quay maneuvered with extraordinary facility and was more tractable and approachable than Platt. It was rumored often that Quay himself was disposed to join the movement to McKinley, but Quay's allegiance was chiefly to the old guard, and he herded with them up to the final stages of the pre-nomination campaign. Before the game was played out in Pennsylvania, Quay found it necessary to bring himself forward as the favorite son of the

Keystone state. By this maneuver the Pennsylvania delegation was pledged to cast its votes for him, and Quay would have a certain bargaining advantage in the convention.

To the McKinley people, who watched with sharp-eyed caution every move of their opponents, another development of this spring campaign seemed also to be an inspiration of "the combine." Shortly before the Illinois Republican convention met McKinley was subjected to a concerted attack from an exceedingly dangerous source—the American Protective Association (APA)—an attack which again he turned to his advantage. The APA had never been particularly friendly to McKinley, because in Ohio they considered Foraker to be a more trustworthy friend and servant.[5] On the other hand, the APA was usually loyal to Republicans; and though it had made violent attacks on Cleveland and Bland, never before had it made such a violent attack on a prominent Republican as it now made on McKinley. On March 24 and 25 the National Advisory Board of the Supreme Council of the APA met in Washington, D.C., to make plans for a May meeting of the Supreme Council. Since the APA planned to take a part in the political canvass of 1896, the Advisory Board undertook a preliminary screening of the Republican presidential candidates. (They decided that there was no apparent Democratic candidate except Cleveland and that the objections to him were so obvious that they required no analysis.)

On April 10 the chairman of the Advisory Board, J. H. D. Stevens, released for publication a letter in which he stated that while the Advisory Board had found all other Republican candidates acceptable, they had found that McKinley was not because he and his friends were anti-APA and pro-Catholic. Stevens' letter stated that Grosvenor had snubbed a sub-committee of the APA Advisory Board when they attempted to interview him on McKinley's religion, that the Ohio APA chapter had produced evidence that McKinley while governor had appointed Catholics to posts to which he had promised to appoint APA people, that the daughter of his secretary, James Boyle, had married a Catholic, that his Missouri friend, Richard Kerens, was Catholic, that the child of his West Virginia friend, Stephen Elkins, had married a Catholic, and so on.[6] Soon, of course, wilder accusations were abroad to the effect that McKinley, Hanna, and Boyle were Catholics, that

McKinley had two children in a Catholic preparatory school, that he had fired APAs and Protestants in order to make jobs for Catholics, and that his grandfather was buried in a Catholic cemetery.[7]

Men as intimate with McKinley as Boyle and Joe Smith believed that the APA attack had received some if not all of its inspiration from the old-line boss "combine." They placed the chief blame on Congressman Aldrich, the Illinois organizer for Reed, believing that in a recent visit to Columbus he had incited the Ohio APA to an overt demonstration of its latent hostility to McKinley.[8] The letters of Clarkson and General Dodge revealed that they were prepared to use APA support in the interest of their candidate, but otherwise evidence that the combine actually employed the APA is circumstantial.[9] James Boyle, much aroused by the APA attack on himself and McKinley, made a three-day personal investigation in Columbus, where he believed the attack had originated; and he said he was convinced that Aldrich was involved.[10]

The more astute members of the McKinley organization recognized that in some quarters at least, and perhaps generally, the APA attack on McKinley could do more good than harm. Dawes concluded that in Illinois the attack was likely to benefit the McKinley cause, particularly because of the editorial treatment which it was receiving in the Illinois press; and he advised rather than any attempt to refute the APA charges point by point, a policy of "dignified silence."[11] Writing from Washington, Grosvenor expressed optimism: "The APA matter in my judgment will be the death blow to the opposition to McKinley. The American people are not quite ready to endorse a warfare upon an American citizen because of his religious belief."[12]

It remained for the political genius of William McKinley to find the words that would express correctly the patriotic sentiments that would serve to turn the attack upon his opponents and to reveal the depths of his own Americanism:

The course [of the APA] is extraordinary in American politics and I can not but think that it will react upon its authors and others related to it. Think for a moment—the leaders of a secret order seeking through its organization to dictate a presidential nomination. A committee sitting in secret judgment on a public man and whose report and judgment are to be binding upon all its membership. It may hurt locally here and there but in the broad sense it cannot hurt. But whether it does or not, we can not afford for any stake to narrow our platform, or consent to countenance any abridgement of the constitutional guarantees of religious freedom.

He concluded with the typical McKinley comment that the record of his past, an open book to all men, must be the answer to all inquiries on this matter.[13]

At another level the McKinley organizers were employing their political skills to get inside the APA and stop altogether the attack upon their man. In Ohio Boyle had friends who were in the APA. He used them to establish contact with A. J. Boyer, editor of the *United American*, a nativist journal which had called Hanna a Catholic and had published some of the most scurrilous literature about McKinley.[14] Soon Boyer visited Hanna in Cleveland, and Hanna sent him on to Canton, with a letter of introduction, "I want him to meet and *know* you. . . ."[15]

Previous to his visit with Hanna and McKinley, Boyer had announced in Washington that the action of the Advisory Board was merely a recommendation which would be acted upon by the Supreme Council of the APA when it met in May.[16] When the Supreme Council met, the growing popularity of McKinley, combined with the inside work of Hanna,[17] resulted in a rejection of the Advisory Board's recommendations. A special committee was appointed to visit McKinley in Canton, and they reported a satisfactory interview. The Supreme Council did not directly repudiate the work of the Advisory Board but concluded that the Board had acted properly in rejecting Mc-Kinley on the information they possessed in March. That information, however, had since been proved inadequate and inaccurate. New and complete information on McKinley proved him to have the record and qualifications satisfactory to the APA; and therefore the APA found it possible to endorse all the Republican candidates for the Presidency.[18] McKinley did not find it expedient to appear too sympathetic and cooperative with APA actions and publicly denied press reports that he had been interviewed by a special APA committee in Canton.[19] By this time it was evident that APA opposition was helpful in certain areas; and McKinley felt it unnecessary to capitulate in any way, at least in public, to an organization which had made such vicious personal and political attacks on him.

In New England the bosses looked to Manley to control that section for Reed. In fact, at the opening of the campaign it was anticipated that Republican politics in New England in 1896 would be comparatively dull, not because New England's candidate, Thomas Bracket

Reed, was in any sense a dull man of undefined views; but because it was assumed that New England was unreservedly for Reed and that its convention votes were already wrapped and sealed for delivery to him. New England anticipations, like those in Iowa, Nebraska, and Minnesota, were based on an inadequate evaluation of the intentions and energies of the McKinley-Hanna organization. In New England the steps in the disintegration of local confidence in the inviolability of the local man's pre-eminence were much the same as in the Middle West: first, the realization that McKinley was unexpectedly popular; next, the appearance of evidence that certain factions were encouraging public and party support of McKinley; third, the act of desperation, intended to weaken McKinley, but instead turning back upon the anti-McKinley men to divide them.

In the Middle West the acts of desperation had been the bringing forth of Davis, Manderson, and Cullom as favorite sons. In New England the act of desperation was a letter written by New Hampshire's erratic Senator William E. Chandler and released for publication on March 16, 1896. In one way there was a difference between Chandler's act and the acts of the favorite sons in the Middle West. There was little doubt that Chandler was sincere. He was thoroughly, wrongly, sincerely—and indiscreetly—angry. He believed that Hanna was using money in unprecedented amounts and in unprecedented ways to win convention delegates pledged to McKinley. He had written letters over the country asking for evidence to document his suspicions and he had received replies which convinced him that what he had suspected was true, that in the South and West particularly, Hanna was buying delegates on a scale never hitherto known in American politics.[20]

The publication of Chandler's letter produced a storm of indignation among the newspapers and the politicians but it attracted no new support of any significance to Reed. It caused considerable amusement in those quarters where Chandler's own political methods were most intimately known and understood.[21] Its major effect was to give McKinley supporters, who had until now been uncertain of the grounds upon which they could campaign for McKinley in New Hampshire, justification for working more actively and openly for him there. Chandler, detained in Washington by his senatorial duties, was not well informed of the growth of McKinley support in New Hampshire. When he came home late in March to manage the New Hampshire Republican convention, he was unprepared to deal with the maneuver by which the pro-McKinley elements, in spite of the fact that Chandler was chairman of the convention, gained control of the resolutions committee and brought to the floor of the convention a resolution naming both Reed and McKinley as acceptable candidates.[22] Later in a letter to Reed Chandler blamed himself for the defection in New Hampshire, claiming that the development came so suddenly that he was caught off his guard and capitulated without fighting the McKinley resolutions as he ought to have.[23] It was more likely that Chandler did not resist because he had evidence that in a direct match with McKinley Reed would lose New Hampshire's support altogether.

New England leaders, trying to soften the blow to Reed's candidacy, characterized the New Hampshire action as more anti-Chandler than pro-McKinley.[24] This was not in the main true. Undoubtedly McKinley and Hanna and their New England workers were glad to have an opportunity to take Chandler down a notch, but they always kept their attention chiefly on McKinley's nomination. Here as elsewhere the politicians opposing McKinley had failed to appreciate the extent of his popularity among the people and the manufacturers. Also in New England, as elsewhere, Hanna and McKinley carefully organized and marshalled whatever support they discovered. Osborne was working on a national scale and was not often in Boston in the early months of 1896, but his contacts in the New England states were useful.

Jacob Gallinger, junior senator from New Hampshire, in comparing the Reed and McKinley campaigns shortly before the national nominating convention put his finger accurately on the sources of McKinley's strength and Reed's weakness:

> [McKinley] has a thorough organization, which is not true of any other candidate, and in politics organization counts for more than anything else. Mr. Reed made a great mistake when he was nominated for Speaker in not taking a more aggressive attitude on public questions. Had he declared that it was the duty of Congress to revise the iniquitous Wilson-Gorman bill, and thus rescue the country from the disasters that the Democratic legislation had brought upon it, he would have aroused the attention of the American people and would be much stronger as a candidate than he now is.[25]

Theodore Roosevelt also thought that Reed should have spoken out more boldly on public issues, but he believed that the emphasis should have been put on the financial question. Roosevelt found in conversations with eastern Republicans of convictions similar to his own that they had gained the impression from Reed's statements favoring international bimetallism that he was trying "to straddle the Silver Question."[26] The economist, David A. Wells, reported that he had discovered that eastern industrial and financial interests distrusted Reed's views on finance.[27] Roosevelt tried to counteract the belief that Reed was unsound on money in an article which he wrote for Century magazine on the 1896 campaign. "No man," he wrote, "deserves more at the hands of believers in sound money than Mr. Reed; and his views are the views of the great mass of Republican voters."[28]

The journalist, Walter Wellman, an astute political observer, said that Reed at the beginning of his campaign had judged his reputation as "a man of too much boldness of action, of too grasping and original a character" to be a liability and had set out deliberately to become "conservatism personified."[29] If so, Reed had succeeded too well. In February 1896, the *Atlantic,* analyzing his campaign, concluded that he would never do as president because it was "wholly as a party leader that he has risen above the rank and file. He has never identified himself with any great cause; he has never set a moral force in motion."[30] A month later Theodore Roosevelt sadly recorded his feeling "that Tom Reed has missed his opportunity this winter. He is trying to make a reputation as a conservative economist, and has merely succeeded in giving the idea that he has turned timid."[31] Meanwhile, the bold man, the man of ideas, the champion of the people against the bosses, appeared to be William McKinley of Canton, Ohio.

There was little more than the assessments of Gallinger and T. R. to be said for the failure of Reed's campaign; it lacked organization and it lacked popular appeal. Reed's followers acknowledged early in the campaign that he was comparatively unknown outside of New England; but following the Republican victory in the House of Representatives in 1894 they anticipated that as Speaker of the House he would have opportunities for bold action that would bring him national attention.[32] Exactly how they expected these opportunities to develop it was difficult to see. The position of Speaker of the House had not in earlier years proved a particularly good post for the grooming of presidential hopefuls; and during the months of 1895 and 1896 in which the office would be occupied by Reed it seemed unlikely that any legislative sensations would develop to draw public attention favorably to the Speaker. It was hardly a post to be sought by a man seriously aspiring to the Presidency. The most he could do would be to give committee assignments in exchange for convention support. There was little evidence that Reed attempted this;[33] yet there was no doubt that Reed was seriously a candidate for the nomination. Reed's fault was that he placed too much confidence in Manley and his political maneuvers, and Manley in turn put too much trust in traditional machine politics.

It was essential to Reed's campaign that Congress adjourn early in 1896, so that the Speaker could carry his campaign actively to the country. Instead Reed was held inactive in Washington as a "do-nothing" Congress protracted its sessions up to the eve of the Republican convention.[34] Reed, watching from the capitol the accelerating progress of McKinley's campaign, fussed and raged, helplessly. Tentative arrangements with the bosses and state organizations, which Manley should have been able to hold and strengthen, gradually disintegrated. Two points of great strategic value, Illinois and New York, appeared in 1895 to be points which Reed would definitely control. In Illinois the Chicago *Tribune* was friendly; the Cook County machine was also kindly disposed; and John R. Tanner was interested. By the turn of the year into 1896 the *Tribune* was flirting with McKinley, and Tanner and the Cook County machine were bringing out Cullom because Reed had not developed sufficient strength to hold Illinois against McKinley. In the East both Platt and Quay were sympathetic to Reed's candidacy, but again he did not develop sufficient strength to draw them deeply into his campaign.

The cup of Reed's humiliation was not yet emptied in New England. Late in April at the Republican convention in Vermont the Republicans of that state adopted resolutions not of instruction but of preference for McKinley. The man chiefly responsible for the Vermont action was Senator Redfield Proctor, an opportunist, impressed by McKinley's popularity among the people and the industrialists of his state and influenced by the McKinley organization.[35] This action by Vermont Republicans had a psychological value, for it was announced at the time that Illinois Republicans were convening at Springfield.[36] Massachusetts and Rhode Island did instruct their delegates to vote for Reed, though not without determined opposition both within and outside the conventions. In Boston the Home Market Club, a protectionist organization which had entertained McKinley in 1894 and listened to one of his major speeches on the tariff, loudly and persistently shouted its hero's virtues.[37]

FIGURE 1.
William McKinley, *c.* 1896.
Courtesy
Chicago Historical
Society.

FIGURE 2.
Mark Hanna, *c.* 1896.

FIGURE 3. A typical day in Canton in the summer of 1896.

FIGURE 4. Campaign Glee Club singing before McKinley at his house in Canton, October 27, 1896. Courtesy Chicago Historical Society.

FIGURE 5. Republican broadside, 1896. Courtesy Chicago Historical Society.

"HOW CAN HE LOSE ME?"

FIGURE 6. Cartoon by Homer Davenport, published October 18, 18[ ] in the New York *Journal*, giving the Democratic view of the McKin[ ] Hanna relationship.

FIGURE 7. Cartoon published September 26, 1896, in the San Francisco *Chronicle*, giving the Republican view of elements in the Democratic party.

Make a Cross at One Emblem, and at Only O

Party	President / Vice-President	Emblem
Republican Party.	For President of the United States, WILLIAM McKINLEY. For Vice-President of the United States, GARRETT A. HOBART.	
People's Party.	For President of the United States, WILLIAM J. BRYAN. For Vice-President of the United States, ARTHUR SEWALL.	
National=Silver Party.	For President of the United States, WILLIAM J. BRYAN. For Vice-President of the United States, ARTHUR SEWALL.	
Silver=Populist Party.	For President of the United States, WILLIAM J. BRYAN. For Vice-President of the United States, ARTHUR SEWALL.	
Democratic Party.	For President of the United States, WILLIAM J. BRYAN. For Vice-President of the United States, ARTHUR SEWALL.	
National Party.	For President of the United States, CHARLES EUGENE BENTLEY. For Vice-President of the United States, JAMES H. SOUTHGATE.	
Socialist=Labor Party.	For President of the United States, For Vice-President of the United States,	
National=People's Party.	For President of the United States, WILLIAM J. BRYAN. For Vice-President of the United States, THOMAS WATSON.	
Silver=Republican Party.	For President of the United States, WILLIAM J. BRYAN. For Vice-President of the United States, ARTHUR SEWALL.	
Water=Consumers' Ticket.		
Prohibition Party.	For President of the United States, JOSHUA LEVERING. For Vice-President of the United States, HALE JOHNSON.	

FIGURE 8. Sample ballot which appeared in the *Weekly Rocky Mountain News,* October 31, 1896.

FIGURE 9.
William Jennings Bryan, *c.* 1896.
Courtesy
Chicago Historical Society.

IF BRYAN SHOULD BE ELECTED ALTGELD WILL BE "THE POWER BEHIND THE THRONE."

FIGURE 10. Cartoon published October 29, 1896, in the Chicago *Tribune*, showing the Republican view of the Bryan-Altgeld relationship.

FIGURE 11. Cartoon published in *Coin's Financial School* (1894), showing the farmers' view of their relationship to Eastern bankers.

FIGURE 12. Cartoon published in *Coin's Financial School* (1894), showing the silverites' view of the potential effect of the free coinage of silver.

In Republican politics in 1896 the pivotal states of Pennsylvania and New York were a law unto themselves. Though in 1895 both Matthew Quay and Thomas C. Platt had won control over the Republican organizations in their states, the factions which had opposed them remained active. In both states the opposition factions were pro-McKinley, and this tended to put Quay and Platt in a posture of opposition to McKinley. Throughout the campaign McKinley tried to keep in contact with these two bosses, while at the same time remaining on intimate terms with the leaders of the factions opposing them. He had no difficulty in retaining his contact with Quay. In fact, McKinley's associates understood that some working agreement existed between Quay and McKinley which prevented them from invading Pennsylvania as aggressively as they might have.[38]

At the beginning of 1896 McKinley had tried to establish liaison with Platt through several agents, including Chauncey Filley and Joseph B. Foraker; but Platt was not in a receptive mood. Tom Platt proved to be McKinley's most resourceful and most stubborn opponent. Platt's enemies characterized him as a man who had cynically devoted his career to the achievement of power and the corrupt use of power. Platt might well have felt justified in whatever cynicism about politics he may have possessed as he studied his relations in 1895 and 1896 with men in New York who thought themselves superior to him as honest and respectable men. Levi Morton found himself bound inescapably to Platt and his organization through his ambition to be president. Platt inevitably would control the larger part of the New York delegation, and Morton could get nowhere without that.

In New York Platt played relentlessly upon Morton's presidential ambitions to persuade Morton to sign bills and make appointments which would help Platt to consolidate his power in that state. In December 1895, Platt wrote to Morton in regard to an appointment recommended by Platt but opposed by the reform Republicans close to Morton: "It is quite important that Mr. Stewart whom Mr. Lauterbach & I suggested for Inspector of Gas Meters should be appointed. Failure to do so would much embarrass us as to some National delegates."[39] Platt's henchman Lauterbach also wrote a letter urging the appointment of Stewart, threatening that any other action would have dire political results for both Platt and Morton and promising that if Morton did act as Platt wanted he would have "as faithful, loyal and impregnable a body-guard of devoted followers as ever came to the

support of any governor, statesman or politician."⁴⁰ Morton usually
made the appointments which Platt recommended; and, after considerable soul-searching, he signed the major pieces of legislation which
Platt wanted. The anxiety that the most important of these bills
caused Morton he himself described in a letter to Platt:

> I presume you know, though perhaps you scarcely realize what it imposes
> upon me, that Mr. Vanderbilt, Pierpont Morgan, and every man with whom
> I have had business, social and club relations, practically the whole group
> of my closest friends of the last forty years, are bitterly hostile to this
> measure [the Raines Liquor Control bill]. . . . What with the Raines bill,
> the greater New York bill and the Albany police bill I cannot avoid saying
> that I have serious forebodings that we may lose the State this fall.⁴¹

To the very end, however, Platt made use of the advantage which
he had. In a letter asking Morton to sign the Greater New York bill
he said, "I am exceedingly anxious to have this out of the way, so far
as I am concerned, so I can devote all my energies to the national
campaign."⁴² In another letter expressing his relief that Morton had
made two appointments which he had recommended Platt said, "Any
other course would have been most unfortunate for yourself, ourselves and the Party." That he was thinking primarily of Morton's
candidacy he left no doubt when further on in the letter he wrote:

> However, I have learned a lesson, and that is never again to attempt to
> manage the affairs of any man's canvass, no matter how good a friend he may
> be. I shall go on and do my utmost to advance your interests in the present
> canvass for the Presidency, but I shall take pains to give no assurances and
> make no promises for the future: then there will be no danger of accusations
> such as have come to my ears as emanating from men close to you, that
> I am "putting the Governor in a hole."⁴³

If Platt needed any other fuel to feed the cynicism which he was
alleged to possess, he must have found it in 1896 in his relations with
Theodore Roosevelt. Roosevelt passionately desired the nomination of
Thomas Reed. At first he played along with Platt because he thought
that Platt, too, favored Reed's nomination, even though he believed
that in the history of politics no one had surpassed Platt in "fraudu-
lent management" and "stuffing and padding."⁴⁴ When Platt scheduled legislation which would deprive Roosevelt of his office as Police
Commissioner of New York City and brought out Morton as a candidate for the Presidency, Roosevelt refused to break with the party
or to join the anti-Platt faction in New York, because as he explained
to Henry Cabot Lodge he would not join in "a bolt which would be
sure to turn out anti-Reed as well as anti-Platt."⁴⁵

The finesse with which Tom Platt united disparate elements in New York revealed, at least in a small arena, political artistry of a high order. Platt's talents applied on a larger scale in national politics in 1896 were confined and frustrated by circumstances largely beyond his control; yet his talents and his stubborn persistence made him in the end the leader in the fight to defeat McKinley. At first he was just one of the group of eastern bosses, of somewhat lesser stature and national experience than Manley or Clarkson and without a candidate. In January 1896, he brought out Morton as his candidate, and by February he had become the chief co-ordinator of the fight against McKinley. By April he had become the storm center of the bitter, last-ditch resistance to McKinley's nomination.

Even though he managed Morton's campaign it could be said that Platt never had a candidate. There were several people acceptable to him—Allison, Reed, Manderson, Davis, and Morton—and he helped them all in one way or another. In cooperation with Quay he even managed to raise money which he distributed not chiefly to help Morton but to help the anti-McKinley cause wherever there was hope it would succeed.

In February the anti-McKinley "combine," calculating that there would be some 150 disputed delegate seats in the convention, became concerned about the attitude of the National Committee. The National Committee would "try" all of the disputes before the convention opened and draw up a provisional list of delegates. Although the convention itself would make the final decision on these disputes, the action taken by the National Committee would probably influence the votes of the delegates. Therefore, the nomination, with so many disputed delegations to be acted upon, might be decided in the National Committee.[46] The "combine" developed an impression that some work ought to be done among the members of the National Committee in the western states and territories. They sent James Clarkson and a group of New York and Pennsylvania politicians into the Far West to interview the National Committeemen and others.[47] General Dodge, Platt, and Quay saw to it that Clarkson was supplied with money to be used to draw the westerners away from McKinley. At the same time they arranged to supply money to Tanner to carry on his desperate fight against McKinley instructions in Illinois.[48] Reporting to Allison after his return from his western trip Clarkson indicated that he had canvassed the Pacific Coast and Rocky

Mountain states thoroughly, that he had found them drifting rapidly toward McKinley, and that he believed he had stopped this trend and had persuaded them to send uninstructed delegations to St. Louis.[49]

By the time of the national convention Platt virtually alone was carrying through the struggle to bring contesting Reed and Allison delegates to St. Louis from western and southern states. He forwarded money to Clarkson to be turned over to the leaders of the various state delegations; and Clarkson reflected bitterly on the fact that money raised by Platt in the East had to be used to bring to St. Louis Allison delegates from the South and West over railroads which ought to have provided transportation and much besides in the interest of Allison.[50]

Tom Platt recognized the importance of money in managing a successful political campaign, but no more than McKinley did he believe that the main reliance could be put on money. He recognized that ideas and issues were the chief sources of McKinley's strength. As the campaign developed he became convinced that this was also the area in which McKinley was most vulnerable. When the success of the free silver propaganda caused public opinion to focus with increasing sharpness on the issue of the currency, it was generally recognized that this was a development potentially harmful to McKinley's campaign because of the fact that he had concentrated on the tariff issue to the exclusion of all others. His statements and actions on the money question had varied widely from time to time (there were few men in any party of which this was not true); but mostly he had tried to occupy middle ground and had not pretended to any special knowledge of finance. This was, of course, where the development of public sentiment made him particularly vulnerable. People everywhere were adopting sharply defined polar points of view on the question of money; so that any man who attempted to take a position of moderation and compromise became, both in the eyes of the silverites and the "sound money" men, a weak man, a "straddler."

Eastern Republicans were, when the circumstances of politics enabled them to speak candidly, of many points of view as to what the monetary policy of the nation should be. Few were free silverites but many were bimetallists. Some of the bimetallists, of whom Senator Chandler was an excellent example, were concerned that the growth of free silver sentiment in the West and Middle West would not only split the Republican party but defeat it in the general election. Chandler and men like him wanted the party in 1896 to adopt a money plank declaring for both silver and gold and capable of as many different interpretations as sentiment in the various regions of the nation demanded. Other Republican bimetallists like Hay, Reed, and Roosevelt reacted to the hysteria of the money debate by taking the side of Cleveland and gold—the so-called "sound money" position. On the other side, at least one Republican bimetallist concluded that the only way to achieve international bimetallism was to encourage the free silver enthusiasm.[51] The largest segment of the Republican party in the East, however, was made up of "gold-bugs," and among these Governor Levi P. Morton, so closely allied to eastern banking and investment interests, was conspicuous.[52]

In the last phases of the campaign, as one by one the favorite sons of the West capitulated to McKinley, while Clarkson and Manley made the half-hearted gestures of men already beaten and Quay made a pilgrimage of capitulation from Pennsylvania to Canton, Platt emerged aggressively in a final, hard-slugging effort to strike down McKinley. Candidates one by one and severally had contended against the Canton champion and had retreated ingloriously. The new contender which Platt brought forth was an issue—the financial question. Platt was distributing money over the country to bring contesting delegates to the convention and seat them, in the desperate hope that he could thereby prevent McKinley's nomination on the first ballot. He sought also to bring the issue of "sound money" into the convention as another ally in his drive against McKinley.

The logic in Platt's maneuver was that if the platform adopted by the convention emphasized the money issue, McKinley's candidacy would appear incongruous; and the convention would seek another candidate. In mid-May Platt gave two press interviews in which he attacked McKinley on three grounds: his tariff views were too radical, his currency views were unsound, and Hanna's political methods were corrupt.[53] He said that the McKinley slogan, "The people against the bosses," was a subterfuge and that the McKinley people had tried to get the support of the bosses. "They have not omitted," he said, "even so humble a person as myself from those whose influence they sought." [54] He appealed "to the business-men of this country, whose sentiment can always control a nominating convention, that they had better do something between now and June 16 on other subjects

than the silly twaddle of newspapers about 'bosses' and 'boss rule.'"
Platt's remarks, like the statements in Chandler's letter published several weeks earlier, were harsh and indiscreet; but now all the state conventions had met, the McKinley juggernaut seemed rolling irresistibly to victory, and Platt spoke in the language of a soldier at the last barricade:

> The methods that have been used to work up the "McKinley cyclone" may be all very well for the lily-souled mugwumps and that sort, but they make a so-called "unscrupulous boss" like myself stand rather aghast. The financial question cannot be ignored. A protective tariff is only half our task, and much the lesser half, because much the less difficult of accomplishment. The great question is the financial question, and nobody can look at Mr. McKinley's record and read the conflicting and generally flabby things that he has said on that subject, without perceiving that he has no fixed opinion about it, and that he has been turned and twisted by every changing wind of what he thought was public opinion. It is time, and high time, for the business men of this country to wake up to what is going on in the effort to rush the nomination of McKinley through the Republican convention, with a whoop and a hurrah. The Republican party is not in favor, as Mr. McKinley says he is, of the double standard. It does not want, as he says he does, to give silver equal credit and honor with gold. It is without disguise a gold standard party.[56]

The Platt campaign against McKinley's monetary views sparked hope along the eastern seaboard from New York up into New England that a new departure had been found upon which McKinley could be beaten and Reed or Morton nominated.

Less than a week after his press conference blast at McKinley and Hanna, Platt was in Washington at the call of his ally, Matthew Quay, to learn that Quay had abandoned the fight and was planning a visit to McKinley in Canton. There was never any doubt, at this or any other time, that Quay and Platt thoroughly understood and accepted each other as pragmatic politicians. At the beginning of his nomination campaign, McKinley, on the basis of an understanding with Quay had kept his managers from pressing a full-scale campaign in Pennsylvania. When this understanding began to break down, Quay acted decisively to stop a thorough McKinley penetration of Pennsylvania by becoming a candidate for the convention votes of that state.

Now in the middle of May, with the convention only a month away, there was no danger that Quay would lose control of the Pennsylvania delegation, but Quay was aware that McKinley as the convention victor would have control of a powerful campaign organization and probably after the election would be president of the United States.

From Quay's point of view the moment had arrived when he must use the power he had established in Pennsylvania in his own interest; in the future that power would inevitably be dissipated if it were not allied with the power wielded by McKinley. Platt could see the logic for Quay in Quay's action, but there was also a potential advantage in it for Platt. Earlier in the campaign Quay, through his understanding with McKinley, had acted as a go-between for the two men. After he made his pilgrimage to Canton, he became a useful instrument for this service again, and the subsequent actions of McKinley and Platt left little doubt that they both desired such a liaison as Quay's friendship afforded. As the press announced Quay's plans to visit Canton, newspaper men found an opportunity to interview McKinley as to his reaction to this news. McKinley's discreet comment, "I am always ready to receive visitors," reflected the confident and forgiving spirit of victory which now pervaded the McKinley camp.[57] Reporters noted that when Quay's train arrived at Canton, McKinley was waiting at the station platform with outstretched hand and that McKinley himself in his private carriage drove Quay to his home and back.[58] A few hours after Quay left Canton McKinley took the train north to Cleveland to spend the weekend with Hanna, and a few days later Platt journeyed to Washington to interview Quay.

Platt's tour de force against McKinley was an unusually able performance in American political strategy, but the McKinley campaign suffered little, if at all, as a result of it. McKinley had the delegates; he had public opinion, money, organization, and he was unbeatable. In fact, McKinley and Hanna succeeded in turning Platt's attack on McKinley's currency policies to McKinley's advantage. At least one observer believed that McKinley by refusing to speak out in the currency debate and thereby drawing the attacks of the eastern gold men was making a sagacious move. This commentator believed that when he had drawn them out sufficiently McKinley could achieve a coup by capitulating to their demands. Better yet, he concluded, McKinley's waiting game was drawing the eastern bimetallists to a sound money policy in a way which would unite the Republican party upon a gold standard platform. The effect of this would be to encourage the Democrats to adopt a free silver platform at Chicago, thus ruling out of the presidential contest all of their strong men, who were tied to Cleveland and the gold standard.[59] There was no evidence that McKinley and Hanna deliberately maneuvered with all the intentions which this analyst described, but he did forecast perceptively the benefits which the McKinley campaign reaped from Platt's attacks.

If Platt did not harm McKinley, he did not harm himself, either. He consolidated his control over his own state and added to his prestige throughout the eastern seaboard, so that by the time of the convention, because of public opinion and organization, he was as unbeatable in New York as McKinley was at St. Louis. This was a reality with which McKinley would have to deal in the future. Even the conservative and Democratic *New York Times,* long a bitter critic of Platt, described him as having proved himself in the silver fight as "better than his party." [60]

Thus, as the Republican convention neared and McKinley became with increasing prominence the candidate favored to win the nomination, it was around him that the debate over the money question swirled. Republicans at either extreme of the issue accused him of playing a pusillanimous, two-faced game; and Republicans in the middle, who still hoped that they could nominate another candidate, nourished their hopes on the extremist attacks.[61]

McKinley made no public reply to his western free silver critics and made no attempt to appease them. The eastern criticisms were another matter, for McKinley could not afford to be regarded there in any general way as a candidate who was unsound on money. He did not, nevertheless, choose to answer his eastern critics directly. Attempts to interview him on the financial issue elicited only the reply that during his public career he had spoken and acted in such a way as to define his position, and he referred his critics to that record.[62] He did arrange to have others speak more explicitly for him. He persuaded Senator Sherman, whose reputation as a sound money man was unassailable, to write for publication a letter in which Sherman stated his confidence that McKinley's views on currency were sound.[63] In addition, McKinley's secretary, James Boyle, compiled a pamphlet anthology titled, "McKinley for Sound Money." This pamphlet, which was composed of some of McKinley's speeches on the money question, was distributed mostly in the East, where McKinley was being criticized. To make certain that the ground was covered thoroughly, a delegation of McKinley's middle western friends spent several days in New York seeking interviews with the city's business leaders and assuring them that McKinley had no harmful views on money.[64]

No doubt McKinley regretted the turn of events which robbed the tariff issue of its dominant position in the campaign; but once it was evident that the monetary issue would be inescapably a prominent feature of the campaign, McKinley had no doubts that he must shape his policy in such a way as to reassure the business men of the country, and particularly those in the East and Middle West. The crucial battle ground, certainly, would be the Middle West, with its large electoral vote and its intermediate position between East and West and between industry and agriculture. It was a battle field which McKinley knew well, and he was prepared to fight hard to control it. There were indications that he was beginning that fight even before the convention when, on being shown a Chicago *Tribune* cartoon of himself holding a banner on which was inscribed these words from his Marquette Club speech, "No man need be in any doubt about what the Republican party stands for. It stands now, as ever, for honest money and a chance to earn it by honest toil," McKinley commented, "That's business." [65]

Still the eastern critics, led by Tom Platt, argued the necessity that McKinley and the Republican convention speak out strongly in favor of gold. On the other side of the debate, the silver Republicans, led by Senator Teller, continued resolutely their movement to put their party to the test on the question of free silver. The result of this double-headed agitation was that by early June the country had become deeply interested in the drama of the Republican debate on the money issue. This had the effect of drawing to the convention much more attention that it might otherwise have attracted, for the success of the McKinley canvass had made it certain that he would win his party's nomination on the first ballot.

12

The Republican Convention

It was inevitable that the McKinley-Hanna organization should dominate the Republican nominating convention in St. Louis in much the same way that it had earlier dominated the presidential canvass. Newspaper reporters, at St. Louis to cover the convention, noted that McKinley buttons, McKinley canes, and McKinley posters were to be seen everywhere. McKinley's name appeared to be on every man's lips. The delegates from South Carolina had invented a drink, composed largely of bourbon whisky, which they labeled "the McKinley." [1] Soon the reporters were complaining that McKinley's domination had deprived the convention of all interest, that it was the least contentious and dullest convention they had ever seen. [2] It was true that, if not for the struggle over the money plank of the platform and the departure from the convention of the free silver men of the West, the event would have been utterly lacking in drama. From first to last there was never any doubt that the McKinley-Hanna group had absolute control. They decided all questions regarding organization, platform, nominees, and the new national committees.

Even the opposition of the other contenders for the nomination was concentrated on McKinley in such a way as to make his ascendancy evident. Men like Henry Cabot Lodge and Thomas C. Platt, who were at this time trying to concentrate the attention of the party on the issue of free silver, in the hope that they could beat McKinley on this issue but also with the sincere conviction that a declaration for sound money was necessary on principle, directed their discussion almost solely to McKinley's attitudes. If the convention had been held in

Boston or New York, the hostility along the eastern seaboard to Mc-
Kinley's equivocal views on finance might conceivably have defeated
him; but the convention was in St. Louis and there the attacks of men
like Lodge and Platt stirred sympathy rather than hostility for their intended victim.

A contretemps aboard the Massachusetts train, bearing Lodge and
other Reed delegates to St. Louis, illustrated the pervasiveness of the
McKinley feeling. After riding for several hours across the country, in
what they believed to be an entourage demonstrating their solid support for Reed, they discovered that the car of the Boston Home Market Club, hitched to their train, was flamboyantly decorated on the
exterior with McKinley pictures and slogans.[3]

In New York Tom Platt continued his fight to get a platform declaration for sound money, a fight heavily weighted with innuendo that
McKinley was not an acceptable candidate for the presidential nomination because of the uncertainty of his financial views. In New York,
however, McKinley had strong newspaper support in the New York
Tribune, published by Whitelaw Reid, who had climbed on the Mc-
Kinley bandwagon early in the campaign. The *Tribune* asserted editorially that the tariff was a more important issue than money and
that, in any case, McKinley's views on finance were perfectly sound.

The strongest attack on McKinley came from a Democratic newspaper, Pulitzer's *World,* which early in June and only a few days before the convention, published a sensational series of articles by James
Creelman, quoting from McKinley's letters and speeches in his congressional campaign in 1890. McKinley was quoted as saying, in a
letter written that year to the secretary of the Stark County Farmers'
Alliance, "I am in favor of the use of all the silver product of the
United States for money as circulating medium. I would have gold
and silver alike." [4]

In spite of much prodding by the *World* and other newspapers, Mc-
Kinley did not comment on these articles; but Hanna, after a telephone conversation from Cleveland with McKinley, stated, "That
letter was written nearly six years ago. Gov. McKinley stands on his
record." [5] Later, after further discussion with McKinley, Hanna said
that he found nothing in McKinley's quoted statements which indicated that he favored the free coinage of silver. The editorial comment of the *World* revealed that its interest in McKinley's earlier ideas
on finance was that of the conservative eastern Democrat; for it pre-

dicted that under McKinley's leadership the Republican platform would "straddle" the currency issue and thus give the Democratic party an incentive to declare for sound money.

Perry Heath, of the Cincinnati *Commercial Gazette,* characterized the attack on McKinley's views as originating in Wall Street and said: "Wall Street has attempted to run every convention held since I have known anything about national conventions"; but this year, he predicted, it would fail.[6] Apparently that year McKinley could eat his cake and have it too; for several days prior to Heath's portrayal of McKinley as the anti-Wall Street champion, J. P. Morgan was quoted as saying in a United Press dispatch from London that McKinley was an altogether acceptable candidate for the Republican nomination.[7]

To those who were watching the pre-convention activities in St. Louis it was evident that the McKinley forces were on the ground earlier and more aggressively than anyone else. Their objectives now were to obtain McKinley's nomination on the first ballot, to assume effective control of the machinery of the campaign, and to mold the platform in such a way as to make it possible for McKinley and the party to win the election. Though the convention was not scheduled to begin until Tuesday, June 16, Perry Heath was in St. Louis by June 5, handling public relations problems and establishing the communications facilities for the McKinley-Hanna organization.[8] On Sunday, June 7, ex-Congressman A. C. Thompson, of Ohio, who for six weeks had been collecting and organizing the material to be used in defending the right of McKinley delegates to convention seats in those cases where there were contests, arrived in St. Louis. A few hours later, Congressman Charles Grosvenor, who had worked closely with Thompson in preparing the briefs on the contesting delegations, also arrived, to take up the task of meeting delegates and to help Thompson in the presentation of his arguments. By Wednesday, June 10, six days before the opening of the convention, all of the leading managers of the McKinley movement, including Hanna, Dawes, Joe Smith, and Osborne, were in St. Louis and working at a pace which, if possible, exceeded that which had marked the earlier stages of their campaign.[9]

Though McKinley remained in Canton, the overall strategy and the decisions on all important matters were in his hands to the very last. Hanna and the other members of the McKinley team were entrusted with the work of guiding the McKinley forces in the convention, as they had been entrusted with the work of the pre-convention canvass, only after receiving careful, detailed instructions from McKinley. Thus, each of the McKinley workers at St. Louis went to Canton to talk with McKinley before he went to the convention. On the weekend of June 6 and 7, in fact, there was virtually a convention of McKinley workers at Canton as Hanna, Dawes and other key members of the organization came into town for a final conference with McKinley.[10]

In reality, though the nation did not know it at the time, all the important decisions of the Republican convention were made at McKinley's home—the platform, the temporary and permanent chairmen, the vice-presidential candidate, practically all the details, large and small, were approved at Canton before they were acted upon by the convention in St. Louis. At the convention city Perry Heath made elaborate preparations to assure speedy communication between McKinley's home and his convention headquarters. Two separate telegraphic installations were secured from the convention into the McKinley home, and direct telephonic communication was established between Hanna's headquarters office and McKinley's bedroom.[11] After Hanna and the others had left for St. Louis no calm descended on the McKinley house. Delegates en route to St. Louis stopped off in great numbers; and on June 12 the young Indiana Republican, Charles W. Fairbanks, who had been chosen by McKinley to deliver the keynote address, spent several hours at Canton conferring with McKinley on the details of his speech.[12] A few days before the convention McKinley summoned Richard C. Kerens of St. Louis to Canton to make certain that there would be no hitch in the local preparations in the convention city itself.[13]

It was a measure of the perversity and perseverance of the American politician that anything whatsoever remained of the organizations of McKinley's rivals to bring into the Republican convention. Their prospects of winning the nomination appeared nil; and the likelihood, for most of them, that they would show sufficient strength to gain any last minute concessions from McKinley was slight, indeed. Yet Allison, Morton, Reed, and Quay headquarters were set up in St. Louis; and the managers made the traditional gestures at "booming" their candidates.

The awesome proportions which the McKinley steam roller must have assumed in the eyes of these men was revealed in the sudden capitulation of Reed's manager, Joe Manley. Manley came to St. Louis when the Republican National Committee was in the midst of deciding upon the preliminary arrangements for the convention. On every hand he found evidence of McKinley's strength: his forces controlled the National Committee; a large majority of the delegates favored him, his managers were shaping all of the decisions of the National Committee in his interest, and his name appeared to dominate all conversation in the convention city. Momentarily shocked by what he saw and heard, Manley in a public interview conceded that McKinley would be nominated on the first ballot.[14]

Henry Cabot Lodge was on the Massachusetts train en route to St. Louis when the newspapers published Manley's statement. As yet he had been exposed to no more than the rarefied atmosphere of the Boston Home Market Club car and had been spared the heavy McKinley atmosphere of St. Louis. No doubt, therefore, he sincerely believed his public statement that Manley had been misquoted. In Washington, D.C., Tom Reed reacted as Lodge had and said that the report of Manley's interview was a lie. Manley immediately recognized that he had committed a political *faux pas* and within hours penned an abjectly apologetic letter to Reed:

> I am in receipt of your letter. I did make the statement attributed to me. It was a great mistake and I shall regret it all my life. I was so surprised at the action of the Committee and the open announcement that they were to practically seat all the McKinley contestants—have the Committee on Credentials adopt the National Committee's report—both chairmen of the Convention, that I felt it was all over and everyone in the Country I thought would so understand it. I have never been disloyal in thought, word, or deed to you. What more can I say? I have suffered more than you can ever know because of my mistake. . . .[15]

Tom Platt arrived in St. Louis on Thursday, June 11, only twenty-four hours after Hanna. He was now the central figure in the anti-McKinley agitation and was so recognized by the McKinley leaders. No sooner had Heath established headquarters in St. Louis the preceding week than he had begun to send out public dispatches and private letters warning that Platt was planning a coup to steal the nomination from McKinley.[16] Platt himself continued to concentrate on the monetary issue, asserting, as he departed from New York and when he arrived in St. Louis, that his chief object was to insert in the platform a plank which committed his party to sound money.

At the time Platt arrived in Chicago the National Committee was already well along with the task of hearing and acting upon the arguments of the contesting delegations. Since the opposition to McKinley was able to muster but seven votes within the National Committee, the McKinley-Hanna team had everything its own way; and it took full advantage of the power which it possessed. When Platt learned how the cases were being decided in McKinley's favor, he accused the National Committee of ignoring the will of the people. He said that the New York delegation would be justified in leaving the convention if, when the Committee arrived at the New York contests, it treated the Morton delegates as it had treated anti-McKinley delegations from other states.[17] Platt, like Manley, must have abandoned all hope of defeating McKinley as soon as he arrived at St. Louis. But Platt was made of sterner stuff than Manley, and he fought tenaciously to keep intact at least the remnants of an opposition to McKinley.

The managers of the "combine" which had fought McKinley since the beginning of the canvass hoped up to the last minute that somehow they could slow up the movement toward the Ohio man, prevent his nomination on the first ballot, and swing the nomination to one of their own men. Their hopes rested in great part on the action to be taken by the National Committee on the 158 contested delegates. On this matter again they worked as a "combine." The task of preparing the briefs in the delegate contests was placed in the hands of James Clarkson, while Platt undertook to raise money to pay the expenses of the contestants who came to St. Louis. It became evident early in the convention preliminaries that all the effort and money expended by the "combine" in these contests had been wasted, because the McKinley-Hanna organization had absolute control of the Republican National Committee. When the National Committee voted to hear the contests in plenary sessions rather than to assign the task to a sub-committee, their decision was interpreted as meaning "that McKinley has absolute control of the National Committee." [18] When, after hearing the first contests from Alabama, the National Committee seated the McKinley slate of delegates by a vote of 38 to 7, it was evident that the McKinley-Hanna organization was unbeatable.[19]

The "combine" was handicapped by the fact that Clarkson, who had worked up the evidence on the contesting delegations, became ill on the eve of the convention. The men who substituted for him in presenting the arguments of the "combine" were often badly prepared.[20] They were handicapped also by the frustration and defeatism which spread through their ranks after Manley's indiscreet capitulation. They used these handicaps as excuses for their failure to control the convention. The truth was that they had been thoroughly beaten.[21]

Two of the leaders of the opposition to McKinley, Platt and Lodge, did manage to salvage some political prestige by claiming that they were responsible for securing a platform pledge for the gold standard.[22] Doubtless many people in the Atlantic seaboard states were persuaded to believe this was so. In reality the platform, including the phrase pledging the party to maintain "the existing gold standard," was written by the McKinley-Hanna organization before Lodge reached St. Louis and without any consultation on the subject with Platt.[23] Since at this time the party's financial policy had become a major factor in the scramble for the Republican nomination, it was not to be expected that any faction in the party (except the western silver group) was dealing with it openly and frankly at the time the convention began in St. Louis. Even while the convention was in session the truth about the origin of the wording of the currency plank became obscured as various persons with various political and personal motives laid claim to the authorship of it.

There was further confusion about the financial plank of the Republican platform because of the evident uncertainty in McKinley's mind and the division among his advisers about the use of the word "gold." This was in no sense an uncertainty or division over financial policy; it was rather a question of convention and campaign strategy. It came down quite simply to this: should the platform pledge the party to the maintenance of "the existing standard" or should the word "gold" be inserted to make the pledge read, "the existing gold standard?" It made no difference in the meaning of the phrase to include "gold," for the existing standard everyone knew to be a gold standard. Furthermore, throughout the canvass there had been no doubt among the McKinleyites that their platform would declare for the prevailing standard, linked perhaps with a promise of negotiation to achieve bimetallism through international agreement.

Yet to many people the insertion of the world "gold" did sharpen and strengthen the Republican declaration for sound money, and to many it seemed to be a refreshing departure from McKinley's tendency to compromise and equivocate. While it attracted eastern voters, it repelled westerners. How it would affect middle western voters was uncertain. Why had the McKinley organization taken such a bold departure at this juncture? The answer lay in two important strategic objectives.

First a declaration for gold by the Republican party would tend to drive the Democrats toward a strong declaration for the free coinage of silver. Long before the convention it had become evident that the Republican party could appease the western dissidents in its own ranks only by an outright stand for the free coinage of silver. This the party could not do. The West, therefore, had to be discounted. If the Democratic party declared for free silver, a serious sectional split was likely to occur in that party. Even if the Democrats did not split, defections from a free silver Democratic party in the eastern states would benefit the Republican party only if the party had clearly and definitively declared for sound money. Already the eastern Democratic press had become deeply involved in the Republican platform debate and applauded the phraseology of the financial plank which the convention adopted. There was now little doubt that a declaration for free silver by the Democrats would make the East solidly Republican.

With the East Republican and the South and West Democratic, the Middle West would become the decisive battle ground; and it was the recognition of this that formed the second strategic basis for McKinley's decision to declare for gold. Free silver doctrine was a product of pre-Civil War Jacksonian politics, readjusted to suit agrarian needs in the post-war era. It had proved its appeal in the agrarian areas of the West, South, and Middle West. William McKinley, with his industrial constituency in Canton, and Mark Hanna, the iron manufacturer, were representative of the new industrial Middle West, just as William Jennings Bryan, with his agricultural constituency in Nebraska, or James Weaver in Iowa and Ignatius Donnelly in Minnesota, represented the old agricultural Middle West.

The McKinley strategy was based on the belief that the votes of the industrial workers combined with the votes of those conservative farmers who would remain Republican would carry the Middle West and give the Republicans sufficient electoral votes to win. A campaign linking sound money with protective tariffs might even succeed in winning the electoral votes of some of the states of the upper

South, where industrialization was creating new classes of potentially Republican voters. A campaign on the currency issue to win the votes of the industrial workers and to hold the votes of the conservative farmers would necessarily be an expensive campaign of education. Large sums of money would have to be raised in the East to finance such a campaign, and the phraseology of the Republican platform ensured an enthusiastic response among wealthy easterners to the solicitations of party fund-raisers.

McKinley was persuaded to adopt a strategy based on a strong pronouncement for gold only after a prolonged and lively debate among his managers and only a few days prior to the opening of the convention.[24] McKinley's first thoughts about the platform and the campaign were that the emphasis should be placed on the tariff issue, while the currency issue should be handled as in previous campaigns—on general terms which would appeal to all factions. Thus the Ohio State Republican platform, carefully devised earlier in 1896 to reflect McKinley's point of view, was worded as a declaration for sound money, but also in such a way as to seem to carry promises of concessions to the silverites.[25] It had been universally condemned in conservative Republican and Democratic quarters in the East.

No doubt McKinley earlier felt about the currency issue very much as Joseph Benson Foraker, who was chosen by the McKinley-Hanna organization to be the chairman of the resolutions committee. In mid-May Foraker wrote that if the Republicans declared for a single gold standard and the Democrats declared for the free coinage of silver at 16 to 1, "We would then have a sharp issue, and one that would in my judgment give us the hardest and most doubtful fight since the war." What he much preferred was a campaign in which the Democrats declared for free silver, which he described as the equivalent of silver monometallism, while the Republicans declared against free silver and for bimetallism achieved through international agreement.[26] Nevertheless, by the time the convention met Foraker had, like McKinley, become persuaded that the platform must declare for gold.[27]

McKinley's own uncertainty about the currency plank and the importance which he attached to it are shown in the method he used in its preparation. He, Grosvenor, and Foraker solicited suggestions on the currency plank from a number of Republican friends.[28] He then wrote out a rough draft which declared for sound money with no mention of gold, but expressing strong opposition to free coinage at 16 to

1. It supported the restoration of bimetallism by international agreement but made no promise to lead in any effort to obtain it.[29] He submitted this draft to several of his supporters and managers, asking them to advise him on it and to submit their own platforms or reconstructions of his, as they desired. Subsequently McKinley received advice on the platform from men representing all the important Republican constituencies of the nation. Whitelaw Reid, who stopped off in Canton en route from Arizona to New York, took away a copy of McKinley's draft, which he submitted to J. P. Morgan. On the basis of conversations with Morgan, Reid developed a memorandum summarizing his own and Morgan's ideas about the currency plank, which he mailed to McKinley on June 13.[30] Reid's memorandum came too late; before it was mailed the McKinley-Hanna organization had framed the financial plank which the convention would adopt.

It was the inner circle of McKinley's middle western advisers that persuaded him to accept a platform statement specifically naming gold. It was not Hanna who did so; for, though observers agreed that Hanna was a gold man, he left in the hands of McKinley and his political entourage the decisions regarding the ideas of the campaign. Afterwards several members of the McKinley inner circle claimed credit for persuading McKinley, Hanna, and the others that the word, "gold," must be inserted to make the platform declare for "the existing gold standard." Leading claimants to the honor were Henry C. Payne of Wisconsin and Herman Kohlsaat of Chicago. Also working within the inner circle which shaped up the final version of the financial plank were ex-Senator W. R. Merriam of Minnesota and Senator Redfield Proctor of Vermont, Charles G. Dawes, Myron Herrick, and Melville E. Stone, all of whom favored the gold standard.

Under the circumstances it was probable that the decision for gold was the decision of the group, and in retrospect an individual member of the group found it easy to exaggerate his personal contribution. In any case, these men with remarkable unanimity recalled that the decision on the use of the word, "gold," had been made by Friday, June 12. All who recounted the story also agreed that "gold" had gone into the platform only after Hanna had conferred with McKinley by telephone and McKinley had given his consent to its inclusion.[31]

It was probable that McKinley on this question, which he had not thoroughly mastered, leaned heavily on the advice of men like Payne and Kohlsaat, who claimed some authority on the subject; but it was also probable that when McKinley assented to this fundamental alteration in the platform, he understood clearly the significance it would have in the strategy of campaign politics. Another consideration that must have carried much weight in bringing him to the decision finally was the fact that the men who were pressing it upon him were the middle western business men whom he so much admired. He must also have considered that the middle western politicians who pressed for the use of the word, "gold," were men like Dawes, Merriam, and Payne, who had already proved their political sagacity.

It was generally overlooked by the public in 1896 and by historians subsequently that while the McKinley platform boldly embraced gold, it also made a firm pledge that the Republican party would "promote" an international agreement to restore the use of silver. It was ironic that the public should have overlooked this, for it was this pledge rather than the declaration for gold which was included in the platform at the behest of men such as Lodge who were outside the McKinley-Hanna organization. Senator Chandler, who believed that the phrase pledging the party to promote international bimetallism had saved it in the West, began while the convention was still in session an inquiry to discover the authorship of it.[32] In 1902 Chandler, after seeing himself that the significant words had been written into the original draft of the platform in Henry Cabot Lodge's hand feted Lodge at a dinner to show his gratitude.[33]

Though bimetallists like Senator Chandler hoped to hold western converts to silver in the Republican party through a platform pledge to promote bimetallism by international agreement, a small group of Republicans from western states was prepared to demonstrate dramatically at St. Louis that in their judgment further compromise on the financial issue could not be tolerated. These men, who looked to Senator Teller for leadership, came to St. Louis keenly aware that they were the central participants in a dramatic moment in their party's history —a moment of drama which, at its conclusion, would find them outside their party, adrift in a no-man's land of inter- and intra-party hostilities. As these western dissenters came into St. Louis one by one they were questioned by the newspaper reporters about their plans. Each of them refused to be interviewed and replied only that the completion of their plans and their organization waited upon the arrival of Senator Teller.[34]

Teller did not arrive until the evening of Saturday, June 13, and through Sunday he secluded himself in a private house in St. Louis. On Monday, June 15, he emerged from seclusion to enter into a hurried round of activities. He was, first of all, the only free silver member of the sub-committee of nine which was set up to write the platform. On his shoulders alone fell the task of introducing and defending in the sub-committee a plank calling for the free coinage of silver at 16 to 1. He was hopelessly in the minority, and his resolution was voted down eight to one. His efforts did not end here. He carried his resolution as a minority report into the plenary session of the Resolutions Committee. He was not the sole free silver representative here, but again it was upon him that the chief burden of presenting the argument for free silver fell. Here again the vote against the free silver plank, forty-one against to ten for, revealed how distinctly the silver men were in the minority. In this debate Teller cleared the air by speaking out frankly about the intentions of the free silver advocates: "The time has come when I shall be obliged to leave it [the Republican party] if it declares for the single gold standard." [35]

Teller and his friends now prepared to make their last stand in the convention itself, by bringing their minority report before the assembled delegates and forcing them to vote for or against it. There was no doubt of how the vote would go. Observers noted that the decisions of the National Committee on the contesting delegations favored gold as well as McKinley.[36] By a great majority the convention would vote for the resolution pledging the Republican party to preserve "the existing gold standard." Teller was now leading the western silver men in a series of conferences in which they concerted their plans for presenting their arguments in the platform debate and in which they discussed the manner of their withdrawal from their convention and from their party.[37]

From the moment the convention opened on Tuesday morning, June 16, it was securely under the control of the McKinley-Hanna organization. Without a hitch the plans which had been perfected in Canton were effected upon the dais of the convention. The opening prayer, intensely partisan and frequently applauded, was delivered by Rabbi Sale of St. Louis, through an arrangement made at Canton between McKinley, Richard Kerens, and a St. Louis Jew, Nathan Frank, who had accompanied Kerens to Canton at McKinley's request.[38] The American Protective Association had been claiming that it would control the Republican convention, and these threats had stirred anxiety among Catholics. By having a Rabbi deliver the opening prayer McKinley deflected the criticism he would have suffered from the APA or the Catholics if he had chosen a Catholic or Protestant to open the convention. The extraordinary nature of the proceedings was indicated, of course, in McKinley's assumption that he would be held responsible personally for the convention's choice of a chaplain. It was true that he would be and was,[39] just as in the days before the convention, when Negro delegates were denied accommodations in St. Louis hotels and restaurants, McKinley and Hanna were blamed, although the McKinley-Hanna organization had opposed the choice of St. Louis when the National Committee acted upon the convention site.[40] McKinley recognized that his pre-eminence was his Achilles' heel; and, therefore, he tried to avoid any possible embarrassment by planning and controlling every minute detail of the convention.

After the applause for the opening prayer subsided, the convention proceeded to carry out the next step in McKinley's plans by electing as temporary chairman Charles W. Fairbanks of Indiana. Fairbanks' keynote speech was a pedestrian, unimpassioned effort which aroused little enthusiasm among the delegates. It would serve its major purpose as a campaign document printed in pamphlet form, for distribution over the country. A few days earlier Fairbanks had spent several hours in consultation with McKinley in Canton, and doubtless the speech reflected the pose which McKinley intended to strike during the campaign. Fairbanks devoted his speech to the discussion of two issues, tariffs and finance; but the major emphasis was placed on the tariff. He began by attacking the Democratic Wilson bill, recalling Cleveland's characterization of it as a child of "perfidy and dishonor" and concluding: "A Bill that is too base for Mr. Cleveland to approve is too rotten for the approval of the American people." He blamed the depression on the Wilson bill in these words: "Suffice it to say, that it has been the great and original factor in breaking down confidence, checking progress, emptying the treasury, causing continued deficits and enforced idleness among millions of willing workers."[41]

In his discussion of the currency issue Fairbanks claimed that "the present currency system was the fruit of Republican wisdom" and that the Republican party was not opposed to the use of silver under a policy which would keep both gold and silver in circulation. He asserted that the Republican party was opposed to the free coinage of silver and gold at 16 to 1, because the actual commercial ratio between the two metals was 30 to 1. Free coinage under these circumstances would drive gold out of circulation. Free coinage of silver would have other adverse effects. It would result in the curtailment of foreign and domestic credit; the amount of money in circulation would decrease because of the withdrawal of gold from circulation; enterprise throughout the nation would be discouraged; business demoralization would be increased; and laborers, farmers, merchants, and others would suffer more grievously than they did at present.[42]

On the second day the McKinley-Hanna plan called for a departure from the usual order of procedure. When the convention was called to order by Fairbanks, a McKinley delegate moved that the report from the Committee on Permanent Organization be presented and acted upon before the reports of the Committees on Credentials and Rules were heard. A delegate from Maryland objected violently and repeatedly to this departure from the usual order of procedure, but he was voted down. With the adoption of the report on Permanent Organization Senator Thurston of Nebraska, one of the original McKinley men, became the permanent chairman of the convention. Later in the day the Committee on Credentials reported that they had adopted, with two exceptions, the slate of delegates approved earlier in the week by the Republican National Committee; and the convention approved their report.[43]

One event occurred in the convention on Thursday, the third day, which McKinley and Hanna had anticipated and discounted but which they could not control—the bolt of the silver Republicans of the West. While Senator Foraker presented the majority report on the platform, Senator Teller was on the stage beside him; and when Foraker was done, Teller moved to the front of the stage to present the minority report. Teller knew, as did everyone present, that he was pleading a lost cause. In reality he did not so much plead his cause as plead for understanding by the convention of the action he was about to take. Tears welled in Teller's eyes as in passages that appealed more to the emotions than the understanding he explained his departure from his party. He said: "I say to you now, ... that with the solid conviction upon me that this plank means ultimate disaster and distress to my fellow-men, I cannot subscribe to it, and if it is adopted I must, as an honest man, sever my connection with the political organization which makes that one of the main articles of its faith." [44] There was little more than this that needed saying but Teller talked on, recalling his earlier loyalty to the party and his previous satisfaction with its achievements. The convention grew impatient but respected the courage and integrity of the white-haired man from Colorado, who had been to many of them for many years, in the Senate and in party conferences, an honored and trusted colleague. When Teller concluded, the vote on the platform was taken; and the McKinley plank, supporting the "existing gold standard," was adopted by a vote of 818½ to 105½.[45]

Senator Teller remained on the platform and was joined by Senator Frank Cannon of Utah. After the vote had been taken, Teller stepped forward, was recognized by the Chairman on a question of personal privilege, and introduced Cannon to the convention as the spokesman for the departing silverites. Cannon was a young man, new to the party. The convention did not respect him as it had Teller. His attempt to create a moving rhetorical effect was broken by a shout from the galleries of "Goodbye, my lover, goodbye!" Cannon's statement was long; it was emotional; and the Chairman found it increasingly difficult to restrain the delegates. As Cannon read on, shouts of "Put him out," "Let him print it," "Go to Chicago," and "Goodbye" were heard through the hall and in the crowded galleries.[46]

The statement which Cannon read to the convention had been prepared and signed by the silver men who planned to leave the convention and the party. As Cannon read, these men moved forward from their seats in the hall to stand near the platform. At the end, as Cannon read out the names of the signers, loud hisses and groans arose from the floor of the convention as each name was read. Now Teller and Cannon stepped forward, shook hands with Thurston, and then slowly walked down to join their friends waiting below the stage.

The convention was at an emotional pitch not easily contained. Every man was on his feet, many were standing on chairs; they were shouting and singing and swearing, waving flags, handkerchiefs, and umbrellas, tossing papers in the air. At first the band struck up "Columbia," then "The Red, White, and Blue," as the departing men walked up the center aisle and members of their state delegations moved out of their seats to join them. Eventually twenty-one men joined Teller and Cannon, both of whom were again in tears, as they moved toward the main doors at the rear of the hall.[47]

As he neared the door, Senator Fred Dubois of Idaho was met by Senator Proctor, who grasped him by the arms and said, "Oh, Fred, don't leave; go back, go back and stay where you belong." Dubois walked on, answering, his voice breaking, "I hated to do it, but as an honest man, true to my people and my convictions, I must go." [48] When the silver men reached the main door at the rear of the hall, the delegates watching their departure were in a frenzy, shouting, singing patriotic songs or the words of "Goodbye, my lover, Goodbye." One of the delegates from Ohio, Mark Hanna, was observed standing on a chair, his face contorted with anger, as he screamed, "Go! Go! Go!" [49]

The silver men walked out of the convention at about 1:30 on Thursday afternoon, June 18; and the convention without a pause went on that day to nominate its presidential and vice-presidential candidates and to adjourn. The delegates in the convention and the general public were given little time to speculate upon the meaning of the withdrawal of the silver men; for the issues of the newspapers that carried the story of this event also carried the news of the nominations of McKinley and Hobart, usually with large front page pictures of McKinley and headlines announcing his convention victory.

Though the monetary plank received widest attention, the Republican platform contained a comprehensive review of all major public issues. In fact, the tariff issue received greater emphasis than the money question. The policy of protection was strongly endorsed, and the Wilson tariff was described as "sectional, injurious to the public credit and destructive to business enterprise." The principle of tariff reciprocity was defended as were special tariffs to protect and build the merchant marine. On other domestic issues the platform condemned lynching and declared the party's support for "fair treatment and generous recognition" of veterans of the Union Army.

Special support was also promised for the civil service law, the free ballot, arbitration of industrial disputes, efforts to lessen and prevent evils of intemperance, and measures to protect the rights and interests of women. On overseas policies the platform asked for United States control of Hawaii, a Nicaraguan Canal to be built, owned and operated by the United States, the purchase of the Danish Islands for use as a naval station, governmental efforts to end the massacres in Armenia, the assertion of the Monroe Doctrine "in its full extent," and the union of all English-speaking parts of the American continent by free consent. The Republican platform also expressed sympathy for Cuba and declared that the United States should use its influence to restore peace and give independence to that island. The platform called for enlargement of the navy, improvement of coastal defenses, and the admission of the territories at the earliest practical date.[50]

There was drama in the ritual through which the Republican convention chose McKinley as its presidential candidate only if one appreciated the hero-worship among the men who had worked with McKinley to make this action within the convention inevitable. There was none of the drama usually associated with the nomination of presidential candidates, nothing whatsoever of the usual trading in votes, the exerting of subtle and not so subtle pressures, the tense moments of uncertainty while the votes of a delegation hung in balance between two candidates, none of the spontaneous shouting when convention action finally released pent-up emotions. It was an extraordinarily orderly convention, for from the first there was no doubt that it was McKinley all the way. True, the gesture was made of placing other candidates in nomination, but no one thought these nominations to be more than a tribute to the "also rans."

As the roll of the states was called for the nominations, no state responded until Iowa was reached. Then John Baldwin of Council Bluffs, Iowa, speaking from the platform, placed Senator William B. Allison in nomination. Baldwin said that Allison believed in a tariff "for Protection and Revenue jointly." On the money question he said, "For Senator Allison you cannot build too strong a platform for sound money, and if you place him upon it he will see to it that the dry rot of 16 to 1 does not steal through its staunch timbers." The Iowa delegates whipped up a demonstration of respectable proportions and artificially sustained it for several minutes.[51]

The next state to respond was Maine, which with Henry Cabot Lodge as its spokesman, put Thomas Brackett Reed in nomination. Lodge emphasized Reed's soundness on the tariff and money issues, though he did not specifically mention the gold standard. There was a brief demonstration for Reed.[52] Next to respond was New York. As Chauncey Depew came forward to nominate Governor Levi P. Morton, the delegates settled back, pleasurably anticipating a rhetorical, "spread-eagle" speech. They were not disappointed. Depew paid slight attention to specific policies or issues. Instead he damned the Democrats and praised Morton in emotional and effective language. The convention enjoyed it immensely, but the demonstration which followed gave little evidence of enthusiasm for Morton.[53]

The next state to present a candidate was Ohio. Joseph Benson

Foraker strode to the platform and in an exceedingly effective address, which concentrated on Democratic mistakes and McKinley's qualities of leadership, placed the Ohio candidate in nomination. Necessarily and inevitably the demonstration which followed his speech was the most enthusiastic and prolonged of the afternoon, but it was far short of sensational. After the demonstration several delegates from other states, including Thurston and La Follette, gave brief speeches seconding McKinley's nomination. After the roll call of the states was concluded, a Negro delegate from Louisiana spoke briefly about McKinley as "that man who is in the hearts of my race." [54]

One more name was placed in nomination before the balloting began. When Pennsylvania was called, Governor Hastings spoke from the platform to nominate Matthew Quay. His speech was an eulogy of Quay. He made no attempt to discuss the issues of the campaign or Quay's attitude toward them.[55]

Very quickly it was all over. To the delegates in the convention making penciled tabulations of the balloting and to McKinley at Canton totaling up the votes as they were given to him by telephone directly from the convention hall, it was evident that the McKinley totals were mounting rapidly on the first ballot. When Ohio cast its votes for him, he had won the nomination, a symbolic event which pleased McKinley and his organization.

After a brief demonstration, the convention, on the motion of Senator Lodge, proceeded immediately to the nomination of the vice-presidential candidates, under a rule that nominating speeches could be no longer than five minutes. Again the process was orderly and speedy because the McKinley-Hanna organization had chosen Garrett A. Hobart of New Jersey as McKinley's running mate several days earlier. They probably would have preferred Reed, but he was unwilling to accept the vice-presidential nomination.[56] Tom Platt would have liked to put Levi Morton in the second spot on the ticket, but McKinley did not want him and Morton refused to be a candidate.[57] Henry Clay Evans of Tennessee wanted the vice-presidential nomination; and the theme of his campaign, that his candidacy would be a deserved recognition of Republicanism in the South, was popular in the convention.[58]

It was evident, however, that the McKinley-Hanna organization had chosen Hobart, barring the availability of Reed, before they came to St. Louis. Senator Thurston arrived in St. Louis wearing a McKinley-

Hobart button; Senator Proctor was sporting such a button before the convention opened; Dawes recorded in his journal that Hanna commissioned him to line up the Illinois delegation for Hobart; Hobart stopped off at Canton en route to St. Louis; and Hobart's letters to his wife from the convention confirm that McKinley and Hanna wanted him.[59]

Hobart was chosen by the convention on the first ballot.[60] Though several men were put in nomination, only Evans had given him competition of any significance.[61] Hobart was a good running mate from the McKinley point of view. He was popular in New York and throughout the East. He would help to hold traditionally Democratic New Jersey in the Republican column. Though he was not closely associated with the anti-McKinley factions, he was not hostile to the Reed, Morton, and Quay forces. As one observer put it, he would add little to the ticket, but he would not detract anything either. With the nomination of a vice-presidential candidate the Republican convention had completed its work, and on the evening of that eventful Thursday it adjourned.

The convention had contributed much to the making of myths about McKinley. To those who fell under his spell, and obviously they were many, he appeared to have an almost mystic hold upon the people. Even hardened politicians became convinced that the McKinley steamroller was not so much the result of ordinary political maneuver as it was the result of McKinley's popularity at the grass-roots. Newspaper editorials asserted this repeatedly, and politicians in their personal letters stated it as a fact.[62] Perhaps the most interesting statement of the theme was made by Mark Hanna in the convention at St. Louis. After McKinley was nominated, General Henderson of Iowa, an Allison supporter, spoke to the delegates in this fashion: "The Republicans, the rank and file, have made the nomination this afternoon, and not Mark Hanna or General Grosvenor. . . ." Hanna replied:

> I am glad that there was one member of this Convention who has the intelligence at this late hour to ascertain how this nomination was made. By the people. What feeble efforts I have contributed to the result, I am here to lay the fruits of it at the feet of my party and upon the altar of my Country.
> I am now ready to take my position in the ranks alongside of my friend General Henderson. . . .[63]

There was no reason to doubt that Mark Hanna believed what he said, though it directly contradicted another myth that was being constructed about McKinley, the myth that he was a creation and a puppet of Mark Hanna, in what one newspaper man referred to as a new "Hannaverian dynasty." [64] The convention had been attended by influential and widely syndicated reporters of the eastern press. They came to St. Louis with preconceptions about the relationship between McKinley and Hanna; and they found in Hanna's domination of the convention proof that their preconceptions were correct. An important element in the myth was the belief that Hanna was a genius of organization, who was in absolute control of the McKinley organization. James Creelman's articles for the New York *World*, which were widely copied, bore heavily on this theme.[65] Alfred Henry Lewis went a step further and linked Hanna's domination of the convention with control of McKinley in passages such as this:

> Bucked and gagged behind doors, barred against all visiting questions, McKinley is left in Canton. Hanna owns McKinley and what was the price? One hundred and eighteen thousand dollars worth of McKinley-Walker notes, paid off and up by the great McKinley syndicate. Where are the notes? Ask Hanna, ask Herrick, ask any of them. They won't answer, but they know. They are not canceled, those notes; they are not destroyed; they exist in force and effect. Hanna, as he strutted through the Southern Hotel today, could have begun suit against his candidate for $118,000 and interest thereon, and taken judgment. When the convention meets next week Hanna can begin that suit for $118,000.[66]

It early became a part of Democratic strategy to view the convention as an occasion on which Mark Hanna had assumed a dictatorial role within the Republican party. Governor Altgeld struck some of the most telling blows in this direction, as in the newspaper interview in which he summarized his impressions of the Republican convention thus: "The convention was one of the most mediocre in character ever held by that great party, and showed that the party is now at the opposite pole from what it was when it nominated Lincoln. The convention was noted for the scarcity of statesmen and orators, and was manipulated in such a way that it will be known in history as 'Mark Hanna's trust.'" [67]

As the years passed the myth of Hanna's domination of McKinley grew. This myth, based on an exaggerated estimate of Hanna's abilities as a politician and a failure to appreciate the consummate mastery of politics possessed by William McKinley, assumed such proportions that it was all but forgotten that a majority of the nation in 1896 conceived of McKinley not as the bossed candidate, but as the candidate who was the champion of the people against the bosses.

13

The Democratic Search for a Candidate to Hold the Standard

While the Republican canvass seemed at times to concentrate on the candidates virtually to the exclusion of issues, just the opposite condition appeared to exist in the Democratic party. The conservative Democrats, who supported Cleveland's financial policies, sometimes blamed the fact that no candidates of their kind emerged on Cleveland's failure to speak out as to whether or not he was a candidate for a third term. This explanation was little more than an excuse. This group of Democrats knew that anyone who campaigned on Cleveland's program with Cleveland's blessing would be making a campaign of sacrifice for the party with no hope of victory.

The Cleveland Democrats from the first committed themselves to a program of defeat. All they hoped to do was to keep the party united on the Cleveland program of revenue tariffs, sound money, and opposition to all forms of governmental paternalism. Party unity, they were fond of stating, necessitated in 1896 the nomination of a western Democrat. Therefore, though all the prominent leaders of the Cleveland Democracy in the East and South, including William E. Russell, Richard Olney, William C. Whitney and John G. Carlisle, were discussed as potential Democratic candidates, not one of them developed a vigorous campaign to win the nomination.

Early in the canvass, in fact, all the leading conservatives firmly withdrew their names from consideration.[1] Whitney and Russell said that they recognized that this year the nomination must go to a westerner. All of them said that they were subordinating any thought of personal ambition to the struggle over issues in the party, that their major concern was to keep the party sound on money. It appeared very much as if they were quite willing to let a western candidate make the sacrifice for the party on a platform dictated by themselves. One potential presidential candidate among the conservatives, Grover Cleveland, did not make an early positive withdrawal. All men intimate with Cleveland knew that he did not want and would not accept the nomination. Eventually Cleveland recognized that he had hurt rather than aided the cause of sound money by postponing a definite statement, but he did not withdraw because no strong conservative leader other than himself emerged and he believed that the continuing discussion of his name gave some aspect of leadership and strength to the sound money cause.[2]

Democrats in the West and South who opposed Cleveland's monetary policies were, in their belief, engaged in a delicately balanced struggle for the preservation of their party, a struggle which from their perspective demanded that the party commit itself to the free coinage of silver at 16 to 1. They, too, insisted that personal ambitions for office must be subordinated to the issues—or *the* issue—of the campaign. The importance in the West and South of wooing into the Democratic party ex-Democrats, ex-Republicans, and political independents who had joined the Populists seemed to require suppression of extreme partisanship.

The emergence of the silver issue in the West and South as early as 1895 as the dominant issue in the minds of what appeared to be a majority of the people of those sections did, however, favor the discussion as a presidential candidate of one man who had prominently associated himself with free silver in the past. No man of any party had been more consistently or conspicuously an advocate of the free coinage of silver than Richard Parks Bland. He had been born in 1838 in Kentucky, and there he had grown up. When he was a young man he had settled briefly in Missouri and then in 1855 had moved west to California, where he had tried his hand at mining. Shortly he moved to Nevada, where he studied law and was admitted to the bar. He practiced law in Nevada for a while; then in 1867 he returned to Missouri and set up a law office, at first in partnership with his brother at Rolla but soon on his own in Lebanon. Here as a lawyer, a farmer, and a politician Bland spent the remainder of his life. For many years he was the representative from his district in the Congress of the United States.

From the first he had championed the free coinage of silver. Because of his authorship of the Bland-Allison Silver Purchase Act of 1878 his name became a household word, and he was known nationally as "Silver Dick" Bland. In any other year the geographical location of Missouri would have been a major handicap to Bland, but in 1896 it could be argued that Missouri was in a strategically advantageous position between North and South. It possessed some of the characteristics and knew some of the problems of both sections. Bland, too, because of the background of his experience, was in a position to understand the problems and attitudes of both sections.

Bland believed passionately that events which had happened in the last decade had combined to make 1896 the year in which the West and South could be reunited within the Democratic party. He believed that since the Civil War the South had been tied politically to the East because the eastern-southern alliance, the basis of Democratic strength, was necessary for the preservation of white supremacy in the South. The West had been a political province of the Republican party and, therefore, hostile to the South. Since 1890 evidence had accumulated that the attitude of the West had changed. First concrete evidence of this was the refusal of western Republican senators to vote for the Force Bill in 1890. Now the fight over the silver issue was creating an insurmountable barrier between the East and West at the same time it was uniting the West and the South. This, Bland believed, would give the Democratic party a new freedom. It was no longer dependent upon the votes of a few city wards in the East. On the broader base of the agrarian and working class electorate of the South and West it would become the party of the common man.[3] Bland, a truly Jacksonian Democrat, appeared to be a logical leader of the emerging sectional coalition.

Certain factors did not favor Bland's candidacy. His most important liability, perhaps, was the fact that he was a staunch Democrat. A liberal Democrat he was, indeed; and it was said that Governor Altgeld favored him because he had opposed Cleveland's use of federal troops in the Pullman Strike. His liberal sympathies had also brought him to the defense of Jacob Coxey when the latter was thrown into jail for walking on the Capitol lawn. True, Bland had stated in recent months that he could not act with his party if his party declared for gold. Yet in Missouri politics Bland had not cooperated with the Populists or with other third party movements. In his long career he had consistently been a Democrat. It was clear in 1896 that the Populists found none of the attractions in Richard P. Bland which they found in such a man as Bryan.

Another liability possessed by Bland in 1896 was his wife's religion. Bland himself was a Presbyterian, but he had married a Catholic and his children had been raised as Catholics. In another year, perhaps, not much attention would have been given to this factor; but the American Protective Association early in its career had singled out Bland as one of its chief targets and claimed that it had been responsible for his defeat in his campaign for Congress in 1894.[4] From the first the Bland campaign was met with such crude attacks as this: "If you want to see a confessional box in the White House vote for Bland."[5]

The West produced one major rival to Bland's presidential aspirations—Horace Boies of Iowa. Boies had originally been a Republican, but in the late 1880's he had left the Republican party because locally it had taken a position favoring Prohibition and nationally it had become more extreme on the tariff issue than he approved. In 1889 Iowa Democrats had nominated Boies for the Iowa governorship; and his victory, in a traditionally Republican state, had brought him immediately into discussion as a presidential candidate. He was a man of impressive appearance, with a countenance so prepossessing that the newspapers referred to him as the man with the "affidavit face," or merely "Affidavit" Boies. He had proved willing to subscribe to the liberal programs of western Democrats but tended to associate himself with the moderate side of their proposals. In 1891, when he campaigned for a second term, Iowa Democrats adopted a platform calling for effective control of railroads, free coinage of silver, the Australian ballot, and direct election of United States Senators. In addition the platform opposed alien ownership of land and denounced monopolistic trusts. Yet in his campaign Boies emphasized the tariff and prohibition issues, the issues on which he had campaigned in 1889.

When the entire Democratic ticket was elected in Iowa in 1891 further attention was given to Boies as a potential national leader.

Early in 1892, replying to an inquiry as to the issues he believed the party should emphasize in its national campaign of that year, Boies again revealed his moderation. He said that he was a bimetallist but that bimetallism should be "approached by degrees" without injuring the business interests of the country. He was opposed to making the silver issue a major campaign issue in 1892 because of the way in which the party was divided on it. Turning to the tariff, he said that he was not an extreme free-trader and that he favored such protection as would promote home industries.[6]

Since 1892 Boies had kept in step with the Democrats of his state and section, and by 1896 he had announced that he favored the free coinage of silver at 16 to 1.[7] His earlier moderation, however, was remembered and was considered by many to be his major liability. Both his opponents and his friends recalled that he had been a Republican before he was a Democrat, his opponents to suggest that his moderation had a source in a tradition alien to their party, his friends to suggest that his candidacy would tend to draw non-Democrats into the party.

Both Bland and Boies were avowed candidates, and for months prior to the nominating convention they had organizations working through the country to secure delegates pledged to vote for them. There was nothing spectacular about either organization. Neither had much money, and neither was staffed with personnel of outstanding political reputation or ability. Nevertheless, their very existence was unique within the Democratic party that year; and Bland and Boies were the leading candidates for the Democratic nomination—if free silver Democrats controlled the nominating convention.

Bland and Boies by no means had the field to themselves. Inevitably events playing upon the chaotic disorganization of the Democratic party brought ambitious men forward. For example, in Kentucky a violent struggle for control of the Democratic party on the money question resulted in the victory of the silver element; and Joseph C. S. Blackburn, their leader, was elected to the United States Senate. Immediately Blackburn was discussed nationally as a Democratic presidential possibility, and Blackburn did everything possible to encourage such discussion.

There were several prominent midwestern Democrats, known as moderates, who had never taken a rigid position either for or against free silver, and who therefore were considered to be available for the nomination. Illinois provided two such Democratic personalities, Vice President Adlai E. Stevenson and Senator William R. Morrison. It was clear that Stevenson would have welcomed the nomination on a compromise or a free silver platform; and when it became evident that the free silver group would control the convention, Stevenson attempted through the press to get before the people his past speeches and actions which had favored silver. The Altgeld organization, which controlled Democratic politics in Illinois, showed no inclination to back Stevenson; but they did investigate thoroughly the possibility of cooperation with Morrison. As it developed, no such cooperation was forthcoming; because Morrison, though a moderate, was opposed to the free coinage of silver. When it became evident to him that the state Democratic convention in Illinois would adopt a platform favoring the free coinage of silver, Morrison firmly withdrew his name from consideration.[8]

In Indiana Governor Claude Matthews, elected in 1892, was, by virtue of the four-year gubernatorial term in that state, one of the few Democratic governors in the North. His name figured repeatedly in the discussions of presidential candidates; and in December 1895, Indiana Democrats responded by initiating a formal movement to secure his nomination. Matthews, like the other ambitious moderates, became progressively more sympathetic to free silver as it showed its strength;[9] but it was assumed among his Indiana supporters that his major appeal lay in his neutrality. Indiana Democrats in launching his campaign carefully avoided defining his position on specific issues contenting themselves with stating: "We know that he is thoroughly devoted to the fundamental principles of the Democratic party, which must endure as long as our republic stands. Like Jefferson and Jackson, he has come into official life from among our agricultural people, and is broad and liberal in his view concerning all the great interests that go to make up our active, progressive and patriotic nation." [10]

From Ohio came another compromise candidate in the person of John R. McLean, wealthy editor of the Cincinnati *Enquirer*. Like Matthews he leaned silverward more decidedly as public opinion shifted, but his strength in the competition for the nomination was assumed to lie in his moderation.

All of these moderate middle western candidates expected to trade heavily in the advantages they derived from their geographic location. They could claim to be western but not too far west. The chairman of the Indiana State Democratic Committee summed up this aspect of the campaign in these words about Matthews: "It must be accepted as a fact, if we hope to win in the coming contest, that the Democracy must look to the Great West for a leader who will impress the whole country as a wise, able and conservative man, a man in close touch with the masses. Indiana believes that the tide will be irresistible for a western man, and that in the person of Governor Matthews the ideal candidate is presented." [11]

Since among silver Democrats in the West and South there was no dominant candidate with an aggressive organization, practically every Democrat of any prominence in the silver movement was a potential candidate if the Democratic convention adopted a free silver platform. Thus, in the months preceding the convention the names of Senators Benjamin Tillman of South Carolina, John W. Daniel of Virginia, James K. Jones of Arkansas, Stephen M. White, of California, Governor James Hogg of Texas, and many others appeared in public discussions of prospective Democratic nominees. The name of Governor Altgeld was also mentioned in discussions of presidential figures until it was understood that his foreign birth made him ineligible.[12]

There was one other name which appeared in the discussions of Democratic candidates, apparently as casually as any of the others, and with no recognition that its possessor that year was marked for special distinction. That was the name of ex-Congressman William J. Bryan. From the perspective of 1896 Bryan was in no sense a conspicuous candidate for the Democratic nomination before the July convention. From the perspective of the present day it can be seen that though Bryan was more actively a candidate than the other "dark-horses" it was a necessary part of his campaign strategy to remain inconspicuous until developments in the conventions at St. Louis and Chicago made his emergence possible.

There is no doubt that Bryan had self consciously organized a campaign to win the Democratic nomination. James A. Barnes has described Bryan's organization as so thorough that it created a machine which "has, perhaps, never been exceeded in pre-convention politics." [13] This was not so. In the year 1896 itself the Bryan pre-convention campaign was far from matching the thoroughness or aggressiveness of the McKinley-Hanna organization. In spite of its earnestness the Bryan campaign was no more than a gamble for which most politicians at that time would have given Bryan very small odds, if any. Bryan himself knew this and was made further conscious of it in the answers which he received from correspondents to whom he intimated his intentions to make a trial of winning the nomination. Several of the men to whom Bryan wrote or talked about his candidacy thought him ridiculously presumptuous; and, though a number of influential and strategically placed leaders joined the Bryan campaign, he could win the nomination only if events developed in such a fashion as to make the "logic" of Bryan's nomination virtually self-evident. Up to the eve of the convention it was essential to his strategy that he remain, at least in appearance, a minor challenger to the leading contenders for the nomination.[14]

The Bryan campaign organization was composed of himself, his wife, and a small clerical staff. Very little money was used or needed. The only expenses were those of mailing Bryan's speeches, clippings from the *World-Herald,* his photographs, and the characteristically brief letters, all of which were sent in great quantity to correspondents over the nation. His traveling expenses were usually paid by those who asked him to come to speak. In fact, Bryan tried to collect fees in addition to his traveling expenses, and in most cases he did.[15]

In the Bryan campaign three different approaches were used to keep his name before the public as a factor in the free silver agitation. First, Bryan wrote letters to Democratic silver leaders in all states asking for the names of the delegates elected to the national convention from their districts. Once he had the names of the delegates he wrote to them urging them to back free silver to the last, and, to inspire them, sent copies of his speeches, *World-Herald* clippings, and his photographs. He also sent to silver leaders copies of the silver plank written by himself and adopted by the Nebraska Democrats in 1894, expressing the belief that they would find this a model for the silver plank they would write for their state platforms.[16] He wrote to such candidates as Boies and Sibley catechizing them on their beliefs and, in the case of Sibley, inquiring into the nature of his investments.[17] This was the sort of work which the Democratic Bimetallic Committee operating out of Washington had undertaken to do and was doing with notable effect; but Bryan had adopted the role of a one-man force to effect free silver and he played that role with perseverance and uninhibited presumption to the very end.[18]

Second, Bryan continued to act as an intermediary between silver Democrats and the silver men in the other parties. He believed that this role was played most persuasively by continued insistence that principle was more important than party and that he and other silver Democrats must abandon their party, at least temporarily, if it declared its support for Cleveland's financial policies.[19] A letter in Bryan's files indicated that he was trying to get Populists to work for his nomination by pointing out his availability from the Populist point of view. In a letter apparently written by Nebraska Populist, John Burrows, to James B. Weaver, it was argued that it was essential to the Populists that the Democratic convention nominate a Democrat like Bryan, who was acceptable to the Populists. Speaking of Bryan the letter said: "He is practically a Populist, except in name. He has considered it wise to remain in the democratic party. He has done so against the urgent solicitations of his many populist friends in this State." Further on the writer of the letter reviewed Bryan's career:

I believe he is the only democrat who has made a record in congress in favor of the total abolition of all banks of issue. He has on several occasions acted with the populists of this state. He aided in the election of Mr. Allen. He nominated Mr. Holcomb for governor in a democratic state convention after he had been made the populist candidate. In a democratic meeting in a southern state he said he would not vote for a democrat who was in favor of the gold standard.[20]

Third, in late spring Bryan began discreetly to hint to certain correspondents that he was himself a candidate for the Democratic nomination and would welcome whatever support they would give him.[21] The Nebraska State Democratic convention had moved to instruct its delegation to the national convention to vote for Bryan, but Bryan had persuaded the convention to rescind this action so that he might be free to attend the convention as a delegate from Nebraska. However, Bryan pointed out that this demonstration of support in Nebraska gave him a base upon which to build in the convention.[22]

Bryan undoubtedly believed, as he said to many people at the time and as he later wrote, that his real strength sprang from "the logic of the situation." [23] The two front-runners among the silver forces—Bland and Boies—were about equal in strength and likely to cancel each other from the race. Furthermore, each of them had liabilities which caused him to be of limited availability in 1896. Bryan, though pressed to throw his support to both Bland and Boies, avoided any necessity of speaking on the qualities and characteristics of either by adopting a position of neutrality.[24]

Bryan suffered from none of the liabilities of Bland or Boies, and he possessed many assets. Among his assets those of greatest value were his ability to arouse popular enthusiasm for a cause through the exuberance of his personality and the inspiration of his speeches and his ability to win the confidence of the silver Republicans and the Populists. He was idolized as a public speaker for the silver cause in large areas of the South and West. In the past year he had spoken in virtually every state in the Union. No other protagonist of free silver had traveled so widely or had met and spoken to so many people as Bryan.

There was for Bryan one major danger. He could easily have destroyed all hopes of winning the nomination by mounting too early too ambitious a campaign. It was essential for him that the great majority of Democrats not become aware of him as "the logic of the situation" until the time of the nominating convention. Yet he had to develop some public awareness of his availability and marshall a nucleus of supporters. He, therefore, struck a precarious balance between active candidacy and passive availability. A month before the convention Bryan, stopping in Chicago, visited the office of the *National Bimetallist,* which had become a clearing-house for information about the free silver movement. The editor of the *Bimetallist* commented: "We know Bryan and like him. He is brilliant, able, brave and true. He took up the issue when it was apparently a losing cause and he has fought for it with unshrinking courage ever since. He has been a power not only through the columns of his paper, the World-Herald of Omaha, but upon the rostrum as well. We incline to the opinion that Mr. Bryan would rather like to be a candidate, although he is a little shy about saying so." [25]

A letter from Josephus Daniels in April indicated how coyly Bryan was replying to inquiries regarding his candidacy: "I think you are right in saying that we ought not to go to Chicago thinking much about men, but of the platform, but you will have many friends who will want you to go on the ticket and most of the North Carolina people feel that way about it." [26] It was not until the end of May, however, that Bryan began to send out letters openly soliciting support for himself as a candidate in the Chicago convention. [27]

For several months past Bryan had been mentioned in newspapers, public addresses, and private correspondence as a presidential candidate. These occasional notices did not signify that Bryan was a leading candidate for the nomination, but they did reveal that in various places in the South and West he had friends who considered him worthy of the presidency. Perhaps the most useful notice of this nature was published sometime in April 1896, in the Little Rock (Arkansas) *Tribune*. Said the *Tribune*, "Young, superb, coming from the geographical center of the nation, his record clear and unambiguous, William Jennings Bryan, stands today the embodiment of Young America in this great struggle for the emancipation of the common people and he is their idol." [28] This announcement followed shortly upon a visit which Bryan made to Little Rock in March, a visit in which he had deeply impressed the Arkansas men with whom he had talked, including the governor of the state and Senator James K. Jones and his brother, Dan.[29]

In North Carolina Josephus Daniels, fledgling editor of the Raleigh *News and Observer*, published in his newspaper such notices as the following: "It is evident that the democracy of the West and South are in the mode to nominate Hon. W. J. Bryan of Nebraska, for president." [30] In letters to Bryan Daniels pledged his support and that of the North Carolina delegation.[31]

In Texas Charles M. Rosser and George Carden, along with other friends whom Bryan had made in his speaking trips into that state, were prepared to work to bring the nomination to him. In Alabama John W. Tomlinson, one of the most influential silver men in the South, was working for Bryan in the belief that his nomination "would create great enthusiasm with the young democracy of the nation, who really do the work of the campaign." [32] Tomlinson arranged to have the Little Rock *Tribune*'s announcement for Bryan reprinted with favorable comment in Alabama and other points in the South.[33]

Bryan had family connections and boyhood friends in Illinois who early began to work for him, but his most influential connection was with William H. Hinrichsen. Hinrichsen worked consciously in Bryan's interest but without an open declaration for him. He arranged to have Bryan speak at the Democratic silver convention in Springfield in 1895, and the two men maintained a friendly correspondence by virtue of which Bryan received much useful information regarding Democratic politics in Illinois. In April the chairman of the Warren County, Illinois, Central Democratic Committee wrote Bryan that he had heard him speak at the Springfield silver meeting in 1895 and that for some time he had wanted to write Bryan to urge him to become a candidate for the presidency.[34] It was clear that Bryan replied to this letter promptly, for only a week later he received another letter from the same source saying that Bryan's letter "and also your speeches" had been received. The nature of Bryan's reply was indicated in the writer's report that he had just written to Hinrichsen to get the names of all the chairmen of the county committees "who are silver's friends" for the purpose of writing them to suggest that they send delegates to the national convention uninstructed for any candidate.[35] This correspondent, acting on Bryan's instructions, addressed a letter to all of the Democratic county chairmen in Illinois asking them to send uninstructed delegations; but he went further and suggested that the nominee of the convention should be a western man. He then added that William J. Bryan was a native-born Illinois man "who possesses all the desired attributes." [36]

There were other friends in Tennessee, Georgia, Oklahoma, Wisconsin, Kansas, and the delegations from the Pacific Coast states. In fact, there was virtually no delegation from any of the western and southern states and territories which did not have one or several members who were enthusiastic about Bryan's potentialities for national leadership in the silver cause and who were ready to act in his interest. Thus, though Bryan on the eve of the convention had little visible support and was in no way evident to the ordinary citizen a leading candidate for the nomination, should his name come before the convention in a dramatic fashion, a small but strategically placed, able, and enthusiastic body of workers was prepared to spring into action for him.

Undoubtedly at this time Bryan was working as hard and as purposefully as William McKinley. Yet Bryan had a freedom of action, a freedom of movement and speech, which McKinley did not. The most striking evidence of this was the fact that in mid-June Bryan was at St. Louis observing the stirring scenes of the Republican convention, while McKinley was tied by the properties of politics to his home in Canton. Bryan went to St. Louis as the correspondent of the Omaha *World-Herald;* and, as a practicing newspaper man, he had a good seat on the floor of the Republican convention. It was clear that Bryan had an enjoyable time in a personal sense at St. Louis, but it was also evident that he worked hard and had a chance "to make hay" in a political sense for himself and his party. He was in the convention hall when the silver Republicans bolted under the leadership of Senator Teller, and observers noted that he was deeply moved.[37]

Silver leaders of all parties, anticipating the silver bolt, had come to St. Louis to confer among themselves and with the silver Republicans as to their future course of action.[38] Bryan had access to these men and undoubtedly made advantageous personal and party use of their presence in St. Louis. Bryan was free to do this sort of thing because he was hardly as yet an acknowledged candidate. Furthermore, as a candidate, he wanted to develop a public image of himself as a free-swinging, free-moving man of ideas and action, a typical man of the West and of young America. In Canton McKinley, assured of the nomination, was already deeply involved in establishing himself as a symbol as fixed as the Constitution or the flag, as unchanging as a monument.[39] Therefore, his movement, physical or intellectual, was strictly limited to the confines of Canton and the orthodoxies of tariff protection.

It is also worthy of note that the strategies of the McKinley and Bryan campaigns in the pre-nomination period were in sharp contrast. While McKinley was striving to make himself so conspicuously the center of the Republican picture that the public images of the other Republican candidates would be blurred, Bryan was attempting to keep his candidacy subordinate to the crucial struggle over free silver. While McKinley was fighting everywhere to win convention delegates strictly instructed to vote for him, Bryan was working to get uninstructed delegates into the Democratic convention. This contrast signified that in the Republican party McKinley was successfully controlling developments to suit his purposes. In the Democratic party Bryan could only hope that events would occur in such a way as to make him "the logic of the situation." His power to control developments was very limited, indeed.

14

The Increasing Domination of Silver in the Democratic Ranks

It is only in retrospect that one is justified in dwelling long on the pre-convention campaign of William Jennings Bryan or any other candidate for the Democratic nomination in 1896. At that time Democrats of all persuasions, from conservative "gold-bugs" to radical free silverites, firmly believed that this year candidates were subordinate to issues.[1] Therefore, while the candidates for the Democratic nomination set up slight or embryonic campaign organizations, if any at all, the factions which opposed each other so bitterly on the issue of the party's financial policy constructed comparatively active and thorough campaign machinery.

The free silver Democrats put their main reliance upon the Democratic National Bimetallic Committee, developed in the summer of 1895, under circumstances which have already been described. Inspired by the early success of their organization as well as their continued devotion to the cause of free silver, the leaders of the Democratic Bimetallic Committee permitted no let down in the morale or the activity of their group. Keeping in view always their major objective of capturing control of the national party organization, they left the propaganda aspects of the free silver movement mainly to the independent silver organizations and to individual Democrats like Bryan.

The Democratic National Bimetallic Committee concentrated its efforts on organization, first to capture control of the individual state machines and then to get control of the national party organization at the national convention. It established state organizations in every state west of the Alleghenies and south of the Potomac. These states were then organized thoroughly from the precincts up.[2] In most states thus worked the silver Democrats gained control of their party's state organization, adopted resolutions declaring for the free coinage of silver at 16 to 1, and elected solid silver delegations to the national convention. In states where they did not succeed in establishing control they had complete organizations parallel with the regular organization, in readiness to take control of the state machinery and constantly on the alert to seize any opportunity to do so.

Conservative Democrats had no such group as the National Bimetallic Committee working in their interest, and they had among them few people with the energy or devotion to principle that were found so abundantly among the Democratic bimetallists. In the summer and autumn of 1895 the conservatives had made some attempt to organize resistance to the spread of free silver ideas and organization, but a few minor successes had convinced the majority of them that free silver was defeated and on the decline. In the early spring of 1896, as pre-convention activity began, the strength shown by free silver within the party in the West, Middle West, and South came as a shocking revelation of how wrong they had been in their easily won self-confidence. As they awoke to the realization that the free silver men of the South and West were virtually in a position to control the party and commit it nationally to the free silver doctrine, they determined that they must attempt a desperate effort to prevent it. They looked to Cleveland and his administrative family for leadership; but Cleveland now was a bitter man, who trusted few men in his party. He was tired, tending toward defeatism, and looking to retirement, apparently more concerned in the spring of 1896 with how the fish were biting off the New Jersey coast than the discouraging details of the Chicago convention.

The diary of William L. Wilson, Cleveland's Postmaster General, is a revealing commentary on Cleveland's actions and attitudes at this time. On Sunday evening, February 16, Wilson was with Cleveland reviewing post office appointments, and the talk turned to politics. During the conversation Cleveland expressed it as essential to his party that it not declare for free silver. He recognized that defeat seemed inevitable in 1896 and that a declaration for sound money would cause some defection from the party in the South and West; but the defectors would return; and, meanwhile, the "integrity of the party would be preserved." [3] Thus, the President showed little understanding of how vulnerable the Democrats in the South and West felt as they watched an angry electorate drift toward Populism.

In the following days Wilson's diary reported meetings with Cleveland in which cabinet members and other Democratic leaders were present and in which various aspects of the money question were discussed, but it was clear that nothing like positive leadership was emerging from within the administration. On April 10, Wilson recorded that Cleveland had invited him to dinner, where he had found Whitney, Justice Peckham, Olney, Carlisle, Lamont, Harmon, and Thurber. There was, he recorded, plenty of good talk, political and otherwise, "but nothing whatever as to plans for the future. The newspaper men would write columns if they knew of this gathering." [4] The following day the newspapers did report the dinner, describing it as a "secret political conference" devoted to the discussion of ways to control the Chicago convention.[5]

Wilson's journal recorded in the days that followed casual White House conferences and desultory cabinet conversations with no clear direction, in which Cleveland alternately expressed confidence and despair. Then came the crucial month of June, with the convention scheduled for early July. On June 20 Wilson wrote, after a political discussion with Cleveland: "He does not comprehend the madness of the free silverites nor the hopelessness of trying to accomplish anything by reason, appeal or entreaty. Yet he is not especially hopeful of staying the lunacy of the convention." [6] On June 22 the journal read: "Came down to Washington on the midday train. The President and Carlisle are off fishing; Smith, Morton, Harmon, and Lamont are out of the city, so the summer break has begun." [7] On June 24, "The President and Carlisle are still away on their fishing trip. . . ." [8]

On June 29 Wilson spent four hours at the White House working with the President on post office appointments. On the following day he drove up to the White House expecting to see the President and other cabinet members; but he was told by the doorman that the President had left the city for the summer. Wilson confided to his journal that he was "surprised and disappointed." [9] He was mollified, perhaps, by a letter which he received shortly from the President which said, among other things, that the President was still getting a heavy volume of work from Washington but that he did not mind this as long as it did not "interfere too much with the duty he owes the fish." [10] On the day that Wilson made this entry in his journal, July 7, free silver Democrats in Chicago were taking control of the party. Cleveland's failure to his party nationally had been his failure to understand the import of the social and economic changes which were taking place in the nation at the end of the nineteenth century. His failure to his own faction within the party had been a failure in leadership.

In the last weeks before the Chicago convention there were many spasmodic, uncoordinated efforts among the conservatives to salvage the situation, some of which achieved notable local success; but overall they were singularly futile. The Far West, never a Democratic stronghold anyway, was lost to the conservatives. A few Cleveland appointees in that section worked hard to send conservative delegations to the convention; but, with free silver sentiment surging through the West, they fought a losing battle.[11] In fact, both in the West and the South, Cleveland's appointees drifted with the tide of public opinion into opposition to him. As some observers pointed out, Cleveland's civil service reforms militated against him at this juncture; for the some 40,000 government workers whom he had placed on the civil service lists could now oppose him without fear of political retaliation.[12]

Before the convention the Democratic South was swept almost totally into the free silver ranks. In a few isolated sectors men resolutely devoted to Cleveland's monetary policies fought local holding actions, but their isolation served only to emphasize the victory of free silver generally in the South. It will be remembered that Josiah Patterson of Memphis, Tennessee, had made a desperate effort in the summer of 1895 to rally the southern Democrats to free silver. At that time he readily found evidence that the Democratic party in the South and in the nation could be saved for sound money; but on March 25, 1896, he wrote Cleveland that it seemed likely that free silver Democrats would control the Chicago convention. Of his own section he said, "As matters now stand the entire South leaving out Maryland will not send more than fifty sound money delegates to the Convention." [13] When in June William C. Whitney wrote, asking Patterson to come to Chicago at the time of the convention to work for sound money, Patterson replied that he thought such an effort futile, that all he planned to do now was to run for Congress from the Memphis district with the hope that by winning there he could make it "the distinguished exception in the South." [14]

In early June there occurred in Kentucky the culmination of a dramatic fight which the nation had been watching anxiously for several weeks, primarily because the efforts of the sound money faction were being directed by the Secretary of the Treasury, John G. Carlisle. When the silver men, led by Joseph C. S. Blackburn, won a smashing victory, the morale of the administration forces everywhere declined noticeably; but this was especially true in the South. [15]

Democrats, including the President, now recognized that the white metal had a southern ally in white supremacy. [16] The steady growth of the Populist party in that section revealed that, to many southern people in the mid-'90's, the economic issues of poverty and exploitation seemed far more important than racial supremacy. When Populists freely combined with Republicans to win elections and to enact or attempt to enact "fair" election laws, a powerful coalition of Negroes and whites, who were drawn together in agreement on economic issues, appeared to be in the making. If such a coalition materialized, the lines of power upon which an entire generation of southern Democratic politicians had built would be destroyed; and a great revolution would take place in southern politics.

However inadequate, from the perspective of the present, free coinage of silver may seem as the basic solution for poverty and economic exploitation, it was nevertheless true that southerners as much as westerners had reached the conviction that this was so in 1896. This doctrine had been current among southern Democrats for years. In fact, it was much easier for Democrats to adopt free silver as a panacea than for southern Populists, who had a much broader concept of the reforms necessary to improve conditions in the South. This statement by a Texas member of the House of Representatives undoubtedly expressed the feeling of most southern Democratic politicians:

The supremacy of the white man and the Democratic party in the southern states is more important to us than the nomination of anybody at Chicago. Not since the war has there ever been before a doubt about how the southern states would vote on state and national candidates, but there is a doubt now. . . . The only chance I see to avert this danger is the nomination of a consistent silver man at Chicago. Then we will hold our states in line on the state tickets and on the national. Let the Chicago convention, however, nominate a gold standard man, and the party is irretrievably wrecked for years to come. A number of southern states will elect populist or fusion state tickets, and the democratic party will lose its power, prestige and machinery in the south. The republican party will also come to life, and some of the states may land in that column.[17]

He went on to say that if the Democrats nominated a gold candidate the Populist party would win control of Texas and commented bitterly that the eastern Democrats did not seem to understand or care much about the critical situation of their party in the South.

Josephus Daniels wrote to Bryan that in the South a free silver declaration by the Democratic party was requisite "for the preservation of our government in the hands of intelligence."[18] Georgia Democrat, Evan Howell, wrote that silver was the only issue with which there was "any possible chance to regain what Cleveland and his crowd have lost for democracy."[19] In June a North Carolina Democrat wrote to Whitney, "Many Democrats in the South care not a hill of beans for silver; but they are using it as a leverage to disrupt the Populist party and draw its members into the Democratic party."[20]

With the Far West and the South irrevocably lost, the sound money Democrats saw the Middle West as the area of decision. Here they made their last attempts to project and coordinate a campaign to save their party for conservatism. In the end no concerted, thoroughly organized effort was made. Rather the President led in a series of individual efforts, mainly from Washington and New York, to stir middle western sound money leaders to action.

The most impressive victory in the Middle West occurred in Michigan as a result of Cleveland's direct intervention. On March 25 he wrote a personal appeal to his one-time Postmaster General, Don M. Dickinson, saying that the dangers in a declaration for free silver by the Democratic party were so great that "I do not believe the welfare of the country or the life of our party can excuse any relaxation of effort to bring the result suggested." He asked Dickinson to make an effort to see that there be "a majority at least of sound money delegates sent from Michigan to Chicago."[21] From Michigan Dickinson replied that when Cleveland's letter arrived he had been on the verge of abandoning any attempt to save the party for gold but that now he would do what he could to secure a sound money delegation from Michigan.[22] A month later Dickinson was able to report that the Michigan State Democratic convention had adopted resolutions indorsing the financial policies of Cleveland. Cleveland, writing to Dickinson to express his gratitude, said that the Michigan action was "the most important event of the pre-convention period."²³ Subsequently Dickinson began a campaign to advise Democratic friends in nearby states on the strategy of fighting free silver.

Cleveland had no friend in Illinois with the political abilities or power of Dickinson. In fact, Illinois, securely under the control of Altgeld, was beyond salvation as far as the conservative administration forces were concerned; but during March and April eastern Democrats made an effort to win Illinois and expressed considerable confidence that they would succeed. The first step was to have Calvin Tompkins, chairman of the Sound Currency Committee of the Reform Club of New York, visit Chicago and interview Democratic business men, with the object of setting up in Chicago a business men's sound currency committee similar to the one he headed in New York. In the course of time this was done, but not without difficulties which revealed the impossibility of a conservative victory as long as Altgeld headed the Democratic party in Illinois.²⁴

Eastern efforts in Illinois came exceedingly late, for at the very time that they were trying to inspire a Democratic sound money club in Chicago, Democrats in Chicago and Cook County were about to hold their conventions. There was never any doubt that the Altgeld forces would control these conventions and that they would declare for the free coinage of silver. Realistic conservatives like Lambert Tree recognized this long before the conventions met.²⁵ The men who emerged as the leaders of the Chicago sound money committee were the men who had fought Altgeld. Tree believed them to be thoroughly discredited and unreliable men and refused to have anything to do with the sound money committee.²⁶ Under these conditions that committee had slight influence upon Democratic politics in Illinois.

It was likely that eastern Democrats were unduly optimistic about the possibilities of winning Illinois to conservatism, because they did not understand that Altgeld's power in Illinois was based on the respect and affection which conservative as well as liberal Democrats held for him. Lambert Tree, for example, though a conservative on the money issue, was a friend of Altgeld; and though he went to the district convention and presented his views as a conservative, when he was beaten, he stated frankly his belief that Altgeld's victory was legitimate. The Altgeld forces in Chicago in spite of his conservatism would have made Tree a member of the Illinois delegation to the national convention, but he decided not to accept their offer.[27]

The letters from Don Dickinson to Tree doubtless represent the administration's point of view on Altgeld and Illinois. In one letter Dickinson wrote:

Looking at Illinois from an outside standpoint, the party livery doesn't seem to be worn by our party, but through its rents we see the devil—to wit, the embodiment of disorder, public dishonor, populism, and every political vice that popular discontent, distress, and desperation among the ignorant and unreflective have usually evolved in every age. Certain it is that Altgeldism, rightly or wrongly, is a name given by the country at large, and by all who have a stake in the future of the country, and in the stability of society and our political system, to this same devil. The name is rank, and smells in the nostrils of the nation at large. And this is the tab and label (from an outside view) on the organization which Altgeldism has captured. . . . So, if I were a citizen of Illinois, it seems to me that I would keep distinctly out of it. Nay, that I would emphasize my distinction from it by any honorable means in my power.[28]

Working with such misconceptions as these, Dickinson recommended to Tree that conservative Democrats in Illinois set up a completely new party organization and challenge Altgeld by bringing a contesting delegation into the national convention. Conservative Illinois Democrats, knowing full well how inexpedient such action would be, took no serious steps in that direction.[29]

Unexpected success in Michigan had raised the hopes of the Administration that the Middle West could be won. Hopes were further raised by the receipt of information which led them to believe that Illinois certainly would repudiate Altgeld and free silver.[30] Disillusionment came very rapidly as the Democratic conventions in the key states of Illinois, Indiana, and Ohio proved to be firmly under the control of free silver, anti-administration Democrats.[31] Newspaper reports reflected the hostility in these conventions to Cleveland. A great uproar occurred in the Illinois convention when the keynote speaker said:

Four years ago we nominated a man for the Presidency from the State of New York, in spite of the protests of the delegations from that State.

May God forgive us for it. There must be a limit even to divine wrath, for we have since then been beaten as with a scourge of scorpions.[32]

In the Ohio convention one of the delegates, speaking from the floor immediately after the keynote speech, pointed to the decorations over the platform and shouted, "Looking down on this convention is that arch traitor, that Benedict Arnold of the Democratic party, Grover Cleveland."[33] The Ohio convention provided another shock for the conservatives in the fact that it was attended by General Adoniram J. Warner, the Nestor of the independent free silver movement. Warner, a native of Ohio, had left the Democratic party many years before because of his disagreement with it on the financial issue. Now he found it possible to return to his party in Ohio, and the Ohio Democrats symbolized their devotion to free silver by electing General Walker the permanent chairman of their convention.[34]

There were some victories in the upper Middle West for the Administration; but coming in conjunction with the free silver victories in Illinois, Indiana, and Ohio, they were seen as futile holding actions. The Wisconsin convention, safely under the control of Senator William F. Vilas and his allies, declared its support for Cleveland and sound money.[35] Nevertheless, the Wisconsin State Chairman, Edward C. Wall, reported that silver sentiment was growing among Democrats in the state and that the action of surrounding states made it increasingly difficult to keep Wisconsin Democrats in line.[36] In South Dakota a Cleveland office-holder remained faithful and by a great exertion managed to persuade the Democratic convention in his state to declare for the Administration and sound money, even though, as he reported to Senator Vilas, the Democrats in the State, "as a rule," favored free silver.[37] In Minnesota Cleveland's old friend, Michael Doran, succeeded in winning a declaration by the Democrats of that state in favor of the President and his policies. But Doran's decision, after a triumphal journey to Washington and New York, to go to Europe for two months, reflected his conclusion that the sound money cause was lost and that he could contribute nothing to it by remaining in the United States.[38]

It was apparent then in mid-June that only the eastern states north of Virginia and east of Ohio, along with a small group of states in the upper Middle West, would declare for sound money, and that the free silver Democrats would have an absolute majority in the nominating convention. At this late date, with the cause all but lost, the administration forces showed more coordination and energy than they had earlier. Since the victory in Michigan, Dickinson and Cleveland had been corresponding regularly; and in one of his letters Dickinson had suggested that the sound money men organize delegations of conservative business men from various sections of the country to go to Chicago during the convention. He believed that such men, merely by their presence in the hotel lobbies, would impress the naive free silver enthusiasts and perhaps swing enough of them back to sound money to give the Administration control of the convention. Cleveland adopted Dickinson's suggestion and succeeded in persuading various people and organizations, including the Sound Money Committee of the Reform Club of New York, to begin the task of organizing business men's delegations for Chicago.[39]

There was still no central leadership, however, other than the highly informal direction which proceeded from the office of the President until, in a dramatic gesture, William C. Whitney, only a few hours before sailing time, canceled reservations for a trip to England and announced that he was going to Chicago to fight for a sound money declaration by the Democratic party.[40] Whitney's action and the realization that they were about to lose control of their party resulted in a degree of cooperation among the various factions of eastern Democrats to which they had not been accustomed for years. Now Gorman and Hill worked with Cleveland men and with middle western and southern conservatives. Lamont, who traveled to New York to talk with Whitney and then stayed on to help him, reported that Whitney was planning a conference at his house which would include such previously incompatible men as Sheehan, Dickinson, Gorman, Hopkins, Brice, Vilas, and Doran.[41]

The eastern leaders believed it essential to their success that they dissociate themselves from any suspicion that they were ambitious to win the party's nomination; and the two leading eastern presidential figures, Whitney and William E. Russell, again made firm declarations that they did not seek the nomination. On June 21 Whitney made public a carefully prepared statement explaining his recent actions. In this statement he reviewed the disagreement on financial policy existing in the party and expressed fear that the adoption of a free silver platform at Chicago might disrupt the party as in 1860. The tone of the statement was conciliatory. He did not declare opposition to the use of silver as money but stated that his opposition was to the free coinage of silver unilaterally by the United States. He emphasized the desirability of restoring silver as money through international agreement. He tried to indicate a special sympathy and understanding for the South in this passage: "I am not foolish enough to suppose that any Eastern man could be nominated by this convention, much less that I could. I sympathize thoroughly with the feeling in the South that has caused the uprising and will find its expression at Chicago, but as to the principle which the uprising has brought forth and the issues being framed, I entirely disagree." [42]

From Whitney's office letters now went out to conservative Democratic leaders in all sections of the country, inviting them to conferences in New York and exhorting them to organize special delegations to be present in Chicago during the convention.[43] All the administration leaders coordinated their efforts through him and turned over to him communications which they received regarding the work going on in various parts of the country. There was in the letters from the South and Middle West a recurring note of scepticism and opposition based on the fear that the eastern movement headed by Whitney was but a prelude to a compromise settlement with the radical agrarians in their sections. It was evident that a number of determined conservatives in the South and Middle West preferred a break with the silver men and a split in the party to a compromise on basic principles.[44]

Whitney, of course, was well aware of this attitude of intransigent opposition to compromise among both the conservatives and the radicals and knew what dangers it presaged at Chicago; but there was no evidence that he attempted to project his policy beyond the convention. For the moment his eyes were fixed only on reversing the drift toward a free silver decision in Chicago. What he hoped in general he expressed in these words in reply to a newspaper reporter's question, "You do not despair of success then?"

No, we can not yet tell whether the knowledge of the attitude of the Eastern Democrats will affect the determination of the Southern and Western Democrats, who have not known, until within the past week, how strong the feeling here is. The vigorous expression of our position may cause hesitation, especially among the rank and file of the Democracy, who, I can not believe, want to drive all Eastern Democrats out of the party. I know some of the leaders of the movement assume that attitude, but I am not yet convinced that the people are behind them. And, if not, they will make their wishes known and felt.[45]

At the end of June the two Democratic factions began to marshall their forces to make an early appearance and a thorough organization at Chicago. The leaders of the National Bimetallic Committee arranged to have its workers at Chicago several days before the convention was scheduled to open, and the administration forces put sound money delegations aboard special trains, bound for the convention at an early date.[46] By this time a wedge of misunderstanding and hatred had been driven deeply into the party. Because the hostility was so great and because it was organized on sectional lines, observers were reminded of the divisions which had occurred in the party in 1860 and of the national disasters which had followed.

The party split was symbolized in the fact that extremists in both factions preferred Republicans of their own kind to Democrats of the opposite faction. Conservative Democrats made it quite clear that they did not like or much trust William McKinley but that they would vote for him rather than a free silver Democrat. Many free silver Democrats, on the other hand, advocated that their party nominate the Colorado Republican, Senator Teller, as a step toward the political unification of all silver forces.

If one were to judge the prospects for disunion of the Democratic party by the words which men spoke, the future looked discouraging indeed. When Missouri's Senator Vest said in the United States Senate of his party's Secretary of Agriculture, Morton, "The Democratic party has been most unfortunate, not only in the dissensions which exist in its own ranks, but in the fact that the devil, to use a Western phrase, has owed the party a grudge and has paid us in a Secretary of Agriculture," he revealed the intolerance for persons and for ideals which infected both factions of the party.[47] William L. Wilson, accustomed to idolatry from his West Virginia constituents, found, when he visited his home, that his old friends avoided him and fellow Democrats threatened physical violence against him. After a train conversation with Senator Gray in which the Senator had described the unfriendly relations among Senate Democrats, Wilson wrote, "As soon as a man gets thoroughly infected with the silver craze he turns viciously on all, especially those of his own party who do not agree with him." [48]

Senator Tillman, in the Senate and out, continued to assail his opponents with his usual violent language. In a Senate debate David B. Hill suggested that it appeared that if Tillman could not have free silver he would have bloodshed. To this Tillman replied: "Yes, and the blood will be on your hands." In a speech which he delivered en route to the national convention Tillman was quoted as saying, "If the Democratic party doesn't adopt free silver, it ought to die, and I have a knife with which I'll cut its throat." [49] It was not to be wondered that a moderate conservative like Lambert Tree, observing the battle of words, should have reached this gloomy conclusion: "The free silver tide continues to rise and looks to me very much as if it was going to shipwreck the party right in the Convention. The men it is sweeping in will be aggressive and uncompromising." [50]

15

Impact of the Battle
on the Third Parties

It was not only the Republican and Democratic parties which were threatened with disruption in 1896. In the end these two parties would survive the traumatic impact of the struggle over the currency. The Populist party, however, was to be destroyed, and other third party movements were to be seriously crippled by it.

For most of the third parties the popularity of the free silver panacea as a reform movement was both a threat and a promise. The protagonists of free silver, even in the major parties, were rarely men who fixed their attention on this panacea alone. Like Bryan and Teller they were also sympathetic to other reforms. Like Bryan and Teller they were often willing to accept the agitation for free silver as the first step in a broad reform movement.[1]

The career of the Prohibitionist party at this time illustrated very well the disruptive impact of the battle of the standards on third party movements. On one side were those (known as the "narrow gauge" Prohibitionists) who resisted a broadening of the party's platform to include, in any important sense, reforms other than the control of the liquor traffic. On the other side were those (known as the "broad gauge" group) who advocated that the party adopt a program embracing a large number of reforms in addition to prohibition.

As 1896 approached Prohibitionists carried on a debate about the position they should take in the forthcoming presidential campaign. The "broad gauge" men, complaining that "dry rot" seemed about to kill off their party, discussed with Populist and other reform leaders the possibilities of cooperative action.[2] In late June and early July, 1895, they held a National Conference of Reformers in Prohibition Park, Staten Island, New York. Here they adopted a "proposed basis of union" of reformers which included these measures: direct legislation, specifically including initiative and referendum in national and state politics, the imperative mandate, and proportional representation; the ownership of monopolies by the government; direct election of the president, vice president, and United States senators; women's suffrage; no land tenure without use and occupancy; prohibition of sale of alcoholic liquors for beverage purposes and governmental control of distribution for other purposes; all money to be issued by the government alone, to be legal tender, and to be issued in amounts equal to the demands of business; the free coinage of silver at the ratio of 16 to 1.[3]

In the following months "broad gauge" Prohibitionists in letters, speeches, and periodical articles explained the Staten Island proposals and advocated them as the basis for a union of reformers. Frances E. Willard presented them to the national convention of the Women's Christian Temperance Union in her presidential speech in October 1895. In this speech Miss Willard said that the labor movement was the natural ally of the Prohibitionists and described the nation as she then saw it: "We are confronted by a vegetating aristocracy on one hand and an agitating democracy on the other...."[4]

In the early weeks of 1896 the "broad gauge" Prohibitionists organized to control the party's nominating convention.[5] In some states they succeeded in winning control of the state organizations;[6] but when they met in national convention on May 27 in Pittsburgh, it was soon evident that men opposed to any concession to the reform movement retained control of the party. The majority adopted virtually a "single plank" platform on the prohibition question and nominated a coffee merchant, Joshua Levering of Maryland, and Hale Johnson of Illinois as their candidates for the presidency and vicepresidency.[7]

After they failed to persuade the convention to adopt their platform suggestions, about seventy-five of the "broad gauge" Prohibitionists left their party's convention. Led by Helen M. Gougar, John P. St. John, and R. E. S. Thompson of Ohio, editor of the *New Era*, they acquired another meeting hall in Pittsburgh and immediately created a new party—the National party. They nominated Charles E. Bentley of Nebraska for president and J. H. Southgate of North Carolina for vice president. Their platform, in addition to its statements on prohibition, declared for free silver and direct election of president and vice president.[8]

In the months of agitation preceding the disruptive action at Pittsburgh the "broad gauge" Prohibitionists had moved closer to intimate cooperation with the Populists; and, like many of the Populists, they had also moved toward a stronger emphasis on silver as the central feature of the reform agitation. When the "broad gauge" group broke from the party, "narrow gauge" spokesmen predicted that many of the bolters would appear in St. Louis on July 22, when the Populist and Silver parties convened in that city.[9] Events were to bear out these predictions.

Meanwhile, the Populists were rapidly being drawn to that exclusive concentration on silver which many of them had earlier opposed. In fact, the silver Republican bolt at St. Louis set up an almost irresistible current in that direction. Populists saw that the western Republicans who had cast loose from their party might be gathered into the Populist party—if the Populist party concentrated on a program calling for the free coinage of silver at 16 to 1. An even more compelling factor drawing the Populists to silver was the seeming availability of Senator Teller as the presidential candidate of a silver coalition which could be centered upon the Populist party. There was a large delegation of Populists, headed by the party chairman, Herman Taubeneck, in St. Louis at the time of the Republican convention.[10] During the convention they were frequently in consultation with the silver Republicans; and after the silver Republicans walked out of their convention, the Populists worked feverishly to effect a program for coordinated action on the basis of Teller's candidacy.

There were three axes of power in the Populist party at this time. The western axis, which had once rotated around Colorado's Governor Waite, had become so completely engulfed by the free silver issue that it was now dominated by Democrats, like Tom Patterson, publisher of the influential *Rocky Mountain News* (Denver), and ex-Republicans, like Nevada's Senator William Stewart. This group was dedicated first to free silver and second to Senator Teller. They admired Teller; but, if necessary, they would sacrifice him to silver. Teller himself thoroughly subscribed to the order of priority by which they ranked their sentiments.[11]

The middle western axis was dominated by Herman Taubeneck. Taubeneck had decided in recent months that the Populist party must sacrifice much of the Omaha platform and concentrate on the monetary issue, in order to take advantage of the popularity of free silver. Most middle western Populists followed his lead, including the author of the Omaha platform, Ignatius Donnelly. There were islands of opposition, however. Most notably these were in Kansas, where radical agrarian reformers wanted to stick with a broad reform program, and among socialistic Populists in Chicago, Milwaukee, and Indiana.[12] Generally across the Middle West Populists swung with Taubeneck to silver.

The southern axis was led by Senator Marion Butler. Butler was in close touch with Senator Stewart, who represented the western mining interests, and with J. J. Mott, the provisional head of the National Silver party, who was also closely associated with the western interests. Butler was trying to get money from the western mine operators to support Populist activities in the South; and, through his association with these people, he had become committed to a free silver campaign.[13] Of course, the enthusiasm of the southern people for free silver also influenced Butler. Most southern Populists went along with Butler; but a minority, including such articulate men as Tom Watson of Georgia and "Cyclone" Davis of Texas, advocated a broader reform program.

The dilemma in which they were placed by the mounting tide for silver in the Democratic party was the chief factor that made Teller an appealing presidential candidate to the Populist leaders in all sections. During May, when the power of the silver faction in the Democratic party had been visibly on the increase, Taubeneck and Butler had repeatedly issued bulletins reporting that all developments indicated that the "gold-bugs" would control the Democratic party again.[14] They continued to make such statements up to the time of Bryan's nomination by the Democrats.[15] There was a note of desperation in the statements of Taubeneck and Butler, a whistling-in-the-dark quality, revealed in Taubeneck's querulous complaint that the Democrats by taking up silver were stealing the Populist platform. In a specially prepared statement, released to the press right after the Republican convention, Taubeneck analyzed the political situation in the West and South and concluded that the Democrats were distinctly the third party in the area west of the Mississippi River and were rapidly becoming, as the Populist party grew, the minority party in the South.[16]

The truth was, and Taubeneck knew it, that if the Democrats did declare for the free coinage of silver at 16 to 1 and nominated a free silver candidate, they would draw back wandering Democrats in the South and Middle West and draw in Republicans and Populists in the West. There were many Populists who felt, like the Oklahoma man who wrote to Bryan, "We pops are watching your battle and I believe if either yourself or Bland is nominated we can all fall in under your banner and elect you." [17] It was reported from Indiana that 75 per cent of the Populists there were former Democrats and that most of them would return to their former allegiance if the Democratic party declared for free silver.[18]

The Populist leadership saw one opportunity to salvage their position and circumvent the Democratic drive toward domination of the free silver movement—the presidential candidacy of Senator Teller. Of course, their action was politically unrealistic. It served only to reveal more clearly how these men were now caught in a web which they had themselves spun in their earlier mistaken actions.

The Populists who attended the Republican convention had two objectives, to sweep the bolting silverites into their own party and to coordinate a campaign to persuade the Democrats to nominate Teller. After the convention Taubeneck wrote to Donnelly, "we have received the full benefit of the Republican bolt for our party in the future." [19] This was an exaggeration. The silver Republicans had agreed to coordinate their activities with the Populists only in the campaign for Teller's nomination. Otherwise, they had decided to set up and maintain an independent organization, at least until the conventions of all the parties had been held.

The Populists and silver Republicans conferred at St. Louis through specially appointed coordinating committees immediately after the Republican silverites left their convention.[20] Following this conference each group issued a separate and distinct address to the public. The silver Republicans in a statement issued on June 19 emphasized their belief that their break from the Republican party stemmed from a broadly based social discontent and not alone from differences over the silver question. They described the inadequacies of the social policies of the old party organizations, declared that monetary reform was "the first requisite in the great work of social evolution in this country," and stated that they supported Henry M. Teller as the silver candidate for the Presidency.[21] The Populists at St. Louis issued their address on the following day. They explained that they had come to St. Louis to see for themselves the true aims of the Republican party. They reported their findings as follows: "Here we have seen the 'boss' in politics more securely enthroned, more servilely obeyed, and more dictatorial as to candidates and policy than has ever before been witnessed in the field of National politics." Like the bolting Republicans the Populists concluded their address with a declaration urging the nomination by all silver factions of Henry M. Teller.[22]

The Populists, silver Republicans, and the American Bimetallic Union now began a campaign to persuade the silver Democrats to nominate Teller at their convention in Chicago. The silver Republicans talked publicly of the unity of silver forces which could be achieved through Teller's leadership and traveled to confer privately with prominent silver Democrats. Thus, Senator Dubois visited Governor Altgeld at Springfield and Senator Pettigrew went down to Arkansas to talk with Senator James K. Jones and traveled with him from his home to the Chicago convention.[23] The Populist spokesmen, Taubeneck and Butler, adopted a threatening posture toward the Democrats. They declared that Teller was the only silver candidate who could unite all silver factions and intimated that if the Democrats refused to nominate him they would be guilty of betraying the silver cause.[24]

The independent silver men, whose activities were coordinated by the American Bimetallic Union and the National Silver party, joined in the propaganda for Teller; but since their interest was in the success of the issue rather than of parties, they were sympathetic to Democratic action for silver whether or not it embraced Teller.[25] General Warner had returned to the Democratic party even before the Republican convention. The newspapers alleged that he had participated in the Ohio Democratic convention in order to sway it to a declaration for Teller.[26] Warner did declare his interest in gaining Teller's nomination, but he wrote realistically to a private correspondent that "there are difficulties in the way of bringing that about." [27] Marion Butler, ignoring Warner's statements in support of Teller, concluded that Warner had "completely sold out" to the Democrats.[28]

Taubeneck, in his desperation, placed himself in the days immediately preceding the Democratic convention in an impossible position by stating that the Populists could not support Bland, "though he would perhaps suit us better than any other Democrat or old party man." Instead, he declared, the Democrats must meet the Populists half way "on a man like Senator Teller" or be responsible for the division of the silver forces in the coming campaign.[29]

In the preceding weeks Senator Teller himself had been stating in public interviews that he would support Bland or another silver Democrat on a Democratic silver platform.[30] The publication of Teller's statements had aroused the ire of Senator Butler who wrote that he did not believe "our Western friends would betray us in this manner; for it would be nothing short of betrayal." [31] The fact was that a declaration by the Democratic convention for free silver at 16 to 1 and the nomination of a free silver Democrat would almost inevitably make the Democratic party the rallying point for the silver coalition. The desperation of the Populist agitation for the Democratic nomination of Teller was in itself a recognition of that fact.

The silver Democrats, sighting victory, remembered that victory had been achieved by leveling their invective against Cleveland and Wall Street rather than against fellow propagandists for silver, and they did not attempt to reply to the challenges of Taubeneck and Butler. There was no logic in antagonizing those men whom, if all went well, they would soon be gathering into the party fold. They did not, however, go out of their way to appease the Populists. Missouri Democrats working for Bland's nomination had attended the Republican convention and Bryan, as a reporter for the *World-Herald,* had also been there. Taubeneck had found their attitude highly objectionable, reporting to Donnelly that "They have the arrogance to claim that the bolting Republicans ought to join them and that the Populists ought to endorse their National ticket." [32]

Not one of the prominent Democrats, other than a handful in the Far West, declared for Teller prior to the Chicago convention.[33] Many were quite willing to concede that he was acceptable, but no one named him as his first choice. A few days before the convention Governor Altgeld wrote to "Coin" Harvey that most Democrats insisted upon having a Democratic candidate. In his judgment a regular Democratic silver nominee was a strategic necessity. Altgeld even foreshadowed the Democratic campaign line regarding Populist opposition to the Democratic silver nominee by writing that "Wall street men will see to it" that Populist and other third party candidates were launched in order to "divide and conquer" the silver forces.[34] Five days later William Hinrichsen, Altgeld's chief political confidante, when asked by newspaper men if Teller were an acceptable candidate for the Democrats, replied, "Not in a thousand years. We want a Democrat who will get the support of the Populists and Westerners generally." [35]

Bryan probably gave the best expression to what the silver Democrats were thinking when he was approached at the Democratic convention by a delegation of silver Republicans and Populists who asked him to support Teller. Bryan answered their request by saying that while he was willing to vote for Teller because of his belief that the money issue was paramount, he did not think it was possible to nominate Teller in the Democratic convention. Silver Democrats would be guided, Bryan said, by the fact that they had won the fight in their own party, while the silver Republicans had lost their party fight. It would seem logical to the silver Democrats, therefore, that they could bring more strength to the cause of silver by nominating one of their own men. They would also be influenced by the feeling that they could fight the opposition of the gold Democrats more effectively with a nominee from within the party than with an ex-Republican.[36] It was evident that many silver Democrats would be glad to shout the praises of Teller at Chicago; but when the time came to vote in the convention, they would vote for one of their own.[37]

16

The Democratic Convention: Silver Triumphant

As the day for the opening of the Democratic convention neared, Chicago, the convention city, became a Mecca for free silver enthusiasts and for other reformers of all political persuasions. Among the first to arrive were the leaders of the Democratic National Bimetallic Committee. Senator James K. Jones was their acknowledged leader and spokesman. Under his guidance the Committee was planning the final steps by which, in the convention, they would assert control of their party. The Committee's secretary, T. O. Towles, who during the preceding months had handled many of the details of the Democratic silver organization from the Washington office of the Committee, boasted on his arrival at Chicago of their achievement:

> We have done what has never before been done in the history of the country. We have reorganized the party within the party on an economic question. Heretofore when a number of men have found themselves differing radically from the leaders of their party on questions of principle they have found it necessary to separate from the parent organization and to organize a new party. We have revolutionized the Democratic party on the question of currency and are still in the ranks.[1]

Pride of achievement did not prevent the silver Democrats from having a healthy respect for the political guile of their conservative Democratic opponents. The silver men were determined that they would not, by neglect or inadvertence, lose the advantage they had gained. Therefore, Jones and Towles set up shop in Chicago on Monday, June 29, more than a week before the scheduled opening of the convention—Tuesday, July 7.

Already silver Republicans were in town. Senator Pettigrew had come up from Arkansas with Jones; Senator Dubois was in the city, seeking an early interview with him. They were missing no opportunity to impress upon the silver Democrats—and particularly their senatorial colleagues—the availability of Senator Teller.[2]

The Populists were comparatively slow to arrive. Not until Friday, July 3, did Taubeneck, Weaver, Donnelly and the other big guns of the Populist party come into town. By that time it was evident that reformers had seized upon the convention as an occasion to peddle their particular social and economic nostrums. Henry George was in Chicago as a correspondent for the New York *Journal.* He obtained an interview with Governor Altgeld in which he tried to convert the Governor to his single tax views.[3] Coxeyites, Prohibitionists, Women Suffragists, Direct Legislationists, Socialists, Bellamy's Nationalists— all saw in the victory of the Democratic silverites and the resulting division in the Democratic ranks an opportunity to plant their causes in one of the major parties. Representatives of all these movements were in Chicago.

Conservative and prosperous middle-class citizens of Chicago were frightened by the unconventional dress, the angry countenances, and the impassioned speech of the silver Democrats and the other reformers. Not unnaturally their clergy tried to interpret the situation; and on the first Sunday after the convention crowds began to gather in the city, the Reverend Mr. Johnston Myers of the Chicago Immanuel Baptist Church preached a widely quoted sermon in which he said:

This whole Nation is deeply interested in the great convention now assembling in our city. Unfortunately, the Populist and anarchist have come with this great Democratic gathering. They have planned deliberately to use this opportunity to press their dangerous doctrines as far as they may be able. Brave leaders are here endeavoring to thwart their movements. It remains to be seen whether character and principle will triumph, or whether in a disguised form, anarchy and socialism will assert itself. . . . Let nothing be allowed to come into our National Life which will hinder our returning prosperity. The poor of the Nation are eager for restored confidence. The rich are only waiting to invest their wealth when there are sound principles assured. Let this Nation be honest with itself and with other nations. Let the world know the American character, conscience and coin are the very best.[4]

Cleveland's Postmaster General, William L. Wilson, watching from Washington the pre-convention developments at Chicago, reached much the same conclusions as the Reverend Mr. Myers. In a special article for the New York *World* he predicted that a Democratic declaration for free silver would result in a break up of the old parties and the realignment of the politics of the nation along class lines. He wrote: "It cannot be disguised that already under the cry of 'free silver' new forces are rallying to the Democratic standard and aspiring to leadership in the party, whose socialistic or even anarchistic utterances are as antagonistic to the great traditional and conservative principles of the party and as dangerous to republican institutions as privilege or Caesarism would be." [5]

The "Brave leaders" who, according to Reverend Mr. Myers, were trying to "thwart" the schemes of the silver Democrats arrived in Chicago comparatively late. Comptroller of the Treasury, James H. Eckels, a Chicago man and a Cleveland stalwart, was in the city by June 29; but he was virtually alone and was overwhelmed by the silverite avalanche.[6] Not until July 3 did Whitney arrive on his private train, which carried a small army of sound money Democrats from the East and Middle West.[7]

Meanwhile, the Democratic National Bimetallic Committee, beginning on June 30, had held a series of caucuses of silver Democrats and had, by the time Whitney arrived at Chicago, a thoroughly developed strategic plan for taking control of the convention and the party. The roster of men attending these caucuses contained the names of many Democrats who were noted for distinguished service to their party and their country, but it was a strictly sectional roster containing names of southerners and westerners only. There were many senators —Harris and Bate of Tennessee, Turpie of Indiana, Daniel of Virginia, and Cockerell of Missouri. There were Governors Stone of Missouri and Altgeld of Illinois; and there were congressmen, ex-congressmen, congressmen-elect, and prominent state office-holders of all types.[8]

The first concern of the Democratic Bimetallic Committee was that the conservatives who controlled the Democratic National Committee might use their control of that Committee to subvert the majority which the silver men possessed in the convention. It was feared, for example, that the National Committee might select a temporary chairman whose eloquence in the keynote speech would sway the free silver delegates from their convictions, that it would control the selections for other convention offices with similar intent, and that it would act unfairly to seat gold delegates in those cases in which convention seats were in dispute.

In their first caucus the silver Democrats adopted a plan, which had been worked out in Washington weeks earlier. They set up a watch-dog committee of five to maintain a surveillance of the National Chair-man, William F. Harrity of Pennsylvania, and his executive committee "in reference to all questions and matters affecting the temporary or-ganization and proceedings." [9] Senator Harris, who presided over the caucus, appointed Senators Jones, Turpie, and Daniel and Governors Stone and Altgeld to serve on this committee. These men immediately went to the rooms of the Democratic National Committee at the Palmer House and asked for an interview with Chairman Harrity. They were told that Harrity was not yet in town but was due to arrive on the next day, July 1. The visitors made a tentative appointment to see him at 2 p.m. on that day.[10]

In the early afternoon of July 1, as the Executive Committee of the Democratic party opened its first meeting at the Palmer House, the five members of the special silver sub-committee waited in an ante-chamber, hoping to be summoned before the Executive Committee for a hearing. Finally Senator Turpie alone was admitted to the com-mittee room. After five minutes he emerged and led the entire sub-committee before the Executive Committee. Senator Jones told the Executive Committee that the silver Democrats were in the majority in the convention and that they hoped the National Committee would recognize this by selecting a silver man as temporary chairman of the convention. He also discussed the problem of the contested delegations and the question of the roll call on the temporary organization. Harrity replied that he could not act on these questions because they were under the control of the National Committee. Nor could he predict what action the National Committee would take on these questions, other than to promise that whatever they did would be honorable and fair. Both Stone and Altgeld replied to Harrity by serving notice that the free silver delegates planned to run the convention. Governor Altgeld warned the Committee that the silver men were going to supervise every move of the convention to avoid any possibility that the minority gold men should gain control.[11]

On the conservative side of the party Whitney's plans, as far as they had been developed, provided that the sound money pre-convention activity should culminate in a large public meeting in the Auditorium Hotel on Saturday night, July 4. Here, he hoped, the most eloquent speakers of the sound money cause would sum up the arguments with which his associates had been assailing the ears of the delegates for the past several hours.[12] Soon after his arrival in Chicago it must have been evident to Whitney that something was terribly wrong with his plans. Many middle western leaders had not come at all or, like Vilas, did not show up early enough to help.[13] Southern men, like Josiah Patterson of Tennessee and William C. P. Breckinridge of Kentucky, had refused his invitation because they thought his efforts futile.[14] What he had succeeded in doing was gathering together a small band of eastern and middle western conservatives, the men whom the silver Democrats already viewed as symbols of eastern despotism within the party and corporate greed within the nation's economy. Their appearance and activity at the convention served only to convince free silver Democrats of the rightness of their sectional anti-Eastern views and to spur them to more heroic efforts for their cause.

The free silver Democrats were not discreet; they were not polite. Whitney's workers unaccustomed to being "despised and spit upon" in their party's conventions, soon abandoned whatever conciliatory and compromising gestures they may have planned.[15] They resorted now to a stance of cold, disapproving silence or intemperate abuse. The growing factional hostility was evident at the public meeting on the evening of July 4, the meeting which Whitney had so jauntily planned in New York as the capstone of his efforts. The Chicago *Tribune* reported: "A small but riotous minority struck a note of discord with cheers for Gov. Altgeld when his name was mentioned to dispraise, but the great body of the audience drowned out the cheers with their indignant hisses." [16] When Chicagoan Franklin MacVeagh, speaking of the Altgeld free silver victory over the gold men in Illinois, said, "Illinois in this convention is stinking and saturated with fraud," it was clear that something had gone sadly awry with Whitney's plans to conciliate silver delegates and by a cool display of reason bring them to a compromise.[17]

In reality, shortly after arriving at Chicago Whitney and his companions had discovered that the practical question for conservative Democrats like themselves was: what position would they take within the party after the silver men from the West and the South had taken control of it? This was a question which southern and western conservative Democrats had begun to ask many weeks earlier. Even when the answer seemed to be that they must break with the party, they had not found the courage or discovered the need to act until the issues had been defined by the national convention. Their attempts to impress their eastern brethren with the gravity of their situation had failed. Now that the eastern conservatives found themselves face to face with the dread question, what action would they take?

The silver men with little difficulty settled the multitude of minor questions that came with control; but they also found that the major question facing them—who was to be their leader?—had no easy answer. The Bimetallic Committee continued to hold its caucuses and make its plans. On July 3, it adopted a resolution authorizing the special sub-committee, composed of Jones, Turpie, Daniel, Stone, and Altgeld, to act as a steering committee for the silver forces for the duration of the convention.[18] It was early decided, however, that while the Bimetallic Committee would fight with all its resources for the nomination of a silver candidate, it would not attempt through caucus action to recommend any particular man for the nomination. Thus, the field was left open to all silver men, including Senator Teller.

Populist, silver Republican, and independent silver leaders were hard at work in Chicago to win support for Teller's nomination. They soon discovered that they could make little headway in a convention which was aggressively Democratic. After the convention, Charles S. Thomas, a delegate from Colorado, the one state which had cast its votes for Teller in the convention, wrote Teller to explain his failure to secure more votes for him. He said that the general sentiment among the delegates in Chicago was that this was a Democratic convention with able Democratic candidates before it, and they could see little logic in nominating a man so recently a Republican.[19]

At this point the silver Democrats themselves lacked a hero, a Democratic leader with sufficient personal magnetism and stature, to be accepted by everyone as a symbolic representative of the cause for which they were battling. Above all now they needed a positive leader. Up to this time they had fought the battle with close attention to the minute arguments of the monetary controversy and with the negativism of the personal and partisan invective which had marked much of their campaign. Now that they had achieved the victory, what they wanted was a bold leadership, which would set forth the broad social and humanitarian objectives at which they aimed.

Altgeld possessed a profound social consciousness. He was able to convey his ideas in a forceful fashion in public speech, but he was barred from presidential leadership because he was foreign-born. He restricted his personal ambitions to the confines of Illinois. Since he did not find it necessary or desirable to pay court to politicians outside his own state, he was not particularly popular among them. His strength in the convention lay in his firm control over the bloc of Illinois votes.

Bland and Boies had a following, and they had organizations at Chicago promoting their nominations. Bland's promoters were moderately well financed. They rented comfortable quarters in several hotels and decorated them lavishly with posters, distributed buttons and literature, and greeted visitors with the "Bland cornfield handshake." (Visiting delegates were approached by two Bland greeters. One grasped his right hand and shook it; the other put a glass in his left hand and filled it with whisky.) [20] Bland had been the leading candidate for the nomination before the delegates began to assemble in Chicago. His lead increased visibly as his managers worked among the incoming delegates and as caucusing delegations declared their intention to vote for him. One major source of strength for him was the rumor, which Altgeld and other Illinois leaders did not disavow, that the Illinois delegation, voting as a unit, would throw its support to him.[21]

Those who were managing Horace Boies' campaign early became alarmed by the growth of sentiment for Bland. They prevailed upon Boies to spend Saturday, July 4, in Chicago, to talk with the delegates. They hoped that a look at his urbane, prepossessing countenance, the "affidavit face," which contrasted so sharply with the whiskered and horny features of Bland, would sway the delegates.[22] Bland remained at his home in Missouri, and the metropolitan press conveyed to the world an image of farmer Bland in the fields putting up hay while Populistic and socialistic delegates at Chicago prepared to nominate him for the Presidency. In fact, though Bland lived on his farm, he was working as a lawyer and public speaker. He had a law office and campaign headquarters in Lebanon, and he spent his time while the convention was in session in his Lebanon office and at his farm home nervously awaiting news of the proceedings in Chicago. Photographs of him in the hayfield showed a man who had come out to the field dressed in a business suit, removed his jacket and taken up a pitchfork to be photographed.[23]

Neither Bland nor Boies possessed the personal dynamism which sweeps delegates off their feet in a frenzied enthusiasm. The leading compromise candidates, Matthews, McLean, Stevenson, were merely opportunists, who might have had some appeal in a Democratic convention under normal conditions. Conditions in this convention, however, were not normal. The delegates had experienced the heady sensation of winning a victory for an idea. Now they awaited the leader who in his person would become the symbol—the apotheosis— of the idea. "Silver Dick" Bland, "Affidavit" Boies, "Pitchfork Ben" Tillman were good men, certainly; but clearly none of these was the heroic figure which the occasion demanded. It was fitting that in the final battle for the idea, in the fight in the convention itself over the adoption of the monetary plank of the platform, the delegates should find the leader for whom they hungered.

In the early afternoon of Monday, July 6, the full Democratic National Committee convened for the first time. Before them was the task of developing the temporary organization of the convention. Their first action was to extend permission to Senator Jones to speak to them in behalf of the steering committee of the Democratic Bimetallic Committee. He requested that they recognize the silver majority in the convention by giving the temporary offices to silver men. By now the pressure of the silver majority was being felt in the National Committee, and some of the National Committeemen who had acted with the conservatives had begun to defect to the silverites.[24] As a result, the vote in the National Committee between the conservative choice for temporary chairman, David B. Hill of New York, and the silver choice, Senator Daniel, was very close, twenty-seven for Hill to twenty-three for Daniel.

In caucus that evening the Democratic Bimetallic Committee, acting now in effect as the national committee for the silver Democrats, decided that in the convention the following day they would challenge the National Committee's selection of Hill and ask that the delegates vote to substitute Senator Daniel.[25] When, in the convention the next day, after a heated debate over the propriety and legality of the silver substitute, the delegates voted 556 to 349 to have Daniel as their temporary chairman, it was evident to all that in the first test the silver delegates had demonstrated that they had sufficient strength to crush all opposition. When contesting silver delegations which had not voted in this test were seated, free silver would control more than two-thirds of the convention.

At the start of his keynote address Senator Daniel developed a theme which had already become familiar to the silver delegates, that for the past thirty years the agrarian Democrats of the West and South had followed the leadership of the eastern wing of the party. "Do not forget," he said to the easterners, "that we have submitted graciously to your compromise platforms and to your repeated pledges of bimetallism and have patiently borne repeated disappointments as to their fulfillment." Now he said it was time for the eastern Democrats to remember and to apply the Golden Rule. They might, he suggested, also remember "the creed of Jefferson that absolute acquiescence in the will of the majority is the vital principle of the Republic."

Daniel reviewed recent monetary legislation, ascribing it and the dire effects which attended it to the Republicans; but he did not attempt to analyze in detail the economic principles behind the advocacy of the free coinage of silver at 16 to 1. He ended his speech with an attack on the argument that the United States could coin silver only after an international agreement with the major European powers. "No nation," he said, "can call itself independent that cannot establish a financial system of its own." In the final sentence of his peroration he spoke these words:

And as our fathers in 1776 declared our national independence, so now has the party founded by Thomas Jefferson, the author of that declaration, met here to declare our financial independence of all other nations, and to invoke all true Americans to assert it by their votes and place their country where it of right belongs as the greatest, noblest and foremost nation that blesses the life of mankind on this globe.[26]

The keynote address merely repeated in a somewhat pedestrian style arguments and points of view with which the silver Democrats were thoroughly familiar, and it did not arouse them; but the choice of Daniel in place of Hill and the sentiments expressed by Daniel in his speech did embitter the eastern sound money Democrats. Their humiliation was not yet completed. After the keynote speech the convention adjourned to permit the committees on permanent organization, credentials, and resolutions to organize and prepare their recommendations. The members of these committees were chosen by the delegations then seated in the convention; and as a result they contained silver majorities. The conservative easterners now found that their every move was repulsed. The National Committee, in making its preliminary list of delegates, had handled the contests by seating the gold delegations from Nebraska and South Dakota. The committee on credentials reversed this action and recommended the seating of the silver delegations, a recommendation which the convention enthusiastically endorsed. The committee on permanent organization chose California silverite, Senator Stephen M. White, to be permanent chairman of the convention.

The committee on resolutions, headed by Senator Jones, prepared a platform which called for the free coinage of silver at 16 to 1, an increase in the powers of the Interstate Commerce Commission, governmental economy and reduced taxes, and arbitration of industrial disputes. It declared Democratic opposition to "arbitrary interference by Federal authorities in local affairs as a violation of the Constitution of the United States and a crime against free institutions." The platform also opposed government by injunction, "life tenure in the public service, except as provided in the Constitution," a third term in the Presidency, and, until the money question was settled, "any agitation for further changes in our tariff laws, except such as are necessary to meet the deficit in revenue caused by the adverse decision of the Supreme Court on the income tax." In the area of foreign relations it declared that the Monroe Doctrine "is a permanent part of the foreign policy of the United States and must at all times be maintained" and extended sympathy to the people of Cuba.[27]

The conservative sound money minority on the resolutions committee drew up a report stating that they found many planks in the majority report objectionable but that they offered a substitute to it only on the most crucial item in the platform, that dealing with the monetary question. They referred to free silver as an "experiment," which would "retard or entirely prevent the establishment of international bimetallism" and "place this country at once upon a silver basis, impair contracts, disturb business, diminish the purchasing power of the wages of labor, and inflict irreparable evils upon our nation's commerce and industry." In conclusion they repaired a deficiency which they discovered in the majority report by commending "the honesty, economy, courage and fidelity of the present Democratic National Administration."[28]

Observers soon noted that the Democratic convention did not move with the celerity and precision which the Republicans had achieved at St. Louis.[29] The silver men had secured control but they did not have thorough coordination. For many this was their first national convention, and none of them had any experience in the management of such an affair. They hesitated to use the rules and customs established in earlier conventions simply because those conventions had been under conservative control. There was evidence of considerable confusion in the preliminary work undertaken by the various committees. The committee on resolutions, after having completed its preparations to elect Senator White of California as its chairman, was informed that he had been chosen as permanent chairman of the convention by the committee on permanent organization. The committee on permanent organization also met in considerable confusion, and its work was delayed by the discovery that the silver men had not caucused beforehand to name their choice for permanent chairman. As a result, the committee recessed for several hours while the silver Democrats caucused and chose their slate of permanent officers.[30]

As a result of this confusion and disorganization the convention sat through Wednesday, awaiting the reports of the various committees. Mostly the delegates occupied themselves in listening to speeches from the silver orators in the various delegations.[31] The committee on credentials presented its report in installments, bringing its recommendations on the contested delegations to the convention as it completed them. The first report from that committee was on the Nebraska dispute. Bryan had been writing about this dispute to the silver delegates for weeks. The Nebraska silver men had made themselves heard since their arrival in Chicago, so the convention was informed about and intensely interested in the Nebraska dispute. When the credentials committee recommended the seating of the Bryan silver delegation, a voice vote was taken; and the chairman of the convention declared the Bryan group seated by acclamation. William Russell then rose from the floor to challenge this ruling and to move that the convention be polled by states. When a spokesman for the credentials committee informed Russell that the committee had voted unanimously, New York and Massachusetts included, to seat the silver delegation, Russell withdrew his motion.[32]

A few minutes later a band was heard in the rear of the convention hall; and the delegates, turning their heads toward the commotion, saw a gay and noisy Nebraska delegation, led by Bryan, moving down the aisle to take the seats which until now had been occupied by conservatives. A demonstration followed during which the Nebraska delegation displayed banners worded, "The W. J. Bryan Club, 16 to 1." [33] A few minutes later, when the crowd shouted for a speech from Bryan, he was not to be found. The moment for him to present himself in full oratorical perspective to the convention had not yet arrived.

Not until 5:45 that afternoon did the credentials committee deliver its final report to the convention, a recommendation that the silver delegation from Michigan be seated. This touched off a demonstration among the silver delegates, who recognized that the seating of the silver men from Michigan gave silver Democrats two-thirds of the convention votes.[34]

It was at the evening session on Wednesday, the second day of the convention, that the convention seated its permanent chairman. Not until the morning of the third day did the resolutions committee make its report. Hour after hour delegates and visitors sat in the convention hall awaiting the reports of the various committees. They became a captive audience for the numerous delegates who had come to the convention with prepared speeches on the public questions of the day. The speakers for the most part were distinguished and able, but they found it difficult to hold the attention of the crowd and to make themselves heard over the voices of the bored, gossiping delegates. Occasionally a striking personality and strong speech held their attention. Governor Altgeld did so, concentrating his remarks on a closely reasoned discussion of the financial problem, in a speech which the *New York Times* described as the best of that day.[35]

Texas Governor James Stephen Hogg delivered himself of an able attack upon the Republican party. He said that for thirty years the Republicans had appealed to the labor vote with the argument that if the government made the corporations rich by protection "wealth would flow into corporation treasuries and be paid out in high wages." It had now become clear that in reality the flow had been only one way and that the laborer had been abandoned "to protect himself." The resulting impoverishment of the worker was not, according to Hogg, the final objective of the Republican party: "This protected class of Republicans proposes now to destroy labor organizations. To that end it has organized syndicates, pools and trusts and proposes through Federal courts, in the exercise of their constitutional powers by the issuance of extraordinary, unconstitutional writs, to strike down, to suppress and overawe those organizations, backed by the Federal bayonet." [36]

The speakers often expressed the sectionalism, which western and southern delegates felt so keenly and which, more than anything else in the convention, perturbed eastern conservatives. The moderate and more conciliatory silverites tried to soft-pedal sectional feeling, particularly now that the battle had been won; but by this time it had become a figure in the pattern of the agrarian protest and it could not be rubbed out. It was expressed in a most quotable fashion during the Wednesday speech-fest by David Overmeyer of Kansas: "All that I care to say now is that yesterday the seat of empire was transferred from the Atlantic States to the great Mississippi Valley. That the day of the common people has dawned. The state of Kansas ... stands here to welcome its friends from the South and from the Northern States to redeem this good land and turn it back to the way of prosperity and greatness, and to begin the good work by restoring the dollar of the daddies, 16 to 1." [37]

At the end of the second day a keen sense of anticipation had developed among the delegates. The first order of business the next day (Thursday) would be the presentation of the report of the platform committee. It was known that a minority report would be presented by the sound money conservatives and that there would be a formal debate on the financial plank of the platform. It was also known that William Jennings Bryan was to be in charge of the debate for the free silver side and that Benjamin Tillman was to speak for free silver, while David Hill would be one of the speakers for sound money. Delegates who remembered the exchanges in the Senate between Hill and Tillman knew that any platform meeting between these two men was likely to elicit pyrotechnical oratory from Tillman and rapier-like ripostes from Hill. This exchange in itself might well make the debate a momentous occasion.

It was Bryan's performance, however, to which most delegates looked forward with the highest anticipation. His speeches on the tariff and on silver in the House of Representatives and his speaking tours up and down the country had won for him a reputation and a following. It was known to many of the delegates that Bryan hoped to win the presidential nomination from the convention. On the morning that the platform debate was to occur the Chicago *Tribune* published a front-page story headlined, "Bryan, Boy Orator of the Platte in the Presidential Race." This story argued, at length, that much of Bland's support was prepared to shift to Bryan, that Bryan was popular in many delegations, and that his acceptability to the Populists was a major factor in his favor.[38]

Bryan did not have a formal campaign organization working for him at Chicago, other than the Nebraska delegation, which he closely supervised. He took modest hotel rooms and afterwards boasted that he spent less than $100 in the Chicago visit in which he won the nomination. He knew how to get the attention of the newspaper reporters, however; and anyone diligently reading the newspapers in any part of the country would have been aware that Bryan was a conspicuous member of the Chicago gathering. Before the convention opened he gave a newspaper interview in Nebraska in which he denied that he was a candidate for the Democratic nomination. This story, published across the country, must have stirred speculation where none had previously existed.[39] After Bryan arrived in Chicago, the newspapers of the nation—metropolitan and country papers alike—found occasion repeatedly to mention his name. It was rumored that he was to be temporary chairman, permanent chairman, chairman of the platform committee, the vice-presidential nominee, and the presidential nominee. The newspapers told the story of the contest over the seating of the Nebraska delegations, always referring to the silver group as the Bryan delegation. It was indeed true as the Chicago *Tribune* printed on July 9, "William Jennings Bryan is more than a dark horse candidate for the Presidency."

Even if the men who were to take part in the debate had not been figures whose reputations aroused public interest, the platform debate would have been recognized, potentially at least, as an extraordinarily dramatic event. It was on this occasion that the conservative Democrats had chosen to make their last stand, their final attempt to persuade the delegates to adopt a more conservative course. On Wednesday evening, preceding the debate, the conservatives had held a caucus; and though it was rumored that they had decided to stay in the convention, silent and not voting, if they lost the platform fight, there were rumors also that some of them would walk out. It appeared that they themselves were divided and that their action, when the convention finally reached a decision, had not been agreed upon in caucus and could not be predicted before the moment of decision arrived in the convention itself. The drama of the event did not, therefore, depend wholly upon the speakers; but since the event itself was innately dramatic, it could be expected that men whose oratorical abilities had already been proved would make the most of the occasion. Delegates and visitors arrived early; and when the debate began, the great hall was filled.

It must be remembered that up to now the silver majority had not had occasion to celebrate its victory, that, during two long days and nights, the convention had produced no eloquent expression of the positive, broadly humanitarian aspects of the silver cause. How much the delegates wished for such an expression they showed in their reaction to Tillman's speech, which opened the debate. Tillman gave them the fiery, slashing kind of speech for which he was famous and which, on other occasions, had aroused silver men to boisterous enthusiasm. Now the violent language and aggressive sectionalism seemed out of place. He said that the easterners viewed the men of the South and West as "mere hewers of wood and drawers of water, tied in bondage"; and of sectionalism he said, "Some of my friends from the South and elsewhere have said that this is not a sectional issue. I say it is a sectional issue." The convention was taken aback, and the hisses and shouts of protest made it difficult for Tillman to continue.[40] After he had finished, Senator Jones, who had not planned to speak, tried to redeem the situation by denying that the issue in the debate was sectional. He said that he was a southern man; "but above the South and above section, I love the whole of this country." [41]

After Tillman's speech the conservatives had their inning. Their arguments were presented by three speakers, Senators David Hill and William Vilas, and ex-Governor William Russell of Massachusetts. When Senator Hill moved forward to speak, the sound money delegations set up a demonstration which lasted for ten minutes. Compared with Tillman's effort, Hill's speech was moderate but persuasive. He bore down heavily on the argument that free silver was not Democratic policy and that its unorthodox qualities would drive many old-line Democrats from their party. "Be not deceived," he shouted, "Do not drive old Democrats out of the party . . . to make room for a lot of Republicans and Populists and political nondescripts who will not vote your ticket at the polls." [42] Vilas and Russell presented the conventional arguments for a conservative policy and for sound money without arousing explosive hostility or enthusiasm in the convention.

When, at last, the moment arrived for Bryan to make the final speech in favor of convention adoption of the majority free silver plank, the rank and file, who controlled the convention, desperately felt that their true position had not been stated. Later Charles S. Thomas recalled that while Hill was speaking he had leaned over to whisper to Bryan some suggestions as to how to answer one of Hill's arguments. Bryan replied, "I shall not spend a minute arguing those points. I do not intend to make an argument for silver. The time for argument has passed. The time for action has come." [43] Bryan appreciated the mood of his audience. He wrote of the occasion in his memoirs: "After an unsatisfactory opening of the debate and after our side had been pounded unmercifully by the giants of the other side, all that was necessary to success was to put into words the sentiments of a majority of the delegates to the Convention—to be the voice of a triumphant majority."[44] When Bryan moved to the speaker's stand the crowd was beside itself with excitement. He had to wait for several minutes while one after another noisy demonstrations erupted among the seething delegates in the convention hall.

Once Bryan began to speak, however, the great convention was unusually silent. His commanding stage presence, his matchlessly beautiful voice, which without seeming effort he projected to the remote corners of the hall, gave him control of his listeners from the first. He himself wrote that "the audience acted like a trained choir"; and California reporter, George Heazelton, writing a few hours after the event, recorded a similar impression: "As he touched chord after chord they [the audience] responded with magnificent outbursts of approval." [45]

The speech itself suited the occasion to perfection. He began by declaring that in the contest in which they were engaged individuals were humbled and principles exalted. The arresting rhythm and style which characterized the entire speech were present in the opening passages:

> I would be presumptuous, indeed, to present myself against the distinguished gentlemen to whom you have listened if this were a mere measure of abilities; but this is not a contest between persons. The humblest citizen in all the land, when clad in the armor of a righteous cause, is stronger than all the hosts of error. I come to speak to you in defense of a cause as holy as the cause of liberty—the cause of humanity.

He enlarged on this theme for a few minutes, and then he turned to a point made by Russell to the effect that free silver threatened to disturb the business interests of the country. Bryan in reply introduced an argument which had occurred to him only recently and which he had not used in his previous speeches, though he had hinted at it in a newspaper interview at St. Louis at the end of the Republican convention.[46] "We say to you," Bryan said, "that you have made the definition of a business man too limited in its application"; and he went on,

> The man who is employed for wages is as much a business man as his employer; the attorney in a country town is as much a business man as the corporation counsel in a great metropolis; the merchant at the cross-roads store is as much a business man as the merchant of New York; the farmer who goes forth in the morning and toils all day—who begins in the spring and toils all summer—and who by the application of brain and muscle to the natural resources of the country creates wealth, is as much a business man as the man who goes upon the board of trade and bets upon the price of grain; the miners who go down a thousand feet into the earth, or climb a thousand feet upon the cliffs, and bring forth from their hiding places the precious metals to be poured into the channels of trade are as much business men as the few financial magnates who, in a back room, corner the money of the world. We come to speak for this broader class of business men.

These words, spoken simply and forcefully, electrified the audience. They were now completely under Bryan's control, and he carried them from period to period, without release. He turned to Vilas' warning that conditions might create a Robespierre. To this Bryan replied that the people could be depended upon not to create a tyrant and concluded, "What we need is an Andrew Jackson to stand, as Jackson stood, against the encroachments of organized wealth."

He went on to defend the platform and to attack the Republicans; but he spoke only in general terms, citing historical parallels and broad principles. As he approached the end, his perspective widened. He used figures of speech calculated to excite the convention. Contrasting Republican and Democratic philosophies, he said,

> There are two ideas of government. There are those who believe that, if you will only legislate to make the well-to-do prosperous, their prosperity will leak through on those below. The Democratic idea, however, has been that if you legislate to make the masses prosperous, their prosperity will find its way up through every class which rests upon them.

Then, immediately, came one of his most telling thrusts:

> You come to us and tell us that the great cities are in favor of the gold standard; we reply that the great cities rest upon our broad and fertile prairies. Burn down your cities and leave your farms, and your cities will spring up again as if by magic; but destroy our farms and the grass will grow in the streets of every city in the country.

This was the beginning of the peroration, which ended with the sentence:

Having behind us the producing masses of this nation and the world, supported by the commercial interests, the laboring interests, and the toilers everywhere, we will answer their demand for a gold standard by saying to them: You shall not press down upon the brow of labor this crown of thorns, you shall not crucify mankind upon a cross of gold.[47]

The convention at last had found its voice. Bryan had said nothing new; he had made no profound argument which men would remember and cite later. He had said, however, what hundreds of delegates, inarticulate and mute, felt and believed. The failure of the convention to arrive at such an expression earlier had saddened and depressed them. In a few minutes Bryan had set everything right. If the delegates could have cast their ballots at that moment, they would have nominated Bryan for the Presidency on the spot.[48] They did shout, stand on chairs, and finally they picked up their state guidons and marched to the Nebraska delegation, until virtually all the states controlled by silver delegations had planted their banners beside that of Nebraska.[49] There was never any doubt of the results of the voting which followed: 628 delegates voted for the free silver platform, while 301 voted against it. By a similar margin the convention rejected a motion made by Senator Hill to endorse the Cleveland administration. The convention then recessed until 8:00 that evening, when nominations were to be received.[50]

17

The Democratic Convention: Nomination of the "Nebraska Cyclone"

The free silver issue dominated the Democratic convention as thoroughly after it had been acted upon as before. The presidential nominations were made and seconded, not on the basis of the personal qualities and characteristics of individual nominees, but in terms of how the nominee had "squared" himself with the platform. On this basis many "logical" candidates had appeared in the pre-convention canvass; and now even those candidates who had opportunistically pursued the nomination as moderates, stressed their loyalty to free silver. Adlai Stevenson (who was not formally placed in nomination but who did receive a few scattered votes during the balloting) circulated in the convention a letter in which he stated that he had advocated "the remonetization of silver" in 1878.[1] An Ohio delegate, in a speech placing McLean in nomination, said of that recent convert to free silver: "I say to you when the cause of free silver was weak, when the members supporting it were few, John R. McLean was one of the bravest soldiers and the noblest pioneer of them all." [2] Another delegate, seconding McLean's nomination, referred to him as "the peerless champion of free silver." [3]

Little drama attended the nominations. It was Thursday evening. Already the delegates had worked a long and emotionally exhausting day. Mostly they were poor men, and they were conscious of the fact that they were in the third evening of a convention which had moved too slowly. They were intent upon getting the business of the convention done, so that they could go home. In any case, the nominating speeches, though able, were not of a high order of eloquence.

It was fitting that the first nomination should be that of "Silver Dick" Bland. When Arkansas was called she yielded the floor to Missouri. Senator George G. Vest then placed Bland's name before the convention in an uninspiring speech which ended with an attempt at poetry which must have dispelled any spontaneous demonstration that might have erupted for Bland:

> Give us Silver Dick, and silver quick
> And we will make McKinley sick
> In the Ides of next November.[4]

The next man to be nominated was Bryan. Clark Howell, who had swung the Georgia delegation to Bryan, had selected Henry T. Lewis of that state to place Bryan's name before the convention. The delegates were not generally informed that Lewis was planning to nominate Bryan; and when, after a brief speech in which he said he was presenting to the convention a man who needed no "encomium to commend him to the people of the United States," a man whose nomination would "reflect credit upon the party you represent," he named Bryan, there was an attempt to develop a demonstration similar to that of the afternoon. It did not succeed. An artificial demonstration was maintained for twelve minutes, the same length of time that the perfunctory Bland demonstration had lasted.[5]

The next state to respond was Indiana. When Senator Turpie came forward to nominate Governor Matthews, the convention chairman begged for order "because Mr. Turpie had not a very strong voice." [6] He had a weak voice and a weak but rather long speech. The delegates and the visitors in the galleries took to gossiping among themselves and applauded neither the speaker nor his subject when Turpie concluded.

Following this Horace Boies was nominated by an orator who referred to his state as "Iowy" in a clumsy speech in which sentences such as this were typical: "But while we are easily supreme in the corn field, our Democrats have had a hard road [sic] to hoe in politics." [7] No demonstration followed this speech, nor the seconding speech for Boies delivered by a Minnesota delegate. It appeared that, amid the noisy chatter of the delegates, the nomination of the Iowa man was to be unnoticed, when the attention of the crowd was diverted to a young lady dressed in white and waving a white handkerchief from the gallery. The Iowa delegation sent up a cheer, the lady in white was carried in triumph from the galleries to the Iowa section on the floor of the convention. A demonstration lasting fifteen minutes, the longest of the evening, resulted.

When the roll of states was continued, Kentucky placed Blackburn in nomination, and Ohio nominated McLean. The following morning before the balloting began an Oregon delegate without a speech placed his state's ex-Governor, Sylvester Pennoyer, in nomination.[8] Senator Teller was not formally nominated. On the first and second ballots he received the eight votes of the Colorado delegation, but on the third ballot he dropped out of consideration altogether when Colorado shifted its votes to Bryan.

The most important development of Thursday evening was the action taken during the nominations by the conservative eastern delegations. They now assumed the attitude they were to display for the duration of the convention—seated in the convention, coldly observing, but not voting or otherwise participating. In repeated state caucuses and conferences during Wednesday and Thursday the question whether to leave altogether and organize a third party or whether to sit it out while not participating had been debated. Finally on Thursday evening, after the platform defeat but before the nominations began in the evening session, the New York delegation had caucussed in a lounge overlooking the race track at Washington Park. David Hill, Whitney, and the Tammany Hall organization advocated a policy of staying in the convention but not voting. Frederic R. Coudert, Perry Belmont, and others wanted to leave the convention immediately. The delegation voted to follow Hill and Whitney, to stay in the convention, but to explain that they had no candidate to present on the platform which had been adopted.[9]

Soon after the evening session began it was evident that the other eastern delegations had decided to take the same action as New York. When Massachusetts was reached as the roll was being called for the nominations, a delegate responded that Massachusetts had a candidate in ex-Governor Russell but that he did not wish to be nominated on the platform which the convention had adopted.[10] When Wisconsin was called, General Bragg responded, "Wisconsin cannot participate in nominating a Democrat to stand upon the platform." The Wisconsin delegation, however, was not united upon Bragg's declaration. Over his strong opposition two other delegates from Wisconsin spoke, one to second the nomination of Blackburn, the other in support of Bryan.[11]

Only one eastern conservative was formally nominated—ex-Governor Robert E. Pattison of Pennsylvania. The Pennsylvania delegation was instructed to present his name; and apparently, unlike Russell, he was unwilling to release the delegation from these instructions. Shortly before the nominations began or while they were in progress, Whitney telegraphed this message to Pattison: "Is it possible you intend to allow your name to go before the Convention on the platform? You know and I know what your delegation feel." [12] That William F. Harrity, the chairman of the Pennsylvania delegation, hoped to avoid putting Pattison in nomination was indicated by the fact that he did not do so during the regular nominating session on Thursday night but instead, acting at the last minute, put him in nomination on Friday morning, just before the balloting began. Harrity indicated his own feelings in the matter by stating curtly that he was placing Pattison in nomination in obedience to the instructions adopted by the Pennsylvania State Democratic convention.[13] Pattison's name provided a rallying point for conservatives who chose to continue to vote in the convention. During the balloting his highest tally was 100 votes; on the final ballot he received 95.

It was possible but not probable that had the convention proceeded to the balloting on Thursday night Bryan would have been nominated on the first ballot. Such a development was not probable because neither the demonstration in the convention nor the bargaining among the delegations in the intervening hours had produced any stampede of delegates toward him. David Overmeyer of Kansas, writing to Bryan after the convention, said that silver leaders like himself had become distressed during the convention by the great number of candidates for the Presidency. It was feared that this provided an opportunity for the conservatives to maneuver to defeat silver. Therefore, it occurred to him, to Governor Altgeld, and others that they must concentrate the vote of the convention as much as possible from the beginning. Since Bland had the most initial support, he seemed the logical man to support; and the Kansas delegation had voted for him as long as he led in the balloting.[14] The large number of "favorite-son" candidates placed in nomination indicated that the convention was still wide open.

The major effect of Bryan's speech was to hold more securely delegates and delegations already committed to him and to win a number of wavering, uncommitted votes. Also the success of his speech made it likely that on the second and third ballots he would pick up first ballot votes cast for "favorite-sons," along with the votes of wavering delegates.

On the first ballot Bryan got all the votes of Nebraska plus the votes of Georgia, Louisiana, Mississippi, and North Carolina. He also had several scattered votes from other delegations. He received only 137 votes, while Bland had 235, Boies 67, and Blackburn 82. On the next ballot Bryan retained all the large delegations which had voted for him and picked up all the votes of Wyoming, Michigan, and South Carolina, which had cast its first ballot vote for Tillman; and most of the California delegation switched to Bryan. At the end of the second tally the vote stood 197 for Bryan, 281 for Bland, and only 37 for Boies. Both Bryan and Bland had gained, but Bryan at the faster pace. On the third ballot the gradual accretion of Bryan's strength was again evident. Colorado switched to him, as did one-half of the Minnesota delegation and most of South Dakota and Florida, while all the states he had gained in the earlier balloting stayed. The vote was now 219 for Bryan and 291 for Bland. On the fourth ballot a surge toward Bryan at the expense of Bland soon developed. At the very beginning of the roll call Alabama, which on the last two ballots had cast its 22 votes for Bland, switched to Bryan. Idaho and Kansas, which had been Bland states, transferred their votes to the Bryan column. When the results were announced, it was found that Bryan had gone ahead of Bland, with 280 votes to Bland's 241.

It was now that the stampede for Bryan developed. Through the third ballot loyalties developed and expressed prior to the convention had held fairly well. The only major surprise had been the weak showing of Boies, but it was not Bryan who profited from votes which Boies failed to win. Middle western and prairie state votes which Boies did not get went either to Bland or to "favorite-sons," not to Bryan. Bryan's early strength lay in the southern states. This strength he gained at the expense of Bland, for Boies, as an ex-Republican, had little appeal to the South.

At the end of the fourth ballot the convention hall was in an uproar. Delegations were caucusing on the floor, loudly and heatedly debating their fifth ballot action. Bryan and Bland workers were going from delegation to delegation urging them to hold their votes or to change them as the situation dictated. To most delegates it was now evident that Bland could not win and that Bryan could not be defeated. There was then a strong argument for expediency's sake that any particular delegation join the Bryan bandwagon forthwith. Before the fifth ballot began, as individual states completed their caucus, they began to pick up their state guidons and carry them to the Nebraska banner. A rout, a massive demonstration for Bryan, was underway.

At this moment the newspaper reporters and knowing visitors in the galleries watched the activity in the Illinois delegation with particular fascination. Through the first four ballots Illinois had cast its 48 votes for Bland. It was clear, however, from the number of times which the delegation left the hall to caucus after the second ballot that Altgeld was having trouble holding his delegation for "Silver Dick." [15] Afterward members of the Illinois delegation, recalling the Illinois caucuses, said that Altgeld, pale and determined, had been loyal to Bland to the last. He agreed to swing his delegation to Bryan only when it became clear that a great majority of the members wanted to do so and when the argument was advanced that it was not fair to the Illinois delegates to put them in the posture of fighting a nomination which was certain.[16] Thus, before the fifth ballot began one of the Illinois delegates signaled the Illinois decision by running with the Illinois guidon to the Nebraska delegation.[17] During the ballot it was Illinois' vote for Bryan which brought the collapse of all opposition. Immediately, Ohio asked for recognition and switched its votes to Bryan. The convention had found its leader.

Through the excitement of these five ballots the eastern delegations had sat looking upon the convention with cold disapproval, or their empty chairs had stood as mute testimony that their erstwhile occupants were hostile to every sentiment and act of the convention. As the roll was called, spokesmen for the eastern delegations announced that their states would not join in the balloting. The first declination came from New Jersey: "The State of New Jersey respectfully declines to vote." Next came New York, and in response to the call ex-Governor Roswell P. Flower said, "In view of the platform adopted by this convention, I am instructed, as a delegate from the State of New York, to say that the delegates have agreed not to participate in the selection of candidates for President and Vice President, and therefore they decline to vote." [18]

When Wisconsin was called and General Bragg replied that his state declined to vote, the silver men on the delegation protested that they wished to cast their ballots. Bragg replied that the delegation was controlled by the unit rule and that the majority had voted against further participation. Senator White, the chairman of the convention, ruled against Bragg, holding that the unit rule could not be applied to prevent delegates from voting. As a result on the first ballot four Wisconsin votes were entered for Bryan and one for Blackburn. On this ballot 178 delegates were recorded as present but not voting. Subsequently some men in the non-voting delegations broke away and joined the balloting, but on the fifth and final ballot 162 delegates were officially recorded as not voting.

The silver delegates were deeply chagrined by this passive resistance on the part of the conservative minority, but no major outbreak occurred. On the third ballot, when New York was reached, no one remained on the floor to reply to the roll call. As the clerk repeated the call for New York, shouts were heard through the hall, "put them out!" [19] When after the fifth ballot delegates paraded around the hall carrying their state banners to show their enthusiasm for Bryan, a fight developed in the Wisconsin delegation which ended when the silver men tore the state's banner from its moorings and carried it into the parade. General Bragg, beside himself with indignation, protested loudly and violently. A few hours later, at the beginning of the evening session, Bragg spoke from the platform to disclaim the action by which the Wisconsin banner had been carried into the Bryan demonstration that afternoon. Again a silver delegate from his state was on the platform to reply to him.[20] It was evident to the convention that Democrats in many states like Wisconsin faced a bitter struggle for party control in the weeks ahead.

It had been anticipated that in the evening session on Friday the convention would make its vice-presidential nomination and adjourn. Again, however, the free silver majority was disorganized and uncertain of its ground. Bryan's western prairie location made an eastern, middle western, or southern running-mate desirable, but there were very few silver leaders of any availability from these sections. There was already some discussion of nominating Arthur Sewall, national committeeman from Maine, who had declared for silver at Chicago before the convention opened; but few of the delegates knew him. Bland was the most popular of all possible candidates, but his geographic location was not the most advantageous, and there was no certainty that he would accept the vice presidency.

The man whose candidacy was furthest advanced on Friday evening was John R. McLean. As an Ohioan he was well located geographically; and he was ardently pursuing the post, promising handsome campaign contributions and the support of his newspapers in return for the nomination. His candidacy had gained considerable popularity among the delegates, who felt that since Bryan was a poor man it would be desirable to provide him with campaign funds by giving him a running-mate who was wealthy. The only hitch in this plan was that McLean was opposed by Bryan and by all the leading figures in the Democratic Bimetallic Committee.[21] Bryan threatened that, if the convention nominated McLean as his running-mate, he would resign his nomination. John Peter Altgeld growled and fulminated against McLean as a symbol of corrupt wealth, the sort of greedy capitalist against whom their campaign had been organized.[22] Therefore, when the dispute between General Bragg and the silver men in the Wisconsin delegation had been quieted, the silver leadership introduced a resolution to recess the convention until the next morning. There was strong opposition to this move among delegates who did not relish spending another day in Chicago, but the reluctant were whipped into line and the convention approved the resolution.

In his memoirs, written many years after the event, Bryan said that when the party leaders visited him to learn his choice for the vice-presidential nomination he had told them that he had no preference, that he would leave the choice to the convention, and that furthermore a southern man would be wholly acceptable to him.[23] That Bryan recalled the situation accurately seemed amply proven by the pattern which the balloting assumed on Saturday morning, July 11. Overnight the silver leaders had arrived at no concerted strategy. Altogether ten men were nominated for the vice-presidency, of whom two withdrew before the balloting began; and five ballots were necessary to make a choice. Among the nominees were George Fred Williams of Massachusetts, Walter Clark of North Carolina, Joseph Sibley, Richard P. Bland, Arthur Sewall, and John R. McLean.[24]

During the balloting no pattern emerged which showed any kind of pre-nomination arrangement. As the second ballot progressed, a stampede toward Bland began to shape up; but at about that time the head of the Missouri delegation received a telegram from Bland stating that he would not be a candidate for the vice presidency; and he stopped the movement toward Bland by distributing the Missouri votes among the other contestants for the office.[25] After that there was a steady drift toward McLean and Sewall. With that development, it was only a matter of time until the silver leaders threw their support to Sewall. On the fifth ballot Illinois precipitated the inevitable stampede by shifting its 48 votes to Sewall.[26]

It appeared that the "logic of the situation" had also dictated Bryan's running-mate; but it seemed in retrospect a curious logic which gave a capitalist from Maine a leading role in a campaign intended to have a strong appeal to the masses of the South and West, as well as the laboring men of the nation's industrial centers. It could be understood only as the logic of people who were chiefly agrarian in outlook, to whom it did not occur to inquire into the labor record of this New England ship owner. For them it was sufficient to know that he was sound on the silver question.

In one sense Bryan was like his Republican opponent McKinley. His was the kind of personality about which political myths were invented. Before the convention had adjourned the myth that Bryan had been nominated by the concluding sentence of his speech, "You shall not press down upon the brow of labor this crown of thorns, you shall not crucify mankind upon a cross of gold," was taking root in the American political imagination. On the day that Bryan was nominated a New York newspaper man telegraphed from Chicago a story which began, "A phrase has nominated a candidate for the presidency...."[27] Two days later the St. Louis *Post Dispatch* printed this interpretation of the convention's action:

> When the history of the convention is written the historian will have little to say of the great leaders who planned the campaign and wrought out the finer moves upon the convention chess board which eventually gave the Nebraska orator first place.
> There were no leaders; there were no skillfully arranged by plays to give effect to sway the multitude. With his eloquence Mr. Bryan cut his way through and at one bound landed from a possibility into a winner's seat.[28]

Undoubtedly the country generally was surprised by Bryan's nomination. This was not to be wondered at when it became evident that even leading members of the convention had not appreciated the strength which Bryan possessed prior to his speech. For instance, George W. Allen, who had managed Bland's "boom" in Chicago, stated that Bryan had not been in the race before he made his speech but that after Bryan spoke many of the delegates "lost their heads altogether." To illustrate his point he cited the fact that during the demonstration which followed the speech a North Carolina delegate came to him and proposed that Missouri consent to Bryan's nomination "then and there." [29] Allen obviously did not know that the North Carolina delegation had been pledged to Bryan several hours before the "cross of gold" speech, nor did he know that many months earlier Josephus Daniels had pledged to bring to Chicago a delegation which would vote for Bryan.

To dismiss Bryan's nomination with the explanation that his convention address alone won it for him is to underestimate the man, his party, and his times. It may be argued plausibly that his speech did secure the nomination for Bryan in the sense that without it he could not have been nominated; but the speech alone could never have achieved this result. Behind the speech was Bryan's career as a worker for popular reform causes. Bryan was not unknown to the delegates, as the tremors of excitement which ran through the convention when he came forward to speak revealed. When the balloting began the next day, it was apparent that Bryan's speech had caused no major first-ballot movement in his direction among the delegates. The support he received he had won in his own right weeks and months before the convention met.

It was noted by several newspaper men that Bryan's support came first of all from those states in which the Populist movement had been most successful. As the balloting proceeded the states which moved to him most rapidly were the states in which he had strong support before he made his speech—the southern and far western states. Bryan was benefitting from the fact that in those states the keen competition with Populism dictated an increasingly radical Democratic policy. Once silver men controlled the convention a policy of adopting a platform which would appeal to Populists, silver Republicans, and third-party reformers became expedient. More and more "the logic of the situation," as Bryan called it, demanded a candidate known for his appeal to Populists and reformers, a Democratic radical. More than any candidate before the convention Bryan met this requirement. It can not be stated with any certainty that Bryan would have received the Democratic nomination if he had never made his speech, but such an outcome was clearly not improbable.

Did Bryan have any idea that his speech would affect his chances for the nomination? Of course he did. It was also true that the convention could not have escaped hearing Bryan's speech. It was his good fortune to speak under the most advantageous conditions imaginable. Several years later Bryan himself wrote of the speech that he "had no thought of its bringing to me the advantage that it did." At the same time he wrote: "I had thought before the Convention that I might possibly be a compromise candidate, but it was the logic of the situation that led me to believe so not the hope of influencing the Convention by any speech I might make." [30]

What Bryan undoubtedly intended to convey in this reminiscence of the convention was his conviction that his nomination did not depend alone upon his speech. If Bryan had not been aware at the time of the platform debate that his speech might have an influence on the nominations, he would have been one of the few perceptive people in the convention and in Chicago who did not so feel. Charles G. Dawes, who had known Bryan well when he lived in Lincoln, wrote that he personally was convinced that if Bryan spoke to the convention he would receive the nomination. [31] Victor Rosewater reporting on the talk in the Nebraska delegation at an early stage in the convention said that they hoped that Bryan would win the nomination through the effect of his keynote address, if, as they hoped, he were elected temporary chairman. [32]

Bryan knew the power which he possessed over crowds, and he knew that power was one of the bases for his prominence in the convention and in the country at large. He had prepared this speech carefully; he had pondered every nuance, had rehearsed every inflection of his voice, had practiced every gesture, had committed every word to memory. Reporters noticed that he was wearing the familiar black alpaca coat and that he was sucking on a lemon. They took both as signs that he planned a major oratorical effort. [33] Perhaps the attitudes of both Bryan and the convention were summed up in an exchange of messages recalled by Clark Howell. Shortly before Bryan spoke Howell scribbled a note on the back of an envelope and handed it to Bryan: "This is your great opportunity." Bryan wrote in reply, "You will not be disappointed." [34]

Conservative Democrats reached no agreement for concerted action before the convention was adjourned and the delegates dispersed. They had found ready agreement in their indignation over the proceedings; but when they faced up to the question of how they were to act in the future, they soon found that they could not easily unite. Delegations were internally divided. More marked, however, was the sectional division between the East and the rest of the country. This sectional difference was easily explained. Eastern Democrats faced no serious challenge to their control locally. In fact, in states like New York the external challenge of free silver had created a bond of unity among factions that had previously seemed irreconcilable. Eastern Democrats were reconciled to defeat in the election. Many of them talked calmly of voting for McKinley. They knew that after the election their local party machinery would remain intact and firmly in their control.

Western, southern, and middle western conservative Democrats faced quite a different situation. In most cases they had already lost control of their local party organizations; and in the few states where they had not, their defeat appeared imminent. They were literally ejected from their party into a political wilderness. They could, in many cases, contemplate voting for McKinley calmly enough; but after the election they could not anticipate any concessions from the victorious Republicans and the local Democratic machines would remain in control of free silver radicals. Southern conservatives would often not even be permitted the comfort of casting a protest vote for McKinley.

The big question for conservative Democrats was whether they should stay in the party or organize an independent third party movement. It was on this question that sectional differences became apparent. Eastern Democrats concluded that they had better stay in the party and maintain the control which they had established over their local organizations.[35] Western, middle western, and southern conservatives, in a sense already thrust out of their party by the free silver victory, argued that they must organize a third party.[36] The reasons which they advanced for such action were that a party true to original Democratic principles should be maintained in national politics and that Democrats in their sections who would not vote the Republican ticket must have some alternative to the Bryan-Sewall ticket.

Every facet of the Democratic organization now revealed a consciousness of a distinctive sectional and class feeling. Free silver Democrats had transformed the campaign for free silver into a popular movement for social justice. During the final hours of the convention Tom Johnson, a convert to Henry George's single tax, told the delegates that he did not favor free silver but that he had joined the Democratic party because "he believed their movement was for the good of humanity." [37] The program, nevertheless, was old fashioned and primarily agrarian. It had originated in the farm regions and had taken root in soil tilled by the Jeffersonian and Jacksonian Democracy. It had not originated in the new industrial cities and had not yet taken root there. The sectional feeling so closely linked with the agrarianism of the western and southern Democrats who seized control of their party in Chicago was enhanced by the action of the eastern conservatives in the convention and in the campaign which followed.

Conservative eastern Democrats saw the action of the Chicago convention as a revolutionary movement, hostile to the property interests with which they were so closely allied. In recent years they had alienated themselves from the urban laborers with the result that they did not understand this class of men as well as the Republicans did. Therefore, conservative Democrats in an hysterical class reaction viewed the action at Chicago as involving a combination of farmers and industrial workers bent upon destroying the foundations of their world. They saw much besides free silver in the Chicago action. The *New York Times* summarized the dangers thus: "Debased coinage, unlimited paper currency, repudiation of public and private debts, the threat of a packed Supreme Court, spoliation of property, cheating of labor, corruption of the civil service—these are the platform." [38] These fears were echoed in a letter written a few days after the convention by a New York business man:

> The election of the Chicago ticket means a great deal more than free coinage. The platform makes an attack on property, on contract, and on judicial institutions, and on the supremacy of Federal authority.... If Brian [sic] should be elected and a subservient Congress also elected, he would make changes in the Supreme Court by the enforced retirement of a sufficient number of Judges during his term, to bring about a reorganization of that body so as to insure a decision in favor of the Income Tax.... A law would be passed to prohibit the interference of Federal authority during the time of strikes, insurrections, etc. All contracts would be declared payable in silver and in fact the whole spirit of the Government would [be] revolutionized.[39]

The dark forebodings of the beaten conservative Democrats, the utopian aspirations of the free silver victors—both displayed a consciousness of class and section which did not square with political reality. Little wonder that both groups talked freely of the comparison between this election and the disastrous election of 1860. The decisive factor in the election of 1896 would be in the action taken by the industrial worker. Neither of the Democratic factions was in a position to understand or accurately to predict how this group of voters would act. To a very large extent they based both their nightmares and their rosy dreams on mistaken predictions of what he would do. Significantly none of the hysteria that swept through the eastern Democrats appeared in the McKinley-Hanna organization, for the men shaping the Republican campaign had a more profound understanding of the industrial worker. They knew that the Bryan Democrats had not won him yet. They knew that they would have to put up a hard fight to keep the Bryan Democrats from winning him. They were ready for that fight. They were confident they could win it.

18

The Populist and Silver
Parties at St. Louis

The Democratic endorsement of silver and Bryan at Chicago precipitated the disintegration of two third parties—the Populists and the National Silver party. Leaders of the latter organization rejoiced in the Democratic action and proceeded eagerly to make a public declaration of their united support. Immediately after Bryan's nomination General Warner broke into print in an interview in which he stated that the American Bimetallic Union would endorse the Democratic ticket.[1] On July 12, the day following the adjournment of the Democratic convention, the Bimetallic Union issued a formal address announcing unqualified acceptance of the Bryan-Sewall ticket and appealing to the other silver organizations of the country to send delegates to St. Louis pledged to support the Democratic ticket and platform.[2] It was never doubted that the Bimetallic Union spoke for its political counterpart, the National Silver party.

Perceptive men in the Populist party realized at once that the developments in Chicago placed their party in a very difficult position. Herman Taubeneck, who had journeyed to Chicago from Populist headquarters in St. Louis to exert pressure on the Democrats to nominate Teller, returned to St. Louis on the second day of the convention and sullenly refused to be interviewed.[3] Marion Butler, who like Taubeneck had urged the National Silver and Democratic parties to nominate Teller and who up to the last minute had believed that Democratic failure to nominate Teller could be used to brand that party a traitor to the silver cause, recognized that Bryan's nomination created difficulties for the Populists. He continued to attack the Democratic party, recalling its history of "treachery and broken promises"; but in public he carefully avoided speaking anything but praise of Bryan.[4] Privately he was quite candid in his analysis: "it would seem that their [the Democrats] real and underlying purpose in stealing of the People's party platform and in nominating Mr. Bryan for the presidency . . . was done more with a view to crippling the People's party than with a view to uniting the silver forces to win a great victory."[5]

Henry Demarest Lloyd, who had consistently opposed Populistic emphasis of the silver issue, concluded before the Democrats left Chicago that now the Populists had "only the Hobson's choice of sinking ourselves out of sight and resurrection in the Democracy; or, of beginning, de novo, within a few weeks of election, the task of making an issue and finding followers." He blamed the use of the silver issue for the party's dilemma and made Taubeneck the "scape-goat." His words revealed his bitterness: "If we fuse, we are sunk; if we don't fuse, all the silver men will leave us for the more powerful Democrats! And this is what Glaubenichts Taubeneck calls politics! Curious that the new party, the Reform party, the People's Party, should be more boss-ridden, ring-ruled, gang-gangrened than the two old parties of monopoly."[6]

Populists in the prairie and western states shed few tears over the impending demise of their party. With extraordinary unanimity they announced their intention to press for the nomination of Bryan *and* Sewall at their convention in St. Louis. Nor did they wait upon consultation with other leaders before acting. General Weaver announced from the convention in Chicago that he would support Bryan.[7] John W. Breidenthal, chairman of the Kansas Populist organization, stated that he was going to St. Louis to work for Bryan.[8] Thomas Patterson of Colorado announced in his newspaper, the *Rocky Mountain News*, that the Populist party could strengthen itself and make Bryan's election certain by nominating him at St. Louis.[9] Even Davis H. Waite, one of the most consistent supporters of the Omaha Platform, wrote to Ignatius Donnelly that to his "utter surprise" the Democratic convention had returned to the old doctrines of Jefferson and Jackson. They had, he said, "nominated a good & true man on the platform. Of course I support him. . . ."[10]

One of the first results of the Democratic action on free silver was to split the Populist party on sectional lines, west versus south. The founders of the party in the South were caught in a curious dilemma. They had established the Populist party in the southern states only after a bitter struggle against Democrats. Under no circumstances could they envisage cooperation with the hated "Bourbons," who were, they believed, only waiting to destroy them.[11] Yet the rapid growth achieved by the Populist party in the South in recent years had occurred largely through defections from the Democratic party by people who were attracted to the Populist party because of its stand on the financial question. These recent converts had not been in the early fight to establish the party and had no strong emotional attachment to the Populist party as such. It could be assumed that most of them would vote with the party which seemed most likely to achieve free silver. There was every indication that they would swarm back to the Democratic party to vote for Bryan and the Chicago platform. Bryan's speaking tours in the South had made him a well known and heroic figure among the southern people. To them he was an argument in himself for casting a Democratic ballot.

Southern Populist leaders found themselves maneuvering within narrowly circumscribed limits. Like Butler they could curse the Democratic party and remind the voters of its disreputable history, but of Bryan they could speak nothing but praise. Not unnaturally they groped for some compromise by which they could endorse Bryan and still maintain the integrity of their own party. Writing to Senator Stewart a few hours after the Democratic convention adjourned, Butler said that he saw two alternatives for the Populist party. One alternative was to endorse Bryan; the other was to set up a separate ticket, but to try to arrange that, after the election, Populist electors and silver electors of other parties would combine their votes on one acceptable candidate.[12]

Middle western Populists shared much of the western enthusiasm for Bryan; but they understood, too, the dilemma in which the Democratic action in Chicago had placed their party, though not many of them saw so clearly as Henry Demarest Lloyd that opportunistic Populist management, coupled with the Democratic platform and nomination, had virtually destroyed their party. More typical of middle western reaction was the indecision which Donnelly revealed as, prior to his departure for St. Louis, he wrote in his diary: "Exciting times there. Shall we or shall we not endorse Bryan, but I do not feel that we can safely accept the Dem. candidates. I fear it will be the end of our party. The South and East seem opposed to such a choice." [13]

Middle western Populists under the leadership of the party chairman, Herman Taubeneck, looked for a compromise. H. H. McDowell, chairman of the Arkansas Populist State Central Committee, who had been selected to serve as Sergeant-at-arms of the Populist convention, had been working for several weeks with Taubeneck in St. Louis. In mid-July he was quoted as saying that if the Democrats sincerely wanted to defeat McKinley they should say to the Populists, "Give us half the electors and you take the other half and we will have an equal showing in naming the President." McDowell said that Taubeneck was the author of this proposal.[14]

Two days after this interview was published Taubeneck made a hurried, unpublicized trip to Chicago. Subsequently there was considerable newspaper discussion of how the Populist leadership was plagued by the drift of the rank and file to Bryan, but that they were impressed anyway with the necessity to run a separate ticket even if it should name Bryan.[15] It was the national treasurer of the party, Martin C. Rankin, however, who was first reported as giving the opinion that the "practical thing" for the Populists to do in St. Louis was to nominate Bryan, change a few details in the Democratic platform, and then nominate a man from the South as their candidate for the vice presidency.[16]

The West, meanwhile, had become Bryan country. In that section his name alone was achieving a fusion of silver men of all parties. Here, where the question of silver had a direct economic significance, free silver had become the touchstone of partisan activity; and here, as in the South, Bryan's speaking tours had made his name virtually a synonym for free silver. Some hostility—at least a hesitancy to cooperate fully—might ordinarily have been anticipated from the silver Republicans; but Senator Teller announced his intention to back Bryan right after the Democrats made the nomination in Chicago. He immediately went to work to bring more reluctant western Republicans to full cooperation with the Bryan campaign. He also organized pressure on the Populist and National Silver parties to nominate Bryan and Sewall in their conventions at St. Louis.[17] It was probable, because of Teller's leadership in closing all western silver ranks behind Bryan, that Bryan's nomination resulted in a more successful unification of silver forces in the West than would have resulted from Teller's nomination. It was evident, for example, that older Populists, like Davis Waite, would not have been eager to cooperate with Republicans like Teller, who had been fighting them as dangerous radicals since their political origin.

After the Democratic convention Teller established contact with Bryan through Thomas Patterson, who left Denver for the Populist convention at an early date. En route Patterson stopped at Lincoln, Nebraska, where he spent a day with Bryan. He delivered a letter in which Teller told Bryan that he might talk freely with Patterson and that Patterson was inclined and was in a strong position to aid his cause in the Populist convention.[18] Bryan released to the press those portions of Teller's letter in which he pledged his support to Bryan, talked of the difficulties of a campaign in which all the forces of concentrated wealth would be opposed to them, and volunteered his services as a speaker to the Democratic National Committee.[19]

Teller was having difficulty at this time in persuading his Republican colleagues in the West to make a forthright statement endorsing Bryan and the Democratic campaign. They were not as unselfishly dedicated to the silver cause as Teller; they were not convinced that the Republican party, even with McKinley and the St. Louis platform, was defunct in the West; and, above all, they saw no future for themselves politically if they supported the Democratic nominees.[20] Populists like Patterson and Bell, in close touch with the Democratic organization, made promises, which they could support only by referring to Bryan's fair and generous nature, that the Democrats would reward independent political leaders who joined them in the campaign.[21] Most western Republicans wanted something more substantial than such unsupported assurances before abandoning their party completely.

In reality the silver Republicans were caught as neatly as the southern Populists in a web largely of their own manufacture; and now Bryan's popularity, combined with the Democratic platform, drew them irresistibly. A few days before the Populist convention opened Teller managed to bring several silver Republicans together in Colorado for a conference. At its conclusion the conferees issued a "Manifesto" which expounded the free silver argument and ended with a statement that the Democratic party had adopted a platform which was sound on the financial issue and had nominated good candidates, to whom all the friends of gold and silver should give "their hearty support." [22] It was not the strong declaration for Bryan which Teller had hoped to get from the conference, but it was released to the press two days prior to the opening of the Populist convention with the hope that it would influence the actions of that body.[23]

Teller himself had given Patterson a letter which he invited Patterson to show to "any member" of the Populist convention in which he declared that he could not allow his name to be placed in nomination in the convention in competition with Bryan's. He stated: "I will not be a party to any movement to divide the friends of silver in this campaign, and if we fail to concentrate on Mr. Bryan all the opponents to the election of a gold standard candidate the fault will not be with the friends of silver who have heretofore acted with the Republican party." [24]

The Populist and National Silver conventions were not due to open until Wednesday, July 22; but as early as the preceding weekend delegates and observers were streaming into St. Louis. A motley crowd they proved to be. The Populists, themselves a curiously mixed aggregation of individualistic reformers and opportunistic politicians, were now joined by a large number of non-Populists of similar character. It appeared that every reform movement which existed in the United States at the moment sent representatives to St. Louis, hoping to prevail upon the Populists to give a conspicuous place in their party's platform to their social, economic, or political nostrums. They were a wordy and contentious lot. Whenever two men stopped to talk an argument was likely to ensue. Soon a crowd gathered, and the private argument became a public debate. The streets, the public parks, the hotel corridors seethed with crowds involved in a noisy, seemingly endless discussion of public issues.

Men, observing the crowds, reached quite different conclusions. Some saw the gathering as inspiring and inspired; others saw it as grotesquely humorous; yet others as sinister, irresponsible, or revolutionary. From different points of view it was all of these things; and newspaper men, reporting the convention, saw all of these things in it. Every crowd seemed to produce an unconventional personality. Conspicuous on many occasions, for example, was a St. Louis resident, who was a convert to the single tax. Whenever he could gather a crowd he made a speech. Standing before his listeners holding over his head an umbrella from which all the cloth had been removed (to symbolize the sham and mockery of government protection of the poor), he stated that if the Populist convention nominated Bryan on the Democratic platform he would immediately announce himself as a Populist candidate for the Presidency with the Lord's Prayer as his platform.[25]

Eastern newspaper men amused themselves and their readers by describing the whiskers so abundantly in evidence in the Populist gathering. Their amusement, however, was mingled with a feeling that there was something of the sinister in the irregular facial features and hirsute adornments of the delegates. A Boston newspaper man described them thus:

> There is a dangerous glitter in most of the eyes, and nearly every face has some normal feature lacking. Queer chins, queer noses, uneven temples— something out of the common is conspicuous on every hand. The only symmetrical faces in the lot are those of a few leaders, in which shrewdness takes the place of oddity. Among these few the web [sic], fishy eye is a marked characteristic. They are the sort of men on whom an engineer of dubious schemes would not waste an argument, but whom he would proceed at once to purchase on general principles.[26]

James Creelman, writing about the first day of the convention, said that there was a dearth of good noses, but of the chins he was unable he judge because few were in evidence. He concluded that there was "some mysterious connection between Populism and hair." Apparently this aspect of the convention had impressed him deeply for at another point in his story he said: "The vast hall was full of whiskers, although here and there was a shaven man. Long whiskers and short whiskers, red whiskers and black whiskers, forked whiskers and pointed whiskers, and, rising grandly above them all, the powerfully intellectual countenance of Senator Peffer, whose whiskers were three inches longer than any other man's." [27]

Metropolitan reporters also found the women of the convention remarkable, not only because they were numerous but because they were outspoken and conspicuous in the business of the convention. By far the most prominent and colorful woman there was Mrs. Mary Elizabeth Lease. She was an intelligent, well informed woman and possessed that ability absolutely essential to political success in Kansas Populism, the ability to deliver effective speeches.[28] She captured attention in the early stages of the convention when, as a member of the Executive Committee, she took a seat on the platform amid enthusiastic applause from the delegates.[29] Along with the rest of the Kansas delegation she favored the nomination of Bryan and Sewall. On the second day of the convention she issued a long statement attacking Taubeneck and alleging that his opposition to Bryan had been arranged through collusion with Mark Hanna and Wall Street.[30]

Another well known woman in the convention was Mrs. Helen M. Gougar, who had made a career speaking for free silver and prohibition. On the second day she delivered to the convention one of her characteristic effusions in which she said that the saloon-keepers, the rum power, the Anarchists, and the "thieves of Wall Street" were on the side of McKinley and the Republican party.[31] Her statement about the Anarchists and McKinley was one heard frequently in the convention. It was based on the fact that the Anarchist, Johann Most, had recently announced that he planned to vote for McKinley.[32]

A figure whose presence in the convention was made conspicuous by the comments of the metropolitan press was Jacob Coxey of Ohio. He was always available for interviews, and his colorful comments on various subjects, including his plan for issuing bonds to finance public works programs, made good newspaper copy.[33] Nor did the newspaper men neglect to report that he brought his wife and children with him onto the floor of the convention, where the women delegates took delight in cuddling his youngest child, who had been christened "Legal Tender." [34]

One writer, Henry Demarest Lloyd, understood that many of the delegates could ill afford to come to St. Louis; and he attacked the "smart" reporters of the metropolitan press, who "dilated with the wit of the boulevardier" upon the bucolic manners of the Populists in St. Louis. One reporter had scoffed at finding delegates sitting at the curb with their shoes off, to rest their feet and save their shoes, they said. Lloyd explained that several delegates, lacking train fare, had walked to the convention. Many could not afford to stay in hotels or rooming houses and were forced to sleep in parks and other public places. Often they did not have money to buy nourishing meals. When the convention lasted longer than the delegates had expected, their hardship became greater. Thus, the men who were objects of ridicule for one newspaper reporter became to another devoted men making great personal sacrifices for high principles.[35]

The newspaper reporters who gave lengthy notices of the convention antics of people like Mrs. Lease and Jacob Coxey and who let no opportunity escape to mention the presence in St. Louis of Socialists and Prohibitionists paid comparatively little attention to the presence in that city of a much more important gentleman, Senator James K.

Jones, the chairman of the Democratic National Committee. Jones was in St. Louis several days before the convention opened, and his office became a reception center for hundreds of delegates from both the Populist and National Silver party conventions. There was never any doubt that his objective was to persuade the Populist convention to nominate Bryan and Sewall. He found allies in the Populist and Republican leaders from the western and middle western states. Men like Stewart, Patterson, and Weaver spent much of their time in the convention herding delegates into Jones's rooms.[36]

The absence of Eugene Debs from the convention was made conspicuous by the comments of the press. The various factions hostile to Bryan placed Debs high on the list of candidates acceptable to them, and his name was discussed prominently in this connection during the first days of the convention.[37] Several days before the convention he had declared that he thought the silver issue to be of minor importance and that he was opposed to the nomination of Bryan by the Populist party. He said that he hoped the Populist party would declare in favor of a constitutional convention. Elaborating on this idea he said: "What is now required is a new organic law adapted to modern conditions and which cannot be adequately treated by amendments. The basic reform, in my opinion, is that of direct government by the initiative and referendum, which would place this government in the hands of the people." [38]

Debs' statement regarding direct government through the initiative and referendum drew attention to a movement that had been underway for many months and which, under the leadership of Eltweed Pomeroy of New Jersey, had resulted in an embryonic organization to promote the initiative and referendum.[39] Pomeroy, no doubt influenced by the statements of the Omaha platform on this question, had tried to develop the support of the Populists, and particularly of Ignatius Donnelly, for the convening of a direct legislation conference in St. Louis on July 21, the day before the opening of the Populist convention.[40] On April 3 Pomeroy released a printed call for a direct legislation conference at St. Louis on July 21, signed by Donnelly and a number of men associated with various kinds of reform efforts.[41] In his letters to Donnelly Pomeroy said that William S. U'Ren of Oregon, single taxer McParlin of New York, and labor leaders Gompers and Debs, had expressed their support for the conference.[42] The growth in the popularity of the free silver movement absorbed the attentions and energies of reformers who otherwise would have cooperated with the conference which Pomeroy had planned. The conference did not materialize, and Pomeroy at St. Louis was a comparatively unnoticed lobbyist for a comparatively inconspicuous cause, not the leader of an established popular movement.

"Broad gauge" Prohibitionists were at St. Louis, continuing their struggle to get the Populists to adopt a platform resolution condemning the liquor traffic. However, they were diverted from their first enthusiasm by their new found enthusiasm for free silver. They were converts now to a campaign for free silver under the leadership of Bryan and Sewall. They pressed that campaign more strongly than they urged a prohibition plank in the Populist platform.

The only strong organized labor representation in St. Louis was that of the Knights of Labor. The leaders of this organization affiliated themselves with the middle-of-the-road element. They possessed a potentially powerful weapon against Bryan and Sewall in the proposed candidacy of Debs. The possibilities of Debs' candidacy were never to be realized, however. Not only did Debs refuse to run, but men who might have been expected to support him in the convention turned to Bryan. Thus, Clarence Darrow at an early stage announced his support for Bryan and Sewall, arguing that to do otherwise would be to divide forces in "a year in which we are to fight the greatest battle of modern times between the plutocrats and the producers." [43] It was likely that Darrow reflected the thinking of John Peter Altgeld. In no way was labor an outstandingly radical force in the convention. Much better organized and more persuasive was the radicalism of the middle-of-the-road Populists from the South.

Two days before the convention opened all the leaders of the Populist party and the leaders of other parties who hoped to influence Populist decisions were at St. Louis. The city was in a flurry of conferences and caucuses as various parties and factions within parties tried to concert plans by which to achieve their objectives within the Populist and National Silver party conventions.

The Populist party itself was unable to find a national leader, a central coordination, or a national objective upon which to arrive at a general agreement. Western and southern delegates who had been antagonistic before coming to St. Louis found no common ground in propinquity. Men from both sections talked of walking out of the convention if their wishes were not realized in the actions of that body. On the day before the convention opened "Bloody Bridles" Davis H. Waite saw the two sections irreconcilably opposed within their party: "The Southern delegates are not so radical as they were, but they are still sore enough to walk out of the convention if they are not given their own way. On the other hand, the silver men from the West are generally determined to have Bryan or walk out. This is a question that cannot be compromised." [44]

The southern Populists formed the hard center of that group of men who were known as the middle-of-the-roaders, the men who opposed all cooperation with the Democratic party in order to preserve the integrity of their own party. Southern Populists had not always opposed cooperation with outside factions; for earlier in the campaign they had eagerly embraced cooperation with two groups chiefly western in orientation—the silver Republicans and the National Silver party. Further, in local politics they had often worked closely with the Republican party. They did not necessarily insist upon the nomination of a straight-out Populist either; for earlier they had played a major part in agitating for the nomination of Teller. Nor did they insist upon strict adherence to the Omaha Platform; for they had taken a prominent role in narrowing the Platform to a strong emphasis on silver. They were struggling desperately now to escape the inevitable results of their earlier mistakes, as they insisted that the party must nominate a straight Populist ticket on a broad Populist platform.

In caucus on Tuesday, July 21, the middle-of-the-road faction made a final attempt to agree upon a plan of action and a candidate. They were able to agree only upon their hostility to the Democrats and their opposition to the nomination of Bryan and Sewall. If they had developed a leadership to congeal their indignation, they might have controlled the convention even though they were in the minority. The men whose names were suggested in the caucus as candidates whom they might support for the nomination revealed the weakness of their leadership. The strongest man named was Eugene Debs, but they could not agree upon him. Other men mentioned were Paul Vandervoort, an ineffectual anti-Bryan malcontent from Nebraska, Ignatius Donnelly, and Representative Charles A. Towne, a silver Republican from Duluth, Minnesota, who had bolted the Republican convention with Teller. They did finally agree upon a ticket headed by Colonel Seymour F. Norton of Illinois for President and Frank Burkett of

Mississippi for vice president, but the slate aroused little enthusiasm among the middle-of-the-roaders themselves.[45]

The middle-of-the-road faction did succeed in impressing upon the convention one fact—that if they nominated Bryan without any assurance from the Democrats of reciprocity in the electoral college, they would cease to exist as a party. Therefore, while the middle-of-the-roaders had slight success in wooing the delegates from Bryan, they did succeed in swaying the convention to adopt the strategy of nominating a separate ticket in which they would link Bryan with a Populist running-mate. The movement of the delegates in this direction was strengthened by the refusal of Senator Jones and other representatives of the Democratic party in St. Louis to bargain in any way for a division of electoral votes. Pointing to this, the middle-of-the-road men argued that the sole object of the Democratic party was to split the Populist party and destroy it.

The two dominating forces in the convention, therefore, became Bryan, the irrepressible symbol of the united fight for a popular cause, and the nomination of a Populist vice-presidential candidate, as a symbol of the survival and integrity of the Populist party. This was the concept of the compromisers in the convention, men such as Taubeneck and Butler. They saw that the party must recognize Bryan as the symbol of unity in the fight for free silver, but that it must also appease the middle-of-the-road faction, who would bolt the party if it nominated a Bryan-Sewall ticket. To outside observers who watched the convention sway unpredictably from pro-Bryan to middle-of-the-road decisions the delegates appeared an uniquely uncertain and unstable group. They argued savagely; they maneuvered wildly; their actions appeared erratic and unpredictable; but always they returned to the narrow confines of the two necessities—Bryan and, in spite of him, party continuity.

On the first day Senator Marion Butler tried to bring the convention to a policy of compromise in his speech as temporary chairman. He reviewed recent political history to demonstrate that it was when "the great middle classes" had recognized the inadequacy of the two old parties that they had created the Populist party. In 1896 the contribution of that party was evident in the fact that the Republican party had been forced to abandon its customary "straddling treachery" and had gone over "bag and baggage to the great money kings of Wall street and of Europe," while the Democrats committed "petty and grand larceny" by stealing the Populist platform, "almost in its entirety." He went on to argue the necessity for the continued existence of the Populist party. It must, he said, see the battle on the money question, now so close to victory, carried to its conclusion. Meanwhile, even as that issue was being settled, other issues such as the transportation question were forcing themselves forward; and only the Populist party could solve them correctly. He concluded with a plea that they act in the convention to keep the party united.[46]

At the end of the first day newspaper reporters, basing their analysis on Butler's speech and the convention's reaction to it, sent dispatches from St. Louis saying that the middle-of-the-road element appeared to have undisputed control of the convention.[47] That night the middle-of-the-road managers had planned to use the convention hall for a rally against Bryan. The meeting failed because the managers of the hall did not turn on the lights. Middle-of-the-road leaders charged that this fiasco was the result of a deliberate act of sabotage by pro-Bryan men.[48]

The following day the delegates appeared to have made a bewildering reversal as, by a large majority, they elected Senator William V. Allen, Nebraska Populist and an ally of Bryan, as permanent chairman of the convention.[49] Allen's long speech was devoted entirely to the argument that the Populist party must act to serve the causes for which it had been created no matter what sacrifice this might require within the party itself. He repeated the newspaper rumor that the "minions of Wall Street" were active in the convention buying up delegates. The implication here was that Wall Street was backing the middle-of-the-road faction because the action they wanted would split the convention, split the silver forces, and assure a Republican victory.[50] At the conclusion of his speech Allen said that when he returned to Nebraska he wanted to be able to say to the people that the convention had made possible the doctrines which the Populists had been preaching for years. "I do not want them to say to me that the Populists have been advocates of reforms when they could not be accomplished, but when the first ray of light appeared and the people were looking with expectancy and with anxiety for relief, the party was not equal to the occasion; that it was stupid; it was blind; it kept 'in the middle of the road,' and missed the golden opportunity." [51]

At the end of the second day the reporters, noting Allen's election as permanent chairman, the enthusiastic reaction of the convention to his speech, the seating of delegates favorable to Bryan in those few instances where there were disputed delegations, and the assignment of General Weaver to head the platform committee, concluded that the convention was swinging to Bryan.[52] But on the third day, Friday, July 24, the middle-of-the-road men seemed to be in control again. The morning session began with the submission of the report of the committee on rules. There was nothing extraordinary in the majority report, but the middle-of-the-road minority on the rules committee submitted a substitute report recommending that the convention make its vice-presidential nomination prior to making its presidential nomination. A violent but brief debate followed. Then in a confused uproar the convention balloted, and by a small majority approved the substitute presented by the minority of the rules committee. Clearly the Bryanites had lost a crucial round.[53]

The pro-Bryan faction won a round in the afternoon session, which was devoted largely to discussion of the report of the resolutions committee and the adoption of the platform. Bryan men held the majority on the resolutions committee. Under the lead of General Weaver they had shaped a platform emphasizing the free silver issue and had beaten down attempts by Coxey and Schilling to incorporate planks recommending specific programs for employment of the unemployed on public works programs. They also turned down a woman suffrage plank.[54] When the platform was presented to the convention, Coxey again presented an amendment embodying his ideas; and a delegate from Texas, complaining that the platform sounded too much like the Democratic platform, submitted a substitute. But the convention voted down all amendments and all substitutes.[55] Thereby the convention acted to adopt a platform oriented toward the nomination of Bryan.

In the field of money and banking the Populist platform demanded a national money issued by the government without the intervention of private banks, the free coinage of gold and silver at the ratio of 16 to 1, an increase in the amount of money in circulation sufficient to meet the "demands of business and population, and to restore the just level of prices of labor and production," and the establishment of a postal savings bank. It denounced the Cleveland administration's sale of bonds and the resulting increase in the public debt. The platform demanded a graduated income tax and stated that the recent decision of the Supreme Court on that question was "a misinterpretation of the Constitution and an invasion of the rightful powers of Congress over the subject of taxation."

On the subject of transportation the platform declared that the government should own and operate the railroads. In this connection a special section on the Pacific railways declared that as public highways they should be owned and operated by the people. Likewise the telegraph system, "being a necessity for the transmission of news," should be publicly owned.

There were sections in the platform opposing land monopolies and declaring that it was proper governmental policy to distribute the public lands to bona fide settlers. Another plank declared for direct legislation by initiative and referendum and also for direct election of the President, Vice-president, and United States Senators. There was also a declaration for home rule in the territories and in the District of Columbia. Another section declared sympathy for the people of Cuba in their "heroic struggle" and stated that the United States should act to recognize the independence of Cuba. The only direct references to the problems of industrial labor were found in brief planks relegated to the end of the platform. These contained statements that in periods of depression "idle labor" should be employed in public works "as far as practicable," and that the "arbitrary course of the courts" in imprisoning citizens for "indirect contempt" and ruling by injunction should be remedied by legislation. At its conclusion the platform returned to the financial question, stating that it was "the great and pressing issue of the pending campaign" and inviting the cooperation of all organizations and citizens on that issue alone.[56]

The adoption of the minority report of the committee on rules, though it foreshadowed defeat of the pro-Bryan faction, did not entirely destroy the hopes of that group to nominate a Bryan-Sewall ticket. The vice-presidential nomination was still to be made, and it was possible that the delegates could be persuaded to nominate Sewall. The balloting on the vice-presidential candidate was scheduled for the evening session of that eventful third day which had begun with the adoption of the minority report on rules in the morning session. After the adoption of that report had indicated that the delegates were disposed to nominate a vice-presidential candidate from their own party, Senator Jones had telegraphed Bryan, informing him of the convention's action, inquiring if he would accept the Populist nomination with a running-mate other than Sewall, and recommending that he refuse to do so. Bryan had telegraphed in reply that he would not accept the Populist nomination if Sewall were not the vice-presidential nominee. Jones, Patterson, and other pro-Bryan leaders showed copies of this telegraphic exchange to the convention delegates, doubtless believing that since most of them desired the nomination of Bryan, they would be persuaded by reading Bryan's dispatch to nominate Sewall. The middle-of-the-road men reacted, of course, by concluding that this merely proved that the convention must not name Bryan but set up an entirely independent campaign with a Populist ticket.[57]

In the last hours of the convention on Friday night and Saturday morning, in the sessions in which the nominations were made, the Populist convention was a scene of chaos and confusion. Misleading rumors, as much a compound of wishful thinking as of deliberate intent, circulated rapidly among the delegates. It was rumored that the Democrats had agreed that if the Populists nominated Bryan with a vice-presidential candidate from their own party, that the Democrats would take Sewall off their ticket and substitute for him the Populist nominee. Various versions of the telegraphic exchange between Jones and Bryan spread among the delegates and right after them went denials that Bryan had sent any message to St. Louis refusing to run with a Populist vice-presidential nominee, that in fact he had indicated his willingness to do so. There were rumors that various delegations were planning to bolt the convention if it nominated Bryan, or if it did not nominate Bryan. So great was the confusion that it was doubtful that there was any man or group of men in St. Louis at the time the Populist party made its nominations who could boast any general understanding or control of the convention.[58]

The vice-presidential nomination made on Friday evening was dictated by the wishful belief that the act of nominating a man from the Populist party to run with Bryan would unite the party and preserve it for future campaigns. When the roll of the states was called, Sewall was nominated, along with several middle-of-the-road state leaders, who were not nationally well known. The best known among them was Thomas E. Watson of Georgia, and the convention nominated him on the first ballot. He was not at the convention but at his Georgia home, a point to which messages from St. Louis often could be delivered only after a delay of several hours. Apparently he accepted the nomination initially in the belief that the Democratic managers had agreed formally to the withdrawal of Sewall. Subsequently in extensive newspaper discussions he further justified his acceptance as an act which kept the Populist party in the field as a valuable force for liberalism, even when it failed to win elections.[59]

The unrest and confusion which had marked the convention came to a culmination in the final session on Saturday morning, July 25, when the Populists nominated Bryan for the Presidency. The morning newspapers printed versions of the telegraphic exchange between Jones and Bryan, but these reports did not dispel the ugly humors of the preceding days. The delegates were weary and tense, but doggedly determined. The long sessions had produced no satisfactory area of agreement between the western and southern factions. Now it seemed clear that each faction was to win from the convention only its minimum demand: for the West, the nomination of Bryan; for the South, a guarantee of party integrity and survival in the nomination of Watson. If this could be called a compromise, neither faction could take much satisfaction in it; for in neither instance did the terms arrived at promise any degree of success.

The middle-of-the-road men had little difficulty in finding a candidate to beat Sewall, but they were sadly lacking in men of sufficient stature to put up against Bryan. General Weaver, potentially a strong candidate, was a Bryan man. Other nationally known men like Davis H. Waite and Ignatius Donnelly had long since forfeited claim to serious attention through hasty speech or unconventional action. An attempt to place Eugene Debs in nomination was stopped by the reading of a telegram in which he positively refused to be a candidate.[60] In the end the middle-of-the-road men nominated Colonel Seymour F. Norton of Illinois.[61]

Bryan, as "that matchless champion of the people, that intrepid foe of corporate greed, that splendid young statesman," was placed in nomination by General Weaver. Weaver's speech showed a mastery fully equal to Bryan's of the florid rhetorical style of the nineteenth century. All that was lacking was the silver tongue of the Nebraska orator. At the beginning of his speech Weaver referred to the newspaper reports of Bryan's telegram to Jones. He disposed of this by saying that "this question has reached a point where neither Mr. Bryan nor his personal friends have any right whatever to say what

the action of this convention shall be." He said that he had refused
to confer with either Bryan or Jones as to the nominee of the convention. Then came a flow of effulgent phrases: He quoted from Shake-
speare, "There is a tide in the affairs of men. . . ." He spoke of the
"sacred cause," "a new Pentecost," "party fealty subordinate to principle," "the field of glory," "the battlements of the gold power," "the
plutocracy of Christendom," "the subsidized organs," and the "sleuth
hounds of the money power of the world." [62]

Weaver's speech was followed by a noisy and prolonged demonstration. As the delegates paraded around the hall, holding high the
banners of their states, the Texas delegation sat silent, looking on the
wild scene with dark disapproval. Many of the older members of the
delegation were in tears. One white-haired Texan was heard to shout,
"We will not crucify the People's Party on the cross of Democracy!" [63]
Some of the parading delegates tried to invade the Texas area, to seize
their state banner and carry it into the procession. They were pitched
out; there was a brief show of guns by the Texas men; the convention
was close to violence.[64] Individuals and small groups of men from
other delegations moved over to congratulate the Texas delegates and
to stand with them against the triumphant Bryan majority. They talked
of bolting the convention and of organizing another convention to
preserve the party.

After the demonstration for Bryan subsided, General James G. Field
agitated the convention again by proposing that they nominate Bryan
by acclamation. The howls of the middle-of-the-road men made it
evident that the convention was too close to disintegration to attempt
such action. Then almost a score of speakers, including Herman
Taubeneck, Jerry Simpson, Ignatius Donnelly, and Mrs. Lease, seconded Bryan's nomination.[65] Colonel Norton was placed in nomination to oppose Bryan in speeches studded with angry middle-of-the-
road sentiments that again deeply stirred the convention.

The balloting was disorderly, marked by a turbulence compounded
of anger and indecision. Conflicting rumors sped from delegation to
delegation. Middle-of-the-roaders continued to talk about bolting.
Several times the chairman, Senator Allen, was questioned from the
floor of the convention about the messages from Bryan. Was it true
that Bryan had declined the Populist nomination if he were not to
have Sewall as his running-mate? Allen lied in replying that he knew

of no such message from Bryan. Long before the first ballot was completed Bryan had won the nomination. The final tally was Bryan, 1042, Norton, 340.[66]

Before adjourning, the Populist convention gave further indication of its uncertainty and confusion by adopting a resolution giving the National Committee plenary powers to act in all matters as if it were the convention. This was a recognition that the actions of the convention left many issues in doubt. The Populists, when they adjourned at St. Louis, did not know that Bryan would accept their nomination. They wishfully thought that Sewall might be persuaded to withdraw from the Democratic ticket and Watson substituted. Under the circumstances it appeared necessary to give the National Committee broad discretionary powers.[67]

In another hall in St. Louis the National Silver party [68] was holding a series of meetings which they referred to as a convention. History could refer to it as such only out of courtesy. Newspaper men present in St. Louis with less courtesy and more accuracy referred to the meetings as "Bryan hurrah sessions" and "a sort of mass meeting." [69]

Though the Populist and National Silver parties had agreed several months before to set up a joint conference committee to coordinate their actions at St. Louis, not until the third day of their convention did the Populists appoint delegates to such a committee. Even then there was resistance to the committee among the middle-of-the-roaders. When the roll of the states was called for the names of delegates to serve on the committee, Texas replied, "Texas never treats with the enemy. Texas names no member to that Committee." [70]

Later that day, when the conference committees of the two parties did meet, they found that their agreement on free silver and Bryan was not sufficient to achieve the coordination which the managers of both parties had planned months earlier. The question of the vice-presidential nomination now stood as a barrier, which neither side was willing to lower. The National Silver party insisted that the ticket of Bryan and Sewall was essential to the victory of silver; the Populists insisted that the nomination of someone other than Sewall was essential to the survival of their party.[71] The conference announced its futility by adopting an innocuous resolution:

Resolved, That it is the sense of this conference committee that union of all forces, including the People's Party, silver men, free-silver Democrats and

Republicans, is expedient and should be effected at once for the purpose of achieving victory for the advancement of free silver in November.[72]

The National Silver party had been formed by silver protagonists who had doubted that the Republican, Democratic, or Populist parties would ever act upon the silver question in such a way as to combine all silver men in a free silver campaign. The action of the Democrats in Chicago had refuted their predictions. They came to St. Louis with slight interest in preserving their organization, intent solely on persuading the Populists to nominate Bryan and Sewall. They perfunctorily organized and held their "hurrah sessions," but the drama of the Populist meetings drew the crowds, and the National Silver party sessions were thinly attended.

The National Silver party nominated Bryan and Sewall and adopted a silver platform with a sincerity and conviction that compensated for the absence of the noisy demonstrations usually found in American political conventions. They perpetuated their existence not because they hoped to succeed as a party but because they believed they could still be of some value as an independent, essentially non-partisan force working for free silver. They publicized their success in breaking down party lines by releasing the results of a poll which had inquired into the previous political affiliations of the delegates to their convention. The results showed that 528 had previously been Republicans, 134 Democrats, 47 Populists, 12 Independents, 9 Prohibitionists, and 1 a Greenbacker.[73] Now they were quite content to "hurrah" and herd all such mavericks into the party of Bryan and Sewall.

19

The Gold Democrats
Raise a New Standard

The fragmentation of established parties and the coalescence of new political unions, which started actively in the conventions, continued through and beyond the campaign. The Democratic convention had witnessed no dramatic exodus such as Teller had led in St. Louis, but the adoption of its platform and the nomination of Bryan created a serious problem for those Democrats who adhered to the conservative traditions of the party. They had learned to believe that the function of government was severely limited to conventional administrative and regulatory roles, that governmental paternalism in any form was contrary to the traditions of the American Constitution, a threat to freedom, and an affront to common sense.[1] During the campaign these men linked Republican protectionism and Populistic "socialism" as allied forces of evil. One of their common arguments was that the Bryan Democratic-Populist campaign was merely another product of the twisted economy and warped thinking on public policy caused by Republican protective tariffs.[2]

Democrats so opposed to governmental paternalism, who no longer felt at home in their own party, did not find at hand an established political organization in which to take refuge. By this time the Republicans had nominated McKinley, who had become a symbol to conservative Democrats of the evils of protectionism. Moreover, he was generally disliked and distrusted as a person by conservative

Democrats. Richard Olney wrote to Cleveland that "So far as personal qualifications for the Presidency are concerned, I should as soon take my chance with Bryan as with McKinley." [3]

Nevertheless, as the campaign progressed, most conservative Democrats in the eastern states concluded that on the bases of both issues and personalities the victory of the Republican party and McKinley was essential. Many of them concluded to vote for McKinley; a few openly campaigned for him.[4] They felt little need to reorganize their local party machines, and most of them took little interest in creating a national organization to represent their point of view.

Some eastern Democrats did see value in the organization of a third-party Democratic movement. One argument which they advanced for a separate conservative organization was the failure of the McKinley campaign to develop a strong line on the monetary question. Conservative Democrats felt that his emphasis on the tariff at the expense of the financial issue endangered his success by making it difficult for conservative Democrats to vote for him. They felt, therefore, that a separate honest money Democratic organization could exert pressure on McKinley to change his campaign tactics and also draw from Bryan Democratic votes that would not on principle be cast for McKinley.[5] In addition such an organization could conduct a popular educational campaign along lines not possible for other organizations. They also believed that a third-party campaign could affect the make-up of the Congress, a crucial point, for if Bryan were elected, a conservative Congress could prevent him achieving free silver. Further, conservative Democrats did not feel altogether certain that McKinley would veto a free silver bill.[6]

Eastern conservatives soon concluded that McKinley was a certain winner in their states and that the crucial points in the campaign were in the Middle West and the Upper South. In those areas it appeared that Democratic voters were being swayed by the arguments of the free silver doctrinaires; and there, too, hostility to McKinley and Republicanism might give Bryan votes which he would not win only on the basis of his free silver speeches.[7] It was in these areas also that conservative Democrats found themselves totally at odds with their local party machines. It was from the middle western region, in the area between Kentucky and Wisconsin and between Indiana and Iowa, that the movement for a third-party Democratic campaign materialized. It was here that the candidates of the new party were found. It was here that the new party developed its most successful state organizations.

The South did not lack conservative Democrats who found Bryan and his platform distasteful, but few southern Democrats were willing to destroy party unity and invite the breakdown of white supremacy by joining a third-party movement. Local and state machines had long since fallen into the control of the free silverites, and southern opinion strongly favored free silver.[8] In these circumstances the action of southern conservative Democrats was individualistic and diverse. The reactions of southerners in Cleveland's Cabinet were typical of this individualism and diversity. Navy Secretary Hilary Herbert was the first to act. Right after the Chicago convention, without consultation with Cleveland or other members of the Cabinet, he declared that he would not support the Chicago platform or ticket.[9] Postmaster General William L. Wilson, strongly opposed to the action taken in Chicago, elected to remain quiet on intra-party politics, though he continued to speak against free silver.

Secretary of the Interior Hoke Smith who had fought free silver earlier, found it expedient to declare in his Atlanta newspaper that he supported Bryan and the platform. After a painful exchange of letters with Cleveland, Smith resigned from the Cabinet. Though Cleveland expressed some sympathy in the abstract for the southern conservative politician who was torn between the issues of the campaign and the question of continuing local Democratic control, he reflected in writing to Smith his inability to reconcile himself to cooperation by any member of his administration with the forces which had so bitterly attacked him.[10]

Josiah Patterson, who had been the leading southern opponent of free silver, ran for Congress on a sound money platform but supported the regular national ticket of Bryan and Sewall in the interest of party unity and white supremacy.[11] As a result the only Democratic congressional candidate in the South who campaigned for sound money and for the third-party Democratic ticket was William P. Breckinridge of Kentucky.

In the free silver West the local state Democratic machines had not been strong. Therefore, the defeat of the conservative Democrats had but slight impact on that region.

Middle western conservatives, accustomed to looking to the East for leadership, soon discovered that the regular party leaders were either unwilling to lead or lacking in understanding of the local situation in the Middle West. Cleveland was uncertain about his role. Though he detested every aspect of the party's action at Chicago, he regretted Herbert's haste in repudiating it. He felt, and generally the Cabinet agreed with him, that he and his official family should remain comparatively aloof from the political controversy.

William C. Whitney was not persuaded that eastern Democrats should take the lead in organizing opposition to Bryan. They were not threatened by loss of local control, and they had just witnessed at the Chicago convention the strong distrust elsewhere in the country of any movement bearing an eastern label.[12] Other leaders, like Senators David B. Hill, George Gray of Delaware, and Arthur P. Gorman, were restrained from leadership of a third-party movement by recognition of the fact that control over their local organizations was neatly balanced between distaste for the issues of the campaign as defined at Chicago and the attractions of party regularity.[13] In the end men in their positions stayed with Bryan and the party in some fashion or other, Hill by silent acquiescence, Gray and Gorman by active participation in the Bryan campaign. The only eastern Democratic group willing to give consistent and hearty support to a third-party movement proved to be the Sound Currency Committee of the New York Reform Club. This organization provided encouragement and guidance to middle western Democrats who acted to bring an independent political organization into existence.[14]

It was the conservative Democrats of Indiana, Illinois, Wisconsin, and Kentucky who played the major role in developing what became known as the National Democratic party.[15] The regular Democratic machines in Indiana, Illinois, and Kentucky were under free silver control before the Chicago convention; and after that convention the regular organization in Wisconsin had elected to support the Chicago platform and nominations. The result was a division between conservative and free silver Democrats in Wisconsin on the same lines as in other states; and, as elsewhere, the conservatives found themselves without effective party representation.[16]

The first call for a second national Democratic convention was issued from Chicago by the same men who had set up a sound currency propaganda committee there in 1895 at the urging of the New York Reform Club. They now called themselves "The Honest Money Democracy of Illinois."[17] William D. Bynum of Indiana, who during

1895 had been the most ardent middle western agent of the New York Reform Club, picked up the Illinois call and began to agitate for a conference of sound money Democrats of the mid-states region. As a result, on July 23 conservative Democrats from Illinois, Indiana, Iowa, Kentucky, Michigan, Minnesota, Missouri, Nebraska, Ohio, and Wisconsin met in Chicago. At the conclusion of their conference they adopted a resolution, "That it is the sense of this conference that there be a Democratic platform enunciated, and a Democratic ticket nominated...." [18] They arranged for an organizational meeting in Indianapolis on August 7 and declared that they would hold a national nominating convention on or before September 2. They set up an executive committee of five with General Bragg of Wisconsin as chairman and Henry S. Robbins of Illinois as secretary. Bynum was a member, along with William S. Haldeman, editor of the Louisville *Courier-Journal*, and J. O. Broadhead of Missouri.[19]

Eastern conservatives gave their moral support, agreeing readily that such a movement might be useful in swinging middle western and even southern states to McKinley; but they resisted direct involvement. The middle western and southern leaders, already half persuaded by their experience in the Chicago convention that the eastern conservatives were unreliable allies, were actively hostile when it became apparent that eastern conservatives were disposed to urge them on from the sidelines without becoming directly engaged in the contest themselves.[20] Their suspicions were strengthened when, on the very day that the call for a third-party Democratic convention was issued from Chicago, Whitney published in New York a plea to the Republican party to abandon its campaign policy of emphasizing protection and ignoring the financial issue, lest this policy drive conservative Democrats to third-party action. He said that it was apparent that the free silver vote was to be united and that upon McKinley rested the responsibility of organizing a campaign which would unite the sound money vote.[21]

Middle western and southern conservatives did not wait for McKinley to speak out. On July 25 Bynum wrote to President Cleveland on stationery bearing the head, "Sound Money National Democratic Party," and listing the members of the executive committee appointed only two days earlier in Chicago. Bynum wrote that their action might appear ill advised to those not acquainted with conditions in the western states, but to conservatives in that section a third ticket appeared to be necessary to maintain a Democratic organization for the future and to win an electoral victory for sound money in 1896. Without a third-party ticket, Bynum warned, the Democratic silver ticket would win every state west of the Ohio River.[22] On July 27 Henry Watterson wrote to Whitney, "If there be no third ticket the Bryan ticket will carry most of the Southern States. If there be a third ticket it will lose most of them." Watterson also pointed out that if they did not organize now, after the election, no matter what the results were, conservative Democrats would have no place to turn for party affiliation but to the Populists or the Republicans.[23]

Middle western conservatives, having seized the initiative, worked energetically to give substance to the skeletal framework they had constructed. They began a careful canvass of the Middle West and South for candidates for their national ticket. They set up organizations in their own and in nearby states and rallied like minded friends to support of the movement. They discussed the possibility of holding state conventions and running state campaigns to parallel the national campaign. As the time approached for the Indianapolis conference preliminary to the convention, they worried over it, particularly concerned that eastern states should send delegations which would try to discourage them from setting up an independent third party.[24]

Middle westerners in their disappointment that eastern conservatives were not as anxious as they were to set up a third party exaggerated eastern hostility to the movement. Bynum, interviewed in Indianapolis on the eve of the preliminary organizational meeting, said that he expected that of the thirty-five delegations in attendance five or six, all from the East or South, would be hostile to independent action.[25] Actually the conference acted with speed and unanimity to issue a call for a nominating convention at Indianapolis on September 2. Charles Tracey, the head of the New York delegation, proved to be one of the most energetic participants in the conference and became a member of the executive committee which was set up to make the detailed arrangements for the convention.[26]

Once conservative Democrats had decided to hold a third-party convention, they faced two major questions: what men should they put at the head of their ticket? And, should they attempt to set up complete state organizations?

Though the candidates of the new party had no chance to win the election, a number of distinguished Democrats became keenly interested in seeking the nomination. It was early assumed that the best ticket would link a distinguished northern conservative with a similarly distinguished and conservative southerner. It was hoped further that both would be military men, that in fact they might succeed in developing a ticket in which a Union general as presidential nominee would be linked with a Confederate general as the vice-presidential candidate. Thus, Generals Edward S. Bragg of Wisconsin and John M. Palmer of Illinois were leading candidates for the presidential nomination.[27] There was also some discussion of Cleveland, Carlisle, and Morton as potential candidates; but Cleveland, though he approved of the movement, viewed with jaundiced eye active participation in it by members of his administration.[28] Henry Watterson, who was mentioned as a prospective candidate, was in Europe; and his candidacy was hampered by a misunderstanding regarding his availability.[29]

The question of the development of state organizations was for the most part answered in the negative. Time was short, and public support was limited. There was some desire among conservative Democrats in the Middle West and Upper South to have some local party machinery in existence to which to turn after the election, but this objective was shortly subordinated to the uses which were made of the movement in the national campaign to defeat Bryan.

William D. Bynum was appointed chairman of the provisional executive committee which was set up during the Indianapolis conference to manage the movement prior to the nominating convention. He found that all he had to work with were the provisional, self appointed chairmen of the cooperating state organizations. In most instances these men had very tenuous organizations in the states over which they claimed control. They were, however, the only agents available to him. He instructed them that they had the duty of organizing the sound money Democrats in their states and of superintending the election or appointment of delegates to the national convention. He wrote to the state chairmen recommending that they exercise their powers broadly and informally in drawing up lists of convention delegates. He promised them that whatever the method used to select delegates they would be "regularly accredited" in the convention upon the certificate of the state chairman.[30]

The third-party Democrats succeeded in holding a convention and launching a campaign only through the persistence of a few determined but relatively unknown leaders. Few men with prolonged experience in government or professional politics remained in the movement to its end. In Wisconsin, for example, Senator Vilas, who helped create the movement and who served as chairman of the platform committee at the national convention, withdrew in a huff mid-way in the campaign, leaving the battle in that state in the comparatively inexperienced hands of General Bragg and the LaCrosse newspaper editor, Ellis B. Usher.[31] In Illinois the movement found an able and experienced but superannuated leader in John M. Palmer. Palmer was aided by Chicago business men who dabbled in politics but who knew few of the tricks and possessed little of the dogged persistence of the professional politician. The leaders in Indiana, William D. Bynum and John Wilson, were able men but not well known political figures. Across the country in New York Whitney played with the idea of forthright cooperation with the movement, but in the end left such action to men like Tracey, who had no established political reputation. The President and his Cabinet remained aloof.[32]

The convention held in Indianapolis on September 2 and 3 was perfunctory. The platform had been prepared in advance by Senator Vilas at the request of Chairman Bynum.[33] It denounced protection, "and its ally, free coinage of silver, as schemes for the personal profit of a few at the expense of the masses...." It declared for the gold standard and for "a uniform, safe, and elastic bank currency, under Governmental supervision, measured in volume by the needs of business." It praised the Cleveland administration, advocated civil service reform, pledged maintenance of the independence and authority of the Supreme Court, and declared opposition to all forms of governmental paternalism.[34]

The nomination of the presidential candidate produced agitation in the convention only because some of the delegates insisted upon placing Cleveland's name in nomination. Those in the convention who knew Cleveland's attitudes were aware that he would not accept; but not until the chairman of the New York delegation sent a telegram to Cleveland asking him if he would be a candidate and had received the President's reply that he was "unalterably opposed," did the delegates desist.[35] Palmer and Bragg were nominated for the Presidency, and the convention balloted. When Palmer won the nomination, Bragg rose, asked that the nomination be unanimous, and the convention so acted.[36] The nomination of the Confederate general, Simon Bolivar Buckner, as the vice-presidential candidate, completed a ticket composed of venerable heroes of the Civil War. It was believed that they would be useful symbols in a campaign which would bear down heavily on the themes of national patriotism and unity.

After the convention adjourned, the national committee of the new party—the National Democratic party—stayed over another day in Indianapolis to plan the strategy of the campaign. It was decided that Bynum should continue in the office of national chairman. He announced that national headquarters was to be in Chicago and that there would be a branch office in New York. He said that the main fight would be in Illinois, Indiana, Iowa, Kentucky, Michigan, and Wisconsin. Hence the Chicago office was in a pivotal location.[37]

Republicans, particularly in the Middle West, were gleeful over the launching of the new party. Soon after the Chicago convention Senator Allison, writing to General Dodge, had expressed the belief that the western states would be "absolutely safe for us" if the conservative Democrats put up another ticket. He also predicted that this would have an immediate effect on the nation's business, for business men would conclude that the Republicans were going to win and this would result in a business revival.[38] After the Indianapolis convention the young Republican strategist, Charles G. Dawes, wrote: "General Palmer's nomination was surely very pleasing to us all, and of the fact that he will secure a good many votes which otherwise would have gone to the Bryan ticket, there can be no doubt." [39]

Bryan gave little attention to the new party in his campaign. However, on the day the National Democratic party convened in Indianapolis Bryan was speaking in Springfield, Ohio; and on this occasion he ridiculed the new party with the vivid figures of speech which came so readily to his tongue:

> I understand that these gold standard Democrats have declared their emblem to be the hickory tree. We have heard about Satan stealing the livery of Heaven, but we have never before seen men try to use the name of that great hero and statesman to undo all that he tried to do. Talk about Andrew Jackson belonging to the gold Democracy! Go back to the time of Andrew Jackson, and who were arrayed against him? The very classes which, after having failed in their effort to use the Democratic party for private gain, are now trying to elect the Republican candidate for President by nominating a gold standard candidate. Take a hickory stick for their emblem? Why do they not take something more appropriate? Why do they not put upon their

ballot the picture of an owl? Nothing could be more appropriate. It looks wise and does its work in the dark. Or, if they do not like the owl, let them take the mole. It is a smooth animal and works underground all the time. But they ought to spare the sacred memory of the man who was the hero of New Orleans, and whose resting place, the Hermitage, is the Mecca of all who love Democratic principles still.[40]

The National Democrats from the first found themselves uncomfortably in the no man's land of the campaign, open to attack from all sides. Even conservative Democrats, who might at least have refrained from criticism, accused them of harming the cause of sound money by dividing the supporters of McKinley.[41]

There was, of course, little quibbling among the National Democrats over the question of backing McKinley. It was of small consequence that they had their own ticket, for there was no expectation of victory for Palmer and Buckner. Even their presidential candidate, speaking in Missouri in the final stages of the campaign said, "If this vast crowd casts its vote for William McKinley next Tuesday, I shall charge them with no sin." [42] General Edward S. Bragg, who conducted a hard, devoted campaign in Wisconsin, wrote: "There are a good many not yet prepared to swallow McK—but in *private conversation* —I have so far advised it—I come pretty near to it on the platform." [43] At the end of the campaign in West Virginia, Senator Camden advised fellow gold Democrats: "The way to make votes count is to throw them to McKinley." [44]

One factor caused some in the new party to be more reserved in their support of McKinley. That was the hope that this party would become the base for the continuation of the Democratic party, if they accomplished Bryan's defeat. The chairman of the party in Wisconsin, Ellis B. Usher, warned campaigners in that state against "overdoing the McKinley act." He pointed out that under state law the party, to qualify to get on the ballot in the next election, had to poll at least 2 per cent of the total vote cast.[45] There were many like Usher who believed that Bryan's victory in Chicago had destroyed the Democratic party and that they, in their third-party effort, were keeping alight the flickering flame of Democratic opposition to governmental paternalism.[46]

However, the mounting hysteria of the campaign tended to subordinate any thought of party organization for the future to the desperately felt need to win a McKinley victory in November. Most men who joined the National Democratic party were using it chiefly to bring victory to sound money and to McKinley. William D. Bynum, the national chairman of the movement, was interested mainly in the monetary issue. Cleveland and the men associated with him gave verbal support to the movement but did not affiliate directly with it, a strong indication that they envisaged it as of very little use beyond the period of the campaign.

The campaign itself started auspiciously at a notification meeting for Palmer and Buckner in Louisville, Kentucky, on September 12. Bynum invited Cleveland to be present. As a result he was able to arouse the meeting by reading a telegram from Buzzard's Bay expressing Cleveland's regret that he could not be in Louisville but stating: "As a democrat devoted to the principles and integrity of my party I should be delighted to be present on an occasion so significant and mingle with those who are determined that the voice of true democracy shall not be smothered and who insist that its glorious standard shall still be borne aloft as of old in faithful hands." [47]

Bynum and his co-workers, who had so effectively engineered the creation of the new party and the nomination of Palmer and Buckner, failed signally to organize a successful campaign. After the Louisville notification meeting Bynum went to New York, which was designated as an auxiliary to Chicago headquarters. In New York Bynum tried to raise funds, a difficult task in territory already worked over by Hanna for the McKinley cause. Not until late September, with only a month of the campaign remaining, did Bynum arrive in Chicago to set up national headquarters.[48] He found the key midwestern state organizers disgruntled over his prolonged stay in New York.[49] In Chicago he was dependent upon the cooperation of John H. Hopkins, leader of the sound money Democrats in Illinois. Bynum and Hopkins promptly began to feud with each other, a feud which did not end until several weeks after the election, when Bynum succeeded in having Hopkins expelled from the party. Such personal factionalism plagued the movement in other quarters as well and robbed it of much of its vigor in the last month of the campaign.[50]

Any political movement hoping to achieve permanent status in the United States must establish strong state organizations. Only in the Middle West did National Democratic leaders make any effort to establish local machines. But the men working toward this end were either amateurs, like Usher in Wisconsin, or discredited professionals, like Hopkins in Illinois; and all too often personal factionalism vitiated their efforts.

The National Democratic party was then a curious anomaly. It was hardly "national"; it was doubtfully a "party." One, perhaps, credits it with too much influence in calling it a "movement." Its claim to the name, "Democratic," was, of course, the most controversial point of all. In 1900 Ellis Usher described its condition in 1896 in these terms: "Few . . . know how near our National Committee's campaign came to being an utter and transparent farce. . . . A few of us put up a big 'bluff' and did enough to save being caught at it, but the escape was a close call." [51]

William D. Bynum, without speaking so forcefully, implied much the same thing in replying to the request of a journalist for the names of the officers of the state organizations of the party: "Owing to the very short space of time we had, in which to make the campaign, we were unable to perfect state organizations in a very large number of states, but did our work through the National Committeemen. Hence, I do not desire to publish a list of the state committees, as there would appear so many blanks upon the list as to make a bad showing." [52]

In reality the strongest support for the National Democratic party was found in the Currency Committee of the Reform Club of New York. Calvin Tompkins, the chairman of that Committee, became secretary of the State Committee of the New York National Democratic party; and John Hopkins, chairman of the Chicago branch of the Reform Club, headed the new party in Illinois.[53] In the campaign of education the Reform Club circulated few pamphlets and maintained no more than an embryonic speakers bureau. It concentrated its efforts on furnishing stereotyped plates and printed supplements free of charge to smaller weekly and bi-weekly rural newspapers.[54]

As the campaign progressed, it became clear that the National Democratic party was no more than an adjunct to the Republican campaign. It had two objectives chiefly: first, to neutralize or direct to McKinley as many Democratic votes as possible in the Middle West and Upper South; [55] and, second, to supplement the Republican educational campaign on the monetary issue. It was never strongly supported by large numbers of enthusiastic workers, and it was not lavishly financed. As a campaign organization it was a fiasco. At the end of the campaign it quietly withdrew to the periphery of the political scene, having the good fortune to be able to conceal its weakness in the confusion that attended McKinley's victory.

20

The Republican Campaign:
The Patriotic Heroes' Hero

The Republican campaign was managed along much the same lines as the pre-nomination drive for McKinley. While Hanna energetically supervised a coordinated and efficient organization, McKinley calmly and cautiously practiced the role intended to make him a national symbol for prosperity and patriotism. The degree to which he succeeded in developing this role was conceded implicitly by his opponents in their failure to discover an opening for a direct assault upon him. Instead the opposition was forced to turn the attack upon Hanna; and eventually a considerable part of the voting public came to believe the Democratic-Populist claims that Hanna, whom they portrayed as the exploiting capitalist supreme, possessed a domineering mastery of McKinley.

The popularly accepted picture of Hanna's domination was not true. Though McKinley did leave to Hanna the immensely complicated and exceedingly arduous task of organizing the campaign and though he usually deferred to Hanna's judgment in this area, he himself retained control of the general structure and program. Nothing of significance was done without his approval. Hanna raised money, hired men, set up headquarters offices, bought literature, with the same drive and skill that he managed his business. He was confident of his mastery of that kind of operation, but he never ceased to defer to McKinley's mastery of the grand strategy of politics.

On one point only did McKinley and Hanna develop a major difference—the question of whether or not McKinley should go over the country on a speaking tour to reply to Bryan. Hanna, frightened by the size and enthusiasm of the crowds which came out to hear Bryan, had concluded that McKinley and the Republicans must make a similar effort. McKinley was determined that he would not do it. First of all, he believed that he could not compete with Bryan in this sort of thing. According to Herrick, who went with Dawes to Canton at Hanna's request to ask McKinley to go out on tour, McKinley said: "I might just as well put up a trapeze on my front lawn and compete with some professional athlete as go out speaking against Bryan. I have to think when I speak." [1] Beyond this, McKinley believed that the type of campaign which Bryan was conducting disgraced the office which he sought.[2]

The McKinley-Hanna group selected Chicago as national headquarters because of their belief that the upper Middle West was to be the area of decision.[3] For a brief time Hanna played wishfully with the thought that his home, Cleveland, might be the headquarters site; but his co-workers soon persuaded him that Chicago was the essential point.[4] An auxiliary office was established in New York. It was assumed at first that the New York office would be of minor significance. At the beginning of the campaign Dawes wrote that it was to be "more the basis for supplies than anything else." [5] In a sense national headquarters was wherever Hanna happened to be, and he spent a considerable part of his time in New York and Cleveland as well as Chicago. In the final weeks of the campaign, however, he stayed in Chicago, the crucial center of the doubtful midwest.

The axes of the Republican campaign became Canton, Chicago, and New York; and the men who made the grand strategy decisions and who controlled their execution at these axes were the men who had headed the pre-convention organization which had accomplished McKinley's nomination at St. Louis. Hanna was in charge of both the New York and Chicago offices. In Chicago his chief aide and confidante was Charles G. Dawes. His right-hand man in the New York office was William McKinley Osborne. Charles Dick became secretary of the Chicago office; and Perry Heath was placed in charge of publications, an assignment of major significance because of the importance which the distribution of pamphlets assumed in the campaign.[6] Another of McKinley's Ohio friends, William M. Hahn, was put in charge of the speakers bureau at Chicago.

In Canton McKinley's local staff work was under the direction of his secretary, James Boyle, while the staff work on the national level, including coordination with the Chicago and New York headquarters, was handled by Joe Smith. Osborne and Dawes reported regularly to McKinley and Smith and also to Hanna, whenever they were not in personal contact with him; for McKinley and Hanna, as in the pre-nomination campaign, were indisputably in charge of the entire operation all the time. Again their mastery was never prominently in evidence, because they delegated responsibility to their trusted aides in such a fashion that they were never burdened with details.

Several men new to the McKinley organization were brought into the campaign headquarters at Chicago and New York. In the Chicago headquarters Henry Payne of Wisconsin became a valued adviser, and William T. Durbin of Indiana and Albert B. Cummins of Iowa aided Dawes and Hanna in various ways.[7] Expedience dictated more conspicuous use in the New York headquarters of men who had not been on the McKinley bandwagon during the pre-nomination campaign. With some urgency McKinley and Hanna sought the consent of Matthew Quay to serve on the national campaign committee. When Quay agreed, he was placed in nominal command of the New York office.[8] Cornelius Bliss, who worked from the New York office, was made treasurer of the national campaign, an important post at the "basis of supplies." Hobart, Manley, and Nathaniel B. Scott of West Virginia also worked at New York, providing some of the basic concepts upon which the campaign in the East was developed.[9]

Men like Quay and Bliss, who were relative outsiders in the McKinley-Hanna organization, never gained the intimacy with either McKinley or Hanna possessed by Dawes and Osborne.[10] When a private telephone line was established between the New York and Chicago headquarters, the telephones were installed in the offices of Dawes and Osborne.[11] The letter files available show an intimate correspondence among Hanna, Dawes, Osborne, and McKinley in which Quay, Bliss, Payne, and the other newcomers did not share. When Dawes drew money from New York, he preferred to draw it through Osborne rather than Bliss.[12] In mid-October, at the height of the campaign, Quay felt his presence at the New York office of so little consequence that he withdrew and spent the duration of the campaign in Pennsylvania.[13]

There seemed to be no developments which Hanna and his staff in the Chicago office did not anticipate and act to control. They informed themselves on every facet of the campaign, even having spies at Democratic headquarters.[14] The journal, the campaign letterbooks and the other records preserved by Dawes reveal the prodigious efforts of the Chicago group. Dawes, who was in charge of the funds expended from the Chicago office, set up an accounting system similar to that of a private business. He even insisted upon competetive bids in placing contracts for materials.[15]

McKinley would follow his own course at Canton, where he was skillfully tying sound money and protection together and swaddling the hybrid result in the American flag; but the headquarters at Chicago assumed the major responsibility for a popular educational campaign requiring the distribution of millions of pamphlets and the arrangement of the itineraries of hundreds of speakers. From Chicago huge bundles of literature, often in carload lots, were shipped over the country.[16] In his final report on the expenditures of the campaign at the Chicago office, Dawes stated that the total expenses of the literary department for printing alone were $469,079.84, a sum which must have purchased several hundred million pamphlets. A further indication of the immensity of the task of distributing literature from the Chicago headquarters is found in Dawes' final report on the expenses of the shipping department, which were $42,693.84, not including salaries.[17]

From Chicago, too, arrangements were made to send speakers over the country. Thus, Nils Haugen of Wisconsin was employed to go into the state of Washington to speak to the Scandinavians there on the campaign issues.[18] In mid-September Dawes wrote that Chicago headquarters at that time had two hundred and fifty speakers working in the twenty-seven states under its jurisdiction.[19]

Another important feature of the work at the Chicago headquarters office was the organization of specially staffed campaign bureaus and departments to appeal to special interest groups. In his final statement of expenditures Dawes listed the costs of maintaining a "Colored Bureau," a woman's department, an organization for bicycling enthusiasts, a German department, and a traveling salesmen's bureau, all working out of Chicago headquarters.[20] In addition the Chicago office provided $7,775 for the National Republican League and contributed $274,189.64 to the campaign expenses of organizations not directly affiliated with the national or local Republican campaign committees.[21]

The largest expenditure reported by Dawes was in the distribution of money to the state organizations, an amount which came finally to $902,752.54 from the Chicago headquarters alone. There is no record of how these contributions were finally broken down, but Dawes' papers contain a few reports of how the money was distributed among the states in the early phases of the campaign.[22] On September 18 he wrote to Hanna that he had so far sent $140,250 to the states under his jurisdiction and provided the following tabulation of how the money had been distributed: [23]

Illinois	$19,050	Kansas	$14,500
Utah	5,000	Washington	10,000
Nebraska	15,000	Indiana	15,000
Wyoming	5,000	Kentucky	3,500
South Dakota	6,200	North Dakota	2,000
Minnesota	12,200	Oregon	5,000
Idaho	50	Michigan	10,250
Iowa	12,500	Texas	5,000

The money thus sent out to the states was usually, but not always, turned over to the official Republican campaign committee of the state.[24]

In the early stages of the campaign the money which Dawes handled at Chicago was in comparatively small amounts—less than $100,000 a week; but when the campaign was at its peak, he appeared to have an insatiable need for money. Hanna and Bliss saw to it that the supply was equal to his need. His papers contain a copy of a note dated October 20 to Cornelius Bliss saying that on that day he would draw on New York for $200,000 and that for the succeeding three days he would draw $100,000 each day.[25]

Thus, all the exigencies of the middle western campaign were liberally financed. Undoubtedly the amount of money furnished by the Republican national committee to any one of the middle western states greatly exceeded the amount available to the Populist party for its entire national campaign. Under the supervision of Hanna and Dawes nothing was forgotten. Arrangements were made to provide McKinley whatever helpers and money he needed in Canton; and Dawes, under instructions from Hanna, arranged that money from the Chicago campaign fund should be placed in a personal checking account for McKinley in a Cleveland bank.[26] The men who organized the work at Canton for the reception and entertainment of visitors were liberally supplied with funds.[27]

The low order of priority at first assigned to the New York office was based on the assumption that the sections of the country assigned to its jurisdiction—the Atlantic Coast and the southern states to the Mississippi—were either safely for McKinley or incurably Democratic. Later in the campaign some uncertainty developed about the eastern seaboard states and the national campaign committee became convinced that the South was not so unassailably Democratic as had been assumed.[28] As a result the New York office mounted a more extensive campaign than had been planned. For example, the first plan of operation called for all of the literature of the campaign to be ordered and distributed from the Chicago office.[29] When the New York headquarters became committed to a more ambitious campaign, this arrangement proved to be too clumsy; and the New York office made its own contracts for large quantities of literature.[30] Dawes, in his final report on expenditures, estimated that the New York headquarters had spent about $1,600,000 on all phases of its campaign, as compared with the $1,962,325.50 spent at Chicago headquarters; but he did not attempt to give a detailed accounting of how the money had been spent in New York.[31]

One participant in the Republican campaign in Virginia claimed that the Republican national committee gave the Republican state organization $160,000 and in addition provided funds liberally for the gold Democrats.[32] The Republican national committee also had some hopes of carrying Florida, and close observers of the campaign there claimed that the state committee received large contributions from New York headquarters.[33] There was little doubt that this phase of the campaign in the East was handled much as it was west of the Alleghenies, that is, by the lavish distribution of funds to those areas where the result was in doubt but where the possibility of Republican victory existed. On the other hand, areas where there was little chance of victory—most notably certain of the Rocky Mountain states, where in former years Republican funds had been so lavishly available—received virtually nothing.[34]

Hanna and his co-workers planned an extensive campaign of education on the assumption that the nation's business men would duly contribute the necessary funds. In the early stages of the campaign, when business men proved not so willing and protested that they were not able to open their pocketbooks as Hanna and Dawes had anticipated, there was mild alarm at Republican headquarters and some discussion of scaling down their operations.[35] However, when Hanna turned his talents to the management of this phase of the campaign and on a tour in the East centering on New York, Boston, and Philadelphia personally solicited funds, the financial situation rapidly improved. In the final crucial month of the campaign Dawes' papers contain no hint that the campaign lacked funds for any purpose. The last accounting which Dawes preserved indicated that the Republican campaign treasury had a surplus after paying all expenses.[36]

Dawes' papers contain a few records of individual contributions, which reveal the manner in which the money came in. In an entry in his journal on September 11 he said that Hanna, during lunch, handed him an envelope containing fifty $1,000 bills, the contribution of a railroad (unnamed). On the same day he deposited a check for $50,000, which he had received as a contribution from another unidentified source.[37] On October 1 he wrote Hanna that he had received Hanna's letter containing a check for $35,000 from E. H. Harriman,[38] and on October 3 he wrote Hanna that John W. Gates had given him a draft for $12,500.[39] On October 10 he wrote a letter to Marshall Field thanking him for his contribution of $4,000.[40] In a newspaper interview the president of a Philadelphia bank explained that his bank contributed $25,000 to McKinley's campaign to protect the funds of its depositors. "During the ten years I have been president of this institution," he said, "we have never before contributed a cent to politics, but the present crisis we believe to be as important as the war." [41]

It was in this way, day after day, that the money came, not sparingly in small contributions from ordinary people, but in sums of hundreds and thousands of dollars from the wealthy men of the nation. The impression developed in the years following this campaign that it was notable chiefly for Hanna's businesslike expenditure of large sums of money for the usual purposes of politics. It was not, however, for the usual purposes of politics that business men in 1896 made their large contributions to Hanna. These contributors were often men who had not supported the McKinley campaign before St. Louis and who did not particularly like Hanna. Many of them were Democrats. They believed that Hanna had become their leader in the fight which they were forced to undertake to preserve their wealth and the system by which they had accumulated it.

Various estimates of the amount of money spent in the Republican campaign have been published.[42] None can be more than an approximation. The only figures of any reliability are those available in Dawes' papers. They are undoubtedly accurate and virtually complete for the Chicago office but are only a general estimate of the expenditures of the New York headquarters. Dawes' figures indicate a total expenditure by the national campaign committee of between $3,500,000 and $4,000,000. Some additional money was raised by the state committees, but it was not likely that this was a large amount, nor was it likely that much of this money was spent on the national campaign. It must be remembered that the Chicago office alone furnished over $900,000 to the state committees. The known figures from the Dawes papers represent a very large amount, particularly when compared with the pitifully inadequate finances available to the Bryan campaign from Democratic, Populist, or National Silver party headquarters.[43]

With Chicago established as the effective center for the organiza- of the crusade, it was a typical stroke of McKinley's political genius to make Canton a Holy Land for visiting pilgrims. In the weeks prior to the election men by the hundreds and thousands, apparently unbidden, in reality carefully mobilized by the Republican campaign organization, traveled from all sections of the country to visit McKinley in his home town. The delegations came from small towns and large cities, from farms and workshops, as representatives of various groups, political and non-political. They came not for intellectual guidance, not to be informed upon public issues by words of instruction from McKinley, but to worship at the shrine of the man who was becoming known as "the advance agent of prosperity," and to wave flags at the man who aspired to make his own picture interchangeable with the flag as a symbol of patriotism. There, too, through the weeks of the campaign, came many of the leading men of the Republican party. With little of the fanfare of the visiting delegations they came into town, were closeted with McKinley, and then quietly went home.[44] John Hay, who came in mid-October, recorded his impressions in a letter to Henry Adams. He had been dreading the visit, "thinking it would be like talking in a boiler factory." Reality proved to be pleasantly different. Hay described his reception thus: "he met me at the station, gave me meat, and, calmly leaving his shouting worshippers in the front yard, took me upstairs and talked for two hours as calmly and serenely as if we were summer boarders in Beverly at a loss for a means to kill time." [45]

Everything was managed with extreme circumspection at Canton. Information about each visiting delegation was sent to Canton several days in advance of the visit. If possible, copies of the speeches to be made by the spokesmen for the delegations were obtained; and McKinley suggested changes, if he judged that discretion made them desirable. McKinley's staff, working under the direction of Joseph Smith, made notes on the speeches forwarded by those planning a visit and prepared the remarks which McKinley would make in response. McKinley remembered vividly the disastrous effect that such indiscreet remarks as "Rum, Romanism, and Rebellion," had had on earlier elections. He took no unnecessary risk of losing his years of careful preparation on such a mischance.

The people of Canton were pleased and proud that their town should have become a national political shrine. They happily shouldered the burdens of welcoming and entertaining their visitors in such fashion that they would be imbued with the proper reverence for McKinley. A neighbor of McKinley, Harry Frease, organized a uniformed, mounted company, called the "Canton Home Guards." These men met the trains carrying delegations into Canton. Their first job when a delegation arrived was to find the leader, get his name and the name of the delegation. Once this information was received, one of the "Home Guards" would dash off on his horse and through back streets speed to McKinley's home. There McKinley's secretaries would check into their files to find their notes on the delegation and the notes which had been made for McKinley's speech in greeting them. At the train other members of the "Home Guard" would greet the delegation, arrange to feed the visitors if necessary, and marshal them for the parade to McKinley's home.[46]

These visiting delegations often contained hundreds and sometimes thousands of men and women. Often they brought bands with them and they occasionally had horse-mounted units of their own. At the height of the campaign several delegations visited Canton every day. Captain Frease, reminiscing about the campaign many years later, said a decorated arch had been erected over the street leading to McKinley's house. His "Home Guards" halted each delegation at this point to ascertain that the delegation which had just visited McKinley had made its exit through the arch before another delegation was admitted. When delegations arrived in quick succession, those waiting beyond the arch were delayed for considerable periods of time. Frease recalled that a brewery located directly across the street served to relieve the tedium of the wait.[47] Newspaper reporters and McKinley's Canton friends have described how avidly the visitors sought souvenirs of McKinley. They took fence rails, branches and twigs of trees, leaves, shrubs, blades of grass, and whittled away methodically at the front porch.

As men and women left Canton they carried away an image of a kindly, home-loving man, a public-spirited man, a man endowed with a profound understanding of public affairs, a man of almost supernal patriotism. Senator Thurston summed up the impression which was desired when he contrasted the Bryan and McKinley campaigns:

> One has selected for his arena the sand lots—his appeals are to the passions and prejudices of men. The forum of the other is an American dooryard; his rostrum is the porch of an American cottage; his words, simple and forceful, are addressed to the intelligence, the conscience, the patriotism and the common sense of a brave, thoughtful, just and hopeful people.[48]

What direction did McKinley give to the campaign in greeting his visitors at Canton? Typically he made a strong appeal to the patriotic emotions of his audience. Thus, in one of the first front-porch speeches of the campaign, speaking to the "J. B. Foraker Club" of Cleveland, he said, "In this contest patriotism is above party and National honor is dearer than party name. The currency and credit of the government are good, and must be kept good forever." [49] In speaking to a delegation from Holmes County, Ohio, he said:

> Let us settle once for all that this government is one of honor and of law, and that neither the seeds of repudiation nor lawlessness can find root in our soil or live beneath our flag. That represents all our aims, all our policies, all our purposes. It is the banner of every patriot; it is, thank God, today the flag of every section of our common country. No flag ever triumphed over it. It was never degraded or defeated and will not now be when more patriotic men are guarding it than ever before in our history.[50]

In shaping his election campaign McKinley faced much the same problems and met the same criticisms from within his own party as in his pre-nomination battle. His chief problem was to fix the relative emphasis which he would place on the tariff and money questions. The metropolitan newspapers and the influential eastern leaders of the party assumed that the platform adopted at St. Louis established the foundation for a campaign concentrated on sound money, even though the candidate they had nominated was not altogether appropriate to that platform.

McKinley was not completely happy with the eastern policy of campaigning on a sound money policy, particularly when the arguments for that policy implied that "sound money" meant the gold standard. He believed that the nation's tariff policy remained an issue upon which the Republican party could campaign effectively.[51] He was convinced that his own reputation on the tariff question was a valuable asset to his party and to himself. His personal campaign, comprising mostly the brief speeches he delivered to the visitors in his front yard, unfailingly gave central attention to the tariff.

Occasionally in these weeks Mark Hanna granted newspaper interviews in which he expressed his views on the issues of the campaign. At these times his statements reflected McKinley's desire that the tariff issue be kept in the foreground. On June 23 Hanna was quoted as saying, "The people—I mean the masses—are most deeply concerned about the tariff. Give us a chance to earn some money, is what they are saying just now, and they are not grumbling about the kind of money." [52] A few days later he said that the farmers were interested in silver, but he knew from talking to his own employees that the workingmen of the country believed that prosperity would be restored through a protective tariff.[53] Writing to Benjamin Harrison requesting that he speak at an early date in the campaign, Hanna explained: "The situation confronting us will necessitate something of a change in our plans and may call for our *heavy artillery* early in the fight that the issue may not be switched off to silver." [54]

The issue was "switched off" to silver to a degree which gave little pleasure to either McKinley or Hanna. McKinley, however, quickly developed a technique of linking free silver and free trade as equally dangerous allies of Democratic origin. Hanna soon adopted a similar approach. Thus they kept before the public the familiar image of McKinley the champion of protection while linking him also with the theme of sound money. How effectively McKinley succeeded in cementing the two themes is shown in his front-porch speech to a group of wool producers from Harrison County, Ohio:

It was said [by the Democrats in the campaign of 1892] that if we opened up this country to the free use of the wool of the world the farmers would be benefited. It was done, and with what benefit you know better than I can tell you. Now, they tell you that free silver (laughter) is the panacea for all our ills, (renewed laughter) and you have the same money in circulation now that you had four years ago, but the wool growers haven't got as much of it as you had then. (Cries of 'That's right.') As free wool degraded your industry so free silver will degrade your money. (Applause and cries of 'That's right too.') You have already been fleeced by loss on your flocks and you don't propose to be fleeced further by loss on your money. (Great Cheering.) [55]

Speaking to delegations of industrial workers he managed to combine the two issues with equal success, as is shown in this quotation from a speech to a delegation from the Edgar Thomson Steel Works of Braddock, Pennsylvania:

We know what partial free trade has done for the labor of the United States. It has diminished its employment and earnings. We do not propose now to inaugurate a currency system that will cheat labor in its pay. The laboring men of this country whenever they give one day's work to their employers, want to be paid in full dollars good everywhere in the world . . . We want in this country good work, good wages, and good money.[56]

Many eastern Republicans resented the failure of McKinley to grasp the monetary issue as firmly as they believed he should. After the Democratic convention they felt that there was a particular force to their contention that all issues should be subordinated to the monetary question. Not only was there the forthright Democratic platform statement to be combatted, but the defection of conservative Democrats from their own party had to be considered. These Democrats would cooperate with the Republicans, might even join the party, on the money issue; but they would be frightened away on the tariff issue.[57]

William McKinley, with his middle western perspective, saw that west of the Alleghenies just the reverse might occur—that free silver Republicans and independents, attracted to the party on the tariff issue, might very well abandon it for the Democratic party should the Republicans campaign exclusively on money. As McKinley on August 5 wrote to his Chicago friend, Herman Kohlsaat, "There is this consideration I would like to leave with you: That thousands of men who are somewhat tinctured with Free Silver ideas keep within the Republican party and will support the Republican nominee because of the fact that they are protectionists." [58] In newspaper interviews in this period of the campaign Hanna expressed similar opinions.[59] Also the extensive campaign of the billboards and broadsides, with their graphic cartoons and simple slogans, bore down heavily on the theme of McKinley, the protectionist, as "the advance agent of prosperity" and the guardian of "the full dinner pail." Campaign songs, too, emphasized the relationship between protection and prosperity.

Not all eastern Republicans believed that McKinley should abandon the tariff and campaign on a monetary policy which promised the gold standard. A group in New England, for whom Senator Chandler was the spokesman, advocated a campaign in which the party stood squarely for bimetallism. Chandler recognized the difficulties faced by western Republicans and wanted to give them a tool by which to retain as many western silver enthusiasts as possible.[60] Of significance were the reactions of James Clarkson, who had a keen understanding of political attitudes in both the Middle West and the East. In the middle of the campaign his health had improved sufficiently to enable him to travel from Iowa to New York, where he interviewed Hanna. Clarkson believed that in Iowa the people were bimetallists, and he advised Hanna to avoid giving the impression in the West that Mc-Kinley was a gold monometallist.[61]

The relative emphasis given to the tariff and monetary issues varied from section to section. Throughout the campaign the monetary issue was the dominant theme in the East and the South. In the Middle West the tariff issue shared the stage with finance. In fact, as the campaign progressed, increasing emphasis was given to the tariff in the Middle West. The Republican leaders, reacting to adverse findings in their early polls of public opinion, concluded that the tariff issue was to play a decisive role in that crucially important section.[62] In the Far West Republican campaigners soon relegated the monetary issue to a minor position, and the tariff was made the central feature of their campaign.[63]

Actually contention over the issues was kept at a minimum within the party and occurred only in the early stages of the campaign. The program of education from Chicago and New York headquarters was devoted primarily to the monetary issue, and the eastern "basis of supplies" showed no reluctance to support it. Easterners must also have been pleased with the emphasis and tone of McKinley's letter of acceptance, issued on August 26. It was certain to be one of the most widely distributed documents of the campaign;[64] and though it gave due attention to all the subjects touched upon in the Republican platform, mostly it contained a careful, pedestrian exposition of the sound money argument.

It was typical of McKinley's approach to issues that his discussion of the money question in his letter of acceptance contained an appeal directed especially to the farmers and laborers. They, he said, were the first to suffer from cheap money and the last to recover from its effects.[65] But he could not conclude without making a strong reference to the tariff question:

Protection has lost none of its virtue and importance. The first duty of the Republican party, if restored to power in the country, will be the enactment of a tariff law which will raise all the money necessary to conduct the Government economically and honestly administered, and so adjusted as to give preference to home manufactures and adequate protection to home labor and the home market.[66]

McKinley also supervised with great care the preparation of Hobart's letter of acceptance, which was scheduled to be a major campaign document in the East. It, too, was devoted chiefly to the monetary issue, containing some graphic illustrations of the ill effects of the adoption of free coinage at 16 to 1.[67]

There were two related areas of public policy which McKinley followed with special concern—labor and religion. Over the years McKinley had developed friendly relations with many leaders of organized labor, and these he now used to his advantage. The most widely publicized and perhaps the most helpful support within the labor movement came from Terence V. Powderly, the former Grand Master of the Knights of Labor. Powderly's friendship with McKinley dated back to 1881. Through the intervening years McKinley had often asked Powderly to advise him on his speeches and other political activities. In 1896 McKinley asked Powderly to undertake a speaking campaign for the Republican cause in the industrial centers of the country. Powderly toured the country, defending protective tariffs and the stand taken by the Republican platform on money.[68]

Mark Hanna was more sympathetic toward labor, organized and unorganized, than most industrialists. The Democratic and Populist campaigners tried to develop the theme that Hanna exploited his own workers and was hostile to organized labor, but they were not able to present convincing evidence of their accusations. Perhaps the Democrats were somewhat reluctant to put strong emphasis on this theme because their vice-presidential candidate, Sewall, was vulnerable to a similar type of attack regarding his treatment of the men whom he employed on his shipping lines.

McKinley scrutinized the discussion of labor issues in the press and in campaign speeches, and he took care to reply to arguments that might cause laboring men to be critical of him or his party. He took pains also to reply to letters from laboring men requesting information about his policies or criticizing them.[69] For example, when one of his remarks to the effect that working men should be paid in dollars of full value for a full day's labor was construed to make him say that a dollar a day was a sufficient wage for a man, McKinley replied to inquiring working men denying that he had said that a dollar a day was a fair wage and explaining how the misunderstanding had occurred.[70] Typical, too, of McKinley's approach to the labor vote was the careful analysis of the possible impact of Payne's anti-labor reputation before his appointment to the national executive committee was cleared.[71]

With the religious issue McKinley adopted quite different tactics, avoiding comment and dodging explanation as much as possible, making the most of his role as an innocent man under attack by malicious bigots. By the middle of the summer the controversy excited by the activities of the American Protective Association had created a situation highly favorable to McKinley. The only danger which he faced now was the occurrence of some accidental, embarrassing incident which would deprive him of the support of Catholic voters in the urban centers of the nation. The APA itself undoubtedly favored the Republican over the Democratic party and McKinley over Bryan. They held to this attitude throughout the campaign in spite of the fact that the McKinley-Hanna organization openly courted Catholic support. One of the major developments of the campaign was the announcement by Archbishop Ireland of the St. Paul diocese that he supported McKinley in opposition to the "socialistic" proposals of the Democrats.[72] In the years following the campaign rumors persisted that the Republicans in certain areas had given campaign money to the Catholic Church.[73] The McKinley-Hanna organization was aware of the strategic importance of Catholic voters in the nation's urban centers and particularly of the Catholic voters in the growing midwestern cities. The APA attack on McKinley initiated an orientation on the part of these voters toward McKinley and the Republican party. The McKinley-Hanna organization took every step possible to consolidate this drift without at the same time antagonizing the majority Protestant blocs.

One of the major themes of the Republican campaign was the significance of McKinley as a patriotic leader. This emphasis upon McKinley's patriotism was hardly a new departure for his campaign managers. In the St. Louis convention in June Hanna had inaugurated the practice of distributing buttons carrying merely a replica of the American flag as McKinley buttons. From that moment this became one of the major themes of the Republican campaign—that McKinley's patriotism made him a national symbol coequal with the flag. The Republican campaign committee bought millions of flags and distributed them over the country to be used wherever McKinley and Hobart demonstrations were staged.[74]

The emphasis on a campaign of patriotism became particularly popular among upper-middle-class conservatives, Republican and Democratic, in the large urban centers of the country. It was Mark Hanna, however, who first suggested to them a plan of action, which as it was developed, seemed to become for these business and professional men a spontaneous demonstration of their patriotism. What Hanna suggested was the declaration in great cities like New York, Chicago, and San Francisco of a flag day in honor of McKinley, a moment, preferably on the weekend before the election, when the people could demonstrate their Republican convictions by marching under the nation's banner.[75]

The careful guidance and lavish funds usually evident in Republican campaign efforts were not lacking in the preparations for the flag day demonstrations. Flags in all sizes, lithograph display posters, buttons, hats, horns, and all the miscellaneous paraphernalia that go into the making of a successful parade were supplied. Also in evidence was something of greater significance. The dignified, the respectable, the well-to-do in cities the country over joined in the preparations with an air of conviction and sober purpose. It was as if they were entering upon a crusade or rallying for war. And they enlisted their employees in the demonstrations with slight regard for their personal wishes or convictions, assuming that they would be willing to march the streets to show their love of country and McKinley.[76]

In New York, which put on the biggest show, the flag parade was organized by the Business Men's Sound Money Association, acting under the guidance of General Horace Porter. Porter, a protective tariff enthusiast, was one of the original McKinley men in New York.[77] More than 100,000 men turned out to parade in New York on Saturday morning, October 31; and more than 750,000 people crowded the streets to cheer them. The New York *Tribune* published this impression of the occasion:

The flag was everywhere. It flaunted from every window; it waved from every portico; it flew from every roof; it floated over almost every street, and many times in every block. The marching thousands tramped between walls of human faces that were almost entirely folded in the stripes and dotted with the stars, while every man in the whole vast line carried a flag of his own which he held aloft in token that it was for the flag and all that it stood for that he was marching in peace, as he would willingly march in war, if need should be. Many of those who marched yesterday have known what it is to march in war under the same flag that covered the city in its folds yesterday all the day long.[78]

In Chicago one of the principal events of the demonstration was an evening meeting in which the major address was delivered by Mark Hanna. Everyone in the audience was provided with a small flag to wave at the speaker.[79] In San Francisco the great sound money parade lasted four hours.[80] In Canton McKinley made his contribution to the day in speaking to a delegation of the employees of the National Carbon Company of Cleveland. Speaking of the flag, he said:

It is a holy banner. No flag represents as much as it does; it represents liberty, it represents equality, it represents opportunity, it represents possibilities for American manhood obtainable in no other land beneath the sun.

I am glad to know that the American workingmen have arrayed themselves on the side of country, patriotism, peace, progress, protection, and prosperity.[81]

The Republican appropriation of the national flag as their campaign banner left Democratic campaign organizers in an infuriatingly frustrating position. After Hanna issued the call for a national flag day in terms that made it at the same time a demonstration for McKinley, the Democratic chairman, Jones, and Bryan attempted to neutralize the effect of Hanna's action by asking Democrats to join the demonstration as a tribute to the flag and the flag alone.[82] This gesture by the Democratic party had no effect whatever. It was inevitable that some ardent Democrats would resent the display of the flag in connection with the McKinley-Hobart campaign and in anger would tear down flags that were so used. As soon as the Democrats became principals in such incidents, the Republicans pointed to their actions as further proof of the lack of patriotism among the Democrats.[83]

Middle-class conservatives turned so readily to a campaign of patriotism, because they saw in the Bryan movement the threat of revolution. William D. Bynum wrote that if Bryan won, the nation would be unable "to escape the terrors of the mob." He therefore felt that in opposing Bryan he was "engaged in the performance of a patriotic duty." [84] Conservatives who reached such conclusions were stimulated to a more intense patriotic effort when they discovered in the circumstances of 1896 similarities to the Civil War crisis of 1861. "It is a good deal to my mind like the issue of 1861," wrote Senator Spooner of Wisconsin; and Henry Cabot Lodge believed that those who fought Bryan were "fighting to save the country from a disaster which would be second only to 1861." [85]

Under such conditions those who were campaigning against Bryan found it expedient to use surviving soldiers of the Civil War, either Union or Confederate, in conspicuous campaign roles. No opportunity to bring McKinley's Civil War career to public attention was passed up; and, of course, Generals Palmer and Buckner had been chosen in great part because of the unique patriotic appeal, North and South, of their Civil War records.

General Alger devised a novel campaign plan on the theme of wartime patriotism. He drew together a group of Union officers and enlisted men into an organization called the "Patriotic Heroes' Battalion." This group included Generals Daniel E. Sickles and Oliver O. Howard, Corporal James Tanner, "Lem" Wiley, General Sickles' wartime bugler, and many others. The "Patriotic Heroes," traveling on a special train made up of three Pullman coaches and a flatcar on which a cannon was mounted, toured exclusively in the critical Middle West. When they appeared in Indianapolis in mid-October, their cars were vividly decked with banners carrying such slogans as "1896 is as vitally important as 1861," "For the honor of our country," and "The State of Morton will never surrender to the champion of anarchy." [86]

In giving careful attention to emotional appeals to the voters the Republican campaign managers did not neglect the practical necessity of strengthening their ties with the local organizations. Certainly one of Mark Hanna's major tasks in organizing the campaign was to make his peace with Tom Platt and his powerful machine in New York. The anti-Platt faction, led by Warner Miller and John Milholland, assumed that they would be recognized by the McKinley-Hanna organization to head up the campaign in New York, since they had supported McKinley, while Platt had fought him in the pre-nomination canvass. They were to be disappointed. Hanna, ever the political realist, had waited for Miller and Milholland to demonstrate their ability locally to control Republican politics in New York.[87] At every point they failed, while Platt exhibited his mastery. The rude awakening of the anti-Platt faction began when Hanna announced the personnel of his national executive committee. Initially no New Yorker was named to that committee. Hanna had named Hobart to the committee with the anticipation that he would resign at the time it became possible to appoint a New Yorker. In the end Hanna appointed Cornelius Bliss, who was not closely aligned with either faction and toward whom Platt possessed no active hostility.[88]

The rift between Hanna and Platt was healed during Hanna's first campaign visit to New York, which occurred in late July and early August. At first both men stood off and refused to make overtures, but they did meet with mutual friends. Finally Hanna invited Platt to visit him in company with two of his lieutenants, and Platt accepted.[89] A few days later, in a letter to Governor Morton, Platt reported that his interview with "Captain General Hanna" was "eminently satisfactory." He then analyzed Hanna's action:

When you come to think of it, there was nothing else for Mr. Hanna to do except to recognize the regular Organization of the Party in this State or any other State, and particularly in *this* State, at *this* time, when it was evident to the wayfaring man though a free silverite that the Republican Party has continued confidence in its present management, and desires them to remain in control.[90]

Even before this letter was written Levi P. Morton had sent off to McKinley a letter expressing his pleasure in the conduct of the campaign and Hanna's treatment of the New York organization. McKinley replied: "I . . . note what you say about Mr. Hanna, and I am gratified that he has been so successful in bringing into harmonious action the different elements of the party in New York. I assure you that I have the fullest confidence in the enthusiastic support of the Republicans of your State." [91]

One of the major differences of opinion over the conduct of the campaign within the McKinley-Hanna organization occurred on the question of whether any part of the South could be won over and whether the national organization should divert efforts and funds to winning any of the southern states. At first Hanna assumed that southern votes were inaccessibly Democratic, and he opposed spending any other than the usual token funds necessary to appease the local Republican workers. Quay and other advisers in the New York headquarters became convinced, however, that several southern and middle border states were vulnerable. They brought pressure on Hanna to channel large sums of money to Virginia, West Virginia, Tennessee, Kentucky, North Carolina, Alabama, Florida, Louisiana, and Texas.[92]

In all of these states but Florida the chances for a Republican victory were enhanced by the anti-Bryan, third-party activities of either or both the middle-of-the-road Populists and the gold Democrats, though Bryan Democrats then and historians subsequently have exaggerated the direct aid which the McKinley-Hanna organization gave these third-party movements in the South. Neither movement attained the affluence typical of Hanna-supported campaign efforts. Both received some direct help from the McKinley-Hanna organization, but never were large amounts of money involved.[93] The Republican organization did spend large sums of money in the South in the final stages of the campaign, but this money was distributed mainly through established Republican channels, not among Populists or gold Democrats. The flow of money was, in fact, in the other direction as far as gold Democrats were concerned; for wealthy eastern Democrats contributed much more money to the Republican campaign than Hanna in turn gave to the gold Democratic third party.

The Republican campaign organization made extensive use of polls of public opinion to guide them in the shaping of their campaign. Key states in the Middle West were polled again and again to enable the McKinley-Hanna campaigners to inform themselves of subtle changes in public opinion.[94] The first polls in the Middle West were highly disturbing. They showed that in states west of the Mississippi, such as the former Republican stronghold of Iowa, the free silver idea had won over many Republicans, who were planning to vote Democratic. Even more disturbing was what the polls revealed about public opinion in the key states east of the Mississippi in the Ohio Valley and the Great Lakes Region. Both Ohio and Indiana appeared to be doubtful states; Michigan was uncertain; and free silver was sufficiently popular in Illinois to make that state debatable.[95] In fact, of all the states in the area between the Appalachians and the Rockies only Wisconsin appeared to be definitely committed to sound money and safe for the Republican ticket.

It was upon this mid-continent region that the Republican organization centered its campaign of education. It was upon this region, too, that non-Republican allies of the McKinley-Hanna machine concentrated their efforts. It was here that the gold Democrats, who in appearance at least were the major non-Republican allies of McKinley and Hanna, centered their organization and concentrated their campaign efforts. Hanna at Chicago and McKinley at Canton were strategically located where they could spot every shift in midwestern opinion and make the adjustments in campaign strategy which the changing scene demanded.

21

The Democratic Campaign:
Carrying the War to the People

To turn from the campaigns for McKinley to the campaigns for Bryan is to turn from riches to poverty, from meticulous organization to motley confusion, from a self-righteous, dignified retaining action to maintain the status quo to a raucously indignant crusade for social justice. The Democrats and their allies did not have much money, and they lacked an impressive organization. They had little more than a cause and a leader. They depended almost wholly upon the logic of the free silver argument and the persuasive oratory of the silver-tongued Bryan to win the victory they sought.

The silver Democrats, who had successfully won control over enough state organizations to command the national convention, found that organization of party control on a national basis for a national campaign presented difficulties for which they were not adequately prepared. In western and southern states where they were in control the silver Democrats readily established their state campaign committees and appointed their representatives to the national committee; but in most eastern and in some of the strategically important middle western states, where the conservative anti-silver elements had remained in control through the convention, party leaders were typically undecided as to their support of the platform and the candidate. This indecision often caused them to delay in setting up their own state organizations and appointing national committeemen. When they elected national committeemen who were hostile to the Chicago platform and candidate, a new problem not easily resolved was posed for the national campaign committee.[1]

The man who was chosen to head up the Democratic campaign, Senator James K. Jones of Arkansas, was an able man thoroughly representative of the agrarian silver element which had won control of the party in the Chicago convention but with no experience in managing a national campaign. Senator Jones had been a leader in the organization of the Democratic Bimetallic Committee, and his appointment by Bryan to head the campaign committee was a recognition that the Democratic campaign would be, in large part, an extension of the pre-convention activities of that Committee.[2] Jones was from a state in which in recent years the Populist party had grown rapidly. As a Democrat in a state in which his party was in the majority, he had fought the Populists with no thought of seeking an alliance with them, quite unlike Bryan, who, in Nebraska, had found Democratic cooperation with Populists expedient.

The campaign was hardly underway when Senator Jones's attitudes toward the Populists were revealed to the public. In a newspaper interview at Washington shortly after the Populist convention had adjourned Jones was quoted as making disparaging remarks about the Populist leadership. He was particularly vehement in his attack upon the southern Populists; and, according to the reporter who interviewed him, he had said that the southern third-party men ought to go "with the negroes where they belonged."[3] The following day Senator Jones corrected this report, denying that he had made the latter statement. Yet he went on to say that when he was at St. Louis during the Populist convention he had found northern and western Populists to be "more responsible" than their brothers from the South.[4] Jones, in turn, was not trusted by southern Populists. Early in the campaign the following attack on him was printed in Senator Butler's paper, *The Caucasion:* "He is a strong representative of the worst type of Bourbon Democracy, and would rather vote for Cleveland today, and be thick with Whitney, Hill, and Brice, than support Bryan or any genuine reform Democrat."[5]

The meaning of the Jones-Bryan alliance was clear. Senator Jones was a regular Democrat who would be trusted by fellow partisans not to trifle with third-party heresies. Old-line Democrats, particularly in the South, were confident that he would not betray them. Though Bryan, too, was a staunch Democrat, he had proved his willingness to assimilate third-party ideas and to work with third-party leaders. The Jones-Bryan campaign was to be aimed at Populists and silver Republicans as well as Democrats. Their program would be basically agrarian in its appeal (even when they did not intend it to be so), a program congenial to both Jones and Bryan because of their allegiance to the Jacksonian traditions of the Democratic party. It was significant, too, that John Peter Altgeld should have played such a minor role in the shaping of the campaign, in spite of the fact that national campaign headquarters was established in Chicago.

After the convention Bryan made a triumphal journey through Illinois and Iowa back to Lincoln, while Senator Jones went home to Arkansas. Jones remained in Arkansas several days and then traveled to St. Louis to work with the Populists during their convention. Afterwards he returned home. Both en route to St. Louis and home he stopped off in Lincoln to see Bryan. In their discussions at Lincoln the two men appear to have perfected their plans for dealing with the Populists, but they failed to project plans for their own party's campaign.[6]

It was soon apparent that Jones and Bryan would not restrict their campaign to the South and West, where it possessed its greatest appeal, but that they would attempt rather to carry their message to the nation, even into the conservative East. Thus, in the first important decision of the campaign it was concluded that Bryan would accept the nomination of the Democratic party in a speech in Madison Square Garden in New York City.

At the time Bryan made his acceptance speech in New York Senator Jones' indecision and the lack of organization within the Democratic party were painfully evident.[7] Though Jones had a clear mandate to develop the campaign, he had not yet chosen his campaign committee or set up campaign headquarters; and he had not discussed these questions with party leaders other than Bryan. He called a meeting of the Democratic National Committee in New York to coincide with Bryan's visit so that Bryan might advise it of his ideas and plans. National committeemen from several of the eastern states did not appear, and much time was spent discussing the question as to whether the committee possessed the power to appoint committeemen from a state where cooperation was not forthcoming from the regular state organization.[8]

It was soon evident, too, that Bryan would be of little help. He had but slight interest in matters of party campaign organization.[9] All he wanted from the campaign committee was agreement that they would furnish funds for an extensive cross-country tour. Bryan expected that he alone, carrying to the people the message of free silver, would win the election for his party.[10] Thus, while it was decided in New York that, beginning in September, Bryan would undertake a national barnstorming campaign, no decisions were reached concerning the organization of the portion of the campaign which Senator Jones would have in hand.[11]

Senator Jones now traveled from New York to Washington to consult with other Democratic leaders and complete his plans for the campaign.[12] Finally from there in mid-August he announced his plans. Campaign headquarters would be established in Chicago, but there would be auxiliary headquarters as well in Washington.[13] Treasurer for the campaign was to be William P. St. John of New York, who, if he found it inconvenient to establish residence in Chicago, planned to conduct his phase of the campaign from his offices in New York. St. John remained in New York with the result that one of the most vital aspects of the campaign was centered there, where no formal headquarters organization existed.[14]

Even now Senator Jones was not prepared to name all of his campaign committee, because telegrams which were sent out inviting men to serve were not immediately answered.[15] As the campaign developed, this committee proved to be unstable in any case.[16] Nor was membership on the campaign committee necessarily a measure of service performed in the campaign. For example, Senator Gorman was offered a post on the committee but declined it because the headquarters city was too distant from his Maryland home.[17] He did participate actively in the campaign, however, from the Washington office. As an adviser to Jones, Bryan, and others, and as a campaign worker, he performed services of great value.[18]

Considerable pressure was exerted on Jones to appoint free silver men from outside the Democratic party to his campaign committee. The strongest and most persistent requests came from western Republicans, who urged Jones to appoint Senator Dubois. The Democratic chairman refused to make this appointment.[19] Throughout the campaign his committee was manned exclusively by Democrats; but he did take the initiative in the formation of a non-partisan free silver campaign committee composed of Democrats, Populists, silver Republicans, and American Silver party leaders. The men named to this committee worked closely with Senator Jones in Chicago, composing a coordinating committee to cooperate with Democratic headquarters in the campaign for free silver and Bryan.[20]

The activities undertaken at Democratic headquarters in Chicago were similar to those going on at the Republican offices, but the lavish financing characteristic of the Republican campaign was not in evidence among the Democrats. The Democrats recognized that the public demanded a campaign of discussion and education, that there was a great need for speakers and publications.[21] From the first, however, they lacked money to provide these. The campaign leaders borrowed money, called upon the party faithful to volunteer their time and talents in order to keep expenses at a minimum, and often paid the bills for maintaining the campaign offices from their own pockets.[22] They appealed to the masses through sympathetic newspapers to make the sacrifice of small contributions to counteract the Republican campaign which was being financed by wealthy business men.[23]

The response from the people was disappointing. Only William Randolph Hearst succeeded in drawing in popular contributions of any size, through a campaign which he conducted in the New York *Journal.* He promised to match every dollar contributed to the Bryan campaign fund with a dollar of his own. Bryan reported after the election that his campaign fund was enriched $40,000 by Hearst's efforts and that of this amount $15,000 was contributed by Hearst himself.[24] A few well-to-do eastern and middle western Democrats, like Sewall, McLean, and Senator Henry G. Davis, made handsome contributions; but they were not men of great wealth and they were few in number.[25]

The newspapers and the Republican campaigners repeatedly claimed that the Democratic campaign was heavily financed by wealthy western mining interests. Lists of western mining companies were published, showing their values, suggesting the profits they were likely to make from their operations if the free coinage of silver were adopted, and giving the totals of the contributions which they allegedly had made to the Bryan campaign fund. It was claimed that these contributions had reached into the millions and that they made up one of the largest "boodle" funds of American history.[26] Mark Hanna, however, knew from the reports of the observers whom he maintained in the Democratic organization that his opponents' campaign was seriously impoverished and threatened by bankruptcy.[27]

The Democrats did not overlook the possibility of getting funds from the western mining companies, and certainly they did not shun money from this source.[28] The mine operators were not, however, as wealthy or as willing to contribute to Bryan's campaign as the newspapers claimed. The poverty of the Democrats was sufficient evidence of this. There is no available record of how much money the silver mining interest did contribute. In late September Senator Gorman wrote a letter to Marcus Daly asking him to work with other western mining men to raise $350,000 for the Democratic campaign. Gorman assured Daly that with this amount of money at hand in the final phases of the campaign the Democrats could win the election.[29] No evidence exists that Daly was able to forward such a sum to Democratic headquarters, and there was no sign of sudden affluence among the Democrats during the last weeks of the campaign. Even had Daly been able to provide the money asked by Gorman the Democrats as spenders would have been greatly outclassed by the Republicans, who were spending more than this in one week in the Chicago office during the final stages of the campaign.

The most spectacular and significant phase of the Democratic campaign—Bryan's cross-country tours—by its very nature was an economical operation. It was much cheaper to take the candidate to the people than to transport the people to the candidate, as the Republicans did. Also Bryan's appearance in the states and congressional districts, speaking approvingly of Democratic candidates for local offices, took the place of contributions from the national headquarters to the state campaigns.

It was upon Bryan, "the boy orator" and the "Popocrat," [30] as his opponents called him, that the chief burden and the major hope of the Democratic campaign were centered. It mattered little, Democratic strategists believed, that funds were lacking to satisfy the public hunger for pamphlets and platform speakers as long as Bryan was willing to travel over the nation and speak frequently to the immense crowds which met him everywhere.

The use which was to be made of Bryan's voice seemed evident in the first important decision of the campaign, the decision to have Bryan travel to New York to accept his party's nomination at Madison Square Garden. Conservative New Yorkers immediately concluded that Bryan would pronounce radical views in a violent and revolutionary manner. They were afraid that such a speech might have a profound influence upon the New York working people who would come to the Garden to hear him.

Bryan planned quite a different performance, however. He was determined to deliver a carefully wrought speech setting forth the logic of free silver in a fashion so conservative and closely reasoned as to counteract the eastern impression that he was an intellectual "light-weight," who had gained public attention only as an irresponsible representative of the lunatic fringe. He wanted also to develop careful arguments to persuade urban working men that the adoption of free silver would be to their interest.

Bryan wrote his New York speech in Lincoln; and though he worked on it en route to New York, he changed very little.[31] Even had he wished to make major changes, the enthusiastic crowds which greeted him everywhere and their insistence all along the way that he speak would have prevented it. It was not Bryan's wish that the trip to New York become a whistle-stopping display of his oratorical powers; but when the people shouted for him to speak, Bryan found the call irresistible. Therefore, he had to make a speech when he left Lincoln; and he had to speak in Iowa, where he called attention to the audacity of the Democratic party in nominating a man who would have to pass through Iowa to reach the White House.[32] It would have been impossible to keep Bryan from speaking in Chicago, or Indiana, or Ohio, or Pennsylvania.[33] By the time Indiana was reached the pattern had been established.[34]

Bryan's train left Chicago at 11:00 P.M. He anticipated no demonstrations and had planned a night of sleep. When the train reached South Chicago at 12:10 A.M., a large crowd was waiting. Bryan tried to limit his activity on this occasion to a brief appearance on the platform of his car, but steel workers lifted him down to the station platform to shake hands. At 1:35 A.M., when the train reached Valparaiso, Indiana, Bryan was in bed; but state Senator John C. Kern aroused him and persuaded him to make a platform appearance in his nightgown. There were no more interruptions until 5:35 A.M. at Fort Wayne, when Bryan, now fully dressed, appeared to greet a large crowd from the platform of his car.[35]

This kind of campaigning exposed Bryan to the ridicule from the eastern press which he was trying to avoid by reading a carefully written speech in Madison Square Garden. His impromptu remarks were picked up by eastern newspaper men and quoted out of context to make him appear silly, weak-minded, or dangerous. Thus, his reference at Lincoln, Nebraska, to the East as "what now seems to be the enemy's country, but which we hope to be our country before this campaign is over,"[36] was extensively quoted and used against Bryan, through the rest of the campaign.[37] Reporters from the metropolitan papers kept close watch on the "silver-tongued orator's" voice and health. As Bryan neared New York, they gleefully reported that he was hoarse and tired. They seemed relieved to find that the hero of the cause of free silver was subject to human frailties.[38]

New York on August 12, the date of Bryan's acceptance speech, was hot and humid. The uncomfortable weather did not deter New Yorkers from crowding to Madison Square Garden, for they expected a sensational display of oratory. They came early to make certain of a seat, and the Garden was filled with a perspiring crowd an hour before the notification ceremony was scheduled to begin. The meeting began twelve minutes late; and Governor Stone, as spokesman for the notification committee, had prepared a long, typically western speech on free silver, with references to the greed of Wall Street, the subservience of America to English capitalists, and so on.[39] At first his hits drew applause, but the crowd had come to hear and see Bryan. As Stone continued what seemed an interminable speech, they began to chant for the Nebraskan. Stone finally abandoned his speech and introduced Bryan, but already people had begun to leave.

Bryan, who was determined to make no unprepared statements which might be used later to embarrass him, read his speech from beginning to end. He read in an undramatic fashion for two hours.

In a few introductory paragraphs Bryan denied that there was anything radical in the proposals of the Democratic platform. He argued briefly that government had the responsibility to protect the people when their welfare was threatened. He defended the income tax plank of the platform, stating that the adoption of any income tax would remedy the inequitable tax structure then existing. He also defended the criticism made in the platform of the Supreme Court's decision on the income tax. One did not, he said, deny the Constitution or act disloyally in questioning the logic by which the Supreme Court reached a decision.

Most of Bryan's speech was given to a discussion of the monetary issue. In making his arguments on this question Bryan did not altogether abandon his accustomed role as spokesman for the farmer, but the greater part of his speech was directed to a discussion of the effect which monetary reform would have upon urban interests. No mention whatever was made of the tariff.[40] Soon, the people having realized one of their objectives in merely seeing Bryan and sensing that no brilliant display of oratory was likely, began to leave the Garden in groups, with the result that entire sections of the hall were vacant.

On the following day the metropolitan press of the nation generally described the Democratic notification meeting as a "frost," a keen disappointment to the masses who had expected to be thrilled by oratorical fireworks.[41] Reporters seized every opportunity to ridicule Bryan and his wife. The *New York Times*, for example, not only described at length the dissatisfaction of the crowds and the meager attendance at the public receptions for the Bryans, but made fun of Mrs. Bryan's hats and pointedly commented on the fact that she wore the same dress to two different receptions.[42]

This was not the beginning of the campaign of ridicule and slander of the Bryans, for that had preceded his nomination. Now, however, Bryan in his first aggressive campaign action, had invited attack by moving to the chief center of his eastern opposition. When he proved not to be as much the "rabble rouser" as conservative easterners had expected, they heaved a sigh of relief and added more ammunition to the counterattack.[43]

Neither of the Bryans spoke with any bitterness during the campaign about the crude attacks to which they were subjected from the press. In *The First Battle*, published a few weeks after the election Bryan wrote this gentle comment about the newspaper accounts of his first New York visit: "Mrs. Bryan and I were much amused the next morning by a newspaper article which attempted to describe her appearance during the delivery of the speech. It carried her through all the emotions, from ecstasy to despair. If the account had been founded upon fact it would have justified her in claiming pre-eminence among the artists of facial expression." [44]

The Republican and conservative Democratic press the country over gave Bryan exceedingly rough treatment. They called him an anarchist, a socialist, a revolutionist, a "Popocrat," a cheap orator, a mountebank, and a political opportunist. They described him as a tool of Altgeld and a pawn of the western silver miners. They circulated the story that he had been sustained by funds from silver miners in the period after he left Congress. When Bryan issued a convincing denial of this story (so convincing that Senator Thurston of Nebraska, who had been industriously circulating the accusation, immediately announced that he accepted Bryan's explanation and withdrew his earlier allegations),[45] they either did not publish it or buried it inconspicuously on inner pages. The *New York Times* gave a great deal of attention to a story that Bryan had applied for a job as a theatrical agent a few months before his nomination, a story denied by both Bryan and the manager of the theatrical company involved.[46] The *Times* also happily reported that at Peoria, Illinois, a policeman, believing he was a hobo, had turned Bryan away when he tried to push through a crowd waiting to hear him speak.[47]

Probably the most irresponsible development of the entire campaign occurred in the columns of the *New York Times*. On September 27 the *Times* published a letter signed by an "eminent alienist," in which the writer concluded, from an analysis of Bryan's speeches, that his mind "was not entirely sound," that his presence in the campaign created the possibility that there would be a "madman in the White House," and that Bryan was a man of "abnormal egotism." The writer of the letter added that Bryan's father had been a "religious fanatic and crank." In the same issue and on the same page the *Times* editorially expressed its agreement with the writer of the letter. The newspaper, too, found in his speeches the evidence of his mental deterioration. It did not follow, said the *Times*, that Bryan was insane. Nevertheless, they went on to say: "What, however, most of all entitles us to say that Mr. Bryan is of unsound mind, whether we call this condition unsoundness in English or insanity in Latin, is that his procedures are not adaptations of intelligent means to intelligible ends." [48]

Though other newspapers did not generally join the *Times* in this attack upon Bryan's sanity, the *Times* for several succeeding days published a number of letters and interviews in which other "alienists" attested to Bryan's "unsoundness." On September 29, for example, under the heading, "Is Mr. Bryan a Mattoid?" [i.e., insane or a degenerate] they published two columns of interviews with New York psychologists, who in the main concluded that the answer to this question was, "Yes." [49] On the following day they printed two more columns of interviews to the same effect under the heading, "Paranoid or Mattoid." [50]

Though Bryan then meekly turned the other cheek to such campaign blows, there is evidence that they served to reinforce his almost intuitive distrust of the East. In later years he was less reluctant to express his convictions about the baneful influence of the eastern newspapers. In a speech which he gave at a banquet in his honor at Washington, D.C., in 1916 he said:

I love the south and the west, and the ideals to which they are attached; but I would do injustice to the east if I told you that the people of the south and west were at heart different from the people of other sections of our country. It is not a difference in people, it is a difference in their means of information and their environment. In the east, the common man is so overshadowed by concentrated wealth that he has not the freedom of expression or action that he has in the west, and then, too, he is the victim of a press that publishes the truth by accident and falsehood by consistently cultivated habit.[51]

Bryan and the managers of the Democratic campaign were not disappointed with the effect of the Madison Square Garden speech.[52] They felt that the attempt to make Bryan appear the statesman had been a success, that he had positively influenced both eastern and western voters.[53] One sympathetic editorial writer recalled that Cleveland's notification had occurred in Madison Square Garden four years earlier under similar circumstances and that large numbers of the audience had left before the conclusion of Cleveland's speech. Speaking of Bryan's audience he said, "Far from being cold and unresponsive ... [it] was immensely enthusiastic. The vast bulk of the crowd remained to hear the very last word...." [54] Nevertheless, this observer concluded that Bryan had made a "tactical mistake" at Madison Square Garden "in bringing to the chief city of the East a monetary argument adapted to the farmers rather than to the industrial wage-earners."[55]

The Democratic leadership had hoped that Bryan's appearance in New York would force the Democratic leaders of that and nearby states to stand publicly for him. Their hopes were not fully realized. Tammany Hall had earlier declared its support for the ticket (though ignoring the platform),[56] but few New York Democrats of prominence appeared on the stage at Madison Square Garden with Bryan. New York Democrats were deeply divided over the platform and the candidate, and Bryan's visit did not succeed in uniting them. Its only positive influence was to cause Tammany to make an early, firm declaration for party regularity.[57]

Bryan's visit in the East had proved to be remarkably bereft of political achievement. His conferences with the National Committee did not result in a definitive formulation of national campaign plans. He and Mrs. Bryan stayed at the home of William P. St. John, where they were isolated to a considerable degree from contact with regular Democratic leaders. After leaving New York City the Bryans traveled to upstate New York, where they spent several days at the home of a former teacher of Mrs. Bryan.[58] At the end of his stay in upstate New York Bryan was entertained at the summer home of James S. Hinkley, chairman of the Democratic State Committee of New York. At this time Bryan met several prominent New York politicians, but they did not give him an opportunity to discuss with them any of the important aspects of the campaign. At this time, too, the Bryans were invited to have dinner with Senator Hill at his home in Albany. Again the meeting was so arranged that Bryan and Hill had no opportunity for an intimate discussion of politics.[59]

At the time Bryan made his trip to New York he was the Democratic campaign, for the National Committee had not yet selected a campaign site or made the other arrangements necessary for a national canvass. The newspapers gave Bryan's movements remarkably full coverage. Most newspapers were not friendly, but they did print much of the substance and often the complete text of the remarks made by Bryan, both in impromptu whistle-stops and in prepared speeches on more formal occasions. The *New York Times* printed the complete text of his acceptance speech at Madison Square Garden, for example. Thus, the Democrats by exploiting the oratorical fame and the youthful energy of their candidate were able to carry much of their message to the country at a minimum cost to themselves.[60]

On August 25, the Bryans began their journey homeward. They traveled slowly by a circuitous route that took them over a wide area in New York, Pennsylvania, Ohio, Indiana, Illinois, Wisconsin, and Iowa; so that they did not arrive at Lincoln until September 8.[61] In the course of this tour Bryan delivered some of the most important speeches of the campaign. On Labor Day he spoke in Chicago at the special invitation of the Building Trades Council of that city. Here, as in his acceptance speech in New York, Bryan advocated positive action by government to "restrain the strongest citizen from injuring the weakest citizen," but in developing his argument on this point in Chicago he used more colorful language:

An idea is the most important thing that a person can get into his head, and we gather our ideas from every source. I was passing through Iowa some months ago and got an idea from some hogs. I noticed a number of hogs rooting in a field and tearing up the ground. The first thought that came to me was that they were destroying property, and that carried me back to the time when I lived on a farm, and I remembered that we put rings in the noses of our hogs. And why? Not to keep the hogs from getting fat, for we were more interested in their getting fat than they were. . . . But we put rings in the noses of the hogs so that while they were getting fat they would not destroy more property than they were worth. And then it occurred to me that one of the most important duties of government is to put rings in the noses of hogs.[62]

The period of this tour, in the return from New York to Lincoln, was the high point of the Bryan campaign. Bryan was well rested. After invading "the enemy's country," he was returning to his own territory. Wherever his train went people, who had traveled from nearby farms and villages, waved and shouted encouragement. Their enthusiasm at the unrehearsed rear platform appearances and in the formal speeches was spontaneous and contagious. The smell of victory seemed to hang in the air. Perhaps a vote taken then would have given Bryan the election.[63]

At Lincoln on the day following his return, Bryan released his letter accepting the Democratic nomination. At the beginning of the letter Bryan said that he would not, if elected, be a candidate for reelection, explaining that he wished to enter the office, "free from any personal desire except the desire to prove worthy of the confidence of my countrymen." [64]

Because he had discussed the silver question extensively during the convention debate over the platform and also in his acceptance speech in New York, he made slight reference to that subject in his acceptance letter. Emphasis was placed rather on those planks in the platform of particular importance to labor. Thus, he argued against federal interference in the affairs of the states, "except upon application of the Legislature of the State, or upon the application of the executive when the Legislature cannot be convened." [65] "Labor creates capital," he wrote; and he promised "to protect the masses in the free exercise of every political right and in the enjoyment of their just share of the rewards of their labor." [66] He strongly endorsed the plank calling for legislation to provide for the arbitration of labor disputes. He opposed the "dumping of the criminal classes upon our shores," as well as paupers or contract laborers who would compete with American workers. He condemned the recent use of the injunction and called for a bill to provide for trial by jury in certain contempt cases. He declared his hostility to trusts and advocated public control of corporations. He argued the necessity of increasing the powers of the Interstate Commerce Commission "to prevent discrimination between persons and places, and protect patrons from unreasonable charges." [67]

He did comment on certain aspects of the money question. He backed his party's platform declaration against the issue of any more interest bearing bonds, arguing that this had become a necessary expedient only because in recent years the United States government had failed to exercise the option of redeeming its currency in either gold or silver coin. He approved of his party's opposition to the issuance of paper money by national banks. He declared that greenbacks redeemable in either gold or silver were safer and cheaper for the people; for "to empower national banks to issue circulating notes is to grant a valuable privilege to a favored class, surrender to private corporations the control of the volume of paper money, and build up a class which will claim a vested interest in the nation's financial policy." [68]

To the all-important question of silver he referred only briefly in the final paragraph of his letter. He began this paragraph by saying that it was not necessary at this time to discuss the tariff issue, for it had been cast in the shade by the money question. In his concluding sentence he said: "In the presence of this overshadowing issue, differences of opinion upon minor questions must be laid aside in order that there may be united action among those who are determined that progress toward an universal gold standard shall be stayed, and the gold and silver coinage of the Constitution restored." [69]

On September 11, only three days after his return to Lincoln from the East, Bryan was off on a tour which kept him from home until November 1. On this tour which took him south into Tennessee and North Carolina, north into Maine and Minnesota, and west into North and South Dakota he traveled nearly 13,000 miles.[70] Bryan spent the greatest amount of time and did his most extensive barnstorming in the populous states of the mid-continent—Michigan, Illinois, Ohio, Indiana, and Wisconsin. Mrs. Bryan did not accompany her husband at the beginning of this trip. She joined Bryan midway in the tour at St. Paul, Minnesota, and remained with him from that point to the end of the campaign.[71]

Everywhere that Bryan appeared there was a huge outpouring of men, women, and children to see and hear him. As his train whistlestopped across the country crowds gathered at every crossroads. In the towns and cities, where he left the train to speak more formally in auditoriums and halls, throngs greeted him in the streets; and usually the rooms in which he spoke were not sufficiently large to accommodate the people who came to hear him. Nor were these crowds passive and unresponsive. With few exceptions they were noisy, enthusiastic, keenly sympathetic. They caused Bryan and his aides to grow confident of the possibility of victory.

Ignatius Donnelly, who was in St. Paul on the October night that Bryan spoke there, found 10,000 people "jammed" into the city's auditorium, while three times as many were outside. He concluded that Bryan's speeches and the rousing demonstrations that accompanied them made it certain that Bryan would carry Minnesota by 50,000 votes.[72] The men opposed to Bryan were also impressed with the reception accorded him by the people across the country, and feared that it portended a victory for him and his cause.

There was nothing elaborate about the Bryan campaign tour. On the first phase of the trip which carried him south to Tennessee, then across to North Carolina, north through New York to Maine and back into the Midwest, Bryan traveled on regularly scheduled public trains. His own schedule was not rigid; and though he had a general itinerary plotted, he often changed his immediate plans from day to day at the request or suggestion of local leaders.

During the first weeks of this trip Bryan had an inadequate staff. After Bryan visited Washington, D.C., the Populist chairman, Marion Butler, wrote to Senator Jones to suggest that the Democratic National Committee send a manager along with Bryan to handle the details of the tour. Butler wrote that on Sunday evening before leaving Washington Bryan had been forced to look up the schedule to Dover, Delaware. In order to get to Dover by regularly scheduled trains he had left Washington Sunday evening, had gone part way and then stopped in the middle of the night, and then had arisen at six in the morning to catch another train which would give him connections with a local train going to Dover. The newspaper men accompanying Bryan told Butler that this sort of thing happened often, that Bryan sometimes carried his bags from the train, and that on occasion he had walked from the train station to his hotel. Bryan was depending upon the local Democratic committees to organize his reception, but the members of these committees lacked experience and imagination.[73] A North Carolina Populist who had accompanied Bryan's party while it was in his state wrote to Butler: "He is a wonderful man but they will kill him the way they are working him. I think you & Jones ought [to] lighten up on him." [74]

At this time the Bryan party was reorganized to relieve Bryan of the management of routine details. Josephus Daniels accompanied him from North Carolina up into New England. He not only took over the tasks of making travel arrangements, but he substituted as a speaker for Bryan at those stops which occurred when Bryan was resting. When Daniels left the Bryan party, Benton McMillan of Tennessee took his place; and he in turn gave way to John W. Tomlinson of Alabama. All of these men were young southern Democrats who had been among the earliest supporters of the campaign to nominate Bryan for the presidency.

At Chicago on October 7 the Democratic National Committee provided Bryan with a private car, which he retained for the duration of this campaign tour. Now he was able to work out a more flexible schedule and get more rest. [75] By this time, too, Bryan had plotted his itinerary more firmly with the result that local committees were informed well ahead of time that he planned to visit their communities. They could then proceed to organize his reception.

Bryan's speeches did not show the careful staff work evident in McKinley's efforts. Of course, Bryan made polite references to local traditions and spoke in support of local Democratic politicians; but he rarely was able to refer to the local situation with the intimacy McKinley achieved in speaking to the delegations which visited him. Of course, local politicians crowded the Bryan train wherever it moved; but the pace was too fast for Bryan to establish mastery of the local situation.

There was one group of men whom Bryan knew well—the leaders in the free silver movement. He needed no staff to inform him of their background or their work. Wherever he spoke he tried to have the men who had been the leaders in the local movement for silver with him on the platform. He paid slight attention to their previous political affiliations, for he knew that his campaign was drawing silver men of all political persuasions into the Democratic party. [76]

Bryan also sometimes intervened in local political matters to prevent anti-silver forces from exercising control over local machines. Thus, in New York, when the Democratic nominee for governor, John B. Thatcher, announced that he was opposed to free silver, Bryan exerted pressure which resulted in his withdrawal from the campaign. The State Democratic Committee then nominated a new candidate who pledged his support to both the national ticket and platform.[77]

In the discussion of issues the Bryan campaign tour produced no surprises. From day to day, with seemingly infinite variation in phraseology, Bryan spoke on the question of bimetallism and the necessity for restoring silver. He usually tried to direct his discussion of this theme to the special interests of the district in which he was speaking, but he rarely failed to set forth clearly the special interest of the farmer in free silver. Typical of his approach was this passage in a speech made in Dover, Delaware: "I would be willing to place the average farmer against the average banker and turn them loose to discuss monetary science and financial history, and the banker could not hold his own with the farmer. Why? Because the financier thinks that he knows so much that it is not necessary for him to study, while the farmer realizes that he must study in order to know anything about the question." [78]

Often his speeches in eastern cities seemed intended to win the votes of others than those in his immediate audience. Speaking to a crowd of wealthy men in Morristown, New Jersey, he said, "Remember that a financial system that commends itself to the wealthy only is a curse to any land." [79] In Hartford, Connecticut, he noted that the insurance companies were active in opposing free silver and surmised that, "The presidents of these companies are more concerned about their own salaries than they are in protecting the policy holders from the effects of free coinage." [80] In New York Bryan made a direct attack upon Wall Street. Speaking in Tammany Hall he said: "As long as our Government receives its financial inspiration from railroad wreckers and stock jobbers legislation will be such as to make it more profitable to be a non-producer than a producer. In time of peace you cannot trust the financial wisdom of those who manipulate your stock markets, nor can you trust their patriotism in time of war." [81]

Swinging back into the Middle West, Bryan used themes which appealed to the special economic interests of that section. At Minneapolis he referred to the dependence of the merchant and the laboring man upon the farmer. "These cities," he said, "rest upon your broad and fertile plains. . . . Are St. Paul and Minneapolis going to be made prosperous by making the foreign financier prosperous? It is your farmers who are going to buy the things which you produce, and we had better take care of them instead of making legislation to suit the financier." [82]

When he spoke to a crowd of business men in Chicago Bryan said "that in pleading the cause of the farmer and the laborer I am trying to lay a substantial foundation upon which the business of this country can be done." He tried to drive a wedge between business men and bankers by suggesting that bankers "tyrannized over" business men through the power which they possessed over capital: "I believe that the mercantile classes have suffered as much as any other class of people by a government by banks, and when I preach to the common people deliverance from the money changer, I preach to the business man deliverance from the tyranny of the bank." [83]

On the last day of the tour, as his train moved homeward across Iowa, Bryan was still speaking on silver. At Ottumwa he said that his appeal had been "to the great producing masses," and the judgment now lay in their hands. He said that he had been trying to do his share of the work of carrying the fight to the people. Yet he was not exhausted: "My hand has been used until it is sore, but it can handle a pen to sign a free-coinage bill, if I am elected. I have been wearied with work, but I still have the physical strength to stand between the people, if they elect me, and the Wall Street syndicates which have been bleeding this country." [84]

Issues other than silver to which Bryan made major reference during this long tour were the recent Supreme Court decision invalidating the income tax, the question of states' rights and federal intervention in industrial disputes, the coercion of farmers and laboring class voters by bankers and employers, and his opposition to trusts and monopolies. Speaking in Brooklyn, New York, on September 23, Bryan firmly defended the planks in the Democratic platform condemning interference by federal authorities in local affairs and the Supreme Court's decision on the income tax. On both questions he quoted sections from the Republican platform of 1860 which agreed substantially with the Democratic platform statements of 1896.[85]

In mid-October at Detroit Bryan devoted the greater part of his speech to issues other than money. Replying to Republican and gold Democratic charges that the Chicago platform was "lawless" and threatened the "safety of society," he quoted Supreme Court Justice Brown's dissent to the Supreme Court decision on the income tax to prove that criticism of the court was not necessarily anarchistic. He defended also the platform statement on the use of the injunction and states' rights. In conclusion, he promised to enforce the laws against the trusts, to secure better laws if these did not work; "and if the Supreme Court decides that the Federal Constitution prohibits the passage or enforcement of any law interfering with a trust, I will recommend an amendment to the Constitution which will permit the American people to live in spite of trusts." [86]

Toward the end of the campaign as the organizations supporting Bryan found evidence that business men were bringing economic pressure on their employees and other dependents to vote for McKinley, Bryan reminded his listeners that they possessed a secret ballot. In one of his last speeches, at Ottumwa, Iowa, on October 31 he said:

I am not surprised at the means which have been employed because when a party starts out with the proposition that we must submit to such a financial system as money lenders demand, they go further and say that any man who borrows money must submit to dictation from the man who loans to him, and that any man who works for wages must submit to dictation from the man who employs him. This doctrine of submission will be carried all the way down the line until the right of the citizen is lost and until the corporation becomes all powerful. [87]

On October 19 Chairman Jones issued a manifesto addressed to the American people calling upon them to resist the coercion exercised by the great corporations; "for if this conspiracy succeeds government by corporation will have succeeded government by the people." [88]

During his tour only one unfortunate incident of any significance occurred. On September 24 Bryan was in Connecticut and stopped at New Haven, where he attempted to speak from a stand set up in the village green. A crowd of nearly 15,000 was on hand to greet him; but when he stepped forward to speak, the cheers were mingled with hisses and groans from Yale College students in the audience. The heckling increased as Bryan proceeded with his speech; and finally when a band practicing nearby moved so close to the stand as to make it impossible for Bryan to be heard, he abandoned the platform. The anti-Bryan newspapers gleefully reported this incident and published editorials approving the action of the students. [89]

Home at Lincoln on November 1 Bryan was not yet ready to end his campaign travels. On Monday, November 2, he and his wife and their daughter Grace took a train westward across Nebraska, going as far as Grand Rapids. At that point they turned south to Hastings. From there they went eastward to Omaha, where Bryan spoke seven times.

Altogether on that last day Bryan made twenty-seven speeches, completing his work at Omaha a few minutes before midnight. It was a fitting conclusion to the campaign of travel and oratory which Bryan had conducted. Bryan himself referred to it as his fourth tour (the first was the return from the Chicago convention; the second the trip to New York to deliver his acceptance speech and the return; the third, the 13,000 mile tour which took him again to New York and back to Lincoln) and computed the mileage as 344 miles, including the mileage of his return from Omaha to Lincoln early on the morning of election day. According to his own figures, he had traveled altogether 18,009 miles since he had begun the campaign in July on his return trip from the convention to his home in Lincoln.[90]

Bryan and the Democratic National Committee, with the resources at hand, had conducted a geographically well balanced campaign. They could be criticized for using too much of Bryan's campaign time and energy in the East; but this was a criticism valid only if one saw that their campaign was ill balanced in its discussion of the issues. Bryan and his party believed that they were making a strong appeal to the urban labor vote.[91] This explained the great amount of time spent in the urban areas of the East and Middle West. Unfortunately for them most of the time so spent was wasted, for it was used to discuss the issue of the free coinage of silver. It was doubtful that anyone could have put the arguments for free coinage in language which would have successfully countered among the working men the Republican attacks upon it. Certainly Bryan was not schooled in such language. His arguments and his language were derived from the agrarian heritage. His style and his obvious sympathy won a hearing, often an enthusiastic response; but it won over few voters among urban working men.

Not only did the Republicans argue effectively the adverse effects of free silver on urban working men; they had an appealing issue of their own in the tariff. Bryan and the Democrats deliberately ignored that issue, claiming that in 1896 it was superseded by the financial question. Their judgment undoubtedly was that the depression and the unfortunate history of the Wilson Bill made them vulnerable on this issue. Perhaps this was so; but their failure to answer the Republican protective tariff propaganda gave the Republicans a completely unrestricted hand in carrying this issue to the city worker, upon whom it worked most effectively.

The Democratic platform, in its statements on the income tax, federal intervention in state affairs, the use of the injunction, and trust regulation, was calculated to make a strong appeal to labor votes, as were Bryan's acceptance speech and letter and many of his speeches in urban centers. It was not a campaign concentrated solely on free silver. There was no question of the strategy. The failure came in the failure of labor to respond to the Democratic appeal. Bryan was criticized—not altogether fairly—for his emphasis on free silver; but Altgeld, who abandoned free silver in the final month of his campaign in Illinois to concentrate on issues judged to be exclusively of interest to labor fared no better than Bryan in the final results. Florence Kelley described his dilemma a month before the election: "Things are badly muddled, and Governor Altgeld's friends seem few, indeed, in this time of need. The Socialists and labor skates are knifing him alike. The Silver populists and the straight trade-union vote seem to be his main hope besides the farmers. And if the working people allow him to be defeated now, in the face of his record, surely they deserve to have no other friend until this generation dies out and another and better one takes its place." [92]

This statement could very well have served as the epitaph of both the Altgeld and the Bryan campaigns.

22

The Populist Campaign:
Fusion and Confusion

During the campaign Populist party leaders found the opportunities for maneuver and innovation rapidly narrowing. Rank and file Populists viewed party survival as secondary to victory for free silver and Bryan. As a result the party's leaders were unable to use advantageously what they had hoped would be a major asset in bargaining with the Democrats—the nomination of Watson for the vice presidency. In this matter they were handicapped by the fact that Watson did not have a national following. Most of the enthusiasm for him in the South and West had a negative source, stemming from opposition to Sewall; and, as Bryan's campaign gathered momentum, Populist voters concentrated on winning Bryan's election without regard to the vice-presidential issue. If the Populist leaders tried to obstruct Bryan's campaign with the object of forcing Watson upon the Democrats, it seemed likely that the rank and file of the party would, in protest, defect to the Democrats.

The Populist party had never succeeded in establishing a responsible and effective central organization. To some extent this was due to the way in which the party had developed out of state and regional movements of political protest. Partly it was due to the existence in the party of so many individualistic political operators and mavericks like Weaver, Donnelly, Waite, Davis, Lloyd, Debs, and Watson. A third deterrent to effective centralization had been the nature of the leadership which controlled the party after 1892. Herman Taubeneck of

Illinois, the party's chairman in that period, was a devoted Populist and a hard worker; but he did not have the qualities required for the development of national party unity.

Senator Marion Butler of North Carolina, who became chairman of the party after the convention of 1896, was an able organizer. More significantly, he was capable of subordinating his own ego to the needs of the national organization. But he came too late to the leadership of the party. All that he succeeded in accomplishing—and probably no other man in the party could have achieved more than this—was to animate the corpse of his party with some semblance of vitality until the ballots had been cast in November.[1]

Senator Butler established the Populist campaign headquarters at Washington, D.C., in a building also housing the headquarters of the National Silver party as well as offices manned by representatives of the Democratic national campaign committee. Midway in the campaign Butler sent Massachusetts Populist George F. Washburn to Chicago, where campaign offices were established chiefly for the purpose of coordination with the Democratic headquarters.[2]

One of Senator Butler's most important subordinates, the party's treasurer, Martin C. Rankin of Terre Haute, Indiana, did not visit the headquarters at Washington or Chicago during the course of the campaign. As campaign pressure mounted and the shortage of funds in the Populist campaign treasury became more desperate, Butler pleaded with Rankin to come to Washington to conduct a vigorous campaign to solicit public and private contributions. Rankin excused himself on the grounds that personal business made it impossible for him to leave home.[3]

Men who were disposed to contribute to the Populists were poor. Rankin did not carry a vigorous campaign to them to demonstrate the party's needs for the small sums which they could contribute. Senator Butler refused to put the party in debt to finance the campaign, arguing that such a policy would deliver the Populist party into the hands of the monopolistic financiers.[4] As a result, the Populists were desperately short of funds throughout the campaign.

They were able to distribute few pamphlets.[5] Early in the campaign it was ruled that pamphlets would be sent out only when local committees which ordered them paid for them in advance.[6] Great delay in filling orders was experienced because printing was not contracted until orders were received.[7] At the end of the campaign they did order a number of pamphlets printed in the hope that orders for them would come in during the final days of the canvass. These orders did not materialize, and at the end the Populist committee distributed these pamphlets without charge.[8] Often during the campaign Populist headquarters referred writers requesting campaign literature to the Democratic or National Silver party headquarters.[9]

As far as campaign headquarters was concerned, it was a "finance-it-yourself" campaign at every level.[10] There was no money to pay the salaries of party speakers, and only rarely were the traveling expenses of speakers paid.[11] No money was available to aid the state committees; in fact, special appeals were made to the state committees to raise money for national headquarters.[12] Week by week Senator Butler and those working with him in Washington had to dig into their own pockets to pay the expenses of maintaining their headquarters offices. Even this cost would have been unbearable had not much of the office staff been unpaid volunteer labor.[13] Washburn also paid from his personal funds the expenses of the office in Chicago.[14]

If one puts beside the letters between Butler and Rankin those between the Republican campaign managers, Dawes and Osborne, the efforts of the Populists to sustain a campaign in competition with the Republicans appear ridiculous. At the height of the campaign, when Dawes was receiving several hundreds of thousands of dollars each week from New York alone, Butler was writing to Rankin expressing gratitude for receiving weekly remittance checks in sums of one hundred or one hundred and fifty dollars.[15]

A special appeal from Butler to the masses of the Populist party for individual contributions of one dollar produced little money. Though Butler explained in his request that the campaign of the people must be financed by the people to counteract the large sums that were being poured by the wealthy classes into the campaign chests of the opposition, the people either had no money to contribute or decided that it would be put to better use in the hands of the Democratic campaign committee. Money from western silver miners which Populists had received in the past was not forthcoming in 1896 largely because the silver men believed that direct support of the Bryan-Sewall ticket was the best way to aid their cause.[16]

Finally Butler turned to William Randolph Hearst and asked him to share with the Populist party the funds which he was receiving in his special fund raising campaign in the New York *Journal.* Butler argued that a portion of the contributions flowing into Hearst's fund resulted from appeals by the Populist campaign committee.[17] In reply Hearst referred Butler to the Democratic National Campaign committee, saying that he had placed distribution of the funds in its control.[18] Senator Jones was sympathetic to the Populist appeal and arranged before the campaign closed to transfer one thousand dollars of the Hearst funds to the Populist campaign committee. These funds were used to finance the efforts directed from the Washington headquarters.[19] It was, of course, no more than enough to pay accumulated bills and to finance commitments already made by that office.

Butler and the other leaders of the party working in cooperation with Washington headquarters hoped that they could force the Democrats to withdraw Sewall from their ticket and substitute Watson. Sewall's withdrawal was a possibility, however, only if the Populists succeeded in coordinating their own campaign from national headquarters through the states.[20]

Such coordination had never existed. It early became an impossibility for the Populists in this campaign because of the actions taken in two key western states, Colorado and Kansas. Lacking the hostility to the Democratic party which southern Populists felt and thoroughly committed to both silver and Bryan, the Populist rank and file as well as the leader in these states wanted to support the Bryan-Sewall ticket and to ignore Watson. These states and their neighbors in the West had tried to nominate Sewall at the St. Louis convention. Now, as the campaign got underway, they acted in their state conventions to put up electoral tickets pledged to vote for Bryan and Sewall, leaving Watson off the ballot altogether.[21]

Throughout the campaign Butler exerted pressure on Colorado and Kansas Populists to recognize Watson in their electoral tickets, but he did not succeed.[22] Finding that he was, in fact, powerless to dictate policy to any of the state organizations, Butler turned to the unpromising alternative of trying to persuade them to accede to compromise, or "fusion" electoral tickets (to contain both Democrats pledged to vote for Sewall, and Populists pledged to vote for Watson). To achieve such a result, Butler required more than cooperation of the state organizations of his own party; he had also to depend upon the support of the Democratic national committee and the state Democratic organizations.

In September he had a long conversation in Washington with Senator Jones on fusion.[23] They reached an agreement that they would both put pressure on their state organizations to arrange for Democratic-Populist fusion in every state. In general the number of electors to be given each party on the fusion ticket would be in proportion to the votes which that party had received in the most recent election. Butler and Jones also agreed that whenever possible they should try to make fusion agreements on the congressional and state contests in order to avoid having two silver people running for the same office against a gold Republican candidate, but both clearly understood that such local fusion should never be consummated at the expense of Bryan-Sewall-Watson electoral fusion.[24]

Butler's task of arranging electoral fusion was handicapped in the South by the middle-of-the-road proclivities of southern Populists and by the reluctance of southern Democrats to cooperate with the Populists. Butler attempted to set the example in North Carolina, where he succeeded in getting a satisfactory electoral fusion for Democratic and Populist support of a Bryan-Sewall-Watson slate of electors.[25] Attempts to achieve similar Democratic-Populist cooperation on the state ticket failed; and on that level the North Carolina Populists fused with the Republicans, in the traditional alignment which had, in fact, made Butler United States Senator. Later, when the Populists had difficulty persuading Democrats to concede electors to them in Arkansas, Senator Jones's home state, Butler insisted that the failure of fusion in Arkansas was preventing Populist cooperation and fusion in other states. Finally, Jones forced Arkansas Democrats to accede to Butler's demands.[26]

Tom Watson viewed Butler's fusion strategy as a betrayal of the party as well as of himself as the vice-presidential candidate; and when Butler's program was blocked in Colorado and Kansas, Watson inaugurated a vituperative attack upon Butler and the Populist campaign committee. Though living in comparative isolation in Georgia, Watson edited a widely distributed journal, the *People's Party Paper;* and he also had access to the columns of the New York *World* in which Watson interviews and articles, often reprinted from the *People's Party Paper,* appeared frequently.[27]

When Watson's editorials in the *People's Party Paper* became too ill-tempered, Butler asked him to abandon his editorial position on that paper for the duration of the campaign. Watson consented to this; but, inevitably, the *People's Party Paper* continued to carp at

Butler's policies.[28] Likewise, when Watson's articles in the New York *World* grew too bitter, Butler asked Watson to abandon his connection with that paper. Again Watson agreed, but still interviews from Watson embarrassing to the Populist high command continued to appear in the *World*.[29] Watson believed that Butler's repeated "betrayals" of himself and the party freed him of any obligation to keep his pledge of silence.

Watson assumed that he would make an extensive speaking tour of the South and West, and at first this assumption was shared by Butler and his associates.[30] When sharp differences developed between Watson and Butler, Watson's eagerness to get out and meet state Populist leaders and to speak to the people increased, while Butler became correspondingly cool to such an idea.[31] Butler's coolness grew when it became evident that there were two areas in particular to which Watson wished to go; to states like Texas, where middle-of-the-road elements were dominant and Butler was having trouble in arranging fusion; and to states like Colorado and Kansas, where Populists had capitulated to the Democratic party.[32]

Watson doubtless was personally piqued by what he saw as Butler's willingness to sacrifice his nomination for the vice-presidency to political expedience, but he also disagreed with Butler on the strategy necessary to party survival. Watson believed that rigid adherence to traditional principles and a straightforward campaign for the party ticket of Bryan and Watson were necessary to the preservation of party integrity.[33] Thus the dilemma of the Populist party in 1896 was expressed in sharp focus in the feud which developed between Butler and Watson. Both men were right; both were wrong. The hard truth was that the Populist party was beyond salvation.

In September Watson went West to Texas, Colorado, Nebraska and Kansas.[34] Already Butler's fusion campaign was in progress, and Colorado and Kansas Populists had put up their electoral slate for Bryan and Sewall.[35] Interviews by Watson sharply critical of these developments, published in the New York *World*, had been given nationwide publicity; and sharply worded letters had been exchanged by Butler and Watson. Butler, fearing that Watson would harm the party and Bryan's campaign by taking the same tone in his western speeches as in these interviews, traveled down to Atlanta, Georgia, to talk with Watson.[36]

Butler came away from the interview with the belief that he had reached an understanding with Watson and that the latter would make no incendiary or divisive comments on his speaking tour. Watson's subsequent actions made it evident that Butler was mistaken. He stormed through Texas, shouting to cheering throngs his indignation at Butler's policies, attacking Sewall as a representative of monopolistic interests, and urging Texas Populists to stay in the middle-of-the-road.[37] It was announced that middle-of-the-road Populists in Texas were planning to bolt Butler's leadership, that they would repudiate Bryan and fuse with the Republicans in support of McKinley. Correspondence between Butler and the Texas Populists ceased, not to be revived in any satisfactory manner for the duration of the campaign.[38]

By such tactics in Texas, Watson prepared the way for a cool reception in the Mountain and Great Plains states. There he was shunted off to speak in small towns, and in most of his appearances he spoke to discouragingly small crowds.[39] When he visited Populist headquarters in Kansas, he walked through doors over which streamers carried the names of Bryan and Sewall, with no mention of Watson. He wanted to make more speeches in this section. But in most places there was no desire to hear him, and opportunities that might have been created were spoiled by lack of coordination between him and Butler.[40]

Watson spoke in Lincoln, Nebraska, at a time when Bryan was out of town. Here he made a strongly conciliatory speech backing Bryan, and Butler hastened to praise him for it.[41] Yet Butler's office remained anxious that Watson end his tour as quickly as possible. The argument which they carried to Watson to persuade him to return home was the imminence of the election in Georgia and their desire that in this first election in a southern state the Populists should make a strong showing.

Watson returned home, where alternately he sulked and raged. Never again did he make a speech outside of Georgia in this campaign, but he continued to make his views known in newspaper interviews and private letters. He now took the attitude that fusion was altogether a mistaken policy, that the only ticket which a Populist could support was Bryan and Watson. He encouraged middle-of-the-road activities in Texas and elsewhere and worked against fusion arrangements made by Butler and Washburn. He intervened openly to attempt to defeat fusion in Indiana. Butler had achieved fusion in that state after an extended and difficult negotiation, only to find success threatened at the last minute by Watson's intervention. Butler won the battle in Indiana, but the conflict between him and Watson in that state was destructive to their party.[42]

Up to the time that Watson returned in mid-September from his speaking tour West, Butler had continued to hope that he could persuade the Democrats to take Sewall off their ticket and substitute Watson. He sent letters to New England Populists asking them to investigate Sewall's political and business career. He hoped with the evidence thus garnered to go to the Democratic National Committee with the argument that Sewall was a recent and insincere convert to free silver, that he had not been constant in his loyalty to the Democratic party, and that he had been an unpopular political personality in his home community of Bath, Maine.[43]

By the middle of September it was evident that Sewall would not withdraw from the Democratic ticket.[44] Butler now found another expedient to sustain his belief that Watson would become Bryan's vice president. He wrote to Washburn, who was in close touch with Jones in Chicago, that during the September interview between himself and Jones he had told Jones that if Sewall were not withdrawn before the election, he would, after Bryan was elected, formally submit a request that Sewall be withdrawn and Watson substituted. Jones had replied that to withdraw Sewall from the ticket prior to the election would endanger Bryan's chances in pivotal states such as Indiana, Illinois, Michigan, Minnesota, and Iowa.[45] Butler felt, in regard to this argument, that the Populist party must not put itself in a position which would be interpreted after the election as having caused Bryan's defeat. Of course, he had also to admit to Washburn that Jones had made no promises regarding the suggested post-election substitution of Watson for Sewall. Watson's conduct so far had made it impossible, Butler said, to secure Sewall's withdrawal before the election. If Watson continued his course of action, he might make it impossible for Butler to request Sewall's withdrawal after the election.[46]

Butler now concentrated on the one activity which still seemed to offer some chance of party survival—to achieve as many state electoral fusions as possible. Thus, from Butler's office during the final weeks of the campaign issued a stream of letters to state party chairmen, as well as to Washburn and Jones in Chicago, discussing the details of fusion arrangements and pressing for agreements by which Sewall and Watson electors would share a fusion ticket with Bryan. As a result of his efforts fusion was arranged in most of the states of the Union.[47]

By this time Butler had convinced himself that his line of action on fusion was necessary to the preservation of the Populist party, that, indeed, it might be the basis of new growth by the party. Thus, he wrote to one of the leaders of the party in Tennessee:

> The strength of a new party is its capacity to increase its strength at every election. But whenever a new party begins to lose votes then the beginning of the end has been reached, because if you make converts, they will not join a party that is growing smaller. It was this view of the matter nationally that made it imperative for the People's Party to nominate Bryan and Watson. If we had not, our vote over the whole country would have been only about one-half this year of what it was last election. Now, to run a straight Bryan and Watson electoral ticket in any state has just the same effect as if we had not nominated Bryan; but, on the other hand, by nominating Bryan and by running joint electoral tickets in every state, we not only hold all of our own people, but we will actually make inroads into the ranks of the Democratic Party by our contact with them, so that when the time comes to draw the party line between us, in the future, we will take a large part of their rank and file with us.[48]

Butler also worked hard at achieving fusion on congressional and local tickets to prevent competition between men who favored free silver. His major objective here was agreement on a state-wide basis for a division of Democratic and Populist congressmen. When it appeared that this must be achieved by the withdrawal of Democrats in favor of Populists, he pressed Chairman Jones and Senator Faulkner, who was in charge of the Democratic congressional campaign offices in Washington, to intervene locally to persuade Democratic congressional candidates to withdraw.[49] When it appeared that the withdrawal of a Populist candidate was necessary, Butler wrote to the candidate directly, explaining the circumstances which made the action necessary and asking the personal sacrifice in the interest of the party and the cause.[50]

The Butler-Watson feud became increasingly vituperative as the campaign approached its conclusion. Watson complained about the seeming reluctance of the National Committee formally to notify both Bryan and himself of their nominations. He was particularly bitter about the failure to notify Bryan, because he believed that the committee hesitated out of fear of embarrassing Bryan. If Bryan were to be embarrassed by the Populist nomination, concluded Watson, then he ought not to have it at all.[51] Also galling to Watson was the failure of the Populists in Colorado and Kansas to take down their Bryan-Sewall tickets and substitute a Bryan-Watson ticket.[52]

Relations between Butler and Watson were further strained at the end of the campaign by a mixup over the receipt by Butler of Watson's letter of acceptance. In mid-October Butler reported to Watson that the party's campaign book had not been published because they did not yet have Watson's letter of acceptance. When Watson mailed the letter to Butler, announcing publicly that he had done so, Butler failed to receive it for several days.[53] When he had received it and read it, Butler refused to publish it under the auspices of the Populist party until Watson altered it. Butler wrote to Watson that he objected particularly to the stand taken in the letter against the fusion electoral tickets. If enough Populists followed this advice, Butler believed that McKinley would win. Furthermore, the Populists would not win a single vote in electoral college.[54]

Watson's reply was scornfully belligerent. He could not believe, he said, that his letter had been delayed in delivery for lack of postage. He asserted that J. A. Edgerton, Populist party Secretary, to whom the letter had been addressed, had been in possession of the letter all the time and that Butler had known this. He sweepingly condemned Butler's conduct of the campaign: "Instead of managing this great campaign in a spirit of broad patriotism and of courageous loyalty to your nominee and your party, you have allowed your personal ill-will towards me to divert you into a tortuous, narrow, jealous and disloyal policy which has shipwrecked the People's Party and brought the success of Mr. Bryan to a crisis of extreme peril." In reply to Butler's suggestion that he modify the letter of acceptance for publication he said, "my letter . . . must stand just as it is written." [55]

George F. Washburn rounded out the negativism with which the Populist campaign concluded by issuing from Chicago a special address to the voters. It was not a positive challenge to a brave new world but rather a warning to the people that they be "on guard." He quoted Republican threats of forceful opposition to Bryan if he should win the election. Washburn advised the voters that they should pay no attention to sensational reports of violence or coercion and reminded them that the ballot was secret. "Insist on your rights," Washburn admonished.[56]

Early in 1896 the Populist party had lost the initiative to the Democrats. Butler had not succeeded in regaining the advantage which the party had lost. The most that can be said is that under his leadership the party yielded as gracefully as possible to the inevitable. He was probably right when he contended that Watson's middle-of-the-road approach to the party's problems would saddle the party with the blame for Bryan's defeat and result at an early date in the party's demise.

Butler was not responsible for the mistakes in judgment which had brought the party to its destruction. Perhaps no individual in the party should be blamed for that. Once the Democratic party had been captured by the agrarian free silver faction there was little that the Populists could do to prevent the erosion of their membership in all sections of the country. Nevertheless, their failure to recognize this development within the Democratic party until long after it was a fact and their ineptitude in dealing with it prior to the St. Louis convention speeded the inevitable disintegration.

The urban socialist wing of the Populist party was also cast adrift by the decision of the convention in St. Louis and the attitudes adopted in the ensuing campaign. This faction had been conceded nothing in the national convention. It was ignored in the campaign, and socialists were defeated in their attempts to gain the upper hand in the various state organizations. Watson as vice-presidential candidate had no appeal to them. In the period before the convention he had led a fight in Georgia and the South against socialist influence in the party. In the campaign he talked of the Populist party of the future as a party which would win victories by combining the farm votes of the West and the South.[57] Watson, like most of his Populist colleagues, operated from the Jacksonian agrarian tradition.

Butler and the other men in the Populist hierarchy were aware of the importance of the labor vote. They recognized that other issues than free silver, particularly the injunction issue, were potentially of interest to labor. They also believed that the labor vote of the Middle West would be decisive in the election.[58] But for the Populists as for the Democrats the failure in dealing with labor was two-headed. On one side they operated with the belief that an idealistic appeal to class interest would be decisive, that it would outpull the pragmatic Republican appeal. On the other side, they assumed that working men and labor organizations would provide material aid. Labor simply did not respond. The head of the Knights of Labor, James K. Sovereign, established a special Labor Bureau in Chicago to raise money and to carry on propaganda work. He did not get any money, and without money he could not finance propaganda.[59] Eugene Debs gave verbal support, but personally he was more deeply involved in other matters.[60]

A large group of Socialists, including Berger, Lloyd, and Bellamy, between 1890 and 1896 had supported cooperation with the Populist party, though they had not (outside of Chicago) developed a unified, aggressive movement to impose socialist principles upon it. Most of them were disillusioned by the action of the Populist party in the St. Louis convention and did not join the Populist campaign in 1896.[61]

The leaders of the Socialist Labor party, the country's one significant Marxist movement, found nothing in the developments of 1896 to persuade them that such "middle class" organizations as the Populist party offered a prospective base for socialist agitation.[62] It was a foregone conclusion that the Socialist Labor party would nominate an independent ticket and conduct a campaign bitterly hostile to Bryan and free silver.[63] Most of them could not agree with Victor Berger, who was to write a few weeks after the election that "the farmer element of America is revolutionary and apt to listen to new ideas." [64] They saw in the Populist and Democratic platforms and campaigns a betrayal of the working men.[65] In some instances the bitterness of their opposition to free silver caused them to make an open declaration for the gold standard.[66]

Though the National Silver party retained the skeleton of an independent organization, there was no doubt that it unreservedly supported the Democratic ticket. This party remained in existence in part because of inertia, in part because it could serve some usefulness to both the Democratic and Populist organizations by operating outside of them, and in part because an independent silver organization might be desirable in the post-election period. Another factor making continued existence of the party desirable was the original party affiliations of its members. A large majority of its membership had come from the Republican party. If they were cut loose by the dissolution of the party, they might drift back to their former allegiance.[67]

The party set up headquarters in both Washington, D.C., and Chicago. In both cities the liaison with the Populists and Democrats was intimate.[68] In New York William P. St. John, treasurer of the Democratic National Committee, was also the treasurer of the new silver party.[69] Colorado silverite, Isaac N. Stevens, was in charge of the Washington office, while liaison activities in Chicago were under the direction of Senator William M. Stewart.

Because of its close association with the mining interests of the West the National Silver party was more lavishly financed than either the Democratic or Populist parties. Since it was encumbered with no problems regarding its future organization as a political movement, it was able to devote all of its funds to the propaganda for Bryan and silver. Shortly after the election Chairman Stevens wrote to Mrs. Bryan that the committee had distributed ten million documents and had organized five thousand silver clubs, chiefly in the Middle West. They had also financed the tours of several silver speakers.[70]

The propaganda work of the National Silver party had been concentrated heavily upon the city of Chicago, the center of the middle western campaign. There alone over six hundred silver clubs had been organized and there was organized a party auxiliary, the Women's National Silver League. This organization, in the final stages of the campaign, hired several halls in Chicago in which every day they conducted discussion meetings on the silver question beginning at noon and continuing until as late at night as anyone cared to stay.

Both the Populist and Democratic campaign managers, swamped with requests for pamphlets which they could not fill because of their poverty, advised their correspondents to appeal to the National Silver party for literature. This the party did provide in greater quantity than anyone else on the silver side of the debate.

Another source of unreserved support for the Democratic ticket was Senator Teller. He campaigned long and hard, concentrating on Republican areas in the Middle West. The Senator emphasized the financial issue, but he also defended the Democratic platform's criticism of the Supreme Court's income tax decision. He also played an important role in raising money in the West for the Democratic campaign.[71]

Senator Teller also took upon himself the major burden of guiding and protecting the political careers of the silver men who had joined him in bolting the Republican party.[72] It was necessary for him to assume this task because he found that not all of the bolters agreed with him that there was no future in their section for the Republican party. He also felt that he bore a personal responsibility to them for having persuaded them to leave their party.

Teller did not achieve much success either in attempting to guide or to protect fellow Republicans. They could not so readily see the logic of joining the Democratic party when the Republican party in campaigning in their section emphasized international bimetallism and higher tariffs on wool and lead.[73] Also, Teller's work in this respect was handicapped by the refusal of the Democrats to make concessions to silver Republican requests. When Idaho Democrats and Populists refused to cooperate with silver Republicans in support of Dubois' campaign for the Senate, a situation was created which pointed up for silver Republicans throughout the West the difficulties of their position.[74]

The silver Republicans developed embryonic state organizations to represent their special interest in local politics, but on the national level they cooperated with Democrats to support the Bryan-Sewall ticket. It was their relationship with western Populists that posed the most difficult problem, not only because of the vice-presidential question but also because of their historic antagonism. Thus, the campaign and the election of 1896 erected no clear signposts to give direction to the silver Republicans cast adrift by the storm over free silver.

23

Battle's End:
The Issue, the Voter,
and the Election

For the people it was a campaign of study and analysis, of exhortation and conviction—a campaign of search for economic and political truth. Pamphlets tumbled from the presses, to be snatched up eagerly, to be read, reread, studied, debated, to become guides to economic thought and political action. They were printed and distributed by the millions, enough to provide several copies for every man, woman, and child in the country; but the people clamored for more. Favorite pamphlets became dog-eared, grimy, fell apart as their owners laboriously restudied their arguments and quoted from them in public and private debate. They were passed from hand to hand and were used as reference guides in the discussion groups and debating clubs which appeared at crossroads and hamlets across the land.[1] A resident of a small town in Nebraska has described how the citizens of that community reacted:

O'Neill buzzed with political disputation from dawn till next dawn. A bowery had been built for the Fourth of July picnic and dance. Ordinarily, it was torn down after that event. In 1896 it was kept as a forum, and by day and by night men and women . . . met there to talk about the Crime of '73, the fallacies of the gold standard, bimetallism and international consent, the evils of the tariff, the moneybags of Mark Hanna, the front-porch campaign of McKinley. They read W. H. Harvey's *Coin's Financial School* to themselves, their friends, and opponents. They reread Mrs. Emery's *Seven*

Financial Conspiracies. They, like myself, found Tom Patterson's *Rocky Mountain News.* They read Bryan when they couldn't go off to listen to him.[2]

Speakers posing as experts on the money question traveled up and down the land. Free silver orators emulated Coin, organizing their arguments in a kind of question and answer catechism; or they aspired to the eloquence and stage presence of their champion, William Jennings Bryan. The fact that the sound money men possessed no spokesman distinguished nationally for his eloquent defense of their argument did not discourage them from entering upon the oratorical battle field. They utilized the services of such adept phrase-makers as Chauncey Depew and Bourke Cockran and leaned heavily upon the careful arguments of platform pundits like William D. Bynum and Professor Laughlin. They also exploited upon the lecture platform the respectability and patriotic appeal of such men as ex-President Harrison, General Palmer, and Carl Schurz.

The people seem to have listened to speeches as tirelessly as they read pamphlets. Newspapers, diaries, and letters recount how audiences, after listening to one speaker for more than an hour, would call for other orators, a process that often extended meetings for several hours.[3] Perhaps the oratorical endurance record of the campaign was set in Aberdeen, South Dakota, when Bryan spoke there on October 9. He described the event: "I made three speeches to three large audiences, between the hours of half past one and half past two A.M. The first meeting was held in Exposition Hall, where the audience had assembled at seven o'clock. Senator Peffer, of Kansas, Senator Kyle, of South Dakota, and others had spoken during the six hours which elapsed between the opening of the meeting and the arrival of our train." [4]

The newspapers and magazines perforce took up the debate and devoted much of their space to the journalistic process of educating and exciting the public mind. They reported the speeches and published the complete texts of the more striking and important. They printed specially prepared articles setting forth the general and specific arguments of the great debate on money. Their columns were particularly adaptable to arguments addressed to special interest groups, and there were to be found numerous articles describing how free silver would affect the industrial worker, the farmer in and out of debt, the widow living on a pension, the retired and unretired railroad worker, the holder of an insurance policy, and so on.[5]

Employers made arrangements to insure that the process of education and discussion not be suspended while their employees were at work. They printed quotations of the arguments which they favored on placards and posted them in the shops where they could be read by their employees at their machines. They distributed pamphlets among their workers. They hired "experts" on the money question as shop foremen or gave special indoctrination classes to existing foremen and then encouraged their employees to talk with their foremen, if they had any questions about the monetary issue of the campaign. They arranged for speakers to talk to the men during the lunch hour. They slipped leaflets on the money question into the men's pay envelopes or put in little typed slips warning their workers that if Bryan won and free silver were adopted, even if their salaries remained what they were and they retained their jobs, the purchasing power of their wages would be reduced by one-half.[6] They developed sound money clubs among their working men and then exerted pressure on the men to join the club and attend its "educational" meetings. They organized excursions to the front-porch at Canton, gave the men time off, and paid their railroad fares to visit McKinley.[7]

The railroads, more conscious than most industries of the significance of the flow of foreign capital into the country and fearful that it would be discouraged by free silver, conducted a particularly energetic campaign among their employees. Their arguments were directly to the pocketbook. In pamphlets distributed among their employees they pictured their plight if a free silver bill were passed. The railroad business would be threatened with bankruptcy, they argued; because the money which they took in on the basis of current rates and fares would be worth only half of its current value, while rising prices would increase their own costs. If they raised fares, they would lose business. Certainly they would have to curtail, if not entirely suspend, operations. Some, perhaps all, of their men would lose their jobs. Even though wages would have a reduced purchasing power, they would not be able to increase them. In fact, there would be strong economic pressure to reduce them.[8]

Customers and clients of American business organizations also discovered that along with their accustomed goods and services they were to receive a course in education on the campaign issue. Insurance companies, thoroughly frightened by the effect they thought free silver would have on financial stability, sent educational literature and direct warnings to their policy holders. They warned of the necessity of cancelling policies if free silver won and informed those who held equities in insurance policies that their value would be reduced by one-half through the inflation that would accompany free silver.[9] Mortgage companies, also uncertain of the future, reduced their loans, informed men who sought to borrow money that they could get it after election only if McKinley won, and told those to whom they had loaned money that their mortgages would not be renewed if Bryan won.[10]

There seemed for most men to be but one issue in this extraordinary campaign. McKinley and Hanna tried to keep the tariff issue in perspective and at the beginning of the campaign even aspired to make it the major issue; but they made no headway against the floodtide of the free silver debate. During the summer and fall of the campaign the millions of pieces of literature which spewed from Republican campaign headquarters dealt mostly with the monetary question. Though McKinley in his speeches on the front porch continued to bear down heavily on the tariff issue and Republican broadsides pictured protection as the key to prosperity, William Jennings Bryan hardly ever mentioned the tariff, and then usually to explain that he did not consider it to be a question of any importance in the current campaign. Literature sent out to the people from the Democratic and from the allied Populist and Silver party headquarters was devoted mainly to discussion of the financial issue.

Foreign policy issues, too, were almost totally submerged by the debate over free silver. In 1895 there had been considerable speculation about the impact of the Hawaiian annexation problem, the Venezuelan boundary dispute, and the Cuban insurrection on the presidential race in 1896. It was commonly suggested, for example, that Cleveland's aggressive intervention in the Venezuelan dispute was intended to divert national attention from the free silver issue.[11] On most of these foreign policy issues public opinion and party positions were not sharply defined. Recent elections had shown that it was inadvisable for a party to appear to be friendly toward England, and the Republicans certainly recognized the danger of being characterized as pro-English if they attacked Cleveland's Venezuelan policy. When John Hay was questioned by a British politician on McKinley's attitude toward the application of the Monroe Doctrine in the Venezuelan dispute, he took care to state that McKinley would probably follow Cleveland in applying the Doctrine.[12] But the people were more interested in other issues in 1896, and none of the principals in the campaign saw any advantage for himself in diverting their attention to foreign policy.

It was not to be expected that the compaign discussion of the money issue would be restricted to the technical economic principles involved, for both sides in the debate saw the money issue as an ideological question cutting deeply and broadly across the structure of American society. The opponents of free silver believed that policy to be revolutionary, unpatriotic, and immoral—painfully destructive of the intricately woven fabric of American life. They associated it with the quirks of personality and the political programs of men like "Pardon" Altgeld, "Pitchfork Ben" Tillman, and "Bloody Bridles" Waite, whom they believed to be dangerous revolutionaries. They pictured free silver as an ally of the subversive "isms," anarchism, socialism, communism, and Populism. Postmaster General Wilson wrote in his diary that he had concluded that the silver leaders "are socialists, anarchists and demagogues of a dangerous type and a supreme test of our institutions seems ahead of us." [13] The *New York Times* published a letter from "an old Gentleman," who said that "within six months of Bryan's election mobs would be rushing up and down our streets howling for bread." He said further that with Bryan's election "I believe we should have anarchy here," and that "the Republican form of Government is on trial here." [14]

The other election issues of such importance to the conservatives who argued the sound money policy—the question of the income tax, the independence of the Supreme Court, the use of injunctions in labor disputes—were not widely discussed. Generally they were mentioned only as auxiliaries to the free silver "heresy" or as concomitants of the disaster which would strike when free silver was adopted. Sometimes a mere statement of indignation caught public attention. William Allen White's editorial essay, "What's the Matter with Kansas?" was no more than a petulant and superficial attack upon the local leaders of the Populist movement. Yet it had a quality which appealed to the sensibilities of conservatives in all sections, and the Republican campaign committee distributed more than a million copies of it.[15]

Long before the election free silver had become to Andrew Carnegie "a Moral Issue." He wrote to William Ewart Gladstone: "You will be pleased to know that the forces of Law, Order & Honesty in the Republic are on the eve of a remarkable triumph— Not through one party but by a Union of the very best elements of both— It has risen to the level of a Moral Issue & you will hear Novr. 4th of a sweep— I think sufficiently overpowering as to enable us to put the Country on the Gold Standard as firmly as England." [16] Carnegie had expressed in his own fashion one of the major conservative arguments against free silver, that as an inflationary proposal which would take money from the pockets of creditors to benefit debtors it was basically dishonest.

Once the monetary question became a moral issue it was judged by conservatives as being properly within the province of the clergy. Rarely, if ever, have ministers spoken so forthrightly on politics as in this campaign. Generally the press, opposed to Bryan to an overwhelming degree, approved the campaign speeches which the clergymen delivered from their pulpits, often to the applause of aroused congregations. The Chicago *Tribune* editorially praised Chicago ministers "who have started to impress upon their congregations the infamous project of immorality which Bryan is seeking to impose on the people as a national financial principle." In further explanation the *Tribune* said: "It is in no respect a question of politics, but of moral principle. It is taking the commandment, 'Thou Shalt not Steal,' which is a common text, and applying it to the Nation." [17]

When one Chicago minister formally declared himself in favor of free silver and Bryan, the *Tribune*, concluding that he was "adrift from his moorings," hypothesized that his error sprang from immersing himself too exclusively in the spiritual life: "No doubt he has been so busy investigating dogmatic theology and in studying things pertaining to the Kingdom of Heaven that he has had no time to study things which pertain to the kingdom of the earth." [18]

Whatever eloquence sound money lacked on the political platform was more than compensated for in the nation's pulpits, particularly the more influential pulpits of the great metropolitan churches. On a Sunday morning in mid-September the Reverend Cortland Myers, speaking in the Baptist Temple in Brooklyn, New York, said that the Democratic platform had been made in Hell and that Altgeld and his associates had acted as the devil's stenographers and prompters.[19] Two weeks later he preached on the subject of "Anarchy in the Chicago Platform," using as his text the plank in the Chicago platform which denounced Federal interference in strikes and riots. In the course of a passionate denunciation of the Democrats he said: "Surely this is not a platform; it is a scaffold. The only King in this land is King Law. Allow the mob to drag him from his throne and you have riot and bloodshed and mob government." [20]

In Chicago another minister preaching on the theme, "The Immorality of Repudiation," aroused his congregation to applause as he said: "Once more is society rent with strife over not what belongs to ordinary politics, but what belongs to national conscience and to civilization itself. Some there are who do seriously propose to tamper with the monetary standard, upon which innumerable contracts have been made, the change in standards making it possible for men to escape their obligations under the shelter of party and of law, so that fraud may be committed under the genius of perfect equity." [21]

The newspapers and the ministers accused Bryan and his supporters of blasphemy. They were particularly critical of his use of such phrases as "crown of thorns" and "cross of gold." [22]

The propagandists for free silver cared no more than their opponents to restrict their arguments to economic principles. To them, too, it was a campaign involving great social and moral principles—the drift of civilization.[23] Free silver became, to them, a symbol for social progress and social justice. To those who came to free silver through the regular party system, it was sufficiently convincing to relate it to the Jeffersonian and Jacksonian traditions of hostility to monopolistic corporations and bankers. Said lifelong Democrat, Champ Clark, "The people might as well recognize the fact that all the trusts in the land are cheek and jowl with Hanna...." [24] In Wisconsin Democratic State Chairman E. C. Wall wrote, "The fight today is, in my judgment, whether there shall be a republic or not. Whether a few men of wealth shall govern this land or the people." [25] To those who had burst the bonds of traditional politics the fact that men like Edward Bellamy, Eugene Debs, and Henry George, already major symbols of social reform, campaigned for Bryan and free silver was proof that free silver had significance ranging far beyond the principles of money and banking.

Since the major propagandists thought of the campaign in either cataclysmic or paradisiacal terms, it was to be expected that they would refer frequently to the parallels between the elections of 1896 and 1860. In 1860, too, parties had been split on sectional lines over a great moral issue involving the very framework of American society. Free silver Democrats and Populists saw themselves like Lincoln and the Republican party riding on the wave of the future to great glory. Republican conservatives saw free silver as an immoral issue comparable to slavery, justifying, if need be, violent action and personal sacrifice to save the republic. Democrat conservatives saw that, too; but gloomily they saw also the disasters of party and sectional division and the horrors of class and sectional warfare.[26] Under such circumstances, as election day approached the temper of the nation became increasingly feverish. On the weekend which preceded the day of decision the hysteria in many quarters seemed close to the breaking point. The Democrats and Populists (still being referred to as "Popocrats" by their opponents) frantically warned each other and the country at large to beware of Republican election frauds.[27] Newspapers which reflected their thinking reported that in Texas a suit had been instituted against Mark Hanna on the basis of a discovery that he had imported money into that state to buy votes.[28] The St. Louis *Post Dispatch,* which gave a prominent place in its columns to these reports from Texas, concluded in an editorial: "Hanna in striped clothes would be a fitting 'object lesson' for the close of the Wall Street campaign. The penitentiary yawns for him and his confederates." [29]

Bryan's supporters also reported mounting evidence of coercion of the voters by Republican employers, bankers, and businessmen.[30] Doubtless many of these reports were exaggerated, but it was evident that men with large interests to protect did try to influence the votes of men who were their dependents. McKinley's managers and the voters who backed him felt that in the final weeks of the campaign their "Popocratic" opponents had abandoned specific issues for a broadly ideological program intended to pit the masses against the classes. They felt that no holds were barred when their existence was so threatened.[31] There were probably few cases of direct individual threats to call in mortgages or cut off jobs in case of a Bryan victory. Frequently, however, employers and bankers let the word slip out that McKinley's defeat would fall very hard upon their businesses with the result that they would have to cut down operations or reduce their loans.[32]

Many bankers and financiers were on the verge of panic. They were calling in money and building up their gold reserves, attempting to protect themselves against the financial disasters which they anticipated if Bryan should win. As a result, there were heavy withdrawals of gold from the government's sub-treasuries.[33]

There was no evidence that the leaders of the country's Protestant churches attempted to do anything but heighten the hysteria which existed in these final hours of the campaign. Hanna's Flag Day parade occurred on the Saturday preceding the election, and many preachers in their sermons on the following day drove home the point that the flag was a symbol of McKinleyism. Preaching in New York's Madison Square Presbyterian Church Dr. Charles H. Parkhurst said, "the one thing which the solid intelligent integrity of the country has to do this week is to grind its heel relentlessly and unpityingly into the viperous head that is lifting itself up in venomous antagonism not only to this Government, but in venomous antagonism to all government." [34] In the same city that Sunday Reverend Thomas Dixon, Jr., preaching in the Academy of Music on the subject, "The Eve of Battle," gave explicit instructions to his listeners as to their obligations when they entered the polling booth: "We are on the eve of the greatest political battle this country has seen for years, if ever. It is a contest between honesty, national honor and patriotism on the one hand, and dishonesty, repudiation and dishonor on the other. McKinley stands for all the patriotism and honor there is in this campaign, and Bryan for anarchy, repudiation, and national dishonor." [35]

Election day itself proved to be so calm as to be an anticlimax to the hectic campaign. There was undoubtedly an air of tense expectation of most important results, but there was no major untoward incident at the polls. Voting in most sections was unusually heavy, and the total vote greatly exceeded any vote cast in preceding presidential elections. Not until 1908 would as many ballots be cast as in 1896. It was evident that the people felt that issues of great import had dominated the campaign, and they went to the polls with an earnest purposefulness unusual to American politics.

The pro-McKinley newspapers, Republican publicists, and many businessmen had hoped for a vote so one-sided that it would silence forever the doctrines of inflation and "repudiation" upon which the Democrats had campaigned. They proceeded at once to read into the returns the realization of their hopes.[36]

The Democrats, on the other hand, developed the thesis that the Republicans had won the victory by a narrow and uncertain margin and that 1896 was but the "first battle" in the struggle of the people against Wall Street and allied evils.[37] Senator Jones did not permit Bryan to concede the election until the afternoon of the day following the balloting. The Democrats had remained confident of victory to the last minute; [38] and Jones delayed the concession to McKinley, hoping that the rural votes, which were reported slowly, would change the count in a sufficient number of close states to throw the victory to Bryan.[39] For years afterward Democratic commentators (with Bryan setting the pace) comforted themselves by juggling the vote figures to show that changes of a few hundred votes in certain states where the margin of McKinley's victory was narrow would have given Bryan the election, in spite of the fact that McKinley's popular majority was 569,748 votes.[40]

Democratic spokesmen elaborating upon how near they had come to victory claimed that in a fair election they would have won. In private letter and in public print they exchanged information about the use of coercive pressure and ballot fraud and bribery.[41] On the day after election Senator Jones charged: "The result was brought about by every kind of coercion and intimidation on the part of the money power, including threats of lock-outs and dismissals, and impending starvation; by the employment of by far the largest campaign fund ever used in this country and by the subsidization of a large portion of the American press." [42]

In certain respects the victory was everything which the most enthusiastic Republican observers claimed. In the New England and Middle Atlantic states they won overwhelmingly, establishing unprecedented margins of victory and reversing all gains which Cleveland had made in 1892. For example, Cleveland that year had carried one New England state, Connecticut, by a majority of more than 5,000 out of about 165,000 votes. In 1896 Connecticut went Republican by a majority of 54,000 out of 175,000 votes.[43] In 1892 Harrison received 53,405 more votes than Cleveland in New England; in 1896 McKinley's vote there exceeded Bryan's by 172,725.

In the Middle Atlantic states Cleveland carried two in 1892, New Jersey and New York, losing only Pennsylvania, though his margin of victory was so narrow that in the section as a whole Harrison received 3,604 more votes than he did. In 1896 McKinley carried all three states by large majorities, and his vote in the section altogether was 657,336 greater than Bryan's.

In the states of the Old Northwest the change in the vote was equally

decisive and from the perspective of later years of long-range significance. Here in 1892 Cleveland had carried Illinois, Indiana, and Wisconsin; and in the section overall his vote margin had exceeded Harrison's by 21,202. In 1896 Bryan lost every state, and McKinley's
margin of victory was 368,050 votes. Two states won by Cleveland,
Illinois and Wisconsin, gave McKinley his largest victories in this section, with majorities of 142,625 and 102,612 respectively. His majority
in Michigan was also comfortable; but in Indiana he won by only 18,181
votes (out of a total of 637,119) and in his home state by 48,494 (out
of a total of 1,014,295), a result which he found keenly disappointing.[44]

In the North Central section (between the Mississippi and the
Rockies and from the Canadian border to Arkansas) the story was quite
different. Here Cleveland carried no state but Missouri in 1892 and
got 268,396 fewer votes than Harrison. However, Cleveland's name
had not been on the ticket in Kansas or in North and South Dakota.
In these states as well as in Nebraska, where Cleveland's name was
on the ballot, the Democratic National Committee encouraged Democrats to throw their support to Weaver, the Populist candidate. As a
result Weaver won 382,725 votes in that section and the electoral votes
of Kansas and North Dakota.

In 1896 McKinley's vote in the North Central section exceeded
Bryan's by only 41,820; and Bryan won the electoral votes of Kansas,
Missouri, Nebraska, and South Dakota. Further, the margin of Mc-
Kinley's victory in the remaining states of the section—Minnesota,
Iowa, and North Dakota—was very close. It should also be noted that
Bryan did not receive large majorities in those states which he carried.
In fact, even in Missouri his plurality was only 58,727 in a total vote
of 674,030.

The Rocky Mountain states produced a distinctively different pattern
of change. Here in the section overall in 1892, 13,297 votes had been
cast for Cleveland, 77,299 for Harrison, and 86,424 for Weaver. In
Colorado and Wyoming Cleveland's name was not on the ballot. Harrison carried Montana and Wyoming, Weaver the others. In 1896
Bryan's sectional majority was 238,566 out of a total vote of 379,285;
and he carried every state in the section.

On the Pacific Coast no dramatic change occurred. In 1892 Harrison received in that section 17,313 more votes than Cleveland. In
1896 McKinley won 13,160 more votes than Bryan. However, in 1892
there were many Populist votes in all three states of the section; and

Cleveland won the electoral votes of both Oregon and California, though his majority over Harrison in the latter (where 25,312 Populist votes were cast) was only 147. In 1896 Bryan won only in Washington; but there his majority was decisive, while McKinley's majorities in California and Oregon were small.

The returns from the South were generally everything the agrarian Democrats had anticipated. Democratic majorities were sufficiently large to assure the continuation of the "solid South." These majorities were not always larger than the majorities of 1892. In fact, in most southern states the Republican vote increased more than the Democratic vote. The most significant change, however, occurred in the Populist column. In 1892 the Populists had registered a high enough vote to hold the balance of power in Missouri and North Carolina and had registered alarmingly high totals in other southern states. In every southern state the votes recorded for the Bryan-Watson ticket in 1896 were sharply below those cast for Weaver and Field in 1892; and in no state were the Populists, as far as the electoral vote was concerned, in the position of holding the balance of power between the two parties.

Three states in the Upper South—Delaware, Maryland, and Kentucky—carried by Cleveland in 1892, were lost by Bryan, though not by large majorities. Republicans claimed that these victories in the Upper South marked the beginning of the breakdown of the "solid South." Nothing could have been further from the truth. In earlier years the rise of the Populist party had, indeed, threatened to break the "solid South." Now the election returns from the South made certain what the campaign had foreshadowed—that southern Populism was in retreat, and to the Democratic, not the Republican camp.

North Carolina Populists were proud of the maneuver by which they fused with the Democrats on the electoral and with Republicans on the state tickets, for they won the contests in both areas.[45] If all southern Populists had achieved similar results, the story of the party may well have been different. But the North Carolina victory stood alone. Texas polled the largest vote for the straight Populist ticket, a total approaching 80,000; but this was 20,000 less than the vote polled by Weaver in 1892, while the Democrats polled 130,000 more votes than in 1892.

The Democratic ticket, in defeat, won 750,000 more votes than Cleveland, in victory, had won in 1892. In fact, not until 1916 would the votes cast for a Democratic candidate exceed those cast for Bryan in 1896. The Republican ticket received almost 2,000,000 more votes than Harrison had received while going down to defeat in 1892.

Partly the increased votes for the Republican and Democratic tickets came from Populists returning to their traditional party allegiances. In 1892 Weaver had received 1,040,600 votes, while the Bryan-Watson ticket in 1896 received 222,207. In some states, however, Populists refused in protest to vote at all; and in some southern states Negro Populists were denied the right to vote by changes in election laws. In the main the large increase in the number of votes cast stemmed from the fact that the excitement of the campaign drew to the polls men who ordinarily did not bother to vote.

In some states, such as Indiana, Ohio, and Michigan these new voters divided their ballots almost equally between the two parties, showing only a slight preference for the Republicans; but in certain key states of the populous northern sector of the country the swing of the new voters to the Republican party was marked. In Illinois, for example, the Democratic vote was only 30,000 greater than in 1892, while the Republican vote increased by more than 200,000. In Wisconsin the Republican vote increased by almost 100,000, while the Democrats suffered a loss of almost 10,000 as compared with 1892. In Pennsylvania the Democratic votes declined by 20,000, while the Republicans gained more than 200,000 over their 1892 totals. In New Jersey the Republicans gained 65,000, while the Democrats lost 40,000 votes. In New York the Democratic vote declined by slightly more than 100,000, but the Republican vote increased by 210,000.

In this strategic northern sector the marked shift of the urban vote to the Republican side in the states west of the Alleghenies was significant. This urban shift was not so violent in the New England and Middle Atlantic states. In fact, in these states generally the Democratic ticket fared better in the urban than in the rural districts, though rarely in either quarter did it receive as much as 30 per cent of the total vote. In the Old Northwest, however, where the percentage of votes cast for the Democratic ticket was much higher, the Republican vote in the urban districts tended to be considerably higher than in the rural districts. Only in Wisconsin did Bryan do better in the urban than in the rural areas. Yet in none of these states was the urban vote decisive; because in all of them—Indiana, Illinois, Michigan, Ohio, and Wisconsin—McKinley received a majority of the rural as well as the urban vote.[46]

There was only one section of the country in which Bryan won a clear majority of the urban vote—the Rocky Mountain states; and there he carried a higher percentage of the city vote (87.75) than of the country vote (81.54).[47] On the West Coast Oregon was lost to the Democrats through the city vote, for here Bryan won slightly more than 50 per cent of the vote in rural areas but won only 33.88 per cent of the urban vote.[48] In the South the Bryan ticket won 57.96 per cent of the total vote, but it did not carry the urban districts. Bryan received 44.46 per cent of the urban vote in the South, while winning 59.08 per cent of the rural vote.[49]

Thus, in the main the Bryan vote was a rural vote. In this connection the fact that he gained a larger percentage of urban than rural voters in New England was of no significance when it is remembered that he received overall but 27.18 per cent of the total vote of the New England states. It was significant, however, that Bryan lost every one of the highly urbanized northern states from the Mississippi Valley eastward to the Atlantic. The only conclusion to be reached was that the Bryan campaign, with its strong emphasis on the free coinage of silver at 16 to 1, had not appealed to the urban working classes.

In the eastern cities the Democratic vote in 1896 was about the same as in 1892. In New York this reflected the effective work of the Tammany machine in supporting Bryan and in New York, Boston, and elsewhere in the East reflected also the continuing loyalty of the Irish voter to the Democratic party.

It was in those cities (except Milwaukee) in which there was a large German population that the drop in the Democratic vote was most marked; for the election statistics in both the urban and the rural areas make it clear that among German voters there was a decisive shift from the Democratic to the Republican party. During the campaign close observers had noted that Americans of German birth or extraction were repelled by the Democratic financial program. Republicans reported that the defections from their party in rural areas in the Middle West were likely to be matched by the departure of German farmers from their traditional allegiance to the Democratic party.[50] One major German newspaper, the Chicago *Freie Presse*, had supported the Democratic ticket; but generally the German press backed Mc-

Kinley on the monetary issue. Publication of campaign literature in the German language had been a major program of the Republican campaign. The Democratic effort to counter the Republican propaganda against the unsoundness of the Democratic monetary proposals by circulating a statement by Bismarck favoring bimetallism met with little response among the German voters.[51]

Nationality groups from eastern and southern Europe, now moving so rapidly into the cities of the East and Middle West, were also drawn into the Republican party during the campaign of 1896. As among the Germans, their newspapers in the main supported McKinley, and the Republican campaign organization subsidized the circulation of literature in their native languages. Speakers employed by the Republican party addressed them in their native tongues. Among these new voters, who had no experience with American political traditions and no familiarity with traditional political ideologies in the United States, the Bryan campaign, with its strong appeal to the traditions of Jefferson and Jackson, had little meaning.[52] Among these voters the Republicans scored heavily by concentrating on the more pragmatic aspects of their campaign argument, with the promise of increasing prosperity, more jobs, and higher wages. Here, too, the American Protective Association's attack on McKinley had attracted votes to the Republican party, once he was the party's nominee.

The Republican party, under the skillful leadership of McKinley and Hanna, produced a combination of votes which gave it the victory in 1896 and which promised Republican ascendancy for many years in the future. In the East, where the close balance between Republican and Democratic parties in preceding years had proved an embarrassment to both parties, the Republicans strengthened their position. Not until 1932 would New York give a majority of its votes to the Democratic party. (In 1912 Wilson received the state's electoral votes, but he did not have a majority of the popular vote.)

Never again, however, would the electoral votes of New York be the determining factor as they had been in the elections of 1884 and 1888; for it was in the Middle West that the most important accretion in Republican power was achieved. It was in this section in 1892 that the Democrats had made their most impressive gains. It was also to this section that the balance of power in the nation's political life seemed to be moving, as economic expansion and immigration brought ever larger populations to the area.

Here, too, an important shift in population was taking place from the country to the city. The growth of cities like Chicago, Milwaukee, and Minneapolis was quickly bringing about a change in the balance of power within many of the important states of this section. McKinley had understood more accurately than Bryan the psychology of the voters involved in these changes taking place in the Middle West. The Republican appeal was successful in 1896, and the reaction of the new urban voters in the Middle West was of critical importance in the future. Their swing to the Republicans in 1896 was not an ephemeral phenomenon. Illinois, for example, up to 1932 cast its electoral votes for a Democratic candidate only in 1912, when Wilson won the state only because the Republican votes were divided between Taft and Roosevelt. When the Republican vote was united in the following election, the state went Republican again.

Under these circumstances the Republicans could well afford to lose one of their traditional bases of power, the Rocky Mountain region. Here the population was not large. No state had a significant electoral vote. It was clearly not an area likely to have influence of any weight in the future politics of the nation.

Elsewhere the story was not exciting for the Republicans, but neither was it disastrous. On the Pacific Coast they had held their own. In the South they had made no spectacular gains, but they had won in certain key states in the border South and generally through the section they had increased their votes.

It was upon the Middle West, however, that they had concentrated their campaign. It was there and in the populous East that their victory would have its greatest significance for the future.

The Democrats from the standpoint of 1896 alone had achieved a minor triumph in going down to defeat. In spite of the depression and the inroads made in preceding years by the Populists they had won a much larger vote than Cleveland in 1892, had built new positions of strength in the Prairie and Mountain states, and had beaten down the Populist threat in the South. Had the party campaigned on a platform and ticket similar to that of 1892 the defeat certainly would have been of disastrous proportions, and the Populist vote might well have outnumbered the Democratic vote.

The trouble with Democratic success lay in the fact that it had majority support only in certain agricultural and mining areas of the South and West. In gaining this support the party had alienated a strategic bloc of voters in the populous states of the East; and, even more significantly, it had failed to win a majority of either the urban or the rural votes in the all-important Middle West. It was here, of course, that the Democrats in 1896 lost the battles of the future. Here on an agrarian reform program they could hold an impressive bloc of votes, both in the urban and rural districts; but never between 1896 and 1932 were they able to win a majority of the votes in these middle western states.

It has been asserted that the rise in wheat prices which preceded the election was a significant factor in Bryan's defeat in certain strategic farm areas. It was true that the Republicans watched the movement in wheat prices very carefully in the weeks preceding the election. When, shortly before the election, wheat prices rose, the Republicans claimed that this proved the fallibility of the free silver argument; for there had been no corresponding increase in the monetary supply. Nevertheless, the wheat growing sections generally voted for Bryan.[53]

The campaign on free silver in 1896 saved the Democratic party from the crippling defeat it would have suffered had the issues of the campaign been restricted to depression and tariffs; but in 1896 and in future years the party was to suffer a serious handicap in its inability to develop a program which would appeal to a majority of the urban voters. Undoubtedly attitudes developed by urban voters toward the Democratic party during the campaign of 1896 affected elections during the next two decades. Bryan remained a dominant figure in the party until his death in 1925, but with each year he became in his own thinking more hostile to the cities of the East. It was a hostility which the East reciprocated, for he was not loved there as he was by the masses in the rural sections of the West and South. As far as Bryan was concerned, it was in the long run a failure in political understanding and leadership equivalent to Cleveland's failure in the 1890's. A rapidly developing nation was groping for solutions to immediate problems; and for a generation after 1896, pulled in different directions by men reflecting the ideas of Cleveland and Bryan, the Democratic party reacted with less sensitivity than the Republicans to the hopes and fears of the new voters which the new age was producing.

For the victory of free silver had, in one sense, turned the Democratic party to the past rather than the future. Bryan and the other leaders of the movement were not unaware of the new urban classes and their problems. The failure of Bryan and the others lay in their inability to propose solutions which would have a pragmatic significance to the new urban voters. Bryan and his supporters, reshaping the Jacksonian ideology to fit new molds, convinced themselves that it provided solutions for the problems of the 90's. They were satisfied that their program would work, and that their commitment to that program would have influence upon politics in the first decades of the next century. But their program proved to be an ideological construction unacceptable to the urban voter.

The Populist party, too, looked into the nineteenth rather than to the twentieth century for its programs and ideas. It, too, had looked to the farm more than to the city for its votes. Once the Democratic party adopted some of the more attractive features of its program the Populist party was doomed in those agricultural regions of the South and West where it had built its power. After July 1896, there was no need to await the election returns to learn the fate of the Populist party.

The third-party gold Democrats tried to find in the election returns some evidence of the success of their efforts. They sometimes claimed they had changed enough votes in the strategic Middle West and Upper South to carry the election for McKinley. They looked to the Republicans to recognize their contributions by giving them patronage appointments. For the most part they looked in vain. They claimed, too, that they had vindicated Cleveland's policies and that they had succeeded in perpetuating the conservative traditions of the Democratic party. Events, demonstrating the firm control held by the Bryan faction, soon gave the fatal blow to this claim. The gold Democrats talked with exaggerated optimism of continuing their independent organization until they were able to regain control of the Democratic party. Very soon, however, they had to face up to the reality that they had won a minute portion of the vote, that their organization was weak, and that they would have no opportunity to reconstitute the Democratic party as they had known it before 1896.

Thus, "the battle of the standards," which had appeared to offer great opportunities for the third parties because of its apparent capacity to disrupt the old parties, proved in the end to be a consolidating rather than a disrupting force. The chief casualties of "the battle" were the third parties, whose members now found acceptable homes in the two traditional parties. Once again Americans in the great majority had turned to the two great political traditions of the nineteenth century, traditions in which the ideas and programs of Jefferson and Hamilton were still clearly discernible. Both parties had achieved a triumph of political artistry in adjusting old party dogmas to the demands of new times and a new electorate.

Reference Matter

Notes

CHAPTER 1

1   Marion Butler to V. B. Carter, January 6, 1895, Marion Butler papers (Southern Historical Collection, University of North Carolina).
2   St. Louis *Globe-Democrat*, October 3, 1893, 2.
3   *Railway Times*, September 2, 1895, as quoted in James Peterson, "The Workers Divided. Organized Labor and the Election of 1896" (unpublished M.A. thesis, Columbia University, 1941), 48.
4   H. G. Martin, in interview published in Washington (D.C.) *Evening Star*, February 12, 1896, 1.
5   Festus P. Summers (ed.), *The Cabinet Diary of William L. Wilson* (Chapel Hill, N.C., 1957), 64; Festus P. Summers, *William L. Wilson and Tariff Reform* (New Brunswick, N.J., 1953), 240; Boston *Evening Transcript*, April 13, 1896, 1; Washington *Evening Star*, April 13, 1896, 1.
6   Washington *Evening Star*, April 30, 1896, 15.
7   William H. Harvey, *Coin's Financial School* (Chicago, 1894), 95–103; American Bimetallic League, *Facts About Silver* (Washington, D.C., 1895), 29–30; Adoniram J. Warner, *The Monetary Conference of 1881* (Marietta, Ohio, n.d.), 1; Washington *Evening Star*, March 8, 1895, 10.
8   John P. Altgeld, *Live Questions* (Chicago, 1899), 213–4.
9   Harold U. Faulkner, *Politics, Reform and Expansion, 1890–1900* (New York, 1959), 54.
10 Chicago *Tribune*, June 27, 1896, 11.
11 Comer V. Woodward, *Origins of the New South, 1877–1913* (Baton Rouge, La., 1951), 186.
12 Fred A. Shannon, *America's Economic Growth* (New York, 1940), 389, 403.
13 A Kansas banker interviewed in a visit to Boston in July 1896, said of conditions in the West: "The free-silver orator is roaming up and down the land, but the most powerful argument appealing to the Western Granger is wheat at 35 cents per bushel on Kansas farms. At this price no Kansas farmer can get either a gold or a silver dollar or a day's labor, to say nothing of interest on either farm mortgage or cost of machinery." He went on to say that corn was selling at the railroad station in Kansas at 14 to 15 cents a bushel; oats at 12 cents a bushel. Hogs were selling on the farm at 2½ cents a pound, butter at 5 to 8 cents per pound, and eggs at 5 cents a dozen. *New York Times*, July 1, 1895, 5. L. D. Llewelling, "Problems Before the Western Farmer,"

North American Review, 160 (January, 1895), 16–20; Thomas R. Ross, *Jonathan Prentiss Dolliver, A Study in Political Integrity and Independence* (Iowa City, Iowa, 1958), 120–1.

14　Joseph Dorfman, *The Economic Mind in American Civilization,* 3 vols. (New York, 1946–1949), III, 206–12; Richard T. Ely, "Report of the Organization of the American Economic Association," *Publications of the American Economic Association,* I (March, 1886), 5–46.

15　American Economic Association, "Hand-Book of the American Economic Association, 1896, Together with Report of the Eighth Annual Meeting, Indianapolis, December 27–31, 1895," *Supplement to Economic Studies,* I (April 1896), 81.

16　David A. Wells, "Downfall of Certain Financial Fallacies," *Forum,* XVI (October, 1893), 131–49; William C. Cornwell, "International Bimetallism neither Practicable nor Desirable" (Pamphlet, n.p., n.d., in bound volume, *Pamphlets on Finance, Public and Private,* Vol. 69, in Library of the University of Chicago), 7; J. Laurence Laughlin, "The Causes of Agricultural Unrest," *Atlantic Monthly,* LXXVIII (September, 1896), 577–85; J. Howard Cowperthwait, *Money, Silver, and Finance* (New York and London, 1892), 43–7.

17　Edward Atkinson, "The Battle of the Standards and the Fall of Prices," *Forum,* XIX (April, 1895), 147.

18　Atkinson to Editor, *Journal of Commerce,* September 25, 1896, as quoted in Harold F. Williamson, *Edward Atkinson, the Biography of an American Liberal, 1827–1905* (Boston, 1934), 200.

19　Boston *Evening Transcript,* September 9, 1896, 7.

20　H. E. Taubeneck, *The Condition of the American Farmer* (Chicago, 1896), 31–63; Francis S. Kinder, "The Effects of Recent Changes in Monetary Standards upon the Distribution of Wealth," *Economic Studies,* IV (December, 1899), 413–40; American Bimetallic League, *Facts About Silver,* 31–8.

21　*Facts About Silver,* 31–8.

22　*Ibid.,* 25; George Rothwell Brown (ed.), *Reminiscences of Senator William M. Stewart of Nevada* (New York and Washington, 1908) 285–91.

23　Harvey, *Coin's School,* 7–9.

24　St. Louis *Post Dispatch,* September 30, 1893, 2.

25　J. G. Carlisle to Hoke Smith, August 11, 1894, Grover Cleveland papers (Library of Congress, hereafter cited as LC).

26　Francis A. Walker, "The Relation of Changes in the Volume of Currency to Prosperity," *Economic Studies,* I (April, 1896), 26.

27　Harvey, *Coin's School,* 130–6.

28　"Bimetallism and Monometallism," *Coin's Financial Series,* I (December, 1893), 4–7.

29　Washington *Evening Star,* June 28, 1893, 1.

30　Chicago *Record, Free Silver Coinage Debate* (Chicago, 1896), 101; *National Bimetallist,* I (December 25, 1895), 131–2.

31　Henry M. Teller in Introduction to James H. Teller, *The Battle of the Standards* (Chicago, 1896), 13.

32　Moreton Frewen, "The American Farmer and the Silver Question," reprinted from the London *Daily Chronicle,* in *National Bimetallist,* I (September 9, 1896), 750–2.

33 *Ibid.*
34 John R. Commons, *History of Labour in the United States,* 4 vols. (New York, 1918–1935), II, 167, 171, 240–51.
35 Robert P. Sharkey, *Money, Class, and Party* (Baltimore, 1959), 283. Sharkey concluded that "the thread of continuity which linked the old hard-money Democracy of the age of Jackson with the 'Ohio rag-baby' champions of the late sixties was a continuing antagonism toward banks, bankers and particularly bank-notes." In 1895 Ignatius Donnelly wrote: "The Hamiltonian school of politics, with its aristocratic leanings, its distrust of the people, and its legalized separate costumes for the classes, has taken shelter in the national banks. The old she-wolf—Nicholas Biddle's bank—which Andrew Jackson wounded, has crawled out of the bushes, followed by all her whelps, and is ravaging the land." Donnelly, *The American People's Money* (Chicago, 1895), 186. In a letter to Donnelly the Populist Governor of Colorado, Davis H. Waite, said: "I intend in Texas to preach the pure and unadulterated gospel of Jeffersonian and Jacksonian democracy—I believe no union is possible between the South and West except *on that line.* If we can't abolish banks of issue, the country is lost." Letter dated July 10, 1895, Donnelly papers (Minnesota Historical Society).

CHAPTER 2

1 St. Louis *Post Dispatch,* July 25, 1889, 4; July 26, 1889, 4.
2 *Ibid.,* November 6, 1889; November 13, 1889, 3; November 14, 1889, 10; November 22, 1889, 10; November 25, 1889, 5; November 26, 1889, 2; *Proceedings of the First National Silver Convention Held at St. Louis, November 26, 27 and 28, 1889* (St. Louis, 1889), xv, 1–2, 65.
3 St. Louis *Post Dispatch,* November 27, 1889, 2.
4 *Ibid.,* November 28, 1889, 7.
5 *Ibid.,* November 28, 1889, 7; November 29, 1889, 4.
6 William Jennings Bryan, *The First Battle. A Story of the Campaign of 1896* (Chicago, 1896), 153; Leon W. Fuller, "The Populist Regime in Colorado" (unpublished Ph.D. dissertation, University of Wisconsin, 1933), 174–5; George Rothwell Brown (ed.), *Reminiscences of Senator William M. Stewart of Nevada* (New York and Washington, 1908), 318; Harold F. Taggart, "California and the Silver Question in 1895," *Pacific Historical Review,* VI (September, 1937), 250.
7 Washington *Evening Star,* February 22, 1893, 5.
8 *Ibid.,* February 25, 1893, 16.
9 *Address of General A. J. Warner of Ohio, at the First Annual Meeting of the American Bimetallic League, Held at Washington, February 22, 23 and 24, 1893* (Washington, 1893), 1–16.
10 Washington *Evening Star,* June 26, 1893, 1.
11 *Ibid.,* July 3, 1893, 5; July 4, 1893, 1.
12 *Ibid.,* July 22, 1893, 6; August 1, 1893, 2; Chicago *Tribune,* July 30, 1893, 3; August 2, 1893, 1; St. Louis *Post Dispatch,* August 1, 1893, 1.
13 Chicago *Tribune,* July 30, 1893, 12.
14 *Ibid.,* August 2, 1893, 4; Jeannette P. Nichols, "Bryan's Benefactor: Coin Harvey and His World," *Ohio Historical Quarterly,* XLVII (Octo-

ber, 1958), 299–325; Willard Fisher, "'Coin' and His Critics," *Quarterly Journal of Economics,* X (January, 1896), 187–208.

15 Chicago *Tribune,* August 1, 1893, 1.
16 Washington *Evening Star,* August 1, 1893, 6.
17 Chicago *Tribune,* August 3, 1893, 1, 2; St. Louis *Post Dispatch,* August 2, 1893, 1.
18 St. Louis *Post Dispatch,* August 3, 1896, 1.
19 *Ibid.,* October 2, 1893, 1.
20 St. Louis *Globe-Democrat,* October 4, 1893, 3.
21 St. Louis *Post Dispatch,* October 8, 1893, 25.
22 *Ibid.,* October 3, 1893, 1.
23 *Ibid.,* October 8, 1893, 25.
24 Fuller, "Populist Regime in Colorado," 202–5.
25 Davis H. Waite, "Are the Silver States Ruined?" *North American Review,* 158 (January, 1894), 29.
26 St. Louis *Post Dispatch,* October 5, 1893, 4; October 6, 1893, 7.
27 *Ibid.,* October 8, 1893, 25.
28 Washington *Evening Star,* November 2, 1893, 1.
29 *Ibid.,* July 2, 1894, 5.
30 Leaflet, "Silver the Dominant Issue," Luman H. Weller papers (Wisconsin Historical Society); Washington *Evening Star,* August 16, 1894, 2; August 17, 1894, 1.
31 A. J. Warner to Wharton Barker, September 13, 1894, Wharton Barker papers (LC).
32 A. J. Warner to Ignatius Donnelly, November 17, 1894, Donnelly papers (Minnesota Historical Society).
33 Washington *Evening Star,* November 19, 1894, 1.
34 St. Louis *Post Dispatch,* November 27, 1894, 2; November 28, 1894, 2; November 29, 1894, 4.
35 *Ibid.,* November 28, 1894, 7; November 29, 1894, 4.
36 Washington *Evening Star,* March 6, 1895, 1, 6; Bryan, *First Battle,* 154–5; *The American Bimetallic Party. A New Political Organization. Statement of the Issue, and an Address to the People Adopted at a Bimetallic Conference held at Washington, D.C., February 22 to March 5, 1895* (n.p., n.d.), 1–8; Lawrence J. Scheidler, "Silver and Politics, 1893–1896" (unpublished Ph.D. dissertation, University of Indiana, 1936), 165. Joseph Crocker Sibley (1850–1926) was in the oil business where he was engaged in small-scale refining operations. Originally a Republican, he left that party in 1884 on the tariff question and for awhile thereafter voted the Prohibition ticket. In 1892 he was elected to Congress by a combination of Democrats, Populists, and Prohibitionists. From the first, he attracted considerable attention because of his support of free silver. He was defeated for re-election in 1894 and 1896, but in 1898 he was elected to Congress as a Democrat and three successive times after that as a Republican. *Dictionary of American Biography,* XVII, 148.
37 William H. Harvey, *Coin's Financial School* (Chicago, 1894), 155 pp. This was actually one volume of a series, titled *Coin's Financial Series,* which Harvey had begun to publish in Chicago in December 1893.
38 Horace White, "Coin's Financial Fool," *Sound Currency,* II (May 1, 1895), 11, 13, 15.

39 William N. Byers to Benjamin Harrison, December 3, 1894, Harrison papers (LC).
40 Josiah Patterson to Grover Cleveland, April 5, 1895, Cleveland papers.
41 T. C. Catchings to Daniel Lamont, April 6, 1895, Lamont papers (LC).
42 E. C. Wall to Henry T. Thurber, April 19, 1895, Cleveland papers.
43 Ezra Peters to John M. Palmer, April 13, 1895, John M. Palmer papers (Illinois State Historical Society).
44 H. E. Bagley, Mapleton, Minnesota, to editor of *The Outlook,* published in *Outlook,* LII (July 13, 1895), 70, as quoted in Scheidler, "Silver and Politics," 197.
45 Seymour F. Norton, *Ten Men of Money Island* (Chicago, 1891), 87 pp.
46 Ignatius Donnelly, *The American People's Money* (Chicago, 1895), 186 pp.
47 American Bimetallic League, *Facts About Silver* (Washington, D.C., 1895), 90 pp.
48 William H. Harvey, *Coin's Financial School Up to Date* (Chicago, 1895), 205 pp.
49 White, "Coin's Financial Fool," *Sound Currency,* II (May 1, 1895). This was distributed as a reprint by the Sound Currency Committee of the Reform Club of New York, which reported that by August 29, 1895, 300,000 copies had been printed.
50 St. Louis *Post Dispatch,* May 15, 1895, 1.
51 R. C. Chambers to Wharton Barker, July 11, 1895, and Edwin B. Light to Barker, July 19, 1895, Barker papers; Edwin B. Light to Bryan, January 16, 1896, William Jennings Bryan papers (LC). In this letter Light, who was in charge of the Chicago headquarters office of the National Bimetallic Union, wrote that the entire cost of the office, which ran to nearly $5,000 monthly, was borne by two or three western states. Most of the expenses were for publication activities of various kinds through which he estimated they were reaching one million readers regularly. Washington *Evening Star,* April 8, 1895, 1; St. Louis *Post Dispatch,* May 15, 1895, 1; May 18, 1895, 2; *National Bimetallist,* I (October 16, 1895), 10–18; Harold F. Taggart, "California and the Silver Question in 1895," 254.

CHAPTER 3

1 A thorough analysis of the election of 1892 is in George H. Knoles, *The Presidential Campaign and Election of 1892* (Stanford, Calif., 1942).
2 *Ibid.,* 180–7.
3 Washington *Evening Star,* March 8, 1893, 3.
4 *Ibid.,* March 15, 1893, 3.
5 *Ibid.,* March 18, 1893, 3.
6 *Ibid.,* March 6, 1893, 12.
7 *Ibid.,* March 20, 1893, 3.
8 *Ibid.*
9 *Ibid.,* March 22, 1893, 3.
10 *Ibid.,* March 25, 1893, 3.
11 *Ibid.,* March 22, 1893, 3.
12 Raymond C. Miller, "The Populist Party in Kansas" (unpublished Ph.D. dissertation, University of Chicago, 1928), 226–7.

13   Washington *Evening Star*, March 24, 1893, 8.
14   *Ibid.*, April 4, 1893, 9.
15   William A. White, *The Autobiography of William Allen White* (New York, 1946), 262–3.
16   Fred A. Shannon, *The Farmer's Last Frontier; Agriculture, 1860–1897* (New York, 1945), 291–5.
17   St. Louis *Post Dispatch*, September 30, 1893, 2.
18   Bryan to W. S. Bissell, October 24, 1893; Bryan to Grover Cleveland, February 7, 1894, Bryan papers.
19   William Jennings Bryan. *First Battle, A Story of the Campaign of 1896* (Chicago, 1896), 113–4.
20   Bryan to Bissell, October 24, 1893, Bryan papers.
21   Judge J. J. McHatton, Butte, Mont., as interviewed in Washington *Evening Star*, October 24, 1893, 5.
22   Cleveland to John G. Carlisle, January 22, 1893, quoted in James A. Barnes, "The Gold Standard Democrats and the Party Conflict," *Mississippi Valley Historical Review*, XVII (December, 1930), 426–7.
23   Francis B. Simkins, *Pitchfork Ben Tillman* (Baton Rouge, La., 1944), 311–3.
24   Sam Hanna Acheson, *Joe Bailey, The Last Democrat* (New York, 1932), 58–9.
25   Cleveland to T. F. Bayard, February 13, 1895, Cleveland papers.
26   Fred W. Bentley to L. L. Carlisle, July 26, 1894, Cleveland papers.
27   A useful summary of the Treasury's attempt to maintain the gold reserve through bond sales will be found in James A. Barnes, *Wealth of the American People* (New York, 1949), 466–71.
28   John R. Lambert, *Arthur Pue Gorman* (Baton Rouge, La., 1953), 199; Jeannette P. Nichols, "The Politics and Personalities of Silver Repeal in the United States Senate," *American Historical Review*, XLI (October, 1935), 26–53.
29   John P. Altgeld to John M. Palmer, November 18, 1892, Palmer papers.
30   Altgeld to Lambert Tree, November 26, December 24, 1894; September 9, 1895; May 11, 1897; Tree to Altgeld, December 4, 1896, Lambert Tree papers (Newberry Library).
31   Pencilled draft, Tree to Cleveland, June 28, 1894, and manuscript titled, "Resolutions drawn by Lambert Tree and adopted by Illinois State Convention at Springfield of 1894," Tree papers.
32   Francis Lynde Stetson to Cleveland, October 7, 1894; A. B. Farquhar to Henry T. Thurber, November 8, 14, 1894, Cleveland papers; Peter B. Olney to Richard Olney, October 22, 1894, Richard Olney papers (LC); Rev. Jos. W. Hendrick to Daniel S. Lamont, October 27, 1894, Lamont papers.
33   Cleveland to D. S. Lamont, October 12, 1894, Cleveland papers.
34   John P. Altgeld to David B. Hill, October 31, 1894, George A. Schilling Collection (Illinois State Historical Society); Harry Barnard, *Eagle Forgotten, The Life of John Peter Altgeld* (New York, 1938), 321–2.
35   David Francis to Cleveland, May 18, 1894, Cleveland papers; Lambert Tree to Walter Q. Gresham, June 24, 1894, Tree papers.
36   Washington *Evening Star*, November 6, 1894, 6.
37   *Ibid.*, November 12, 1894; A. B. Farquhar to Henry T. Thurber, November 8, 1894, Cleveland papers.

CHAPTER 4

1 Richard P. Bland, "The Hopes of Free Silver," *North American Review,* CLVIII (May, 1894), 560–1.
2 Harold A. Haswell, Jr., "The Public Life of Congressman Richard Parks Bland" (unpublished Ph.D. dissertation, University of Missouri, 1951), 255–6.
3 William Jennings Bryan, *First Battle, A Story of the Campaign of 1896* (Chicago, 1896), 136.
4 *Ibid.,* 146.
5 *Ibid.,* 155–7; Washington *Evening Star,* March 1, 1895, 1; Marian Silveus, "The Antecedents of the Campaign of 1896" (unpublished Ph.D. dissertation, University of Wisconsin, 1932), 28–9.
6 C[harles] R. Tuttle, *Illinois Currency Convention* (Chicago, 1895), 34–6, 72–3; St. Louis *Post Dispatch,* June 5, 1895, 1.
7 Tuttle, *Illinois Currency Convention,* 34–6; Hinrichsen to Bryan, April 15, 1895, Bryan papers.
8 Cincinnati *Commercial Gazette,* April 15, 1895, 1.
9 William D. Bynum to Cleveland, April 15, 1895, Cleveland papers.
10 Bryan, *First Battle,* 160–1.
11 Lyman J. Gage to Cleveland, March 29, 1895, and Everett B. Wheeler to Cleveland, April 2, 1895, Cleveland papers; C. N. Jordan to William E. Curtis, April 8, 1895, William E. Curtis papers (LC); J. H. Johnson to John Palmer, April 10, 1895, Palmer papers; Washington *Evening Star,* April 1, 8, 1895.
12 Washington *Evening Star,* June 15, 1895, 14; Leonard S. Kenworthy, *The Tall Sycamore of the Wabash, Daniel Wolsey Voorhees* (Boston, 1936), 105–7; Allan Nevins, *Grover Cleveland, A Study in Courage* (New York, 1932), 541–2.
13 F. H. Jones to Thurber, April 19, 1895, Cleveland papers.
14 Lambert Tree to Don M. Dickinson, May 25, 1896, Cleveland papers; Tree to William F. Vilas, May 28 and June 3, 1896, William F. Vilas papers (Wisconsin State Historical Society).
15 E. C. Wall to Vilas, June 30, 1896, Vilas papers.
16 St. Louis *Post Dispatch,* March 13, 1896, 4; Lawrence J. Scheidler, "Silver and Politics, 1893–1896" (unpublished Ph.D. dissertation, University of Indiana, 1936), 198; Festus P. Summers (ed.), *The Cabinet Diary of William L. Wilson* (Chapel Hill, N. Car., 1951), 94–7.
17 Washington *Evening Star,* April 29, 1895, 1; July 19, 1895, 1; Comer V. Woodward, *Origins of the New South, 1877–1913* (Baton Rouge, La., 1951), 283–4.
18 A. J. Gross to Cleveland, May 14, 1895, Cleveland papers.
19 *National Bimetallist,* I (October 16, 1895), 1.
20 Summers, *Cabinet Diary of Wilson,* 85–91.
21 J. M. Stone to Cleveland, April 21, 1895, Cleveland papers.
22 Cleveland to Stone, April 26, 1896, Cleveland papers.
23 Nevins, *Cleveland,* 681.
24 James A. Barnes, *John G. Carlisle, Financial Statesman* (New York, 1931), 438–43.
25 Josiah Patterson to Cleveland, April 5 and May 5, 1895, Cleveland

papers; Patterson to Daniel Lamont, April 18, 1895, Lamont papers; Patterson to Richard Olney, June 7, 1895, Olney papers; J. D. Newton, A. W. Stoval, E. L. Bullock, and J. D. Hunt to Bryan, April 22, 1895, Bryan papers; Bryan, *First Battle*, 162.

26 "Annual Report, 1896," *Sound Currency*, III, No. 24 (November 15, 1896), 2; Washington *Evening Star*, April 15, 1896, 1.

27 "Executive Committee Report, August 29, 1895," *Sound Money*, II No. 20 (September 15, 1895), 8 pp.

28 A. Barton Hepburn, *History of Coinage and Currency in the United States and the Perennial Contest for Sound Money* (New York, 1903), 381; Scheidler, "Silver and Politics," 119–22.

29 Washington *Evening Star*, February 5, 1894, 1; September 24, 1895, 1; Horace White, "National and State Banks," *Sound Currency*, II, No. 1 (December 1, 1894), 16 pp.; John Dewitt Warner, "The Currency Famine of 1893," *Sound Currency*, II, No. 6 (February 15, 1895), 20 pp.; L. Carroll Root, "New England Bank Currency," *Sound Currency*, II, No. 13 (June 1, 1895), 32 pp.; Walter Stuart Kelley, "Proposals for Currency Reform," *Sound Currency*, III, No. 22 (October, 1896), 16 pp.; John DeWitt Warner, "Practical Bank Currency," *Sound Currency*, IV, No. 6 (March 15, 1897), 24 pp.; *Review of Reviews*, XI (January, 1895), 7–15.

30 William Jennings Bryan, "The President's Currency Plan," *Arena*, XI (February, 1895), 321–9.

31 Anthony Higgins to Moreton Frewen, September 23, 1895, Moreton Frewen papers (LC); Washington *Evening Star*, October 16, 1895, 6; November 1, 1895, 1.

32 Josiah Patterson to Cleveland, September 12, 1895, Cleveland papers.

33 Cincinnati *Commercial Gazette*, November 7, 1895, 4.

34 Interview with Claude M. Johnson, Chief of Bureau of Engraving and Printing, Washington *Evening Star*, November 7, 1895, 1. Also the *Star*, November 8, 1895, 2; November 13, 1895, 2. Cincinnati *Commercial Gazette*, November 15, 1895, 1.

35 *National Bimetallist*, I (November 27, 1895).

36 Grover Cleveland, "Our Financial Disease," *Sound Currency*, III (December 1, 1895), 11 pp.

37 J. J. Brown to Cleveland, December 4, 1895, Cleveland papers.

CHAPTER 5

1 Henry Jones to Marion Butler, May 31, 1895, Butler papers; Washington *Evening Star*, June 12, 1895, 1; June 13, 1895, 1; June 14, 1895, 1.

2 *Ibid.*, June 12, 1895, 1.

3 *Ibid.*, June 26, 1895, 11; William Jennings Bryan, *First Battle, A Story of the Campaign of 1896* (Chicago, 1896), 162.

4 Washington *Evening Star*, August 15, 1895, 1.

5 *Ibid.*, 3.

6 *Ibid.*, August 13, 1895, 1.

7 *Ibid.*, August 15, 1895, 3.

8 Later the executive committee was expanded to include Governor William J. Stone of Missouri, Congressman Charles F. Crisp of Georgia, and

T. O. Towles of Missouri, who acted as secretary. William J. Stone to W. J. Bryan, August 26, 1895, Bryan papers; Bryan, *First Battle*, 162–3.

9 Edgar Lee Masters, *The New Star Chamber and Other Essays* (Chicago, 1904), 185–6; Willa Cather, "The Personal Side of William Jennings Bryan," *Prairie Schooner*, XXIII (Winter, 1949), 331–7. In the concluding sentence of this essay (which was first published in *Library,* in Pittsburgh, Pa., on July 4, 1900) Willa Cather said: "So I think William Jennings Bryan synthesizes the entire middle west; all its newness and vigor; its magnitude and monotony; its richness and lack of variety; its inflammability and volubility; its strength and its crudeness; its high seriousness and self-confidence; its egotism and its nobility." Hamlin Garland to Henry George, November 10, 1896, Henry George papers (New York Public Library).

10 Bryan, *First Battle,* 78.

11 *Ibid.,* 84.

12 *Ibid.,* 81.

13 *Ibid.,* 114.

14 G. P. Keeney to Bryan, October 22, 1895, Bryan papers.

15 Charles B. Spahr to Bryan, September 12, 1894, Bryan papers.

16 J. A. Turley to Bryan, October 19, 1894, Bryan papers.

17 James C. Dahlman to Bryan, November 15, 1894, Bryan papers.

18 Guthrie (Okla.) *Daily Leader,* June 27, 1895, as quoted in Norbert R. Mahnken, "William Jennings Bryan in Oklahoma," *Nebraska History,* XXXI (December, 1950), 251–2.

19 Chicago *Times-Herald,* June 6, 1895, as quoted in Harvey Wish, "John Peter Altgeld and the Background of the Campaign of 1896," *Mississippi Valley Historical Review,* XXIV (March, 1938), 509.

20 Paolo E. Coletta, "William Jennings Bryan and the Senatorial Election of 1893," *Nebraska History,* XXXI (September, 1950), 199–200.

21 Wayne C. Williams, *William Jennings Bryan* (New York, 1936), 123.

22 Bryan to E. G. Wilson, October 26, 1893, as quoted in New York *World,* July 20, 1896, 1.

23 Charles M. Rosser to Bryan, February 3, 1896, Bryan papers.

24 Rosser to Bryan, November 23, 1895, Bryan papers; Charles M. Rosser, *The Crusading Commoner; A Close-up of William Jennings Bryan and His Times* (Dallas, Texas, 1937), 34–5.

25 Bryan to Ignatius Donnelly, January 1, 1896, Donnelly papers; James B. Weaver to Bryan, January 3, 1896, and Marion Butler to Bryan, January 8, 1896, Bryan papers.

26 In a letter of November 13, 1895 (now in Donnelly papers) Bryan wrote to Ignatius Donnelly: "I cannot say as much editorially [about the union of silver men of all parties] as I would like to because I am now doing what I can to get the silver democrats to capture the national convention. I have stated in answer to inquiries that I shall not support a goldbug for president. I think that is as far as I ought to go in public statements at present."

27 J. C. S. Blackburn to Bryan, August 24, 1895; W. H. Hinrichsen to Bryan, January 29, 1896; William J. Stone to Bryan, February 28, 1896; David Overmeyer to Bryan, February 29, 1896, Bryan papers.

28 Omaha *World-Herald,* February 26, 1896, as quoted in Bryan, *First Battle,* 125–6.

29 David Overmeyer to Bryan, February 29, 1896, Bryan papers.
30 George A. Carden to Bryan, February 25, 1896, Bryan papers.

CHAPTER 6

1 Richard Hofstadter, *Age of Reform* (New York, 1955), 101–2; Washington *Evening Star*, October 3, 1893, 4.
2 George H. Knoles, "Populism and Socialism, with Special Reference to the Election of 1892," *Pacific Historical Review*, XII (September, 1943), 299.
3 J. Laurence Laughlin wrote in 1896: "It is precisely the expansive, optimistic, speculating American-born in whose minds these erratic movements have taken deepest root. Our less mercurial Germans and shrewder Scandinavians are safer than our Americans, in this day of crazes." "Causes of Industrial Unrest," *Atlantic Monthly*, LXXVIII (November, 1896), 585. For a different point of view see John Higham, *Strangers in the Land, Patterns of American Nativism, 1860–1925* (New Brunswick, N.J., 1955), 7–8. Here Higham said: "And since the flexibility of American institutions has continued to discourage extreme dissent, America's most uncompromising radicals have in fact come from abroad. This persistent contrast between a generally hopeful psychology of mobility in America and the more desperate politics born in class-ridden Europe has fostered the belief that violent and sweeping opposition to the status quo is characteristically European and profoundly un-American. Thus, anti-radical movements in America, like anti-Catholic ones, have had a singular propensity to assume a nationalistic form."
4 Samuel Gompers, *Seventy Years of Life and Labor*, 2 vols. (New York, 1925, II, 87–9; John R. Commons, *et al.*, *History of Labour in the United States*, 4 vols. (New York, 1918–1935), II, 509–14; IV, 6–7, 10, 150, 514; Harold U. Faulkner, *Politics, Reform and Expansion, 1890–1900* (New York, 1959), 88–90; James Peterson, "The Workers Divided. Organized Labor and the Election of 1896" (unpublished M.A. thesis, Columbia University, 1941), 28–36. The manuscript collections of the leading Populist figures reveal little interest in establishing a working relationship with labor, and frequently comments on the prospect of labor cooperation are negative or pessimistic. Thus, in December 1894, Davis H. Waite wrote to Ignatius Donnelly that in the November election the working men of Denver had sold their votes to the Republicans in spite of the policies favorable to labor which Waite had adopted in his administration. He doubted the desirability of catering to them any longer and concluded: "If we cannot win the great *middle classes,* there is no hope for our country." Waite to Donnelly, December 11, 1894, Donnelly papers.
5 Raymond C. Miller, "The Populist Party in Kansas" (unpublished Ph.D. dissertation, University of Chicago, 1928), 272–80; Frederick E. Haynes, "The New Sectionalism," *Quarterly Journal of Economics*, X (April, 1896), 277–80.
6 Joseph F. Steelman, "The Progressive Era in North Carolina, 1884–1917," (unpublished Ph.D. dissertation, University of North Carolina, 1955), 54–6; Philip J. Weaver, "The Gubernatorial Election of 1896

in North Carolina" (unpublished M.A. thesis, University of North Carolina, 1937), 20–9.

7 Haynes, "The New Sectionalism," 277–80; John D. Hicks, *The Populist Revolt, A History of the Farmers' Alliance and the People's Party* (Lincoln, Nebraska, 1961), 333–4, 337–9.

8 William A. Mabry, "Negro Suffrage and Fusion Rule in North Carolina," *North Carolina Historical Review*, XII (April, 1935), 83; Comer V. Woodward, *Origins of the New South, 1877–1913* (Baton Rouge, La., 1951), 275–6.

9 Washington *Evening Star*, November 10, 1894, 1.

10 *Ibid.*, November 13, 1894, 1.

11 Waite to Donnelly, August 25, 1895, Donnelly papers.

12 George Wilson to Marion Butler, May 30, 1896, Butler papers.

13 Flower to Marion Butler, December 14, 1894, Butler papers.

14 Washington *Evening Star*, January 1, 1895, 2.

15 Letter from Weaver, published in *Farmers' Tribune*, March 27, 1895, quoted in Herman C. Nixon, "The Populist Movement in Iowa" (unpublished Ph.D. dissertation, University of Chicago, 1925), 104–5.

16 Henry Demarest Lloyd to John Burns, February 6, 1895; Lloyd to Andrews, February 19, 1895; Thomas Morgan to Lloyd, July 6, 1896, Henry Demarest Lloyd papers (Wisconsin Historical Society); Russel B. Nye, *Midwestern Progressive Politics. A Historical Study of its Origins and Development, 1870–1950* (East Lansing, Mich., 1951), 81–3; Willis J. Abbott, "The Chicago Populist Campaign," *Arena*, XI (December, 1894–February, 1895), 330–7; Chester McA. Destler, "Consummation of a Labor-Populist Alliance in Illinois, 1894," *Mississippi Valley Historical Review*, XXVII (March, 1941), 589–602; Edward B. Mittelman, "Chicago Labor in Politics, 1877–96," *Journal of Political Economy*, XXVIII (May, 1920), 423; Peterson, "Workers Divided," 62–6.

17 Commons, *et al.*, *History of Labour in the U.S.*, IV, 224–9. In 1897 Berger wrote to Henry Demarest Lloyd that the farmers, though still individualistic about production on farms, were willing to have collective ownership of industries where production was now on a collective basis. "Every thinking Socialist in this country," he wrote, "ought to be glad that the farmer element of America is revolutionary, and apt to listen to new ideas." Berger to Lloyd, January 11, 1897, Lloyd papers.

18 Ira Kipnis, *The American Socialist Movement, 1897–1912* (New York, 1952), 47–50.

19 For evidence of Prohibitionist interest in Populism see John P. St. John to T. C. Richmond, January 16 and May 17, 1895; Edward Evans to Richmond, January 18, 1895; Richmond to Samuel Dickie, April 22, 1895, Thomas C. Richmond papers (Wisconsin Historical Society); E. J. Wheeler to Lloyd, July 30, 1895, Lloyd papers; Washington *Evening Star*, October 18, 1895, 3; St. Louis *Post Dispatch*, April 9, 1896, 6. For evidence of interest among single-taxers in Populism see Thomas G. Sheaman to George, November 4, 1896, George papers; Thomas L. Johnson, *My Story* (New York, 1911), 54–5, 108–9; Arthur N. Young, *The Single Tax Movement in the United States* (Princeton, N.J., 1916), 242–3; J. Martin Klotsche, "The United Front Populists," *Wisconsin Magazine of History*, XX (June, 1937), 378–80. Interest on

the part of the direct legislation reformers is evident in Eltweed Pomeroy to Ignatius Donnelly, February 8 and April 3, 1896, Donnelly papers; *Weekly Rocky Mountain News*, February 13, 1896, 4; Eltweed Pomeroy, "The Direct Legislation Movement and its Leaders," *Arena*, XVI (June–November, 1896), 29–43. See also, Edward Bellamy to Lloyd, December 5, 1896, Lloyd papers; William P. St. John, "A National Platform for the American Independents of 1896," *Arena*, XVI (June–November, 1896), 67–9; Canton *Repository*, November 8, 1894.

20   Call, signed by H. E. Taubeneck and dated December 10, 1894, in Lloyd papers.

21   Weaver to Donnelly, January 13, 1895, Donnelly papers.

22   Butler to V. B. Carter, January 6, 1895, Butler papers.

23   St. Louis *Post Dispatch*, June 4, 1895, 1.

24   Jo A. Parker to N. A. Dunning, October 11, 1895; C. H. Ellington to Butler, January 3, 1896, Butler papers.

25   J. H. Edmisten to Butler, August 14, 1895; J. H. Hobson to Butler, January 8, 1895 [1896], Butler papers; H. E. Taubeneck to Donnelly, August 31, 1895; Thomas V. Cator to Donnelly, December 17, 1895; E. M. Wardall to Donnelly, December 19, 1895, Donnelly papers; J. B. Weaver to Bryan, December 31, 1895, Bryan papers; Cincinnati *Commercial Gazette*, November 16, 1895.

26   Washington *Evening Star*, January 2, 1896, 3; Chester McA. Destler, "Western Radicalism, 1865–1901: Concepts and Origins," *Mississippi Valley Historical Review*, XXXI (December, 1944), 366–7. Destler said that the Populist decision to concentrate on silver was guided in part by fear of the rise of socialism in the party. It is true that the silver issue had overshadowed socialism both within and outside the Populist party by 1896, but this was due largely to the success of the independent free silver propaganda, not to any conscious strategy within the party. At the time the Populist Executive Committee met to arrange the details on its nominating convention Thomas Watson was conducting a vigorous campaign against the influence of socialism in the party; but Watson, rather than being a silverite, was an ardent "middle-of-the-road" man. In a mid-December meeting of the Populist party of Georgia, Watson obtained the adoption of a platform which he hoped to make the platform of the national convention. The Georgia platform, in part, called for direct issue of all money by the government, the abolition of all banks of issue, the free coinage of gold and silver at 16 to 1, a graduated income tax, government ownership of railroads, canals, telephone and telegraph, the prohibition of alien ownership of land, direct election of the United States Senators, the perpetual separation of Church and State and the enactment in each state of an honest election law. *People's Party Paper*, December 27, 1895, 1; Watson to Butler, December 23 and 28, 1895, Butler papers. In an editorial on the action of the convention Watson said: "Georgia is Populistic for *Reform*, not for *Revolution*. She stands for the doctrines of Jefferson, not for those of Karl Marx." *People's Party Paper*, December 27, 1895, 1.

27   Thomas V. Cator to Donnelly, November 13, 1895; William M. Stewart to Donnelly, December 20, 1895, Donnelly papers.

28   Taubeneck to Donnelly, December 16, 1895, Donnelly papers.

29   M. C. Rankin to Donnelly, December 16, 1895, Donnelly papers.

30 Thomas V. Cator to Taubeneck, December 16, 1895, Donnelly papers.
31 St. Louis *Post Dispatch,* January 17, 1896; 3; January 19, 1896, 9; January 20, 1896, 3; Washington *Evening Star,* January 21, 1896, 1; New York *Tribune,* January 22, 1896, 1.
32 Bryan to Donnelly, January 1, 1896, Donnelly papers.
33 Weaver to Bryan, December 31, 1895, Bryan papers.
34 Weaver to Bryan, January 3, 1896, Bryan papers.
35 Washington *Evening Star,* November 15, 1895.
36 *Proceedings of the Bimetallic Conference Held at Washington, D.C., January 22 and 23, 1896. Including Resolutions and Address to the People of the United States* (Chicago, 1896), 3–15; New York *Times,* January 24, 1896; Washington *Evening Star,* January 24, 1896, 1; *National Bimetallist,* I (January 29, 1896), 212–15.
37 St. Louis *Post Dispatch,* January 20, 1896, 3.
38 Marion Butler to Edward B. Light, February 7, 1896, Butler papers. Butler wrote that it was certain that the Republican party would act unfavorably to silver and that the Democratic party was so situated that it would be split whether its actions were favorable or unfavorable to silver.
39 Elmer Ellis, *Henry Moore Teller, Defender of the West* (Caldwell, Idaho, 1941), 265–6.
40 *Ibid.,* 194–201; William V. Byars, *An American Commoner, The Life and Times of Richard Parks Bland* (St. Louis, 1900), 121; 186–93.
41 George P. Keeney to Bryan, January 2, 1896, Bryan papers. An "eminent" but otherwise unidentified Populist interviewed at the St. Louis meeting of the Populist National Committee said that either Bland or Bryan would be acceptable candidates of a silver fusion campaign. St. Louis *Post Dispatch,* January 19, 1896, 9.

CHAPTER 7

1 Leon W. Fuller, "The Populist Regime in Colorado" (unpublished Ph.D. dissertation, University of Wisconsin, 1933), 25.
2 Lawrence J. Scheidler, "Silver and Politics, 1893–1896" (unpublished Ph.D. dissertation, University of Indiana, 1936), 83–92.
3 *Ibid.;* C. E. Perkins to William B. Allison, May 19, 1894, Allison papers (Iowa State Department of History and Archives); Washington *Evening Star,* May 2, 1894, 3; May 3, 1894, 1.
4 Washington *Evening Star,* June 1, 1894, 1.
5 *Ibid.*
6 Fred Wilmot Wellborn, "The Silver Republicans, 1890–1900" (unpublished Ph.D. dissertation, University of Wisconsin, 1926), 117–9.
7 Washington *Evening Star,* September 4, 1894, 1; September 5, 1894, 5.
8 *Ibid.,* August 20, 1894, 1. Teller in an interview with a *Star* reporter had indicated that he was not speaking only of the need to defeat Waite: "It is not a question of the defeat of any one individual, but of the entire party."
9 *Ibid.,* August 4, 1894, 1; September 8, 1894, 1.
10 *Ibid.,* June 1, 1895, 1; June 3, 1895, 1; September 17, 1895, 2; *New York Times,* February 10, 1896, 1; St. Louis *Post Dispatch,* February

13, 1896, 2; March 30, 1896, 7; J. S. Clarkson to William B. Allison, June 4 and June 7, 1895, Allison papers.

11 Washington *Evening Star,* January 9, 1896, 1.

12 *Ibid.,* March 20, 1896, 11; St. Louis *Post Dispatch,* March 20, 1896, 1. Senator Teller was quoted in the Boston *Evening Transcript,* March 31, 1896, 1, as saying: "I see a good many letters that lead me to believe that Eastern manufacturers are dropping onto the idea that in no way can they meet the Asiatic competition, except by giving up the old standard. As one Eastern manufacturer said the other day, a tariff of one hundred and forty per cent would hardly do it, and this is impossible to get. The only way to meet Asiatic competition is to adopt the same monetary standard they use, and then our tariffs will amount to something."

13 Scheidler, "Silver and Politics," 243–4; Washington *Evening Star,* March 31, 1896, 1; Boston *Evening Transcript,* March 31, 1896, 1.

14 Edw. O. Wolcott to Moreton Frewen, February 7, 1896, Frewen papers.

15 Washington *Evening Star,* April 30, 1896, 15.

CHAPTER 8

1 Joseph L. Bristow, *Fraud and Politics at the Turn of the Century, McKinley and his Administration as Seen by his Principal Patronage Dispenser and Investigator* (New York, 1952), 27.

2 Samuel R. Thayer to Davis, April 4, 1895, Cushman K. Davis papers (Minnesota Historical Society); Collis P. Huntington to Elkins, June 25, 1894; T. H. Norton to Elkins, June 11, 1895, Stephen B. Elkins papers (West Virginia Collection, West Virginia University Library); Elkins to A. B. White, December 5, 1894, Governor A. B. White papers (West Virginia Collection, West Virginia University Library); Oscar D. Lambert, *Stephen Benton Elkins* (Pittsburgh, 1955), 200–2.

3 Cincinnati *Commercial Gazette,* November 7, 1895, 1; November 8, 1895, 1; December 6, 1895, 1; St. Louis *Post Dispatch,* January 1, 1896, 1.

4 S. B. Elkins to H. G. Davis, March 2, 1894; J. H. Manley to S. B. Elkins, August 29, 1894, Elkins papers; H. G. Davis to S. B. Elkins, May 3, 1896, Henry Gassaway Davis papers (West Virginia Collection, West Virginia University). Manley in his letter to Elkins said that he understood he was to receive $1500 a month for his services.

5 Nelson W. Aldrich to Levi Morton, n.d. [1895], Morton papers (New York Public Library); Washington *Evening Star,* January 11, 1894, 2; September 10, 1894, 9.

6 J. S. Clarkson to Allison, October 15, 1894 and January 5, 1896, Allison papers; Jacob Rich to C. K. Davis, January 3, 1896, Davis papers; Jacob Rich to E. W. Keyes, January 14, 1896, Elisha W. Keyes papers (in Wisconsin State Historical Society); Chicago *Tribune,* January 8, 1896, 3; Washington *Evening Star,* January 14, 1896, 3.

7 William D. Washburn to Allison, August 10, 1895, Allison papers; Theodore Roosevelt to Henry Cabot Lodge, December 2, 1895, in Elting E. Morison (ed.), *The Letters of Theodore Roosevelt,* 8 vols. (Cambridge, 1951), I, 498; William M. Osborne to McKinley, January 16, 1896, McKinley papers (Library of Congress); Washington *Evening Star,*

February 6, 1895, 1; July 6, 1895, 2; Boston *Evening Transcript*, February 11, 1896, 1.

8   T. B. Reed to Chandler, April 10, 1895, William E. Chandler papers (LC); Robert M. McMurdy to Foraker, November 12, 1895, Joseph B. Foraker papers (Historical and Philosophical Society of Ohio); Charles M. Pepper to Joseph Morgan, November 29, 1895; J. E. Blythe to Allison, October 6 and November 15, 1895; G. B. Pray to Allison, October 12, 1895, Allison papers; William A. Robinson, *Thomas B. Reed, Parliamentarian* (New York, 1930), 330–5.

9   J. S. Clarkson to Allison, March 3, 4, 5, July 7, August 25, 1895; M. B. Madden to Allison, January 21, 1896; Robert Patterson to Allison, January 30, 1896; H. G. McMillan to Allison, April 3, 1896; Jacob Rich to Allison, March 27, 1896, Allison papers. John S. Miller to Aldrich, January 22, 1896, James Franklin Aldrich papers (Chicago Historical Society).

10 Charles M. Pepper to Joseph Morgan, February 28, 1895, Allison papers; Miller to Aldrich, January 22, 1896, Aldrich papers.

11 J. S. Clarkson to Allison, n.d. [1895?], July 7, August 31, 1895, Allison papers; C. H. Grosvenor to J. H. Gallinger, September 23, 1897, Jacob Gallinger papers (New Hampshire State Historical Society).

12 W. P. Hepburn to Allison, November 22, 1895; Clarkson to Allison, November 28, December 14, 1895, January 5, 28, 1896, Allison papers; G. M. Dodge to Alexander G. Cochrane, January 3, 1896; Dodge to Roswell Miller, February 6, 1896; Dodge to R. R. Cable, January 8, 1896; Clarkson to Dodge, January 20, 1896, Grenville M. Dodge papers (Iowa State Department of History and Archives).

13 Thomas Beer, *Hanna* (New York, 1929), 110–3; Herbert Croly, *Marcus Alonzo Hanna, His Life and Work* (New York, 1912), 120–39, 140–63.

14 Col. T. Bentley Mott, *Myron T. Herrick, Friend of France; An Autobiographical Biography* (Garden City, New York, 1929), 59–63. Herman H. Kohlsaat, *From McKinley to Harding; Personal Recollections of our Presidents* (New York and London, 1923), 30–1.

15 Kohlsaat, *From McKinley to Harding*, 1–9.

16 Washington *Evening Star*, February 21, 1893, 6; February 27, 1893, 2; February 28, 1893, 6; Kohlsaat, *From McKinley to Harding*, 10–7; Mott, *Herrick*, 48–56; Croly, *Hanna*, 169–70. The best account of this episode is in H. Wayne Morgan, "Governor McKinley's Misfortune: The Walker-McKinley Feud of 1893," *The Ohio History Quarterly*, LXIX (April, 1960), 103–20.

17 Washington *Evening Star*, March 10, 1893, 9.

18 *Ibid.*, March 24, 1893, 8.

19 *Ibid.*, March 30, 1893, 7.

20 *Ibid.*, November 8, 1893, 1; December 7, 1893, 2; December 30, 1893, 1.

21 Frank G. Carpenter in story datelined, Columbus, Ohio, January 8, 1894, printed in Washington *Evening Star*, January 13, 1894, 7.

22 Beer, *Hanna*, 110–3; Croly, *Hanna*, 140–63.

23 Joseph Benson Foraker, *Notes of a Busy Life*, 2 vols. (Cincinnati, 1917), I, 452–6; Winfield S. Kerr, *John Sherman, His Public Life and Services*, 2 vols. (Boston, 1908), II, 348–9.

24 Congressman Grosvenor, interviewed in Washington, D.C., said that he, Hanna, and all the other representatives of McKinley's interests had said that Foraker should be elected to the Senate; and he knew that Foraker had stated, though not in public, that McKinley ought to have a united delegation from Ohio to the presidential convention. He was quoted as saying at this point: "And the idea that Gov. Foraker would first receive the unanimous support of the republicans of Ohio for Senator at the opening of the legislature in 1896 and then turn around and with the weapon of the election in his hands, use it to defeat Gov. McKinley is not attributing high motives and generous purposes and political wisdom to Gov. Foraker...." Washington *Evening Star*, February 4, 1895, 9; February 6, 1895, 1; March 13, 1895, 1; Canton *Repository*, February 7, 1895; February 28, 1895.

25 Kurtz to Foraker, January 28, 1896; copy, Foraker to McKinley, January 28, 1896, November 7, 1896, Foraker papers; Foraker, *Notes of a Busy Life*, I, 456–7. Washington *Evening Star*, February 4, 1895, 9; February 6, 1895, 1; Canton *Repository*, February 7, 28, 1895.

26 Foraker to McKinley, January 28, 1896; Foraker to Little, January 28, 1896; McKinley to Foraker, January 31, 1896, Foraker papers.

27 Foraker to McKinley, March 13, 1896, Foraker papers.

28 McKinley to Foraker, January 29, 1896, McKinley papers.

29 Foraker to Herrick, December 30, 1895, as quoted in Marian Silveus, "The Antecedents of the Campaign of 1896" (unpublished Ph.D. dissertation, University of Wisconsin, 1932), 72; Foraker to McKinley, January 28 and February 4, 1896, Foraker papers. In the letter of January 28 Foraker said: "You must have noticed that the occasion of my visit [to Platt] made at your request and in your interest was seized upon by the papers all over the country for talk about plots and schemes, knives, razors, intrigues, treachery, etc. These, and such articles as in this morning's Tribune, confirm me in the idea that I am in great danger if I go to the St. Louis Convention of being crucified again, as I was in 1888, if your candidacy should fail."

30 Foraker, *Notes of a Busy Life*, I, 460–1.

31 Copy, Foraker to McKinley, November 7, 1896, Foraker papers.

32 Washington *Evening Star*, February 7, 1894, 11.

33 Kerr, *Sherman*, II, 367.

34 Charles S. Olcott, *The Life of William McKinley*, 2 vols. (Boston and New York, 1916), I, 246; William A. White, *The Autobiography of William Allen White* (New York, 1946), 249–52.

35 Robert P. Porter, *Life of William McKinley, Soldier, Lawyer, Statesman, With a Biographical Sketch of Hon. G. A. Hobart* (Cleveland, 1896), 226–29.

36 Canton *Repository*, February 15, 1894.

37 Maud Cuney Hare, *Norris Wright Cuney, A Tribune of the Black People* (New York, 1913), 178–81.

38 McKinley to Col. J. F. Hanson, February 27, 1895; McKinley to A. B. Casselman, December 20, 1894, McKinley papers; Hamilton Disston to M. S. Quay, April 1, 1895, Matthew S. Quay papers (in Library of Congress); Washington *Evening Star*, April 1, 1895, 1.

39 Hanna to Daniel Joseph Ryan, March 17, 1895, Daniel J. Ryan papers (in Ohio Historical Society).

CHAPTER 9

1. McKinley to J. W. Brown, February 8, 1896, McKinley papers. In this letter McKinley wrote: "Of course, I do not want anything done in the state of Iowa which will, in any way, conflict with those [sources of support in the national convention] of Mr. Allison. He is your State man and he should have your united and hearty support and the support of your delegation. It is very gratifying to me to know that after Mr. Allison, the sentiment is so favorable to Ohio." The tone of this letter is quite different from McKinley's replies to pledges of support from Pennsylvania, also in the McKinley papers. Writing on March 2, 1896, to William A. Clark, he said: "Of course, I want the friendship of the people of Pennsylvania, and in saying this, I fully recognize the obligation of your State to your distinguished Senator." In a letter of March 10, 1896, to Charles A. Snyder, he said that the growth of support for him in Pennsylvania was embarrassing, but it appeared that nothing could be done about it. "I fully recognize," he wrote, "that the people have the issue in their own hands." Washington *Evening Star*, April 4, 1896, 1.

2   Theodore Roosevelt to Anna Roosevelt, May 27, 1894, in Elting E. Morison (ed.), *The Letters of Theodore Roosevelt*, 8 vols. (Cambridge, 1951), I, 382.

3   Samuel R. Thayer to Davis, April 4, 1895, C. K. Davis papers; Clarkson to Allison, June 17, 1895, Allison papers; brochure, "Senator Davis and the Presidency," in Henry A. Castle papers (Minnesota Historical Society); Washington *Evening Star*, April 12, 1895, 1.

4   W. Gage Miller to Davis, March 27, 1895; Samuel R. Thayer to Davis, April 17, 1895, C. K. Davis papers; John H. Keatley to Dodge, January 7, 1896, Dodge papers; Washington *Evening Star*, September 12, 1895, 8.

5   J. A. Tawney to H. A. Castle, January 10, 1896, Castle papers.

6   C. K. Davis to H. A. Castle, March 12, April 6, 19, 1896, Castle papers; *New York Times*, March 25, 1896, 5.

7   B. G. Dawes to Charles G. Dawes, February 2, 8, 1896; F. W. Collins to Charles G. Dawes, February 8, 1896, Charles G. Dawes papers (Northwestern University Library).

8   B. G. Dawes to Charles G. Dawes, February 8, 1896; F. W. Collins to Charles G. Dawes, February 8, 1896, Dawes papers; Charles G. Dawes (Bascom N. Timmons, ed.), *A Journal of the McKinley Years* (Chicago, 1950), 69–70; Chicago *Tribune*, February 15, 1896, 6; Boston *Evening Transcript*, March 3, 1896, 1; March 7, 1896, 11.

9   Typewritten sheet, corrections in Harrison's hand, dated February 3, 1896, in Harrison papers.

10 *Ibid.*

11 J. S. Clarkson to Allison, June 4 and June 17, 1895, Allison papers (LC).

12 L. A. Coolidge to Chandler, July 24, 1895, Chandler papers.

13 McKinley to Holloway, February 5, 1896; M. A. Hanna to Holloway, February 8, 1896, as given in A. Dale Beeler, "Letters to Colonel William R. Holloway, 1893–1897," *Indiana Magazine of History*, XXXVI

(December, 1940), 375–6; New York *Tribune*, February 4, 1896, 1; Canton *Repository*, February 6, 1896, 4.

14 E. H. Nebeker to Dunlap, February 8, 1896, Morton papers.
15 Harrison to John H. Gear, May 8, 1896, Harrison papers. Twice in this letter Harrison explained his inaction in terms of his fear that action would renew speculation about his own candidacy. Explaining why he had not opposed McKinley in Indiana, he said: "I did not see how I could do anything that would not tend to bring me into the field—a thing I was utterly unwilling to do." Explaining why he had not declared for Allison, he said: "I should have been charged at once with trying to bring about a situation that might result in my nomination." Harrison to S. B. Elkins, April 28, 1896, Harrison papers.
16 W. A. Sutherland to Morton, March 8, 12, 1896; Morton to Rev. J. A. Wood, February 5, 1896, Morton papers.
17 M. A. Hanna to Holloway (undated), in Beeler, "Letters to Holloway," 381.
18 F. B. D[awes] to Dawes, June 21, 1896, Dawes papers.
19 Entry dated May 9, 1896, in Dawes, *Journal*, 82–3.
20 Edens to Dawes, December 23, 1895, Dawes papers.
21 Dawes to M. A. Hanna, March 9, 1896, Dawes papers.
22 F. W. Collins to Dawes, January 6, 1896; Dawes to F. W. Collins, January 9 and March 9, 1896; Dawes to W. F. Calhoun, February 24, 1896; Joseph P. Smith to Dawes, March 3 and April 1, 1896, Dawes papers; J. W. Gates to Allison, February 17, 1896, Allison papers; W. M. Osborne to Hanna, March 11, 1896, McKinley papers.
23 S. M. Cullom to Joseph W. Fifer, February 4, 1896, Joseph Fifer papers (Illinois State Historical Society); St. Louis *Post Dispatch*, January 27, 1896, 5; Chicago *Tribune*, January 29, 1896, 1, 3, 4; Dawes, *Journal*, 66–7.
24 Hanna to McKinley, January 20, 1896, McKinley papers; Charles G. Dawes to Beman C. Dawes, February 4, 1896, Dawes papers; Cincinnati *Commercial Gazette*, January 28, 1896, 1; February 1, 1896, 1; February 3, 1896, 1; Chicago *Tribune*, January 28, 1896, 4; January 31, 1896, 4; Dawes, *Journal*, 66–7.
25 Joseph P. Smith to Dawes, January 27, 1896, Dawes papers; entry dated January 29, 1896, in Dawes, *Journal*, 66.
26 Dawes, *Journal*, 66.
27 Clarkson to Allison, February 3, 1896, Allison papers.
28 Entry dated February 3, 1896 in Dawes, *Journal*, 67.
29 Entry of February 4, 1896, *Ibid.*, 67–8.
30 Entry dated February 5, 1896, *Ibid.*, 68.
31 Joseph P. Smith to A. B. White, February 15, 1896, White papers.
32 Canton *Repository*, February 16, 1896.
33 *Ibid.*, February 13, 1896.
34 P. S. Grosscup to Herrick, March 16, 1896; Herrick to McKinley, March 17, 1896; S. Cullom to [Grosscup], April 4, 1896; Grosscup to McKinley, April 8, 1896; Charles G. Dawes to McKinley, April 9 and 10, 1896; John McNulta to McKinley, April 9, 1896, McKinley papers. Joseph P. Smith to Dawes, April 3, 1896; W. M. Osborne to Dawes, April 6, 1896, Dawes papers. Dawes, *Journal*, 74–6.
35 Entry dated April 28, 1896, in Dawes, *Journal*, 78–9.

36 Joseph P. Smith to McKinley, April 10, 1896, McKinley papers.
37 Elisha Keyes to Jacob Rich, January 31, 1896, February 4, 1896, Keyes papers; Spooner to H. M. Kutchin, April 26, 1896, John Coit Spooner papers (Library of Congress).
38 La Follette to [McKinley], January 29, 1896, Robert M. La Follette papers (in Wisconsin Historical Society); Jacob Rich to Allison, January 30, 1896, Allison papers.
39 Copy of letter, unsigned, on La Follette stationery, addressed to Lewis Baker, dated February 18, 1896, La Follette papers; Keyes to Philetus Sawyer, February 5, 1896, Keyes papers.
40 Nils P. Haugen to McKinley, April 8, 1896, Nils P. Haugen papers (Wisconsin Historical Society).
41 Joseph P. Smith to Dawes, April 1, 1896, Dawes papers.
42 Osborne to McKinley, March 15, 1896, McKinley papers; Dawes to Hanna, March 16, 1896, Dawes papers; Dawes, *Journal*, 72–3.

CHAPTER 10

1 McKinley to Hanna, February 25, 1895; McKinley to Sen. J. C. Pritchard, April 13, 1895; McKinley to Rev. I. Dawson, April 15, 1895; McKinley to Dr. C. C. Stewart, June 12, 1895, McKinley papers; Washington *Evening Star*, March 13, 1895; Robert P. Porter, *Life of William McKinley, Soldier, Lawyer, Statesman, With a Biographical Sketch of Hon. G. A. Hobart* (Cleveland, 1896), 347–52.
2 Quoted, without date, in Maud Cuney Hare, *Norris Wright Cuney, A Tribune of the Black People* (New York, 1913), 178–81.
3 James S. Clarkson to Dodge, February 18, 1896, Dodge papers; Hare, *Cuney*, 182–88.
4 Dodge to Allison, March 26, 1896, Allison papers.
5 N. B. Moore to D. B. Henderson, December 24, 1895; Henderson to Moore, December 29, 1895, Allison papers; Hanna to McKinley, February 28, 1896, McKinley papers.
6 McKinley to John Grant, April 2, 1896, McKinley papers; Marian Silveus, "Antecedents of the Campaign of 1896" (unpublished Ph.D. dissertation, University of Wisconsin, 1932), 283; Hare, *Cuney*, 182–8; Chicago *Tribune*, March 27, 1896, 2.
7 Emory F. Skinner, *Reminiscences* (Chicago, 1908), 261–75.
8 T. C. Platt to Clarkson, May 27, 1896, James S. Clarkson papers (in Library of Congress); Clarkson to Dodge, May 28, 1896, Dodge papers.
9 W. S. Reese to Chandler, February 19, 1895, Chandler papers (LC); Washington *Evening Star*, March 27, 1894, 16; March 28, 1894, 6.
10 Morton to Youngblood, January 9, 1896, Morton papers.
11 Youngblood to Morton, February 28, 1896, Morton papers.
12 The Reed forces in Alabama were guided by Dr. Robert A. Mosely, Chairman of the State Executive Committee. Youngblood, who headed the McKinley drive, was national committeeman from Alabama. *New York Times*, April 12, 1896, 2; Chandler to R. A. Mosely, June 3, 1896, Chandler papers (LC). Chandler wrote, "If Mr. Hanna has covered every district in the United States in the manner that he did those in Alabama McKinley will be nominated, indeed that is the outlook now."
13 McKinley to Senator J. C. Pritchard, April 13, 1895; Pritchard to James

H. Ramsey, February 27, March 4, 1896, James Graham Ramsey papers (Southern Historical Collection, University of North Carolina).

14 H. C. Warmoth to Chandler, February 23, 1895, February 4, 1896, Chandler papers (LC).

15 J. R. G. Pitkin to Harrison, December 22, 1895, Harrison papers.

16 McKinley to Warmoth, December 30, 1895; McKinley to W. M. Osborne, December 30, 1895, McKinley papers.

17 H. C. Warmoth to Chandler February 4, 1896; Chandler to Warmoth, February 17, 1896, Chandler papers (LC); Clarkson to Allison, February 6, 1896, Allison papers; John C. Daugherty to Elkins, March 18, 1896, Elkins papers; F. N. Wicker to C. S. Kelsey, May 20, 22, 1896, McKinley papers.

18 Clarkson to Allison, April 9, May 18, 1896, Allison papers; Daugherty to Elkins, May 18, 1896, Elkins papers.

19 Elkins to Harrison, April 18, 1896, Harrison papers.

20 McKinley to Elkins, March 21, 1896, Elkins papers; McKinley to Elkins, April 7, 1896, McKinley papers.

21 McKinley to Charles Burdette Hart, April 22, 1896, McKinley papers.

22 Elkins to White, April 10, 15, 25, 1896, White papers.

23 McKinley to Charles Burdette Hart, April 22, 1896; McKinley to John W. Mason, April 26, 1896, McKinley papers.

24 Elkins to White, May 15, 1896, White papers; *New York Times,* May 15, 1896, 1.

25 McKinley to Bradley, July 19, July 23, 1895, McKinley papers; Canton *Repository,* November 10, 1895; Washington *Evening Star,* March 30, 1896, 1; St. Louis *Post Dispatch,* August 16, 1896.

26 C. K. Davis to Castle, January 30, 1896, Castle papers. Davis wrote that he had just returned from St. Louis and after giving details about the antagonism between Kerens and Filley concluded: "There is going to be a regular old-fashioned Missouri fight, the right of which no man can find out."

27 McKinley to Kerens, December 4, 1895; McKinley to Brownell, December 18, 1895, McKinley papers.

28 Chauncey I. Filley, *Some Republican History of Missouri* (St. Louis, 1898), 181–5. Filley blamed the break-down of negotiations to ally McKinley with Quay, Platt, and the others on Hanna and said that in February, 1896, he informed McKinley in person that he could not head up his campaign in Missouri. McKinley to Filley, April 24, 1896, McKinley papers.

29 J. M. Blythe to Allison, n.d., Allison papers. In a letter dated February 24, 1896, to Grenville Dodge, Blythe said that he believed that Filley was disposed to aid Allison, "but his methods are past my understanding." Letter in Dodge papers.

30 McKinley to John Hay, April 13, 1895; McKinley to Hanna, April 13, 1895; McKinley to James A. Gary, April 13, 1895, McKinley papers.

31 Horace Baker to Allison, April 30, 1895, July 4, 1895; Clarkson to Allison, June 17, 1895, Allison papers.

32 R. F. Patterson to Allison, August 12, 1895; Ben M. Samuels to Allison, October 3, 1895, Allison papers; Hanna to J. C. Napier, April 15, 20, 1896, McKinley papers; Cincinnati *Commercial Gazette,* November 12, 1895, 2; Washington *Evening Star,* February 18, 1896, 1.

33 J. N. Dolph to Allison, January 24, 1896, Allison papers; James A. Waymire to McKinley, April 13, 1896; McKinley to Waymire, April 20, 1896, McKinley papers; *New York Times,* May 7, 1896, 5; Chicago *Tribune,* May 11, 1896, 4; *Oregon State Journal,* February 29, 1896; Harold F. Taggart, "The Party Realignment of 1896 in California," *Pacific Historical Review,* VIII (December, 1939), 438–40.

34 Chicago *Tribune,* May 16, 1896, 5.

35 St. Louis *Post Dispatch,* March 19, 1896, 12.

36 Boston *Evening Transcript,* March 24, 1896, 1.

37 William M. Stewart to McKinley, April 28, 1896, McKinley papers.

38 *National Bimetallist,* I (May 20, 1896), 492.

39 Teller to Irving Howbert, May 11, 1896, quoted in Thomas F. Dawson, *Senator Teller, A Brief Account of His Fifth Election to the United States Senate....* (Washington, D.C., 1898), 9–10.

40 *New York Times,* May 16, 1896, 2; *Chicago Tribune,* May 16, 1895, 5; Elmer Ellis, *Henry Moore Teller, Defender of the West* (Caldwell, Idaho, 1941), 253–4; Fred Wilmot Wellborn, "The Silver Republicans, 1890–1900" (unpublished Ph.D. dissertation, University of Wisconsin, 1926), 123–7.

CHAPTER 11

1 Foraker to W. C. Doane, April 6, 1896, Foraker papers.

2 J. S. Clarkson to Allison, January 5, 1896, Allison papers; Chicago *Tribune,* January 8, 1896, 3; Washington *Evening Star,* January 14, 1896, 3.

3 Clarkson to Allison, December 14, 1895, Allison papers. Clarkson, reporting on interviews he had with Quay, Platt, Fessenden, and Hobart, said: "They say they are banking all the votes possible against McKinley under the Reed strength in the East. Fessenden, as you know is outright for you. So is Hobart and they will give their states solid for you when chance comes if you can show strength in the northwest." Later in the letter he quoted Platt as saying to him every day: "We are holding the situation in the East against McKinley; you must hold it in the Northwest."

4 Clarkson to Allison, December 14, and December 23, 1895, Allison papers; Clarkson to Grenville Dodge, February 18, 1896, Dodge papers.

5 McKinley to Rev. James Curry, January 2, 1896, McKinley papers; D. C. Meeker to Foraker, January 17, 1896, Foraker papers; Washington *Evening Star,* September 4, 1893, 3.

6 Printed letter signed by J. H. D. Stevens, Chairman, and James B. Dunn, Secretary, National Advisory Board of the APA, to members, April 10, 1896, McKinley papers; Washington *Evening Star,* March 23, 1896, 3; March 26, 1896, 2; April 6, 1896, 1; St. Louis *Post Dispatch,* April 13, 1896, 2; Chicago *Tribune,* April 16, 1896, 3.

7 James Boyle to Samuel J. Roberts, April 10, 1896; Boyle to John K. Gowdy, April 13, 1896; Boyle to Samuel G. McClure, April 14, 1896, McKinley papers. In 1897 newspaper reports were published claiming that Aldrich was responsible for the APA attack on McKinley. In a letter to Herman Kohlsaat, Aldrich protested the publication of such a report in the Chicago *Times-Herald.* Aldrich said that he had been approached by Ohio APA men, that he had stopped in Columbus at their

request to talk with them; but he had spurned their proposals that he join them in establishing an APA literary bureau, which would be used to support work in Ohio, Michigan, Kentucky, and one or two other states. Copy, Aldrich to Kohlsaat, February 2, 1897, Aldrich papers.

8   Boyle to D. K. Watson, April 9, 1896; Boyle to A. C. Caine, April 14, 1896, McKinley papers; Moses [Handy] to Hanna, April 22, 1896, Dawes papers; *Kansas Semi-Weekly Capital,* April 21, 1896, 5.

9   Hervey Lindley to Allison, January 21, 1896; Clarkson to Allison, January 28, 1896; J. W. Gates to Allison, April 18, 1896, Allison papers; Dodge to C. E. Perkins, April 10, 1896; Dodge to Jonathan G. Gear, April 10, 1896, Dodge papers.

10   James Boyle to Charles G. Dawes, April 21, 1896; Joseph Smith to Dawes, April 16 and 22, 1896, Dawes papers.

11   Dawes to Joseph P. Smith, April 17, 1896; Dawes to James Boyle, April 17, 1896, Dawes papers.

12   C. H. Grosvenor to William Holloway, April 16, 1896, William Holloway papers (Indiana State Library)

13   McKinley to William Osborne, April 17, 1896, McKinley papers.

14   James Boyle to Chas. H. Grosvenor, April 11, 1896, McKinley papers.

15   Hanna to McKinley, April 21, 1896, McKinley papers.

16   A. J. Boyer to Washington *Evening Star,* published April 17, 1896, 10.

17   George Hester to McKinley, December 18, 1896, McKinley papers.

18   St. Louis *Post Dispatch,* May 12, 1896, 9; May 14, 1896, 5; May 16, 1896, 2; Washington *Evening Star,* May 13, 1896, 1; May 14, 1896, 1; May 16, 1896, 2; Chicago *Tribune,* May 15, 1896, 3; May 17, 1896, 2; *New York Times,* May 14, 1896, 1; New York *World,* May 17, 1896, 1.

19   L. T. Michener to Tibbot, May 19, 1896, Harrison papers; Washington *Evening Star,* May 16, 1896, 2.

20   Chandler to A. L. Conger, March [?, 1896], Chandler papers (LC); A. F. Howard to Chandler, March 23, 1896, Chandler papers (New Hampshire Historical Society, hereafter designated as NH).

21   Leon Burr Richardson, *William E. Chandler, Republican* (New York, 1940), 335–6; New York *Tribune,* March 21, 1896, 1.

22   New York *Tribune,* March 21, 1896, 1; *New York Times,* April 1, 1896, 5.

23   Chandler to Reed, November 9, 1896, Chandler papers (NH).

24   Boston *Evening Transcript,* April 1, 1896, 1, 4. One New England congressman was quoted: "It seems to me that this must be more a bit of local politics than anything else. Senator Chandler has many enemies in his State, and they may have taken this occasion to show their disapproval of his course in attacking McKinley." *New York Times,* April 1, 1896, 5.

25   J. H. Gallinger to Marseilles, May 30, 1896, Gallinger papers.

26   Theodore Roosevelt to Henry Cabot Lodge, July 30, 1895, in Elting E. Morison (ed.), *The Letters of Theodore Roosevelt,* 8 vols. (Cambridge, 1951), I, 470.

27   Wells to Allison, November 12, 1895, Allison papers.

28   Theodore Roosevelt, "The Issues of 1896. A Republican View," *Century,* LI (November, 1895), 70–1.

29   Canton *Repository,* March 1, 1896.

30 *Atlantic*, LXXVII (February, 1896), 250–6.
31 Theodore Roosevelt to Anna Roosevelt Cowles, March 9, 1896, in Morison, *Letters of T.R.*, I, 520.
32 Nils P. Haugen to Robert La Follette, December 18, 1894, Haugen papers; Theodore Roosevelt to Henry Cabot Lodge, June 5, 1895, in Morison, *Letters of T.R.*, I, 460–1.
33 Clarkson to Allison, December 23, 1895, Allison papers; John Abel to McKinley, March 8, 1896, Dawes papers.
34 St. Louis *Post Dispatch*, January 5, 1896, 24.
35 Boston *Evening Transcript*, May 1, 1896, 1; *New York Times*, April 30, 1896, 5.
36 Boston *Evening Transcript*, May 4, 1896, 4.
37 Washington *Evening Star*, June 15, 1895, 9.
38 William M. Osborne to McKinley, January 16, 1896. Osborne wrote that Quay was fighting the selection of McKinley delegates in Pennsylvania and concluded, "I have thought for some time that he was stringing us and I am now satisfied of it—I think we had better make an open campaign in every district. . . ." John Hay to Hanna, January 27, 1896. In a letter to McKinley, dated February 19, 1896, C. H. Grosvenor wrote, "I am not to decide questions of so much importance, but I want to suggest to you whether we should coddle Quay any longer, or whether by some step to be taken not from here an open fight should be organized in every district of his State." All these letters are in the McKinley papers.
39 T. C. Platt to Morton, December 11, 1895, Morton papers.
40 Edward Lauterbach to Morton, December 14, 1895, Morton papers.
41 Morton to Platt, March 20, 1896, Morton papers.
42 Platt to Morton, April 23, 1896, Morton papers.
43 Platt to Morton, April 28, 1896, Morton papers.
44 Theodore Roosevelt to Henry Cabot Lodge, December 2, 20, 1895, in Morison, *Letters of T.R.*, I, 498–501.
45 Roosevelt to Lodge, January 19, February 25, 1896, in Morison, *Letters of T.R.*, I, 517–8.
46 J. S. Clarkson to Allison, February 26, 1896, Allison papers.
47 J. S. Clarkson to Dodge, March 6, 1896, Dodge papers. Clarkson said that it had been decided in Washington the night before by Platt and Quay that Clarkson was to go to the West Coast to "look after" the delegates and the National Committeemen. He spoke of money being raised for him to use on the trip. W. M. Osborne to McKinley, March 15, 1896, McKinley papers. Washington *Evening Star*, March 13, 1896; New York *Tribune*, March 14, 1896, 4.
48 Clarkson to Allison, February 10, 1896. Clarkson said that he had received acknowledgement of a draft forwarded by him and that Tanner had enough money to take care of Chicago but he needed more for the rest of the state. J. W. Gates to Allison, February 17, 1896. Gates said that Tanner had received a check from Clarkson for $10,000, which was all the aid he had received until then. Clarkson to Allison, February 25, 1896. Clarkson identified General Dodge as the man who had given help to Tanner. All the above letters are in the Allison papers. Clarkson to Dodge, March 6, 1896, Dodge papers. Clarkson said that $5,000

was needed in Illinois and that Platt and Quay were helping to raise it.
49   Clarkson to Allison, March 29, 1896, Allison papers; Clarkson to Dodge,
     April 3, 1896, Dodge papers.
50   Clarkson to Dodge, May 28, 1896, Dodge papers. In this letter Clark-
     son said that "men like Allison and you have used your influence to very
     little avail," that Platt was furnishing the money to bring Allison dele-
     gates from New Mexico, Arizona, Nevada, and Utah to the convention,
     "when all the country between is filled with railroads that ought to be
     friendly to Allison." T. C. Platt to Clarkson, May 27, 1896, Clarkson
     papers. Platt wrote that he enclosed four checks drawn in Clarkson's
     name. They were for Perry Carson of Washington, D.C. ($300), Cuney
     of Texas ($1000); Beach ($300), and North Carolina ($400). He also
     listed checks which had been drawn for other southern states and for
     a few western states.
51   C. E. Perkins to Allison, May 20, 1895, Allison papers. Perkins wrote
     that he found much ignorance on money among both the free silverites
     and the gold monometallists. "But on the whole the Gold Bugs are
     ahead so far as ignorance goes." In a postcript he added: "You may say
     I encourage the silver monometallists too much. But is not that the
     only way, if there is any way, to hold them till we can get international
     action—And if we cant [*sic*] get such action at all I am a silver mono-
     metallist."
52   Stuyvesant Fish to Allison, April 1, 1896, Allison papers. Fish wrote,
     "In the present Campaign the one question seems to me to be the
     preservation of the single gold standard." On that basis, he explained,
     he had declared for Governor Morton.
53   *New York Times,* May 11, 1896, 1.
54   Chicago *Tribune,* May 14, 1896, 8.
55   *Ibid.*
56   Boston *Evening Transcript,* May 14, 1896, 1.
57   Chicago *Tribune,* May 20, 1896, 3.
58   *New York Times,* May 23, 1896, 1, 5.
59   R. C. Dawes to C. G. Dawes, April 20, 1896, Dawes papers.
60   *New York Times,* June 19, 1896, 4.
61   Jonathan Gear to Dodge, May 8, 1896; Clarkson to Dodge, May 29,
     1896, Dodge papers.
62   New York *World,* May 2, 1896, 1.
63   McKinley to Senator John Sherman, March 22, 1896; McKinley to
     Robert C. Alexander, April 9, 1896, McKinley papers.
64   New York *Tribune,* May 11, 1896, 1; May 12, 1896, 3; New York
     World, May 17, 1896, 1; May 18, 1896, 1.
65   Chicago *Tribune,* May 19, 1896, 1.

CHAPTER 12

1   Cincinnati *Commercial Gazette,* June 14, 1896, 1.
2   James Creelman in New York *World,* June 13, 1896, 1; St. Louis *Post
    Dispatch,* June 17, 1896, 1; New York *Tribune,* June 17, 1896, 1;
    June 18, 1896, 1; Walter Johnson, *William Allen White's America* (New
    York, 1947), 89.

3 Solomon B. Griffin, *People and Politics Observed by a Massachusetts Editor* (Boston, 1923), 344.

4 McKinley to Secretary, Stark County Farmers' Alliance, October 27, 1890, quoted in article signed by James Creelman in New York *World*, June 4, 1896, 1.

5 New York *World*, June 5, 1896, 3.

6 Indianapolis *Journal*, June 6, 1896, 1.

7 New York *Tribune*, May 31, 1896, 1.

8 Louisville *Courier-Journal*, June 6, 1896, 1.

9 St. Louis *Post Dispatch*, June 9, 1896, 3; St. Louis *Globe-Democrat*, June 11, 1896, 1; Chicago *Tribune*, June 11, 1896, 2. An Indiana reporter who swung onto Hanna's special convention-bound train at Muncie, Indiana, as it speeded across the country from Cleveland, found it a beehive of activity. When he interviewed Hanna in the library of his car he found there, around a table, Senator Redfield Proctor, William M. Osborne, Colonel Myron Herrick, Sylvester Everett, William M. Hahn, Abner McKinley, and others, working intently on various convention details. Indianapolis *Journal*, June 10, 1896, 1.

10 St. Louis *Post Dispatch*, June 7, 1896, 1; Cincinnati *Commercial Gazette*, June 7, 1896, 1; Charles G. Dawes (Bascom N. Timmons, ed.), *A Journal of the McKinley Years* (Chicago, 1950), 84.

11 New York *World*, June 14, 1896, 12.

12 New York *Tribune*, June 13, 1896, 3; St. Louis *Post Dispatch*, June 13, 1896, 2.

13 St. Louis *Globe-Democrat*, June 7, 1896, 9; June 9, 1896, 2; St. Louis *Post Dispatch*, June 8, 1896, 1; June 9, 1896, 7.

14 Gallinger to Charles Marseilles, June 18, 1896, Gallinger papers; *New York Times*, June 11, 1896, 2.

15 Manley to Reed, June 12, 1896, quoted in Samuel W. McCall, *The Life of Thomas Brackett Reed* (Boston and New York, 1914), 224.

16 Perry Heath to McKinley, May 29 [1896], McKinley papers; Louisville *Courier-Journal*, June 6, 1896, 1; St. Louis *Post Dispatch*, June 6, 1896, 1; June 5, 1896, 7; New York *Tribune*, June 6, 1896, 1.

17 St. Louis *Post Dispatch*, June 13, 1896, 1.

18 *New York Times*, June 10, 1896, 2.

19 New York *Tribune*, June 11, 1896, 1. The seven who voted against the McKinley slate were Samuel Fessenden of Connecticut, Senator John H. Gear of Iowa (carrying James Clarkson's proxy), Albert H. Leonard of Louisiana, Joseph H. Manley of Maine, William M. Crane of Massachusetts, W. A. Sutherland of New York, and Perry H. Carson of the District of Columbia. Fessenden, Leonard, Manley, and Crane were Reed men; Gear and Carson were Allison men; and Sutherland was for Morton.

20 St. Louis *Globe-Democrat*, June 12, 1896, 3; June 16, 1896, 2.

21 David Magie, *Life of Garret Augustus Hobart* (New York and London, 1910), 79–80.

22 H. C. Lodge to C. K. Davis, June 19, 1896, Davis papers. Lodge claimed responsibility in these words: "I think you will agree there is nothing evasive about the plank we have forced upon them." Garraty, *Lodge*, 167–72; St. Louis *Post Dispatch*, June 17, 1896, 7.

23 In an interview on Friday, June 12, Herman Kohlsaat said that there was no major difference of opinion on the platform such as he had anticipated. He said that he had found that the only question, practically, was whether the phrase "existing standard" or "existing gold standard" should be used. Indianapolis *Journal,* June 13, 1896, 1. On June 13 (p. 1) the Washington *Evening Star* reported that Hanna was now ready to accept a platform declaration for the "present gold standard." In a letter to Charles Marseilles (July 14, 1896, Gallinger papers) Senator Gallinger wrote: "Concerning the money plank of the St. Louis platform I know only this: I arrived at St. Louis on the Friday preceding convention week, and on that very day I was shown a draft of a resolution by Person C. Cheney, Senator Proctor and Henry B. Payne of Milwaukee, exactly alike in each case, and identical in every essential particular with that adopted by the convention. The phraseology was slightly changed; but, as I say, the essential expressions were all retained in the exact language that it was presented to me." Also Redfield Proctor to Gallinger, July 16, 1896, and P. C. Cheney to Gallinger, July 17, 1896, Gallinger papers. Proctor said that he saw the currency plank on Friday morning, June 12; Cheney said that he saw it on Thursday evening, June 11.

24 A. C. Thompson, one of the first McKinley agents to arrive in St. Louis, in an interview there Tuesday, June 9, replied when asked about McKinley's financial plank: "It will be for the single gold standard pure and simple. And to be explicit, I will add that the financial platform of Mr. McKinley always has been the antithesis of what is known as the 16-to-1 silverism, and so it will be through this campaign." Louisville *Courier-Journal,* June 10, 1896, 2.

25 Cincinnati *Commercial Gazette,* March 12, 1896, 4.

26 Foraker to John Little, May 13, 1896, Foraker papers.

27 St. Louis *Post Dispatch,* June 13, 1896, 1; Joseph Benson Foraker, *Notes of a Busy Life,* 2 vols. (Cincinnati, 1917), I, 464–8.

28 W. R. Merriam to Grosvenor, May 25, 1896; C. H. Grosvenor to John Sherman, May 29, 1896, Foraker papers.

29 Memorandum in McKinley's hand and on his stationery, dated 1896, in McKinley papers. Also memorandum attached to letter, Whitelaw Reid to McKinley, June 13, 1896, McKinley papers. Royal Cortissoz, *The Life of Whitelaw Reid* (New York, 1921), 205–8; Col. T. Bentley Mott, *Myron T. Herrick, Friend of France; An Autobiographical Biography* (Garden City, N.Y., 1929), 67–71.

30 Whitelaw Reid to McKinley, June 13, 1896, McKinley papers.

31 Dawes to [G. M.] Lamberton, July 1, 1896, Dawes papers; New York *Tribune,* June 18, 1896, 3; June 19, 1896, 1; Frank G. Carpenter in San Francisco *Chronicle,* June 18, 1896, 1; Washington *Evening Star,* June 19, 1896, 6; June 22, 1896, 1; New York *World,* June 23, 1896, 3; Cincinnati *Commercial Tribune,* June 25, 1896, 1; Dawes, *Journal,* 85; Marcus A. Hanna, *Mark Hanna, His Book* (Boston, 1904), 62–3; Foraker, *Notes of a Busy Life,* I, 464, 467, 468; Griffin, *People and Politics,* 346–7; Herman H. Kohlsaat, *From McKinley to Harding; Personal Recollections of Our Presidents* (New York and London, 1923), 33–48; Nicholas Murray Butler, *Across the Busy Years. Recollections and Reflections,* 2 vols. (New York, 1939, 1940), I, 222–3; Mott, *Her-*

rick, 67–71; Melville E. Stone, *Fifty Years a Journalist* (Garden City, N.Y., 1921), 220–2; Thomas Beer, *Hanna* (New York, 1929), 143–4; Herbert Croly, *Marcus Alonzo Hanna, His Life and Work* (New York, 1912), 198–9; William W. Wight, *Henry Clay Payne. A Life* (Milwaukee, 1907), 92; Cortissoz, *Reid*, II, 205–8; Everett Walters, *Joseph Benson Foraker, An Uncompromising Republican* (Columbus, Ohio, 1948), 130; Marian Silveus, "Antecedents of the Campaign of 1896" (unpublished Ph.D. dissertation, University of Wisconsin, 1932), 132–41.

32   W. E. Chandler to Gen. Chas. H. Grosvenor, June 24, 1896, McKinley papers. H. C. Hansbrough to J. H. Gallinger, August 4, 1896; Gallinger to Chandler, August 9, 1896, Gallinger papers.

33   John A. Garraty, *Henry Cabot Lodge, A Biography* (New York, 1953), 171–2.

34   St. Louis *Post Dispatch,* June 15, 1896, 1.

35   *New York Times,* June 18, 1896, 2; Elmer Ellis, *Henry Moore Teller, Defender of the West* (Caldwell, Idaho, 1941), 258.

36   St. Louis *Post Dispatch,* June 12, 1896, 2; Washington *Evening Star,* June 13, 1896, 1.

37   *New York Times,* June 16, 1896, 1–2.

38   St. Louis *Post Dispatch,* June 8, 1896, 1; Chicago *Tribune,* June 10, 1896, 2; June 17, 1896, 1; New York *Tribune,* June 11, 1896, 2.

39   McKinley was criticized, of course, for choosing a Rabbi. One Methodist minister in St. Louis preached a sermon attacking McKinley's choice of Rabbi Sale, saying, "I think that this is a Christian age, and not a Jewish age and the Republican party that claims always to be in the advance should not have put themselves back more than 2000 years in religion." St. Louis *Globe-Democrat,* June 22, 1896, 7.

40   *New York Times,* June 8, 1896, 5; June 11, 1896, 1; Chicago *Tribune,* June 10, 1896, 2.

41   *Official Proceedings of the Eleventh Republican National Convention.* . . . (n.p., 1896), 27–30.

42   *Ibid.,* 30.

43   *New York Times,* June 17, 1896, 2. The two exceptions were the disputed delegations from Delaware and Texas.

44   William Jennings Bryan, *First Battle, A Story of the Campaign of 1896* (Chicago, 1896), 175.

45   Ellis, *Teller,* 259–61.

46   Washington *Evening Star,* June 18, 1896, 2; Chicago *Tribune,* June 19, 1896, 1.

47   *New York Times,* June 19, 1896, 7.

48   St. Louis *Post Dispatch,* June 18, 1896, 2.

49   William A. White, *The Autobiography of William Allen White* (New York, 1946), 277–8.

50   *Official Proceedings, Republican,* 81–5.

51   *Ibid.*

52   *Ibid.,* 108–12.

53   *Ibid.,* 112–6.

54   *Ibid.,* 117–20; *New York Times,* June 19, 1896, 1.

55   *Official Proceedings, Republican,* 120.

56   Washington *Evening Star,* June 2, 1896, 12; Cincinnati *Commercial*

Gazette, June 4, 1896, 2; June 6, 1896, 1; Chicago *Tribune,* June 10, 1896, 2.

57 Copies of telegraphic exchanges between Morton and Platt and Morton and Depew at the time of the convention, in Morton papers.

58 St. Louis *Post Dispatch,* June 12, 1896, 3; Belle Case La Follette and Fola La Follette, *Robert M. La Follette, June 14, 1855–June 18, 1925,* 2 vols. (New York, 1953), I, 114–5.

59 Washington *Evening Star,* May 22, 1896, 1; St. Louis *Post Dispatch,* June 10, 1896, 2; Canton *Repository,* June 11, 1896; Louisville *Courier-Journal,* June 11, 1896, 1; St. Louis *Globe-Democrat,* June 11, 1896, 1; Dawes, *Journal,* 86; Croly, *Hanna,* 191; Magie, *Hobart,* 78–80.

60 *New York Times,* June 19, 1896, 2.

61 *Official Proceedings, Republican,* 136–43.

62 J. H. Gallinger to Charles Marseilles, June 18, 1896, Gallinger papers. Gallinger wrote, "Whether wise or unwise, *the people* have decreed McKinley's nomination. . . ."

63 *Official Proceedings, Republican,* 130–1.

64 Boston *Evening Transcript,* June 10, 1896, 4.

65 In an article published in the New York *World,* June 18, 1896, 2, Creelman wrote of Hanna, "Having created a popular craze for Mr. McKinley, he had mastered the National Committee, dictated the names of the delegates to the convention, chosen the officers and made all the arrangements to choose the President and Vice-President to-morrow."

66 Louisville *Courier-Journal,* June 13, 1896, 6.

67 Boston *Evening Transcript,* June 20, 1896, 3.

CHAPTER 13

1 Chicago *Tribune,* April 6, 1896, 1.

2 Festus P. Summers (ed.), *The Cabinet Diary of William L. Wilson* (Chapel Hill, N. Car., 1951), 67–8.

3 William V. Byars, *An American Commoner, The Life and Times of Richard Parks Bland* (St. Louis, 1900), 121.

4 Chicago *Tribune,* July 7, 1896, 3.

5 St. Louis *Post Dispatch,* July 9, 1896, 1.

6 Horace Boies to Carter Harrison, February 2, 1892, Carter Harrison papers (Newberry Library).

7 Horace Boies to Bryan, February 28, 1896, Bryan papers.

8 William R. Morrison to Gustave A. Koerner [June 20, 1896], William R. Morrison papers (Illinois State Historical Society).

9 Allen W. Clark to Bryan, May 16 [1896], Bryan papers.

10 Sterling R. Holt to A. L. Smith, January 24, 1896.

11 *Ibid.*

12 John P. Altgeld to James S. Hogg, June 8, 1896, quoted in John P. Altgeld, *Live Questions* (Chicago, 1899), 525.

13 James A. Barnes, "Illinois and the Gold-Silver Controversy, 1890–1896," *Transactions of the Illinois State Historical Society for the Year 1931* (Springfield, Illinois, 1932), 54.

14 Josephus Daniels to Bryan, April 30, 1896; George F. Washburn to Bryan, November 4, 1896, Bryan papers; Charles M. Rosser, *The Crusading Commoner. A Close-Up of William Jennings Bryan and His*

Times (Dallas, Tex., 1937), 11–17; Wayne C. Williams, *William Jennings Bryan* (New York, 1936), 124.

15 William Jennings Bryan, *First Battle, A Story of the Campaign of 1896* (Chicago, 1896), 60–3.

16 C. S. Thomas to Bryan, April 13, 1896; Josephus Daniels to Bryan, April 30, 1896; J. S. Hogg to Bryan, May 9, 1896, Bryan papers.

17 Horace Boies to Bryan, February 28, 1896; Joseph C. Sibley to Bryan, March 18, 1896, Bryan papers.

18 William J. Stone to Bryan, February 28, 1896; David Overmeyer to Bryan, February 29, 1896; J. S. Hogg to Bryan, March 2, 1896; Thomas H. Ayres to Bryan, April 7, 1896; W. H. Hinrichsen to Bryan, April 16, 1896; H. H. Seldomridge to Bryan, April 18, 1896; M. A. Miller to Bryan, April 20, 1896; John E. Osborne to Bryan, May 23, 1896; George W. Allen to Bryan, May 27, 1896, Bryan papers.

19 George A. Carden to Bryan, February 25, 1896, Bryan papers. In an editorial in the Omaha *World-Herald*, published on February 26, 1896, Bryan declared for bolting a Democratic convention controlled by "gold-bugs." He asked, "If to continue Mr. Cleveland's financial policy is to declare war against the common people, What friend of the common people would be willing to enlist in such warfare, even at the command of his party?" Editorial quoted in Bryan, *First Battle,* 125–6. Bryan arranged for wide distribution of this editorial.

20 [J. Burrows?] to James B. Weaver, May 23, 1896, Bryan papers.

21 C. S. Thomas to Bryan, April 18, 1896, Bryan papers.

22 W. J. Bryan to Miller, April 23, 1896, Bryan papers.

23 [J. Burrows?] to J. B. Weaver, May 23, 1896, Bryan papers; Champ Clark, *My Quarter Century of American Politics,* 2 vols. (New York, 1920), I, 401–2; Melville E. Stone, *Fifty Years a Journalist* (Garden City, N.Y., 1921), 222.

24 George W. Allen to Bryan, June 5, 1896, Bryan papers.

25 *National Bimetallist,* I (June 3, 1896), 526.

26 Josephus Daniels to Bryan, May 9, 1896, Bryan papers.

27 J. D. Calhoun to Bryan, June 8, 1896; John H. Atwood to Bryan, June 8, 1896; George A. Carden to Bryan, June 8, 1896; John P. Altgeld to Bryan, June 9, 1896; Walter Allen to Bryan, June 11, 1896, Bryan papers.

28 Quoted in *Oregon State Journal,* June 13, 1896, 1; C. S. Collins to Bryan, April 26, 1896, Bryan papers.

29 Charles S. Collins, *The Genesis of the Campaign of 1896* (Little Rock, Ark., [1906?]), 14–5; St. Louis *Post Dispatch,* April 19, 1896, 3.

30 Quoted in *Oregon State Journal,* June 13, 1896, 1.

31 Josephus Daniels to Bryan, April 30, and May 9, 1896, Bryan papers.

32 John W. Tomlinson to Bryan, May 13, 1896; J. F. Johnston to Bryan, April 25, 1896, Bryan papers.

33 Tomlinson to Bryan, May 26, 1896, Bryan papers.

34 F. Regnier to Bryan, April 8, 1896, Bryan papers.

35 Regnier to Bryan, April 15, 1896; W. H. Hinrichsen to Bryan, April 16, 1896, Bryan papers.

36 Copy, dated April 30, 1896, in Bryan papers.

37 Chicago *Tribune,* June 15, 1896, 2; St. Louis *Post Dispatch,* June 19, 1896, 1; July 14, 1896, 1; William Jennings and Mary Baird Bryan, *The*

Memoirs of William Jennings Bryan (Philadelphia, 1925), 99–100.
38 H. E. Taubeneck to Ignatius Donnelly, June 22, 1896, Donnelly papers.
39 At a later date William Allen White recorded his impressions of Mc-
Kinley when he visited him at Canton: "We were just not meant for
each other—William McKinley and I. He was destined for a statue in
a park, and was practicing the pose for it." White, *Autobiography of
William Allen White* (New York, 1946), 292.

CHAPTER 14

1 Canton *Repository*, March 26, 1896, 6. Tom Johnson, interviewed in
Cleveland about Democratic candidates, replied, "I don't think the
matter has gone far enough yet. There isn't enough interest in the thing
yet in this year when the Republicans will win the election."
2 T. O. Towles to Bryan, March 26 and April 9, 1896, Bryan papers; New
York *Tribune*, March 5, 1896, 1; St. Louis *Post Dispatch*, March 14,
1896, 7; Washington *Evening Star*, March 4, 1896, 1.
3 Festus P. Summers (ed.), *The Cabinet Diary of William L. Wilson*
(Chapel Hill, N. Car., 1951), 27–8.
4 *Ibid.*, 62–3.
5 New York *Tribune*, April 12, 1896, 1.
6 Summers, *Cabinet Diary of Wilson*, 105.
7 *Ibid.*, 106.
8 *Ibid.*, 107.
9 *Ibid.*, 110.
10 *Ibid.*, 114–5.
11 A. S. New to Cleveland, March 31 and May 25, 1896, Cleveland papers.
12 St. Louis *Globe-Democrat*, June 8, 1896, 4.
13 Patterson to Cleveland, March 25, 1896, Cleveland papers.
14 Patterson to Whitney, June 29, 1896, William Collins Whitney papers
(LC).
15 William F. Vilas to Usher, June 4, 1896, Ellis B. Usher papers (Wisconsin Historical Society); Louisville *Courier-Journal*, June 4, 1896, 1;
Chicago *Tribune*, June 4, 1896, 3; June 5, 1896, 3; *New York Times*,
June 4, 1896, 1, 5; Summers, *Cabinet Diary of Wilson*, 95.
16 Josiah Patterson to Whitney, March 25, 1896, Whitney papers. Patterson
wrote, "The situation is serious and to the South it means everything.
We must stand with the organization for white supremacy and good
government. Carry the convention for free silver and the sound money
men in that section must either submit to republican rule or remain
with the party. They will remain with the party...." Summers, *Cabinet
Diary of Wilson*, 68; St. Louis *Post Dispatch*, March 22, 1896, 11; New
York *Tribune*, June 9, 1896.
17 Washington *Evening Star*, April 27, 1896, 1.
18 Daniels to Bryan, April 30, 1896, Bryan papers.
19 Howell to Bryan, May 13, 1896, Bryan papers.
20 Chas. E. Turner to Whitney, June 30, 1896, Whitney papers.
21 Cleveland to Dickinson, March 25, 1896, Cleveland papers.
22 Dickinson to Cleveland, March 31, 1896, Cleveland papers.
23 Cleveland to Dickinson, May 1, 1896, Cleveland papers; Summers,
Cabinet Diary of Wilson, 73–4; *New York Times*, April 30, 1896, 5.

24 Calvin Tomkins to Cleveland, March 24, April 17, and May 21, 1896; Henry S. Robbins to John G. Carlisle, April 18, 1896, Cleveland papers; John P. Hopkins to Whitney, April 10, 1896, Whitney papers; Chicago *Tribune*, May 5, 1896, 7; May 6, 1896, 2.

25 Lambert Tree to Don M. Dickinson, May 25, 1896, Cleveland papers; Tree to Vilas, May 28 and June 3, 1896, Vilas papers; Summers, *Cabinet Diary of Wilson*, 78.

26 Tree to Vilas, May 28 and June 3, 1896, Vilas papers.

27 Tree to Vilas, June 3, 1896, Vilas papers.

28 Dickinson to Tree, May 28, 1896, Cleveland papers.

29 Dickinson to Cleveland (posted June 12, 1896), Cleveland papers.

30 Summers, *Cabinet Diary of Wilson*, 70, 74, 78.

31 John J. Lentz to Whitney, June 23, 1896, Whitney papers; Cincinnati *Commercial Tribune*, June 22, 1896, 1; Chicago *Tribune*, June 23, 1896, 2, 3; June 24, 1896, 1; St. Louis *Post Dispatch*, June 23, 1896; Boston *Evening Transcript*, June 23, 1896, 1; *New York Times*, June 24, 1896, 5; Indianapolis *Journal*, June 25, 1896, 1.

32 Alexander M. Bell, quoted in St. Louis *Post Dispatch*, June 23, 1896, 1.

33 Chicago *Tribune*, June 25, 1896, 3.

34 Washington *Evening Star*, June 24, 1896, 1.

35 Chicago *Tribune*, June 24, 1896, 3.

36 E. C. Wall to Vilas, June 8, 1896, Vilas papers.

37 M. W. Sheafe to Vilas, June 8, 1896, Vilas papers; A. D. Tinsley to Thurber, May 23, 1896, Cleveland papers; C. Boyd Barrett to Bryan, June 4, 1896, Bryan papers; Chicago *Tribune*, May 21, 1896.

38 Telegram, M. Doran to Thurber, June 12, 1896, Cleveland papers; Doran to Cleveland, June 22, 1896, Cleveland papers; *New York Times*, June 12, 1896, 1; Louisville *Courier-Journal*, June 12, 1896, 1.

39 Cleveland to Dickinson, June 10 and 17, 1896; Dickinson to Cleveland, June 12, 1896, Cleveland papers; Wm. A. McCorkle to Lamont, Lamont papers.

40 William F. Sheehan to Whitney, June 17, 1896, Whitney papers; New York *World*, June 18, 1896, 1; Allan Nevins, *Grover Cleveland, A Study in Courage* (New York, 1932), 694–5.

41 [Lamont] to Cleveland [June 18, 1896]; Daniel Lamont to Cleveland [c. June 21, 1896], Cleveland papers.

42 Cincinnati *Commercial Tribune*, June 22, 1896, 1; Lamont to Cleveland [c. June 21, 1896], Cleveland papers.

43 John E. Russell to Whitney, June 18, 1896; William E. Russell to Whitney, June 20, 1896, Whitney papers; Whitney to Vilas, June 19, 1896, June 21, 1896; Lamont to Vilas, June 21 [1896], Vilas papers.

44 Wm. C. P. Breckinridge to Vilas, June 20, 1896, Vilas papers.

45 Cincinnati *Commercial Tribune*, June 28, 1896, 1.

46 W. C. Whitney to Vilas, June 26 and 27, 1896, Vilas papers; William Jennings Bryan, *First Battle, A Story of the Campaign of 1896* (Chicago, 1896), 188; New York *Tribune*, June 30, 1896, 1; July 1, 1896, 1.

47 St. Louis *Post Dispatch*, February 6, 1896, 8.

48 Summers, *Cabinet Diary of Wilson*, 80.

49 Francis B. Simkins, *Pitchfork Ben Tillman* (Baton Rouge, La., 1944), 332.

50 Lambert Tree to Vilas, June 25, 1896, Vilas papers.

CHAPTER 15

1 D. Leigh Colvin, *Prohibition in the United States. A History of the Prohibition Party and of the Prohibition Movement* (New York, 1926), 255.
2 John P. St. John to Richmond, May 17, 1895, Richmond papers; E. J. Wheeler to Lloyd, July 30, 1895, Lloyd papers; E. Evans to Donnelly, March 31, 1896, Donnelly papers.
3 Wheeler to Lloyd, July 30, 1895, Lloyd papers.
4 Washington *Evening Star*, October 18, 1895, 3.
5 Evans to Donnelly, March 31, 1896, Lloyd papers.
6 St. Louis *Post Dispatch*, April 9, 1896, 6; Colvin, *Prohibition in the United States,* 255.
7 St. Louis *Post Dispatch,* May 27, 1896, 1; May 29, 1896, 7; Chicago *Tribune,* May 28, 1896, 3, 7; New York *Tribune,* May 29, 1896, 5.
8 St. Louis *Post Dispatch,* May 29, 1896, 7; July 16, 1896, 2; Chicago *Tribune,* May 30, 1896, 9.
9 Chicago *Tribune,* May 30, 1896, 9.
10 M. C. Rankin to Donnelly, June 9, 1896; H. E. Taubeneck to Donnelly, June 10, 1896, Donnelly papers; St. Louis *Globe-Democrat,* June 15, 1896, 3; John D. Hicks, *The Populist Revolt, A History of the Farmers' Alliance and the People's Party* (Lincoln, Nebraska, 1961), 351.
11 *Weekly Rocky Mountain News,* May 21, 1896, 4; St. Louis *Post Dispatch,* June 15, 1896, 1; St. Louis *Globe-Democrat,* July 11, 1896, 3.
12 *New York Times,* June 25, 1896, 5; New York *Tribune,* June 26, 1896, 3.
13 J. J. Mott to Butler, June 21, 1896, Butler papers.
14 H. E. Taubeneck to Donnelly, May 15, 1896, Donnelly papers; Butler to Wm. M. Stewart, June 24, 1896, William M. Stewart papers (Nevada State Historical Society); St. Louis *Post Dispatch,* May 1, 1896, 1.
15 Marion Butler to W. J. Peele, July 8, 1896, William J. Peele papers (Southern Historical Collection, University of North Carolina).
16 Manuscript notes stapled to letter, Taubeneck to Donnelly, June 29, 1896, Donnelly papers; New York *World,* June 21, 1896, 1.
17 W. L. Cundiff to Bryan, June 4, 1896, Bryan papers.
18 St. Louis *Post Dispatch,* June 6, 1896, 2.
19 Taubeneck to Donnelly, June 22, 1896, Donnelly papers.
20 *Kansas Semi-Weekly Capital,* June 23, 1896, 2; *People's Party Paper,* June 26, 1896, 8.
21 St. Louis *Post Dispatch,* June 19, 1896, 1.
22 Taubeneck to Donnelly, June 22, 1896, Donnelly papers; St. Louis *Post Dispatch,* June 20, 1896, 1; *New York Times,* June 22, 1896, 9.
23 Elmer Ellis, *Henry Moore Teller, Defender of the West* (Caldwell, Idaho, 1941).
24 H. E. Taubeneck to Donnelly, June 20, 1896, Donnelly papers; H. E. Taubeneck to Butler, July 2, 1896, Butler papers; St. Louis *Post Dispatch,* June 18, 1896, 11.
25 Washington *Evening Star,* April 18, 1896, 2; June 2, 1896, 13; St. Louis *Post Dispatch,* June 9, 1896, 4; *National Bimetallist,* I (June 10, 1896), 544.
26 Cincinnati *Commercial Tribune,* June 22, 1896, 1; Washington *Evening Star,* June 24, 1896, 1.

27 A. J. Warner to Moreton Frewen, June 28, 1896, Frewen papers.
28 Butler to Wm. M. Stewart, June 29, 1896, Stewart papers.
29 Chicago *Tribune,* July 2, 1896, 3; Cincinnati *Commercial Tribune,* July 2, 1896, 2; *New York Times,* July 2, 1896, 1.
30 Ellis, *Teller,* 268–71.
31 Butler to Wm. M. Stewart, July 6, 1896, Stewart papers.
32 Taubeneck to Donnelly, June 22, 1896, Donnelly papers.
33 *New York Times,* June 8, 1896, 1.
34 Altgeld to W. H. Harvey, June 25, 1896, in Altgeld, *Live Questions,* 526–7.
35 New York *Tribune,* July 1, 1896, 3.
36 William Jennings and Mary Baird Bryan, *The Memoirs of William Jennings Bryan* (Philadelphia, 1925), 105–6.
37 New York *Tribune,* July 6, 1896, 1.

CHAPTER 16

1 Washington *Post,* June 30, July 1, 1896, quoted in Lawrence J. Scheidler, "Silver and Politics, 1893–1896" (unpublished Ph.D. dissertation, University of Indiana, 1936), 285.
2 St. Louis *Post Dispatch,* June 30, 1896, 7.
3 Chicago *Tribune,* July 5, 1896, 3.
4 Article signed by W. H. Eggleston, in Cincinnati *Commercial Tribune,* July 6, 1896, 1.
5 New York *World,* July 6, 1896, 1.
6 New York *Tribune,* June 30, 1896, 1; *New York Times,* July 1, 1896, 2.
7 *New York Times,* July 2, 1896, 2; Allan Nevins, *Grover Cleveland,* A *Study in Courage* (New York, 1932), 698–9.
8 New York *Tribune,* July 1, 1896, 1; *New York Times,* July 1, 1896, 2.
9 New York *Tribune,* July 1, 1896, 1.
10 *Ibid.,* 1, 3; *New York Times,* July 1, 1896, 2.
11 Chicago *Tribune,* July 2, 1896, 2; *New York Times,* July 2, 1896, 1; New York *Tribune,* July 2, 1896, 1.
12 Telegram, Whitney to Vilas, July 1, 1896; E. C. Wall to Vilas [July] 2 [1896], Vilas papers; New York *Tribune,* July 4, 1896, 1, 2.
13 Illinois conservative John M. Palmer wrote that he had not come because he was certain that the silver leaders "would force their program through." Palmer to Whitney, July 6, 1896, Whitney papers.
14 Josiah Patterson to Whitney, June 29, 1896; Wm. C. P. Breckinridge to Whitney, June 29, 1896, Whitney papers.
15 Chicago *Tribune,* July 6, 1896, 2; July 8, 1896, 1.
16 *Ibid.,* July 5, 1896, 1.
17 *Ibid.;* Cincinnati *Commercial Tribune,* July 5, 1896, 1; Nevins *Cleveland,* 700.
18 St. Louis *Post Dispatch,* July 4, 1896, 2.
19 C. S. Thomas to Teller, July 14, 1896, Teller papers (Colorado Historical Society); St. Louis *Post Dispatch,* July 7, 1896, 2.
20 *New York Times,* July 3, 1896, 2; New York *Tribune,* July 4, 1896, 1.
21 *New York Times,* July 1, 1896, 12. The conservative metropolitan papers, such as the Chicago *Tribune* and the *New York Times,* developed the theme that the Democratic convention was bossed by Altgeld, who was

to them a symbol for anarchism and other types of radical subversion. Recent historians have also seen Altgeld as the dominant influence in the convention. See, for example, Harry Barnard, *Eagle Forgotten, The Life of John Peter Altgeld* (New York, 1938), 345–73; Ray Ginger, *Altgeld's America, The Lincoln Ideal versus Changing Realities* (New York, 1958), 175–6; Harvey Wish, "John Peter Altgeld and the Election of 1896," *Journal of the Illinois State Historical Society*, XXX (October, 1937), 355–8, 363–4; and Wish, "John Peter Altgeld and the Background of the Campaign of 1896," *Mississippi Valley Historical Review*, XXIV (March, 1938), 512–3.

22 Chicago *Tribune*, July 4, 1896, 1; July 5, 1896, 4.
23 St. Louis *Post Dispatch*, July 8, 1896, 4.
24 *New York Times*, July 7, 1896, 1.
25 *Ibid.*, 2; St. Louis *Post Dispatch*, July 7, 1896, 3.
26 The text of Daniel's speech is in William Jennings Bryan, *First Battle, A Story of The Campaign of 1896* (Chicago, 1896), 189–95.
27 Bryan, *First Battle*, 406–9.
28 *Ibid.*, 198–9.
29 Chicago *Tribune*, July 9, 1896, 4.
30 *Ibid.*, July 8, 1896, 3; *New York Times*, July 8, 1896, 5.
31 *New York Times*, July 9, 1896, 2.
32 *Ibid.*
33 *Ibid.*
34 *Ibid.*
35 *Ibid.*
36 *Official Proceedings of the Democratic National Convention Held in Chicago, Ill., July 7th, 8th, 9th, 10th and 11th, 1896* (Logansport, Ind., 1896), 116–7.
37 *Ibid.*, 125; New York *Tribune*, July 9, 1896, 1.
38 Chicago *Tribune*, July 9, 1896, 1
39 *Ibid.*, July 1, 1896, 2.
40 *Official Proceedings, Democratic*, 198–209; Francis B. Simkins, *Pitchfork Ben Tillman* (Baton Rouge, La., 1944), 532–7.
41 *Official Proceedings, Democratic*, 209–10.
42 *Ibid.*, 218–9.
43 Wayne C. Williams, *William Jennings Bryan* (New York, 1936), 140.
44 William Jennings and Mary Baird Bryan, *The Memoirs of William Jennings Bryan* (Philadelphia, 1925), 114.
45 San Francisco *Chronicle*, July 9, 1896, 2; Francis E. Leupp, "The Convention of 1896," first printed in the *Outlook* and reprinted in *The Commoner*, June 21, 1912, 5, 10–11.
46 St. Louis *Post Dispatch*, June 19, 1896, 1; Bryan, *Memoirs*, 104.
47 The text of Bryan's speech is in Bryan, *First Battle*, 199–206.
48 *New York Times*, July 10, 1896, 1.
49 Chicago *Tribune*, July 10, 1896, 9.
50 *New York Times*, July 10, 1896, 1.

CHAPTER 17

1 *New York Times*, July 3, 1896, 2; July 7, 1896, 2; Chicago *Tribune*, July 6, 1896, 1.

2 *Official Proceedings of the Democratic National Convention Held in Chicago, Ill., July 7th, 8th, 9th, 10th and 11th, 1896* (Logansport, Ind., 1896), 290.
3 *Ibid.*, 298.
4 *Ibid.*, 258–65. Throughout the convention the Bland "boom" was plagued by incredibly bad poetic efforts. Kansas City Bland enthusiasts went through the streets of Chicago shouting these words:

> Ha! Ha! Hee!
> Who are we?
> We are the Bland Club
> Of K.C.
> We're hot stuff;
> That's no bluff.
> Vote for silver
> And we'll all have stuff!

Chicago *Tribune*, July 7, 1896, 4.
5 *New York Times*, July 10, 1896, 2; William Jennings Bryan, *First Battle, A Story of the Campaign of 1896* (Chicago, 1896), 213.
6 *New York Times*, July 10, 1896, 1–2.
7 *Official Proceedings, Democratic*, 279.
8 *Ibid.*, 298.
9 *New York Times*, July 10, 1896, 1; Perry Belmont, *An American Democrat, The Recollections of Perry Belmont* (New York, 1940), 422–3.
10 *New York Times*, July 10, 1896, 2.
11 *Official Proceedings, Democratic*, 295–6.
12 Whitney to Pattison [July 10, 1896], Whitney papers.
13 *Official Proceedings, Democratic*, 298.
14 Overmeyer to Bryan, July 16, 1896, Bryan papers.
15 *New York Times*, July 11, 1896, 2.
16 Henry W. Clendenin, *Autobiography of Henry W. Clendenin, Editor* (Springfield, Ill., 1926), 222–3; Wish, "John Peter Altgeld and the Election of 1896," *Journal of the Illinois State Historical Society*, XXX (October, 1937), 363–4.
17 *New York Times*, July 11, 1896, 2.
18 *Ibid.*
19 *Ibid.*
20 *Ibid.*, 3.
21 Charles M. Rosser, *The Crusading Commoner; A Close-Up of William Jennings Bryan and His Times* (Dallas, Texas, 1937), 42; Melville E. Stone, *Fifty Years a Journalist* (Garden City, New York, 1921), 222–31.
22 *New York Times*, July 11, 1896, 5.
23 William Jennings and Mary Baird Bryan, *The Memoirs of William Jennings Bryan* (Philadelphia, 1925), 116–7.
24 *New York Times*, July 12, 1896, 2.
25 *Ibid.*; William V. Byars, *An American Commoner, The Life and Times of Richard Parks Bland* (St. Louis, 1900), 296–7.
26 *New York Times*, July 12, 1896, 2.
27 John Russell Young in New York *Herald*, reprinted in St. Louis *Globe-Democrat*, July 11, 1896, 5.

28 St. Louis *Post Dispatch*, July 12, 1896, 1. In his speech placing Bryan in nomination at the National Silver party convention in St. Louis Senator Stewart said: "He was nominated before he left the stand. He went upon the stand not as a candidate, but as the advocate of reform; and in advocating the cause of reform he was made the leader of the cause by the audience." *Ibid.*, July 24, 1896, 1, 6.
29 Interview in Chicago *Tribune*, July 14, 1896, 4.
30 Bryan in Introduction to Farrar Newberry, *James K. Jones, The Plumed Knight of Arkansas* (n.p., 1913), 328. Bryan in an interview in 1925 said the same thing to Mark Sullivan. Elmer Ellis, *Henry Moore Teller, Defender of the West* (Caldwell, Idaho, 1941), 273.
31 Charles C. Dawes (Bascom N. Timmons, ed.), *A Journal of the McKinley Years* (Chicago, 1950), 88, 89.
32 Story signed by Victor Rosewater and reprinted from Omaha *Daily Bee* in Chicago *Tribune*, July 7, 1896, 4.
33 Boston *Evening Transcript*, July 9, 1896, 1; *The Commoner*, June 21, 1912, 5.
34 J. C. Long, *Bryan, The Great Commoner* (New York, 1928), 84.
35 Roswell P. Flower to Williams, July 2, 1896, T. S. Williams Collection (New York Public Library); *New York Times*, July 6, 1896, 1.
36 James D. Hays to Whitney, June 27, 1896; D. C. Woods to Whitney, June 29, 1896, Whitney papers.
37 *New York Times*, July 12, 1896, 2. New York journalist, John Russell Young, analyzed the action of the convention in these words: "The West is swept with a wave of discontent. The wave takes the form of silver. . . . This discontent is based upon the indifference at Washington to any interest but those of monopolies. Corporate schemes are so multiplied and vast that they block the way in Congress. Neither party takes a proper interest in measures of vital interest to the people. The result is a rebellion, expressed in the nomination of Mr. Bryan—this and nothing more." Reprinted from New York *Herald* in St. Louis *Globe-Democrat*, July 12, 1896, 6.
38 *New York Times*, July 11, 1896, 4.
39 Stanley J. Folmsbee and Marguerite B. Hamer (eds.), "The Presidential Election of 1896 as Reflected in the Correspondence of Charles McClung McGhee," *The East Tennessee Historical Society's Publications*, XXII (1950), 163–4.

CHAPTER 18

1 St. Louis *Post Dispatch*, July 11, 1896, 1.
2 *New York Times*, July 13, 1896, 1; New York *Tribune*, July 16, 1896, 5.
3 St. Louis *Post Dispatch*, July 8, 1896, 5; July 13, 1896, 1.
4 Marion Butler to W. J. Peele, July 8, 1896, Peele papers; Butler to W. M. Stewart, July 13, 1896, Stewart papers.
5 Marion Butler to Samuel A. Ashe, July 13, 1896, quoted in Joseph F. Steelman, "The Progressive Era in North Carolina, 1884–1917" (unpublished Ph.D. dissertation, University of North Carolina, 1955), 139–40; Florence E. Smith, "The Populist Movement and its Influence in North Carolina" (unpublished Ph.D. dissertation, University of Chi-

cago, 1929), 145–6. Tom Watson was less restrained than Butler in his public comments: "Dressing Billy Bryan up in Populist raiment makes Billy an attractive figure to our admiring gaze; but, as long as he remains mixed in with the scrub sheep of the Democratic flock, we are much inclined to say to him, in the language of the ancient anecdote, 'We love you, Billy, but d—n your company.'" *People's Party Paper,* July 17, 1896, 4.

6   Copy, Lloyd to R. I. Grimes, July 10, 1896, Lloyd papers.
7   St. Louis *Post Dispatch,* July 11, 1896, 2.
8   *Ibid.,* July 12, 1896, 9.
9   *Ibid.,* July 16, 1896, 4.
10   Waite to Donnelly, July 12, 1896, Donnelly papers.
11   New York *Tribune,* July 11, 1896. A Populist from Alabama was quoted as saying that the Democrats "have counted us out down there three times" with the result that feeling between Populists and Democrats was very bitter. *Ibid.,* July 21, 1896, 2. Texas Populist, "Cyclone" Davis was quoted: "If the Populists are swallowed bag and baggage by the Democratic party the Bourbon Brigadiers will lord it over us Populists in the South more than ever. They don't think we are anybody now, and if we endorse their candidate we will get swallowed sure." In a statement to a Chicago *Tribune* (July 20, 1896, 1) reporter he said: "The plan of the Bourbons is to turn over the remnant of the Northwest Democracy to the Populists and silver folk for the indorsement of Bryan, obliterate the Populist party in the South, and have the Southern Bourbon in the saddle." North Carolina Populist, Richmond Pearson, wrote to Marion Butler: "How can the People's Party be fools enough to walk through the open mouth of Democracy into their merciless maw?" Pearson to Butler, July 13, 1896, Butler papers. Henry Demarest Lloyd wrote that after the Populist convention nominated Bryan a southern Populist said to him: "This may cost me my life. I can return home only at that risk. The feeling of the Democrats against us is one of murderous hate. I have been shot at many times. Grand juries will not indict our assailants. Courts give us no protection." Lloyd, "The Populists at St. Louis," *Review of Reviews,* XIV (September, 1896), 299–300.
12   Butler to Stewart, July 13, 1896, Stewart papers. John P. Buchanan, a Populist from Tennessee, proposed a similar plan, which was known to newspaper readers as the "Tennessee plan." St. Louis *Post Dispatch,* July 15, 1896, 3.
13   Entry dated July 18, 1896, in Donnelly diary, Donnelly papers.
14   *Kansas Semi-Weekly Capital,* July 17, 1896, 2; New York *Tribune,* July 17, 1896, 4.
15   St. Louis *Post Dispatch,* July 17, 1896, 7; July 18, 1896, 8; Chicago *Tribune,* July 19, 1896, 1.
16   St. Louis *Post Dispatch,* July 18, 1896, 2. The Indianapolis *Journal,* August 1, 1896, 1, said that Samuel W. Williams, a "middle-of-the-road" Populist from Indiana, was the originator of the plan to nominate the vice-presidential candidate first. It was Williams who presented this plan to the convention. Shortly after arriving in St. Louis Boston Populist, George Washburn, said that the practical thing to solve the party's dilemma appeared to be the nomination of Bryan and a prominent south-

ern Populist for vice president. "It is clearly our duty to support Mr. Bryan, but at the same time to preserve harmony in our own ranks it may be necessary to take the step just indicated. That will, I think, be the action of the Populist Convention." St. Louis *Post Dispatch*, July 29, 1896, 2.

17 Teller to Butler, July 15, 1896, Butler papers.
18 Teller to Bryan, July 15, 1896, Teller papers.
19 Teller to Bryan, July 22, 1896, Teller papers; *New York Times*, July 19, 1896, 3.
20 Telegram, Fred T. Dubois, F. Pettigrew, Chas. A. Towne, and Chas. A. Hartman to Teller, July 7, 1896, Teller papers; Elmer Ellis, *Henry Moore Teller, Defender of the West* (Caldwell, Idaho, 1941), 273–4.
21 St. Louis *Globe-Democrat*, July 20, 1896, 3.
22 The signers were, in addition to Teller, Fred T. Dubois, Lee Mantle, Charles S. Hartman, Charles A. Towne, Edgar Wilson, John F. Shafroth, and A. M. Stevenson. Chicago *Tribune*, July 21, 1896, 2; *New York Times*, July 21, 1896, 3.
23 Teller to Bryan, July 22, 1896, Teller papers; *New York Times*, July 21, 1896, 3; Ellis, *Teller*, 276.
24 Teller to Thomas M. Patterson, July 16, 1896, Teller papers.
25 New York *Tribune*, July 21, 1896, 2.
26 Boston *Evening Advertiser*, July 21, 1896, 10.
27 New York *World*, July 23, 1896, 1. A *New York Times* (July 22, 1896, 2) reporter made a similar observation: "There unquestionably is a tendency of whiskers to Populism, for even the colored delegates to the convention displayed beards of the orthodox, tangled, contentious, and cranky pattern."
28 During the campaign Mrs. Lease spoke at Cooper Union in New York where she referred to the "grand" principles of socialism, called the Prince of Wales a "debaucher" and said that Queen Victoria was "no longer regarded as made even of common clay, but of common mud." *New York Times*, August 11, 1896, 3.
29 *Ibid.*, July 23, 1896, 2.
30 Chicago *Tribune*, July 24, 1896, 2.
31 *Ibid.*
32 *New York Times*, July 23, 1896, 2.
33 Chicago *Tribune*, July 20, 1896, 2.
34 New York *Tribune*, July 23, 1896, 2.
35 Henry Demarest Lloyd, "Populists at St. Louis," 298–9.
36 Chicago *Tribune*, July 20, 1896, 3; *New York Times*, July 22, 1896, 2; St. Louis *Globe-Democrat*, July 23, 1896, 3.
37 Chicago *Tribune*, July 20, 1896, 2; St. Louis *Post Dispatch*, July 22, 1896, 7. Henry Demarest Lloyd wrote that his favorite ticket was Debs and Coxey because their record proved them to be "indomitable and incorruptible." Copy, Lloyd to R. I. Grimes, July 10, 1896, Lloyd papers.
38 New York *Tribune*, July 18, 1896, 3.
39 Eltweed Pomeroy, "The Direct Legislation Movement and its Leaders," *Arena*, XVI (June–November, 1896), 29–43.
40 Pomeroy to Donnelly, February 8, 1896, Donnelly papers.
41 Printed Call for Direct Legislation Conference at St. Louis, July 21, 1896, in Donnelly papers.

42   Pomeroy to Donnelly, April 3 and 24, 1896, Donnelly papers.
43   St. Louis *Post Dispatch*, July 23, 1896, 7.
44   Chicago *Tribune*, July 22, 1896, 1.
45   *Ibid.; New York Times*, July 22, 1896, 1; Comer V. Woodward, *Tom Watson, Agrarian Rebel* (New York, 1938), 295–7. Norton, author of *Ten Men of Money Island* and editor of the *Monthly Sentinel*, was a favorite of the "middle-of-the-road" group because of his opposition to free silver as a monetary panacea. C. B. Matthews to H. D. Lloyd, December 7, 1895, Lloyd papers.
46   William Jennings Bryan, *First Battle, A Story of the Campaign of 1896* (Chicago, 1896), 259–64.
47   *New York Times*, July 23, 1896, 1.
48   *Ibid.*, 2; Woodward, *Watson*, 296–7.
49   *New York Times*, July 24, 1896, 2; Chicago *Tribune*, July 24, 1896, 2.
50   Chicago *Tribune*, July 20, 1896, 1; St. Louis *Post Dispatch*, July 20, 1896, 1; July 21, 1896, 1.
51   Bryan, *First Battle*, 264–70.
52   Chicago *Tribune*, July 24, 1896, 2; *New York Times*, July 24, 1896, 2.
53   St. Louis *Post Dispatch*, July 24, 1896, 1, 2; San Francisco *Chronicle*, July 25, 1896, 1.
54   St. Louis *Post Dispatch*, July 24, 1896, 2.
55   *Ibid.; New York Times*, July 25, 1896, 2.
56   Bryan, *First Battle*, 271–6.
57   St. Louis *Post Dispatch*, July 23, 1896, 1; Chicago *Tribune*, July 25, 1896, 1; *New York Times*, July 25, 1896, 1.
58   Chicago *Tribune*, July 24, 1896, 2; July 25, 1896, 2; Alex M. Arnett, *The Populist Movement in Georgia* (New York, 1922), 199.
59   Woodward, *Watson*, 302–5. In a letter to the New York *World*, dated July 25, 1896, Watson said that he accepted the nomination after dispatches from St. Louis assured him that "my agreement to run with Bryan would harmonize all factions, unite the silver forces and at the same time prevent a possible split of my own party." New York *World*, July 26, 1896, 2. In an article initialed by Watson he said that if the Populist party had failed to nominate Bryan it would have lost the West. The nomination of Watson had saved the party. *People's Party Paper*, July 31, 1896, 4.
60   Telegram, Debs to Lloyd, July 25 [1896], Lloyd papers; St. Louis *Post Dispatch*, July 22, 1896, 7; July 23, 1896, 7.
61   *New York Times*, July 26, 1896, 1, 2. Seymour Lutzky, "The Reform Editors and Their Press" (unpublished Ph.D. dissertation, State University of Iowa, 1951), 278.
62   Bryan, *First Battle*, 276–9.
63   San Francisco *Chronicle*, July 26, 1896, 1.
64   *Ibid.*, Woodward, *Watson*, 299–301.
65   *New York Times*, July 26, 1896, 1, 2; Bryan, *First Battle*, 279.
66   San Francisco *Chronicle*, July 26, 1896, 1; Bryan, *First Battle*, 279; Woodward, *Watson*, 299–301.
67   *New York Times*, August 18, 1896, 8; John D. Hicks, *The Populist Revolt, A History of the Farmers' Alliance and the People's Party* (Lincoln, Nebraska, 1961), 366–7.
68   There was confusion about the name of this party. At the convention in

July it had been officially titled "The National Silver Party." However, General Weaver, in writing the platform, referred to it as the "National Bi-Metallic Party." The name, "National Silver Party," was already being used on the stationery of the organization, and this name was retained through the history of the party. John P. St. John to Bryan, December 9, 1896; Isaac N. Stevens to Mrs. Bryan, December 13, 1896, Bryan papers.

69   *New York Times,* July 2, 1896, 1; Chicago *Tribune,* July 22, 1896, 2; July 23, 1896, 1.
70   St. Louis *Post Dispatch,* July 24, 1896, 1.
71   *Ibid.,* 2.
72   *New York Times,* July 25, 1896, 3.
73   *Ibid.,* July 24, 1896, 2; St. Louis *Post Dispatch,* July 25, 1896, 4.

CHAPTER 19

1   In a special address to Democrats in mid-August the provisional executive committee of the National Democratic party said that the majority at Chicago had violated the rights of the minority and "promulgated a platform at variance with the essential principles of the Democratic party." These principles they defined as individualism, freedom of speech, trade, contract, and conscience, the rule of law, strict observance of the Federal Constitution, and a disbelief in the ability of government, "through paternal legislation," to increase the happiness of the nation. *Campaign Text-Book of the National Democratic Party, 1896* (New York and Chicago, 1896), 2. Sam Hanna Acheson, *35,000 Days in Texas* (New York, 1938), 184–5.
2   *New York Times,* August 18, 1896, 1, 2; Festus P. Summers (ed.), *The Cabinet Diary of William L. Wilson* (Chapel Hill, N. Car., 1951), 93.
3   Copy, Olney to Cleveland, July 11, 1896, Cleveland papers.
4   John K. Cowan to McGhee, July 11, 1896 in Stanley J. Folmsbee and Marguerite B. Hamer (eds.), "The Presidential Election of 1896 as Reflected in the Correspondence of Charles McClung McGhee," *The East Tennessee Historical Society's Publications,* XXII (1950), 161; Edward Yates to Vilas, July 14, 1896, Vilas papers. Yates wrote that Democrats should not organize a third-party movement but vote for McKinley; because "The issue is Americanism against Communism." John Bassell to Alfred Caldwell, July 29, 1896, John Bassell papers (West Virginia Collection, West Virginia University); Dawes to W. A. Sawyer, August 24, 1896, Dawes papers. Summers, *Cabinet Diary of Wilson,* 99.
5   Lynde Harrison to Mac Veagh, July 28, 1896, Franklin Mac Veagh papers (LC); L. C. Straus to Andrew D. White, July 29, 1896, Oscar Straus papers (LC); *New York Times,* July 24, 1896, 4; July 26, 1896, 5.
6   Calvin Tomkins to Bynum, July 17, 1896, William Dallas Bynum papers (Library of Congress); French to Mac Veagh, July 24, 1896, Mac Veagh papers.
7   Usher to Vilas, June 8, 1896, Vilas papers; Frederick M. Grant to Palmer, June 29, 1896, Palmer papers. Grant wrote that he would vote for Tanner, the Republican gubernatorial candidate in Illinois; but "I am

unable—at present—to see it in the light of duty to vote for the high priest of Protection. I can but think that the bestowment of special privileges in a republic of equal rights, upon either mine owners or mill owners, is a violation of the spirit of our Constitution. . . ." William C. P. Breckinridge to Vilas, July 11, 1896, Vilas papers. Conservative Democrats also feared loss of the German vote permanently on the monetary issue. T. J. Mead to Cleveland, August 1, 1896, Cleveland papers.

8 T. C. W. Ellis to B. R. Forman, July 28, 1896, Donelson Caffery papers (Southern Historical Collection, University of North Carolina) Ellis wrote: "I will stand by the party of home rule, tariff for revenue, state rights & white supremacy for the South & oppose the Republican party with its class protection & force bill & nigger equality notions & proclivities." J. W. Hillman to Donelson Caffery August 18, 1896, Caffery papers. W. L. Wilson to Breckinridge, July 30, 1896, Breckinridge papers (LC).

9 Cleveland to D. S. Lamont, July 15, 1896, Cleveland papers. Summers, *Cabinet Diary of Wilson,* 119.

10 Smith to Cleveland, July 20 and August 5, 6, 1896; Cleveland to Smith, August 4, 1896, Cleveland papers. *New York Times,* August 23, 1896, 1.

11 Josiah Patterson to Whitney, July 10, 1896, Whitney papers. Patterson to Cleveland, July 11, 1896, Cleveland papers. Patterson to Lamont, August 10, 1896, Lamont papers. Patterson wrote Lamont that "while voting for Bryan I am praying for his defeat." Patterson to Richard Olney, August 12, 1896, Cleveland papers.

12 George Gray to Whitney, July 29, 1896, Whitney papers.

13 Gray to Whitney, July 15, 29, 1896, Whitney papers. In his letter of July 15, Gray said that because of the growth of silver sentiment, "it will require careful handling on my part not to loose [*sic*] control of the party organization." On July 29 he wrote: "I think the wisdom of going slow in this matter is being daily demonstrated. It is very important for us in this State, as I doubt not elsewhere, to hold influence, if not control, over our party organization." David B. Hill to Chandler, August 1, 1896, Chandler papers (LC). Hill reported that he was following a course popular with neither faction of his party. His only objective, he said, was to keep the party united in New York. Hill to Lamont, September 14, 1896, Lamont papers. Hill, explaining why he could not cooperate with the third-party Democrats, said: "If I withdraw the organization will go into the hands of adventurers and blatherskites." Summers, *Cabinet Diary of Wilson,* 118–9. In this entry, dated July 14, 1896, Wilson said that it was doubtful that such leaders as Hill and Gorman would join the third-party movement, because they were more interested in keeping control of the party machines in their states for the future than in upholding "true party principles." *New York Times,* August 15, 1896, 4; August 22, 1896, 1. Gorman in an interview printed in the *Times* on August 22 said that his only chance of reelection to the Senate was through supporting the Bryan ticket, because his rural constituents were for silver, and he could not win without them. Washington *Evening Star,* July 17, 1896, 3.

14 "Annual Report, 1896," *Sound Currency,* III, No. 24 (November 15, 1896), 9–11.

394   *Notes to Pages 267–273*

15 *New York Times,* August 8, 1896, 2.
16 F. W. McCutcheon to Whitney, July 13, 1896, Whitney papers.
17 "Annual Report, 1896," *Sound Currency;* Chicago *Tribune,* July 14, 1896, 1.
18 Chicago *Tribune,* July 23, 1896, 1.
19 *Ibid.;* telegram, Charles A. Ewing to Usher, July 22, 1896, Usher papers; *New York Times,* July 23, 1896, 1; July 25, 1896, 1.
20 Otto Hoffman to McClellan, July 13, 1896; McClellan to Hoffman, July 20, 1896; McClellan to Henry Oviatt, September 1, 1896, George B. McClellan, Jr., papers (LC); F. W. McCutcheon to Whitney, July 13, 1896, Whitney papers; Tomkins to Bynum, July 17, 1896, Bynum papers; copy, Breckinridge to George M. Davie, July 23, 1896, Breckinridge papers; Summers, *Cabinet Diary of Wilson,* 118–9.
21 *New York Times,* July 24, 1896, 1.
22 Bynum to Cleveland, July 25, 1896, Cleveland papers.
23 Watterson to Whitney, July 27, 1896, Whitney papers.
24 Usher to Vilas, August 4, 1896, Vilas papers.
25 Indianapolis *Journal,* August 7, 1896, 1; New York *World,* August 7, 1896, 1.
26 L. C. Krauthoff to Whitney, August 9, 1896, Whitney papers; "Proceedings of the Conference of the National Committee of the Sound Money Democracy Held at Indianapolis, Indiana, August 7, 1896," in Bynum papers; *New York Times,* August 8, 1896, 2; August 9, 1896, 9.
27 *New York Times,* August 9, 1896, 5.
28 William L. Wilson to Breckinridge, July 30, 1896, Breckinridge papers; Wilson to Cleveland, August 9, 1896, Cleveland papers. Summers, *Cabinet Diary of Wilson,* 126, 127, 130. Chicago *Tribune,* July 29, 1896, 1. *New York Times,* July 30, 1896, August 4, 1896.
29 W. B. Haldeman to Watterson, August 22, October 8, 1896, Henry Watterson papers (LC); St. Louis *Post Dispatch,* September 1, 1896, 1.
30 Bynum to Usher, August 13, 1896, Usher papers.
31 Vilas to Usher, September 5, 16, 22, 1896; Vilas to John B. Webb, October 7, 1896, Usher papers.
32 W. L. Wilson to Cleveland, August 9, 1896; J. Sterling Morton to Cleveland, August 24, 1896, Cleveland papers.
33 Bynum to Vilas, August 14, 1896, Vilas papers.
34 *New York Times,* September 4, 1896, 1.
35 *Ibid.,* 3; St. Louis *Post Dispatch,* September 3, 1896, 1.
36 Cincinnati *Commercial Tribune,* September 4, 1896, 1.
37 *New York Times,* September 5, 1896, 2.
38 Allison to Dodge, July 12, 1896, Dodge papers.
39 Dawes to A. J. Lester, September 9, 1896, Dawes papers; C. H. Grosvenor to Holloway, August 19, 1896, in A. Dale Beeler, "Letters to Colonel William R. Holloway, 1893–1897," *Indiana Magazine of History,* XXXVI (December, 1940), 393. Grosvenor said: "I am . . . of the opinion that the nomination of a second Democratic ticket would be of the greatest benefit to us."
40 William Jennings Bryan, *First Battle, A Story of the Campaign of 1896* (Chicago, 1896), 361; St. Louis *Post Dispatch,* September 2, 1896, 3.
41 J. J. Atkinson to Usher, July 30, 1896, Usher papers; W. Bourke Cockran to C. E. Sanford, August 7, 1896, William Bourke Cockran papers

(New York Public Library). Cockran wrote: "In a fight for honest money and honest principles I believe in honest methods. We are all agreed that a direct support of McKinley is the best method to defeat the socialistic and anarchistic programme adopted at Chicago, and for my part I do not think we should shrink from saying so."

42 St. Louis *Republic*, November 6, 1896, quoted in Homer Clevenger, "Agrarian Politics in Missouri, 1880–1896" (unpublished Ph.D. dissertation, University of Missouri, 1940), 309.

43 E. S. Bragg to Usher, September 24, 1896, Usher papers.

44 Camden to A. M. Lane, October 28, 1896; Camden to W. D. Rollyson, October 30, 1896, cited in Festus P. Summers, *Johnson Newlon Camden, A Study in Individualism* (New York and London, 1937), 514.

45 Usher to E. S. Bragg, September 30, 1896, Usher papers.

46 Samuel O. Pickens to [?], October 28, 1896; T[homas] A. Moran *et al.*, to "Fellow Democrats," October 28, 1896, Usher papers.

47 Bynum to Cleveland [September 6, 1896]; Cleveland to Bynum, September 10, 1896, Cleveland papers. Cleveland had now withdrawn opposition to participation by members of his cabinet in the gold Democratic movement. On September 6 he wrote to Lamont: "I am gratified to know that you are willing to declare your sentiments and the quicker and stronger you or any other members of the cabinet speak the better I shall like it." Cleveland papers. He was still uncertain, however, about his own course. Cleveland to Vilas, September 5, 1896, Vilas papers; entry dated September 25, 1896, in Summers, *Cabinet Diary of Wilson*, 145.

48 Telegram, Bynum to Usher, October 3, 1896, Usher papers. Boston *Evening Transcript*, September 21, 1896, 1; *New York Times*, October 5, 1896, 5; October 6, 1896, 5.

49 Usher to Vilas, September 24, 1896, Usher papers.

50 Usher to Vilas, October 10, 1896, Vilas papers. Bynum to John C. Bullit, December 12, 1896; Bynum to George Foster Peabody, December 12, 1896, Bynum papers.

51 Usher to Stuart MacKibbin, June 11, 1900, Usher papers.

52 Bynum to Henry E. Rhoads, December 21, 1896, Bynum papers.

53 Calvin Tomkins to Bynum, September 28, 1896, Bynum papers. "Annual Report, 1896," *Sound Currency*, 9–11.

54 *Ibid.*, 1–12. The newspapers to which they furnished material in this way had an average circulation of 1,857.

55 Bynum to Thomas F. Corrigan, November 18, 1896, Bynum papers. Bynum said that the campaign was principally fought in Indiana, Kentucky, Michigan, Minnesota, and Kansas. The party's campaign was also of significant proportions in Illinois and Wisconsin.

CHAPTER 20

1 Col. T. Bentley Mott, *Myron T. Herrick, Friend of France; An Autobiographical Biography* (Garden City, New York, 1929), 64.

2 St. Louis *Post Dispatch*, September 6, 1896, 1; *New York Times*, August 14, 1896, 3.

3 New York *Tribune*, July 15, 1896, 1; *New York Times*, July 16, 1896, 5;

C. H. Cromer, *Royal Bob. The Life of Robert G. Ingersoll* (Indianapolis and New York, 1952), 245–6.

4 *New York Times,* July 15, 1896, 1.

5 Charles G. Dawes to Rufus Dawes, July 30, 1896, Dawes papers.

6 Chicago *Tribune,* July 18, 1896, 2; July 21, 1896, 1.

7 William W. Wight, *Henry Clay Payne, A Life* (Milwaukee, 1907), 88; Elbert W. Harrington, "A Survey of the Political Ideas of Albert Baird Cummins," *Iowa Journal of History and Politics,* XXXIX (October, 1941), 344.

8 McKinley to Quay [June 23, 1896?]; McKinley to Hanna, July 7, 1896; Hanna to McKinley, July 8, 1896, McKinley papers; *New York Times,* September 2, 1896, 8.

9 New York *Tribune,* July 10, 1896, 5; July 29, 1896, 1; Chicago *Tribune,* July 29, 1896, 1; July 30, 1896, 3.

10 Clarkson to H. G. McMillan, October 5, 1896, Clarkson papers.

11 Osborne to Dawes, August 8, 1896, Dawes papers.

12 Dawes to Osborne, July 29, 1896, Dawes papers.

13 Quay to McKinley, October 20, 1896, McKinley papers.

14 Samuel Thayer to C. K. Davis, August 31, 1896, Davis papers.

15 Dawes to Hanna, July 30, 1896; Dawes to McKinley, August 1, 1896, Dawes papers; Charles G. Dawes (Bascom N. Timmons, ed.), *A Journal of the McKinley Years* (Chicago, 1950), 90–1; Thomas Beer, *Hanna* (New York, 1929), 165–6.

16 In an interview on August 17, Hanna stated that to that date the committee had distributed 15,500,000 documents. Canton *Repository,* August 20, 1896, 2. On September 3 the Canton *Repository* (p. 5) reported that the committee in Chicago had already sent out 25,000,000 pieces of literature. On September 17 Dawes wrote that Heath had reported to him that they had already sent out from Chicago alone 100,-000,000 pieces of Republican literature. Dawes to C. H. Bosworth, September 17, 1896, Dawes papers. There is no record of how much the committee had spent by that date on contracts for literature; but on September 26 Dawes reported to Hanna that expenses to that time for the printing of literature were $154,232.25. Dawes, *Journal,* 98–9. The chairman of the gold Democratic campaign, William D. Bynum, said early in October that campaign literature was going out of Republican headquarters in Chicago at the rate of three carloads per day. *New York Times,* October 4, 1896, 2.

17 Dawes, *Journal,* 106. The nature of the literature thus printed and distributed was indicated in a newspaper description of 500,000 documents sent out over Illinois between July 22 and August 15. They included speeches by Senator Cullom, Judge Aldrich of Chicago, and Congressman McCleary on money, Secretary Carlisle's speech to the Chicago workingmen, Blaine's reply to Gladstone on the money question, a speech by Reed on the tariff, a speech in German by Babcock on sound money, pamphlets titled, "History of Money," "Money and Silver," "Look Before You Leap," and "Horse Sense." Also on the list were miscellaneous leaflets, lithographs, and posters, and a pamphlet called "Silver Snakes," which was printed in German and Swedish as well as English. Chicago *Tribune,* August 15, 1896, 1. The committee also furnished free supplements to newspapers. Dawes wrote that an

article which he arranged to insert in one of the supplements would have a circulation of 900,000. Dawes to C. H. Bosworth, October 2, 1896, Dawes papers.

18 Nils P. Haugen, "Pioneer and Political Reminiscences," *Wisconsin Magazine of History*, XII (September, 1928), 50–1; Dawes to C. H. Bosworth, September 17, 1896, Dawes papers.

19 Dawes to Bosworth, September 17, 1896, Dawes papers.

20 Frederick W. Holls to Hanna, June 27, 1896, Frederick W. Holls papers (Columbia University); Dawes to M. A. Hanna, July 23, 24, 27, 29 and August 5, 1896; Dawes to Osborne, August 22, 1896, Dawes papers.

21 Dawes to M. J. Dowling, August 12, 1896, Dawes papers.

22 Dawes to Hanna, August 20 and 29, 1896, Dawes papers.

23 Dawes to Hanna, September 18, 1896, Dawes papers; Thomas R. Ross, *Jonathan Prentiss Dolliver. A Study in Political Integrity and Independence* (Iowa City, Iowa, 1958), 125.

24 Clarkson to H. G. McMillan, October 5, 1896, Clarkson papers; A. B. Cummins to H. G. McMillan, September 2, 1896; Cummins to Cyrus Leland, September 2, 1896; Dawes to A. B. Kittredge, September 12, 1896; Dawes to Dexter M. Perry, September 14, 1896; Dawes to W. R. Merriam, September 14, 1896; Dawes to Joseph P. Smith, October 30, 1896, Dawes papers.

25 Dawes to Bliss, October 20, 1896, Dawes papers.

26 Dawes to Judge William L. Day, September 15 and 26, 1896; Dawes to H. E. Bourne, October 24, 1896, Dawes papers; Bess L. Thompson, "Hanna and McKinley, 1892–1897" (unpublished M.A. thesis, University of Wisconsin, 1925), 55.

27 Dawes to Day, September 15 and 26, Dawes papers.

28 William L. Royal, *Some Reminiscences* (New York and Washington, 1909), 202–3; Vincent P. DeSantis, *Republicans Face the Southern Question—The New Departure Years, 1877–1897* (Baltimore, 1959), 258.

29 *New York Times*, July 17, 1896, 2.

30 The Protective Tariff League handled the distribution of Republican literature in the states under the control of the New York office. Osborne to Dawes, August 8, 1896, Dawes papers; Osborne to McKinley, August 11, 1896; Osborne to McKinley, September 1, 1896, McKinley papers; *New York Times*, October 8, 1896, 9; W. B. Shaw, "Methods and Tactics of the Campaign," *Review of Reviews*, XIV (November, 1896) 556.

31 Dawes, *Journal*, 106.

32 Royal, *Reminiscences*, 202–3.

33 De Santis, *Republicans Face the Southern Question*, 255–6.

34 Early in October Senator Thomas H. Carter of Colorado wrote to his wife: "The National Committee having refused to pay expenses the campaign will not amount to much in this state." Letter dated October 7, 1896, Carter papers (LC).

35 Dawes to McKinley, August 1, 1896; Dawes to Hanna, August 24, 1896, Dawes papers.

36 Dawes, *Journal* (entry dated November 22, 1896), 106; Dawes to Hanna, November 12 and 21, 1896, Dawes papers.

37 Dawes, *Journal*, 95–7.
38 Dawes to Hanna, October 1, 1896, Dawes papers.
39 Dawes to Hanna, October 3, 1896, Dawes papers.
40 Dawes to Marshall Field, October 10, 1896, Dawes papers.
41 Boston *Evening Transcript*, September 25, 1896, 3.
42 Depew, *Memories of Eighty Years*, 149–50. Depew said that the campaign cost "nearly five millions of dollars." Herbert Croly, *Marcus Alonzo Hanna, His Life and Work* (New York, 1912), 200. Croly gave the figure of $3,500,000 based apparently on Dawes' official account. Russel B. Nye, *Midwestern Progressive Politics. A Historical Study of Its Origins and Development, 1870–1950* (East Lansing, Michigan, 1951), 118–9. Matthew Josephson, *The Politicos, 1865–1896* (New York, 1938), 699; Harold U. Faulkner, *Politics, Reform and Expansion, 1890–1900* (New York, 1959), 203–4.
43 Dawes, *Journal*, 106.
44 Depew, *Memories of Eighty Years*, 150–2.
45 Hay to Henry Adams, October 20, 1896, quoted in William R. Thayer, *The Life and Letters of John Hay*, 2 vols. (Boston and New York, 1915) II, 153.
46 Interview with Harry Frease, described in Thompson, "Hanna and McKinley, 1892–1897," 45–8; Margaret Leech, *In the Days of McKinley* (New York, 1959), 87–90.
47 Leech, *McKinley*, 87–90.
48 Canton *Repository*, September 20, 1896, 7. Marcus A. Hanna, *Mark Hanna. His Book* (Boston, 1904), 52–3. Hanna wrote of the impression which McKinley made on the visitors: "He not only impressed them by the earnestness and sincerity of his speeches and the wisdom of his words, but there was always present the genial personality of the man that quickly won admiration and respect from everyone with whom he came in contact."
49 New York *Tribune*, July 12, 1896, 1.
50 Canton *Repository*, September 24, 1896, 6.
51 On July 27 McKinley wrote to a Pennsylvania correspondent who had expressed concern at the possibility that the Republican party might abandon the issue of protection, "I assure you . . . that there is no intention in the slightest to compromise with principle or yield up the great cardinal doctrine of protection." McKinley to L. G. Sherman, July 27, 1896, McKinley papers. On July 30 he wrote to Senator Elkins: "I agree exactly with you as to the issues of the day. We should, of course, insist upon sound money, but at the same time we should not forget the overwhelming importance of the tariff issue" (in McKinley papers). On August 1 McKinley wrote that he believed that interest in the silver issue was declining and that before the campaign ended the tariff would be the main issue. McKinley to C. A. Boutelle, August 1, 1896, McKinley papers.
52 New York *World*, June 23, 1896, 3.
53 Washington *Evening Star*, July 26, 1896, 1; Joseph Benson Foraker, *Notes of A Busy Life*, 2 vols. (Cincinnati, 1917), I, 491–2.
54 Hanna to Harrison, July 4, 1896, Harrison papers.
55 Canton *Repository*, September 20, 1896, 7.
56 *Ibid.*, 6.

57 W. J. Curtis to Spooner, July 20, 1896, Spooner papers; Theodore Roosevelt to Henry Cabot Lodge, July 30, 1896, in Elting E. Morison (ed.), *Letters of Theodore Roosevelt,* 8 vols. (Cambridge, 1951), I, 552; George N. Aldredge to John P. Hopkins, October 10, 1896, Usher papers; *New York Times,* July 28, 1896, 1.

58 McKinley to Kohlsaat, August 5, 1896, McKinley papers.

59 New York *World,* August 25, 1896, 2; St. Louis *Post Dispatch,* August 25, 1896, 1; August 26, 1896, 3.

60 Chandler to Charles Emory Smith, July 2, 1896; Chandler to McKinley, July 25, 1896, Chandler papers (LC).

61 Clarkson to H. G. McMillan, October 5, 1896, Clarkson papers.

62 Henry L. Stoddard, *As I Knew Them. Presidents and Politics from Grant to Coolidge* (New York and London, 1927), 241.

63 San Francisco *Chronicle,* July 3, 1896, 6; Herman H. Kohlsaat, *From McKinley to Harding, Personal Recollections of our Presidents* (New York and Philadelphia, 1923), 39; Harold F. Taggart, "The Party Realignment of 1896 in California," *Pacific Historical Review,* VIII (December, 1939), 441–2.

64 W. M. Osborne to McKinley, September 1, 1896, McKinley papers.

65 William Jennings Bryan, *First Battle, A Story of the Campaign of 1896* (Chicago, 1896), 396–7.

66 *New York Times,* August 27, 1896, 1.

67 Garret A. Hobart to McKinley, September 2, 1896, McKinley papers.

68 Terence V. Powderly, *The Path I Trod, The Autobiography of Terence V. Powderly* (New York, 1940), 294–8; Chicago *Tribune,* August 16, 1896, 16.

69 McKinley to Louis Theobald, July 13, 1896, McKinley papers.

70 McKinley to John Gallaher, July 13, 1896; McKinley to C. D. Chipman, July 28, 1896; McKinley to R. A. Jones, September 4, 1896, McKinley papers.

71 Dawes to Hanna, July 24 and 25, 1896, Dawes papers; James Chalmers to McKinley, August 17, 1896, La Follette papers; New York *World,* July 19, 1896, 2; Wight, *Payne,* 88.

72 New York *Journal,* October 12, 1896, 1; James H. Moynihan, *The Life of Archbishop John Ireland* (New York, 1953), 261.

73 Donald L. Kinzer, "The American Protective Association: A Study of Anti-Catholicism" (unpublished Ph.D. dissertation, University of Washington, 1954), 440.

74 Chicago *Tribune,* June 10, 1896, 2; September 18, 1896, 6; Canton *Repository,* September 24, 1896, 6.

75 Chicago *Tribune,* November 1, 1896, 34.

76 San Francisco *Chronicle,* October 22, 1896, 4; Boston *Evening Transcript,* October 28, 1896, 1; *New York Times,* November 1, 1896, 1, 2, 3.

77 Elsie Porter Mende, *An American Soldier and Diplomat, Horace Porter* (New York, 1927), 163–4.

78 New York *Tribune,* November 1, 1896, 1; *New York Times,* November 1, 1896, 1.

79 Dawes, *Journal,* 103–4.

80 San Francisco *Chronicle,* November 1, 1896, 22; Harold F. Taggart, "The Party Realignment of 1896 in California," 446–8.

400 Notes to Pages 292–298

81 *New York Times,* November 1, 1896, 1.
82 Bryan, *First Battle,* 566–7; Chicago *Tribune,* November 1, 1896, 3, 4.
83 New York *World,* October 30, 1896, 4.
84 Bynum to Cleveland, July 25, 1896, Cleveland papers.
85 Spooner to H. M. Kutchin, July 11, 1896, Spooner papers; Lodge to Joseph Benson Foraker, July 14, 1896, Foraker papers.
86 Indianapolis *Journal,* October 14, 1896, 1; Canton *Repository,* October 22, 1896.
87 *New York Times,* June 27, 1896, 1; Boston *Evening Transcript,* July 2, 1896, 6.
88 Hanna to McKinley, July 8, 1896, McKinley papers; *New York Times,* July 14, 1896, 3; Chicago *Tribune,* July 14, 1896, 4.
89 Cincinnati *Commercial Tribune,* July 27, 1896, 2; *New York Times,* August 1, 1896, 1; August 2, 1896, 2; August 3, 1896, 3; August 4, 1896, 2; Chicago *Tribune,* August 6, 1896, 3.
90 T. C. Platt to Levi P. Morton, August 4, 1896, Morton papers; Clarkson to Fessenden, July 21, 1896, October 15, 1896, Clarkson papers.
91 McKinley to Morton, August 7, 1896, Morton papers.
92 W. M. Osborne to McKinley, August 11, September 1, 1896, McKinley papers; Powell Clayton to Chandler, August 26, 1896, Chandler papers (LC); Samuel R. Thayer to Cushman K. Davis, August 31, 1896, Davis papers; Marion Butler to J. H. Lorimer, October 1, 1896, Butler papers; *New York Times,* October 2, 1896, 1; Chicago *Tribune,* October 7, 1896, 2; Royal, *Reminiscences,* 202–3; DeSantis, *Republicans Face the Southern Question,* 255–8.
93 A. T. Wimberley to Percy S. Heath, August 18, 1896; C. M. Puckette to Heath, August 18, 1896, Dawes papers; W. Breidenthal to Butler, September 14, 1896, Butler papers. Breidenthal wrote that he had "absolute proof" that Hanna was using money in Kansas to support the middle-of-the-road Populist opposition to Bryan. Z. T. Vinson to Bynum, October 7, 1896, Bynum papers. James A. Barnes, "The Gold Standard Democrats and the Party Conflict," *Mississippi Valley Historical Review,* XVII (December, 1930), 445.
94 Dawes to C. H. Bosworth, September 17, 1896, Dawes papers.
95 Clarkson to H. G. McMillan, October 5, 1896, Clarkson papers; James Boyle to Holloway, October 17, 1896, William R. Holloway papers (Indiana State Library); John P. Irish to George F. Parker, February 1, 1897, in "Letters Written by John P. Irish to George F. Parker," *Iowa Journal of History and Politics,* XXXI (July, 1933), 450; St. Louis *Post Dispatch,* September 10, 1896, 1.

CHAPTER 21

1 St. Louis *Post Dispatch,* August 13, 1896, 6.
2 William Jennings Bryan, "An Estimate [of James K. Jones] from William Jennings Bryan," in Farrar Newberry, *James K. Jones, The Plumed Knight of Arkansas* (n.p., 1913), 328–30; Willis J. Abbott, "James K. Jones," *Review of Reviews,* XIV (October, 1896), 427–8. Though a leader of the silver Democrats, Jones had devised a currency bill which he hoped would compromise the issue by satisfying both the radicals and the conservatives in his party. Jones to J. N. Camden, May 17,

1896; W. H. Lamar to Camden, May 27, 1896, and attached article, "Solution of the Silver Question," Johnson N. Camden papers (West Virginia Collection, University of West Virginia).

3 Chicago *Tribune*, August 3, 1896, 1.

4 St. Louis *Post Dispatch*, August 4, 1896, 7.

5 Reprinted in Chicago *Tribune*, August 7, 1896, 2.

6 St. Louis *Globe-Democrat*, July 27, 1896, 1; New York *World*, July 27, 1896, 1.

7 *New York Times*, August 3, 1896, 1; August 12, 1896, 8; August 13, 1896, 9; Chicago *Tribune*, August 4, 1896, 3; St. Louis *Post Dispatch*, August 12, 1896, 1.

8 St. Louis *Post Dispatch*, August 13, 1896, 6; August 14, 1896, 1; August 15, 1896, 8; *New York Times*, August 15, 1896, 2.

9 *Ibid.*, August 14, 1896, 1, 2; August 16, 1896, 1.

10 Vilas to Usher, September 25, 1896, Usher papers.

11 St Louis *Post Dispatch*, August 14, 1896, 1.

12 *Ibid.*, August 15, 1896, 7.

13 *Ibid.* There had been some opposition to Chicago, because all the newspapers published there were hostile to Bryan. William J. Stone to James K. Jones, July 31, 1896, Bryan papers; *New York Times*, August 3, 1896, 1.

14 *Ibid.*, August 16, 1896, 1; August 18, 1896, 8; Chicago *Tribune*, August 16, 1896, 1; Indianapolis *Journal*, August 16, 1896, 1.

15 *New York Times*, August 19, 1896, 1.

16 Richardson of Tennessee was a member of the original committee and was placed in command of the Washington office. Later he was brought to Chicago and Clark Howell assumed control of the Washington office. When giving a list of the campaign committee in *The First Battle* (p. 287), Bryan included Howell but not Richardson. *New York Times*, September 8, 1896, 2; Cincinnati *Commercial Tribune*, September 7, 1896, 1; Chicago *Tribune*, September 24, 1896, 3.

17 *New York Times*, August 16, 1896, 1.

18 W. J. Bryan to Gorman, December 13, 1896, Arthur Pue Gorman papers (Maryland Historical Society); *New York Times*, July 15, 1896, 4; August 22, 1896, 9; Washington *Evening Star*, July 17, 1896, 3.

19 James K. Jones to Teller, August 24, 1896, Teller papers; Elmer Ellis, *Henry Moore Teller, Defender of the West* (Caldwell, Idaho, 1941), 277–8.

20 Form letter signed by Charles J. Faulkner and I. N. Stevens, dated September 21, 1896, in scrapbook for campaign of 1896 in Wisconsin Historical Society. New York *World*, September 4, 1896, 6; *People's Party Paper*, September 4, 1896, 6; Chicago *Tribune*, September 5, 1896, 9.

21 St. Louis *Post Dispatch*, August 25, 1896, 1.

22 Chairman Jones in an interview with James Creelman (New York *World*, September 8, 1896, 2) said that his headquarters was not paying the salaries of any speakers, though they were contributing to the living and traveling expenses of a few. On September 11, 1896, George F. Washburn wrote from Chicago to Marion Butler (Butler papers): "If we had done half that we ought to do here, we would have been as badly in debt as Senator Jones is." On September 14 the Boston *Tran-*

script (p. 3) reported that for the past two weeks all the money spent at Chicago headquarters had been advanced by Daniel Campau, wealthy Michigan member of the campaign committee. In a form letter (Usher papers) sent out from Chicago headquarters, signed by F. U. Adams and dated September 16, 1896, this sentence appeared: "Because of our depleted campaign fund it would be helpful if you could help on expenses [of a special press service] but if you cannot we will furnish it free of charge as long as we can." Still the Democratic campaign committee had more money than the Populists. It was able to outbid the Populist campaign committee for Ignatius Donnelly's services. James K. Jones to Donnelly, September 23, 1896; J. A. Edgerton to Donnelly, October 3, 1896; Donnelly to Edgerton, October 9, 1896; James K. Jones to Donnelly, October 17, 1896, Donnelly papers. *New York Times,* September 14, 1896, 1.

23 St. Louis *Post Dispatch,* August 17, 1896, 4; September 10, 1896, 1.
24 William Jennings Bryan, *First Battle, A Story of the Campaign of 1896* (Chicago, 1896), 291–2.
25 Henry G. Davis to Jones, September 29, 1896, Davis papers; Boston *Evening Transcript,* October 3, 1896, 3.
26 *New York Times,* September 14, 1896, 1; Chicago *Tribune,* October 12, 1896, 1; October 16, 1896, 1; November 2, 1896, 1; Canton *Repository,* October 8, 1896, 6; October 15, 1896, 5; "Address to the Illinois Mine Workers and Others Who Toil for Wages" (Illinois Republican Labor League Committee, 1896), appendix.
27 Samuel R. Thayer to Cushman K. Davis, August 31, 1896, Davis papers.
28 James H. Graham to Bryan, July 15, 1896, Bryan papers.
29 Gorman to Marcus Daly, September 29, 1896, Gorman papers. In February, 1908, the New York *World* published a pamphlet titled "The Map of Bryanism. 1907. Twelve Years of Demagogy and Defeat. . . ." Giving figures which were purported to be taken from the books of the Democratic National Committee, this pamphlet claimed that Marcus Daly had contributed $159,000 to the Democratic campaign in 1896 and that altogether silver mine owners from western states had contributed $228,000.
30 Chicago *Tribune,* July 17, 1896, 6. The *Tribune* noted that one of its competitors had initiated the practice of using the term "Popocrats" to designate the Democratic-Populist groups which were supporting Bryan. Noting that it had heretofore used the rather unsatisfactory terms "Demopopulist" and "Dem-Pops," the *Tribune* found "Popocrats" more euphonious and descriptive. From it would be derived other terms: "Popocratic," "Popocratical," and "Popocratism."
31 St. Louis *Post Dispatch,* August 20, 1896, 10.
32 *Ibid.,* August 8, 1896, 1.
33 *New York Times,* August 6, 1896, 2.
34 St. Louis *Post Dispatch,* August 8, 1896, 1; August 9, 1896, 2; August 10, 1896, 1; August 11, 1896, 1.
35 *New York Times,* August 11, 1896, 1, 3.
36 Bryan, *First Battle,* 300.
37 Bryan was not the only one to think in such terms. In a letter to Bryan of July 16, 1896, Joseph C. Sibley of Pennsylvania advocated a hard campaign in the states of Michigan, Pennsylvania, Indiana, Illinois, and

Ohio. He wrote: "the battle ground is not in the South or West; the battle must be fought in the enemy's territory, and it will be won in the enemy's territory." Bryan papers.

38 *New York Times,* August 10, 1896, 1; August 11, 1896, 1, 3; August 12, 1896, 1, 3.

39 *Official Proceedings, Democratic,* 394.

40 New York *World,* August 15, 1896, 6. Bryan, *First Battle,* 337.

41 *New York Times,* August 14, 1896, 1, 2; August 15, 1896, 1; Chicago *Tribune,* August 16, 1896, 1.

42 *New York Times,* August 13, 1896, 3; August 14, 1896, 2.

43 H. V. Boynton to General James H. Wilson, James H. Wilson papers; Theodore Roosevelt to Anna Roosevelt, August 15, 1896, in Elting E. Morison (ed.), *The Letters of Theodore Roosevelt,* 8 vols. (Cambridge, 1951), I, 557; Alexander Dana Noyes, *The Market Place; Reminiscences of a Financial Editor* (Boston, 1938), 128–30.

44 Bryan, *First Battle,* 338.

45 St. Louis *Post Dispatch,* August 18, 1896, 2; August 19, 1896, 1; August 21, 1896, 1.

46 *New York Times,* October 17, 1896, 3, 4; October 18, 1896, 12; October 20, 1896, 1; October 21, 1896, 9.

47 *Ibid.,* October 25, 1896, 2.

48 *Ibid.,* September 27, 1896, 12.

49 *Ibid.,* September 29, 1896, 3.

50 *Ibid.,* September 30, 1896, 9.

51 *The Commoner* (January, 1917), 16–7. In June, 1915, speaking to his neighbors at Lincoln, Nebraska, Bryan said: "I congratulate you upon the fact that you enjoy an environment which lends itself to the calm consideration of the nation's welfare. You are especially fortunate in that you can take counsel of the *Producers of Wealth* and do not have to be irritated daily by the *Producers of Trouble.* It is well that you are thirty-six hours journey from the New York newspapers—the journalistic mosquitoes can not carry the germs of the red fever so far. . . ." *The Commoner* (July, 1915), 11–2.

52 Wayne C. Williams, *William Jennings Bryan* (New York, 1936), 170.

53 Henry M. Teller to Brooks Adams, September 3, 1896, Teller papers.

54 *Review of Reviews,* XIV (September, 1896), 261–2.

55 *Ibid.,* 262–3.

56 George B. McClellan, Jr., to Croker, September 8, 1896, George B. McClellan, Jr. papers (LC); *New York Times,* July 18, 1896, 3; August 1, 1896, 1; St. Louis *Post Dispatch,* August 1, 1896, 2.

57 *New York Times,* August 15, 1896, 1.

58 St. Louis *Post Dispatch,* August 17, 1896, 1; August 18, 1896, 2.

59 Bryan, *First Battle,* 349.

60 Elisha W. Keyes to H. C. Payne, October 28, 1896, Keyes papers. Keyes complained that the extensive newspaper coverage of Bryan's speeches and other activities were helping the Democrats.

61 Chicago *Tribune,* September 5, 1896, 9.

62 Bryan, *First Battle,* 378; Cincinnati *Commercial Tribune,* September 8, 1896, 6.

63 Andrew Carnegie to Wayne Mac Veagh, October 26, 1896, Andrew Carnegie papers. (LC). Carnegie, writing from New York, said, "I un-

derstand you feeling that the Bryan campaign was not to be taken seriously; but I have not met one friend here who does not say that if the election had taken place immediately after the nomination, that light-headed-blathering demagogue would have been President of the United States."

64 George A. Groot to William M. Stewart, August 31, 1896, Stewart papers. Entries dated September 7, 8, and 9, 1896, in Ignatius Donnelly Diary, Donnelly papers; James Manahan to his wife, September 9, 1896, Manahan papers (Minnesota Historical Society); *New York Times,* September 9, 1896, 1. Bryan, *First Battle,* 409.

65 Bryan, *First Battle,* 410.

66 *Ibid.*

67 *Ibid.,* 413.

68 *Ibid.,* 411.

69 *Ibid.,* 414.

70 *Ibid.,* 601.

71 *New York Times,* October 12, 1896, 1.

72 Entry dated October 10, 1896, in Donnelly Diary, Donnelly papers; Theodore Roosevelt to Lodge, October 21, 1896, in Morison, *Letters of T.R.,* I, 563.

73 Butler to James K. Jones, September 21, 1896, Butler papers.

74 B. F. Keith to Butler, September 19, 1896, Butler papers.

75 Bryan, *First Battle,* 534.

76 *New York Times,* October 14, 1896, 2.

77 *Ibid.,* September 21, 1896, 1; September 22, 1896, 1.

78 Bryan, *First Battle,* 467–8.

79 *Ibid.,* 479.

80 *Ibid.,* 489.

81 *Ibid.,* 510.

82 *Ibid.,* 545.

83 *Ibid.,* 583.

84 *Ibid.,* 595.

85 *Ibid.,* 481.

86 *Ibid.,* 565.

87 *Ibid.,* 596–7.

88 *New York Times,* October 20, 1896, 1.

89 *Ibid.,* September 25, 1896, 5; Bryan, *First Battle,* 484–8.

90 *Ibid.,* 604.

91 Robert E. Burke to Bryan, July 27, 1896, Bryan papers; St. Louis *Post Dispatch,* July 18, 1896, 3.

92 Florence Kelley to Henry Demarest Lloyd, October 1, 1896, Lloyd papers.

CHAPTER 22

1 The officers of the Populist National Executive Committee during the campaign were Butler, Raleigh, North Carolina, Chairman; J. A. Edgerton, Lincoln, Nebraska, Secretary; and Martin C. Rankin, Terre Haute, Indiana, Treasurer. The other members of the committee were George F. Washburn, Boston, Massachusetts; James R. Sovereign, Sulphur Springs, Arkansas; C. F. Taylor, Philadelphia, Pennsylvania;

H. W. Reed, Brunswick, Georgia; and John S. Dore, Fresno, California.
2 Butler to Washburn, August 31 and September 5, 1896, Butler papers; Washburn to Watson, September 3, 1896, Thomas E. Watson papers (Southern Historical Collection, University of North Carolina); St. Louis *Post Dispatch*, August 20, 1896, 2.
3 Butler to Rankin, September 11, 1896; Rankin to Butler, September 12, 1896, Butler papers.
4 Butler to E. T. Meredith, September 7, 1896, Butler papers.
5 Butler to Washburn, September 21, 1896, Butler papers; J. A. Edgerton to Donnelly, October 3, 1896, Donnelly papers.
6 Butler to J. H. Burnam, August 31, 1896; Butler to James L. Scott, September 3, 1896, Butler to John W. Breidenthal, September 12, 1896, Butler papers.
7 Butler to Sovereign, September 26, 1896, Butler papers.
8 Butler to Washburn, October 24, 1896, Butler papers.
9 Butler to C. C. Everson, September 5, 1896, Butler papers.
10 St. Louis *Post Dispatch*, August 20, 1896, 2.
11 Butler to Frank J. Thompson, August 31, 1896; Butler to J. M. Leach, August 31, 1896, Butler papers.
12 Butler to J. B. Bradley, August [?], 1896; Butler to J. A. Williams, August 31, 1896; H. W. Reed to Butler, September 4, 1896; Butler to Washburn, September 11, 1896, Butler papers.
13 Butler to R. E. Younger, September 3, 1896, Butler papers.
14 J. R. Sovereign to Butler, September 24, 1896, Butler papers.
15 Butler to M. C. Rankin, August 29, September 11, 17, and October 9, 1896; Rankin to Butler, September 19, 1896, Butler papers. In his letter of October 9, Butler wrote to Rankin: "We are financially stranded at Headquarters. A number of printing bills are now unpaid, and besides we have not a dollar in sight to meet even the incidental expenses of the office." The next day Butler wrote to Rankin acknowledging receipt of $100.
16 Butler to James K. Jones, August 24, 1896; Rankin to Butler, September 12, 1896; Butler to Edward Boyce, October 5, 1896, Butler papers, *New York Times*, September 9, 1896, 3.
17 Butler to W. R. Hearst, October 8, 1896; Butler to William P. St. John, October 10, 1896, Butler papers.
18 Butler to James K. Jones, October 17 and 24, 1896; Butler to C. J. Faulkner, October 17, 1896; Butler to Washburn, October 22, 1896, Butler papers.
19 C. H. Pirtle to Butler, October 27, 1896, Butler papers.
20 Copy, Arthur Sewall to J. K. Jones, August 31, 1896; Sewall to Bryan, September 1, 1896, Bryan papers.
21 John W. Breidenthal to Butler, August 2, and September 14, 1896; H. C. Childs to Butler, August 13, 1896; John C. Bell to Butler, September 7, 1896; Abe Steinberger to Butler, August 26, 1896; H. W. Reed to Butler, September 10 and 16, 1896; Butler to James Gunn, August 29, 1896; Butler to James K. Jones, September 7, 1896; Butler to John W. Breidenthal, September 7, 1896, Butler papers.
22 Butler to Joseph A. Bryan, August 28, 1896; Butler to H. C. Childs, August 29, September 7, 1896; Butler to J. C. Bell, August 29, September 7, 1896; Butler to Abe Steinberger, August 29, 1896; Butler to

John W. Breidenthal, August 29, September 7, 12, 16, 21, 1896; Butler to R. M. Patterson, September 1, 1896; Butler to John D. Haskell, September 7, 1896; Butler to Washburn, October 8, 1896, Butler papers.

23 Charleston (S.C.) *Weekly News and Courier,* September 16, 1896, 1.

24 Butler to J. K. Jones, September 18, 1896; Butler to Washburn, September 18, 1896, Butler papers.

25 Broadside, signed by Hal Ayer, n.d. [1896], Butler papers. Boston *Evening Transcript,* August 17, 1896, 1; Florence E. Smith, "The Populist Movement and its Influence in North Carolina" (unpublished Ph.D. dissertation, University of Chicago, 1929), 14–5; Joseph F. Steelman, "The Progressive Era in North Carolina, 1884–1917" (unpublished Ph.D. dissertation, University of North Carolina, 1955), 138; Philip J. Weaver, "The Gubernatorial Election of 1896 in North Carolina," (unpublished M.A. thesis, University of North Carolina, 1937), 45–62.

26 Butler to Jones, September 24 and 30, October 5 and 6, 1896; Butler to Washburn, September 24 and 29, October 5 and 8, 1896, Butler papers. S. P. Van Patten to Schilling, October 27, 1896, George A. Schilling Collection; Farrar Newberry, *James K. Jones, The Plumed Knight of Arkansas* (n.p., 1913), 214–5.

27 New York *World,* July 27, 1896, 1.

28 H. W. Reed to Butler, July 21 and August 22, 1896, Butler papers.

29 Watson to Butler, August 24, 1896; Butler to Watson, August 27, 1896; Butler to H. W. Reed, September 29, 1896, Butler papers.

30 Watson to Butler, July 28, 1896, Butler papers.

31 Watson to Butler, August 25, 1896, Butler papers.

32 Butler to Watson, August 27, 1896; H. W. Reed to Butler, October 9, 1896, Butler papers.

33 Watson to Butler, September 1, 1896, Butler papers.

34 H. W. Reed to Butler, September 4, 1896, Butler papers.

35 *Weekly Rocky Mountain News,* July 30, 1896, 4.

36 H. W. Reed to Butler, August 27, 1896; Butler to H. W. Reed, August 27, 1896, Butler papers; Reed to Watson, August 30, 1896, Watson papers.

37 Chicago *Tribune,* September 8, 1896, 1. Watson was quoted as saying of Sewall: "He is a wart on the party. He is a knot on the log. He is a dead weight to the ticket." *New York Times,* September 8, 1896, 2. Butler to Watson, September 8, 1896, Butler papers.

38 H. W. Reed to Butler, September 10, 1896; Butler to J. H. Edmisten, October 12, 1896; Butler to Thomas J. Middleton, October 12, 1896, Butler papers. Clipping, Nashville (Tenn.) *Banner,* September 11, 1896, in Butler papers.

39 Breidenthal to Butler, September 7, 1896; H. W. Reed to Butler, September 7, 1896, Butler papers; Raymond C. Miller, "The Populist Party in Kansas" (unpublished Ph.D. dissertation, University of Chicago, 1928), 301–4.

40 Breidenthal to Butler, September 5 and 12, 1896, Butler papers; *Kansas Semi-Weekly Capital,* September 8, 1896, 4; September 11, 1896, 1; September 15, 1896, 5.

41 Butler to H. W. Reed, September 18, 1896, Butler papers.

42 Butler to Washburn, September 29, 1896, October 1, 1896; Butler to Watson, September 30, 1896; Butler to Reed, October 2, 1896, Butler papers; Ernest D. Stewart, "The Populist Party in Indiana," *Indiana Magazine of History,* XV (March, 1919), 56–66.

43 Butler to Washburn, August 31 and September 5, 1896; Butler to L. C. Bateman, August 31 and September 5, 1896, Butler papers.

44 Butler to John S. Dore, September 5, 1896; Butler to Jeff D. Potter, September 5, 1896; Butler to Washburn, September 18, 1896; Butler to J. P. Buchanan, September 14, 1896, Butler papers.

45 Butler to Washburn, September 21, 1896, Butler papers.

46 Butler to Washburn, September 18 and October 6, 1896, Butler papers.

47 Baltimore *Weekly Sun,* October 31, 1896, 2.

48 Butler to J. P. Buchanan, October 19, 1896, Butler papers.

49 Butler to T. St. Clair Thompson, October 10, 1896; Butler to L. K. Taylor, October 12, 1896; Butler to Faulkner, October 12, 1896; Butler to Jones, October 22, 1896, Butler papers.

50 Butler to John O. Zabel, October 2 and 19, 1896; John W. Breidenthal to Butler, September 15, 1896, Butler papers.

51 Watson to Butler, August 24 and 25, 1896, Butler papers.

52 H. W. Reed to Butler, October 9, 1896, Butler papers. In this letter Reed quoted from a telegram which he had sent Butler that afternoon: "Have seen Watson. Unless Kansas and Colorado situation straightened on basis last vote or committee recognize straight ticket immediately there will be trouble."

53 Butler to Dr. C. K. Taylor, October 19, 1896; F. H. Hoover to T. E. Watson, October 19, 1896; Butler to Washburn, October 22, 1896; Butler papers.

54 [Butler] to Watson, October 26, 1896, Butler papers.

55 Watson to Butler, October 28, 1896, Butler papers.

56 *New York Times,* November 2, 1896, 1.

57 Chicago *Tribune,* August 7, 1896, 2.

58 Butler to J. K. Jones, August 29 and September 7, 1896; Butler to Washburn, August 31 and September 28, 1896; Butler to N. E. Baker, September 3, 1896; Butler to Wharton Barker, September 14, 1896, Butler papers.

59 J. R. Sovereign to Butler, August 6, September 24, 28, 1896; Butler to John W. Hayes, September 12, 1896, Butler papers.

60 Butler to Eugene Debs, September 12, 1896; Debs to Butler, September 14, 1896, Butler papers.

61 Ira Kipnis, *The American Socialist Movement, 1897–1912* (New York, 1952), 47–50.

62 Typed Ms., "Report of the National Executive Committee, Socialist Labor Party to the 9th National Convention, July 4, 1896," 7, Socialist Labor Party papers (Wisconsin Historical Society).

63 The Socialist Labor party ticket was for President, Charles H. Matchett, Brooklyn, New York; for Vice-President, Matthew Maguire, Paterson, New Jersey. *Public Opinion,* XXI (July 23, 1896), 105.

64 Victor L. Berger to Henry Demarest Lloyd, January 11, 1897, Lloyd papers.

65 James Peterson, "The Workers Divided; Organized Labor and the Elec-

tion of 1896" (unpublished M.A. thesis, Columbia University, 1941), 102; St. Louis *Post Dispatch*, August 10, 1896, 2.

66 New York *Tribune*, July 23, 1896, 13; *Chicago Tribune*, August 4, 1896, 6.

67 *Ibid.*, August 20, 1896, 2.

68 St. Louis *Post Dispatch*, August 20, 1896, 2.

69 *New York Times*, August 4, 1896, 3.

70 Stevens to Mrs. Bryan, December 13, 1896, Bryan papers.

71 Elmer Ellis, "Silver Republicans in the Election of 1896," *Mississippi Valley Historical Review*, XVIII (March, 1932), 533–4; Elmer Ellis, *Henry Moore Teller, Defender of the West* (Caldwell, Idaho, 1941), 280–3; Daniel J. Campau to Teller, November 2, 1896, Teller papers.

72 Teller to Bryan, July 20, 1896; James K. Jones to Teller, August 24, 1896, Teller papers.

73 Ellis, *Teller*, 279.

74 James K. Jones to Teller, August 24, 1896, Teller papers. Marion Butler to Norman M. Ruick, August 25, 1896; Butler to P. H. Blake, August 27, 1896; Butler to J. K. Jones, August 29 and September 7, 1896; Butler to Fred T. Dubois, August 29 and September 7, 1896; N. M. Ruick to Butler, August 29, 1896; Fred T. Dubois to Butler, September 2, 1896; J. H. Anderson to Butler, September 3, 1896; P. H. Blake to Butler, September 3, 1896, Butler papers. Boston *Evening Transcript*, September 14, 1896, 3; Ellis, *Teller*, 277–8.

CHAPTER 23

1 Chauncey Depew, *My Memories of Eighty Years* (New York, 1923), 149–50; Herman H. Kohlsaat, *From McKinley to Harding; Personal Recollections of our Presidents* (New York and Philadelphia, 1923), 50–3.

2 Arthur F. Mullen, *Western Democrat* (New York, 1940), 100.

3 An Irishman from Minneapolis, James Manahan, was in Lincoln, Nebraska, during the summer of the campaign. His letters to his wife (now in the Minnesota Historical Society) make it appear that Lincoln was the scene of perpetual free silver oratory. All the silver leaders who came to town were expected to speak on the great issue of the day. Manahan reported that on one October evening, when two United States Senators, William V. Allen and William A. Stewart, were in Lincoln, both were scheduled to speak in the same hall. When Manahan arrived at the hall, it was filled; and there was a great crowd in the street outside. Eventually it was arranged that Senator Stewart should talk to the crowd inside the hall, while Allen, standing in a wagon, should address those outside. After speaking for an hour Allen became too hoarse to continue; and the crowd called for Manahan, who spoke to them for half an hour. Manahan to his wife, October 25, 1896, Manahan papers.

4 William Jennings Bryan, *First Battle, A Story of the Campaign of 1896* (Chicago, 1896), 535; New York *Journal*, September 21, 1896, 2.

5 Victor Lawson to H. N. McKinney, November 2, 1896, Victor F. Lawson papers (Newberry Library). Lawson described the educational

campaign which he had conducted in the two newspapers which he controlled, the Chicago *Record* and the Chicago *Daily News*. He reported that in the *Daily News* for the last month of the campaign he had conducted a column under the title, "Should the wage-earner vote for Free Silver?" He said that he had carefully avoided any action which would compromise his newspaper as an independent journal. Yet he believed that this column had caused many workingmen to vote for McKinley. Through the summer and fall of the campaign the *New York Times* carried a column under the heading, "Practical Talks about Silver" and signed "Wage Earner."

6   Chicago *Tribune*, August 6, 1896, 3; August 16, 1896, 15; St. Louis *Post Dispatch*, September 5, 1896, 3; September 6, 1896, 1.

7   George Pullman to Harrison, September 10, 1896, Harrison papers; Chicago *Tribune*, August 6, 1896, 3; St. Louis *Post Dispatch*, August 30, 1896, 1; New York *Journal*, October 13, 1896, 5.

8   Walter M. Raymond to Lloyd, August 27, 1896, Lloyd papers; Leaflet, "To the Employees of the Chicago, Peoria, & St. Louis Railroad," dated September 19, 1896, and signed by C. H. Bosworth, McKinley papers. Dawes to C. H. Bosworth, October 2, 1896, Dawes papers. Dawes told Bosworth that the Republican campaign committee had arranged for the distribution of 900,000 copies of this leaflet. McGhee to Col. E. J. Sanford, July 9, 1896; John K. Cowan to McGhee, July 11, 1896; McGhee to J. W. Thomas, July 16, 1896; McGhee to Cowan, July 19, 1896, in Stanley J. Folmsbee and Marguerite B. Hamer (eds.), "The Presidential Election of 1896 as Reflected in the Correspondence of Charles McClung McGhee," *The East Tennessee Historical Society's Publications*, XXII (1950), 160–3; St. Louis *Post Dispatch*, August 7, 1896, 5; James Peterson, "The Workers Divided. Organized Labor and the Election of 1896" (unpublished M.A. thesis, Columbia University, 1941), 112–3.

9   *New York Times*, July 26, 1896, 4; Chicago *Tribune*, July 27, 1896, 6; July 30, 1896, 12; August 3, 1896, 6.

10   Charles Leonhardt to James Callaway, July 21, 1896, in Folmsbee and Hamer, "The Presidential Election of 1896 . . . ," 164; W. M. Leonard to Dawes, August 8, 1896, Dawes papers. Entry dated October 2 [1896], in Donnelly Diary, Minnesota Historical Society. Boston *Evening Transcript*, September 10, 1896, 10; *New York Times*, October 28, 1896, 1.

11   *People's Party Paper*, December 27, 1895, 4; *Oregon State Journal*, January 4, 1896, 1; George R. Brown (ed.), *Reminiscences of Senator William R. Stewart of Nevada* (New York and Washington, 1908), 320–3; Lawrence J. Scheidler, "Silver and Politics, 1893–1896" (unpublished Ph.D. dissertation, University of Indiana, 1936), 220–1; Walter LaFeber, "The Background of Cleveland's Venezuelan Policy: A Reinterpretation," *American Historical Review*, LXVI (July, 1961), 948, 965. LaFeber concluded that the political situation played no important part in Cleveland's policy in the Venezuelan crisis.

12   John Hay to McKinley, August 3, 1896, McKinley papers.

13   Festus P. Summers (ed.), *The Cabinet Diary of William L. Wilson* (Chapel Hill, N. Car., 1951), 108–9.

14   *New York Times*, August 18, 1896, 3.

15 William A. White, *The Autobiography of William Allen White* (New York, 1946), 284–5.
16 Copy, Carnegie to Gladstone, September 28, 1896, Carnegie papers.
17 Chicago *Tribune*, September 27, 1896, 28.
18 *Ibid.*, October 23, 1896, 6.
19 Boston *Evening Transcript*, September 14, 1896, 3.
20 Chicago *Tribune*, September 28, 1896, 2.
21 *Ibid.*, September 22, 1896, 6.
22 Rev. Henry E. Barnes to Bryan, July 31, 1896, quoted in Canton *Repository*, August 2, 1896, 2; Chicago *Tribune*, August 8, 1896, 12; New York *Tribune*, November 1, 1896, 6.
23 Speaking in Boston during this campaign Bryan said that the silver question was a moral question and that "your financiers will have to study morality before they can preach much finance in this campaign." Bryan, *First Battle*, 501.
24 St. Louis *Post Dispatch*, August 10, 1896, 8.
25 Wall to Vilas, August 13, 1896, Vilas papers.
26 John C. T[omlinson] to Bourke [Cockran], July 16, 1896; Cockran to John H. Lewis, September 10, 1896, Cockran papers; Theodore Roosevelt to Anna Roosevelt Cowles, July 26, 1896, in Elting E. Morison (ed.) *The Letters of Theodore Roosevelt*, 8 vols. (Cambridge, 1951), I, 550; Francis J. Parker to Palmer, October 12, 1896, Palmer papers; Chicago *Tribune*, May 13, 1896, 6; Baltimore *Weekly Sun*, September 19, 1896, 4.
27 Note signed by E. C. Wall, dated November 2, 1896, in "Scrapbook of Campaign Documents—1896," in Wisconsin Historical Society. *New York Times*, November 2, 1896, 1; November 3, 1896, 2.
28 St. Louis *Post Dispatch*, November 1, 1896, 1; New York *Journal*, November 2, 1896, 5; *New York Times*, November 2, 1896, 1.
29 St. Louis *Post Dispatch*, November 2, 1896, 4.
30 Florence Kelley to Henry Demarest Lloyd, October 15, 1896, Lloyd papers; entry dated October 2, 1896, in Ignatius Donnelly Diary, Donnelly papers; New York *Journal*, October 13, 1896, 5; *New York Times*, October 28, 1896, 1; November 2, 1896, 1; James Manahan, *Trials of a Lawyer* (n.p., n.d.), 20–1; Wayne C. Williams, *William Jennings Bryan* (New York, 1936), 190; Peterson, "Workers Divided," 112–3.
31 Henry Cabot Lodge to Cushman K. Davis, November 9, 1896, Davis papers; New York *Tribune*, November 6, 1896, 2.
32 W. A. White, *Autobiography*, 285; Manahan, *Trials*, 21; Charleston (S.C.) *Weekly News and Courier*, October 14, 1896, 1; Chicago *Tribune*, October 23, 1896, 3.
33 William E. Curtis to his mother, October 31, 1896; C. W. Jordan to Curtis, October 30, 1896, Curtis papers; Summers, *Cabinet Diary of Wilson*, 158–9; Barnes, "The Gold Standard Democrats and the Party Conflict," *Mississippi Valley Historical Review*, XVII (December, 1930), 443.
34 New York *Tribune*, November 2, 1896, 2.
35 *Ibid.*
36 Andrew Carnegie to Wayne Mac Veagh, October 26, 1896; Carnegie to J. H. Reed, October 26, 1896, Carnegie papers; entries dated November 2, 3, and 4, 1896, in diary of Henry W. Ball, on microfilm in Southern Historical Collection, University of North Carolina.

37 Bryan to Altgeld, September 29, 1897, John Peter Altgeld Collection (Illinois State Historical Library); St. Louis *Post Dispatch*, November 4, 1896, 4; November 7, 1896, 5; *Oregon State Journal*, November 7, 1896, 5; Boston *Evening Transcript*, November 25, 1896, 1; Altgeld, *Live Questions*, 691–2.

38 Summers, *Cabinet Diary of Wilson*, 64.

39 James K. Jones to Wharton Barker, November 4, 1896, Barker papers; *New York Times*, November 5, 1896, 1; Bryan, *First Battle*, 605.

40 New York *Tribune*, November 21, 1896, 1; *Weekly Rocky Mountain News*, November 26, 1896, 1; Bryan, *First Battle*, 609.

41 Frank Stephenson to Bryan, November 5, 1896; Leon O. Bailey to Bryan, November 9, 1896, Bryan papers; Julius Rosenheimer to Marion Butler, November 9, 1896; Butler to W. J. Peele, November 9, 1896; Butler to F. McQuary, December 14, 1896; Butler to John C. Sutherland, December 15, 1896, Butler papers; A. J. Warner to Moreton Frewen, November 24, 1896; George Fred Williams to Frewen, December 5, 1896, Frewen papers; John P. Altgeld to James K. Jones, December 5, 1896, Altgeld papers; Altgeld to Lambert Tree, May 11, 1897, Tree papers; Altgeld, *Live Questions*, 702–4, 706–22; Chicago *Tribune*, November 6, 1896; Kansas *Semi-Weekly Capital*, November 20, 1896, 4.

42 *New York Times*, November 6, 1896, 5.

43 The election statistics cited here and subsequently are derived, unless otherwise noted, from W. Dean Burnham, *Presidential Ballots, 1836–1892* (Baltimore, 1955) and Edgar Eugene Robinson, *The Presidential Vote, 1896–1932* (Palo Alto, California, 1934).

44 Chicago *Tribune*, November 9, 1896, 6; William T. Kuhns, *Memories of Old Canton and My Personal Recollections of William McKinley* (privately published, *c.* 1937), 61.

45 Hal W. Ayer to Butler, November 7, 1896, Butler papers.

46 William Diamond, "Urban and Rural Voting in 1896," *American Historical Review*, XLVI (January, 1941), 289.

47 *Ibid.*, 286, 293.

48 *Ibid.*, 294.

49 *Ibid.*, 291.

50 John H. Gear to L. T. Michener, July 20, 1896, Michener papers; Washington Hesing to William McKinley, July 25, 1896, and J. I. Irwin to Moses P. Handy, July 25, 1896, McKinley papers; E. J. Burnside to Ellis Usher, July 27, 1896, Usher papers; Ellis Usher to Vilas, July 29, 1896, Vilas papers; Louisville *Courier-Journal*, June 22, 1896, 1; Boston *Evening Transcript*, August 10, 1896, 5.

51 Boston *Evening Transcript*, October 22, 1896, 4; Bryan, *First Battle*, 483.

52 Altgeld, *Live Questions*, 702, 707–8, 814–5; Samuel P. Hays, *The Response to Industrialism, 1885–1914* (Chicago, 1957), 46–7; Frederick J. Turner, *The Frontier in American History* (New York, 1920), 237–9; Chicago *Tribune*, November 4, 1896, 1.

53 Boston *Evening Transcript*, October 20, 1896, 4; October 21, 1896, 4; Thomas R. Ross, *Jonathan Prentiss Dolliver, A Study in Political Integrity and Independence* (Iowa City, Iowa, 1958), 131; Harold U. Faulkner, *Politics, Reform and Expansion, 1890–1900* (New York, 1959), 209–10.

Bibliography

Included here are separate and complete lists of the manuscript collections, newspapers, and unpublished dissertations consulted in the preparation of this book. Provided also is a selected list of published materials on the currency question. For other published materials (such as letters, diaries, biographies, and special studies) relevant to the historical developments covered in *The Presidential Election of 1896,* the reader is referred to the notes.

MANUSCRIPTS

James Franklin Aldrich Papers, Chicago Historical Society.
William B. Allison Papers, Iowa State Department of History and Archives.
John Peter Altgeld Collection, Illinois State Historical Library.

Henry W. Ball Diaries (microfilm), Southern Historical Collection, University of North Carolina.
Wharton Barker Papers, Library of Congress.
John Bassell Papers, West Virginia Collection, West Virginia University.
Breckinridge Family Papers (William C. P. Breckinridge), Library of Congress.
William Jennings Bryan Papers, Library of Congress.
Marion Butler Papers, Southern Historical Collection, University of North Carolina.
William Dallas Bynum Papers, Library of Congress.

Caffery Papers (Senator Donelson Caffery), Southern Historical Collection, University of North Carolina.
Johnson N. Camden Papers, West Virginia Collection, West Virginia University.
Joseph G. Cannon Papers, Illinois State Historical Library.
Andrew Carnegie Papers, Library of Congress.
Edward W. Carmack Papers, Southern Historical Collection, University of North Carolina.
Henry A. Castle Papers, Minnesota Historical Society.
William E. Chandler Papers, Library of Congress.
William E. Chandler Papers, New Hampshire Historical Society.
James S. Clarkson Papers, Library of Congress.
Grover Cleveland Papers, Library of Congress.
William Bourke Cockran Papers, New York Public Library.

Shelby M. Cullom Papers, Illinois State Historical Library.
William Edmond Curtis Papers, Library of Congress.

Cushman K. Davis Papers, Minnesota Historical Society.
Henry Gassaway Davis Papers, West Virginia Collection, West Virginia University.
Charles G. Dawes Papers, Northwestern University.
Alston G. Dayton Papers, West Virginia Collection, West Virginia University.
Charles Dick Papers, Ohio Historical Society.
General Grenville M. Dodge Papers, Iowa State Department of History and Archives.
Ignatius Donnelly Papers, Minnesota Historical Society.

Stephen Benton Elkins Papers, West Virginia Collection, West Virginia University.

Joseph W. Fifer Papers, Illinois State Historical Library.
Albert B. Fleming Papers, West Virginia Collection, West Virginia University.
Joseph Benson Foraker Papers, Historical and Philosophical Society of Ohio.
Moreton Frewen Papers, Library of Congress.

Jacob H. Gallinger Papers, New Hampshire Historical Society.
Arthur Pue Gorman Papers, Maryland Historical Society.
J. Bryan Grimes Collection, Southern Historical Collection, University of North Carolina.

Murat Halstead Papers, Historical and Philosophical Society of Ohio.
Benjamin Harrison Papers, Library of Congress.
Carter Harrison Papers, Newberry Library.
Nils P. Haugen Papers, Wisconsin Historical Society.
John Hay Papers, Library of Congress.
John Steele Henderson Papers, Southern Historical Collection, University of North Carolina.
Frederick William Holls Papers, Columbia University.

David M. Key Papers (microfilm), Southern Historical Collection, University of North Carolina.
Elisha W. Keyes Papers, Wisconsin Historical Society.

Robert M. La Follette Papers, Wisconsin Historical Society.
Daniel S. Lamont Papers, Library of Congress.
Victor F. Lawson Papers, Newberry Library.
John Lind Papers, Minnesota Historical Society.
Henry Demarest Lloyd Papers, Wisconsin Historical Society.

George B. McClellan, Jr., Papers, Library of Congress.
William McKinley Papers, Library of Congress.
Franklin MacVeagh Papers, Library of Congress.
James Manahan Papers, Minnesota Historical Society.

Louis T. Michener Papers, Library of Congress.
William R. Morrison Papers, Illinois State Historical Library.

Knute Nelson Papers, Minnesota Historical Society.

Richard Olney Papers, Library of Congress.

John M. Palmer Papers, Illinois State Historical Library.
Lewis B. Parsons Papers, Illinois State Historical Library.
William J. Peele Papers, Southern Historical Collection, University of North Carolina.
Orville Hitchcock Platt Papers, Connecticut State Library.

Matthew Stanley Quay Papers, Library of Congress.

James Graham Ramsey Papers, Southern Historical Collection, University of North Carolina.
Thomas C. Richmond Papers, Wisconsin Historical Society.
Daniel L. Russell Papers, Southern Historical Collection, University of North Carolina.
Daniel Joseph Ryan Collection, Ohio Historical Society.

George A. Schilling Collection, Illinois State Historical Library.
Robert Schilling Papers, Wisconsin Historical Society.
John Coit Spooner Papers, Library of Congress.
William M. Stewart Papers, Nevada State Historical Society.

James A. Tawney Papers, Minnesota Historical Society.
Judge Robert S. Taylor Mss., Indiana State Library.
Henry Moore Teller Papers, State Historical Society of Colorado.
John Robert Thomas Papers, Library of Congress.
Lambert Tree Papers, Newberry Library.

Ellis B. Usher Papers, Wisconsin Historical Society.

William F. Vilas Papers, Wisconsin Historical Society.

Francis Amasa Walker Papers, Library of Congress.
Henry Watterson Papers, Library of Congress.
Thomas E. Watson Papers, Southern Historical Collection, University of North Carolina.
Luman H. Weller Papers, Wisconsin Historical Society.
Albert B. White Papers, West Virginia Collection, West Virginia University.
William Collins Whitney Papers, Library of Congress.
James H. Wilson Papers, Library of Congress.

NEWSPAPERS

Atlanta (Ga.) *People's Party Paper* [weekly].
Baltimore *Weekly Sun.*
Boston *Evening Transcript.*
Canton (Ohio) *Repository.*

Charleston (S.C.) *Weekly News and Courier.*
Chicago *Daily News.*
Chicago *Tribune.*
Cincinnati *Commercial Gazette.*
Denver *Rocky Mountain News* [daily].
Denver *Weekly Rocky Mountain News.*
Indianapolis *Journal.*
Kansas (Topeka) *Semi-Weekly Capital.*
Louisville *Courier-Journal.*
New York *Journal.*
New York Times.
New York *Tribune.*
New York *World.*
Oregon (Eugene) *State Journal.*
St. Louis *Globe-Democrat.*
St. Louis *Post Dispatch.*
San Francisco *Chronicle.*
Washington, D.C., *Evening Star.*

UNPUBLISHED DISSERTATIONS

Calvin, Elsie Ferguson, "The Candidacy of William McKinley for the Presidency," M.A., University of Wisconsin, 1926.
Clevenger, Homer, "Agrarian Politics in Missouri, 1880–1896," Ph.D., University of Missouri, 1940.
Felt, Thomas Edward, "The Rise of Mark Hanna," Ph.D., Michigan State University, 1960.
Fuller, Leon Webber, "The Populist Regime in Colorado," Ph.D., University of Wisconsin, 1933.
Furst, Ralph Henry, "William McKinley in Relation to the Political Issues, Protective Tariff and Sound Money, 1870 to 1896," M.A., University of Chicago, 1932.
Hantke, Richard Watson, "The Life of Elisha William Keyes," Ph.D., University of Wisconsin, 1942.
Kinzer, Donald Louis, "The American Protective Association: A Study of Anti-Catholicism," Ph.D., University of Washington, 1954.
Leslie, Helen, "The Attitude of the Republican and Democratic Parties Towards Free Silver from 1884 to 1896," M.A., University of Wisconsin, 1912.
Lutzky, Seymour, "The Reform Editors and Their Press," Ph.D., State University of Iowa, 1951.
Miller, Raymond Curtis, "The Populist Party in Kansas," Ph.D., University of Chicago, 1928.
Nixon, Herman Clarence, "The Populist Movement in Iowa," Ph.D., University of Chicago, 1925.
Peterson, James, "The Workers Divided. Organized Labor and the Election of 1896," M.A., Columbia University, 1941.
Schafer, Joseph, Jr., "The Presidential Election of 1896," Ph.D., University of Wisconsin, 1941.
Scheidler, Lawrence John, "Silver and Politics, 1893–1896," Ph.D., University of Indiana, 1936.

Silveus, Marian, "The Antecedents of the Campaign of 1896," Ph.D., University of Wisconsin, 1932.

Smith, Florence Emeline, "The Populist Movement and its Influence in North Carolina," Ph.D., University of Chicago, 1929.

Steelman, Joseph Flake, "The Progressive Era in North Carolina, 1884–1917," Ph.D., University of North Carolina, 1955.

Stevenson, Marietta, "William Jennings Bryan as a Political Leader," Ph.D., University of Chicago, 1926.

Thompson, Bess Lindsay, "Hanna and McKinley, 1892–1897," M.A., University of Wisconsin, 1925.

Tree, Robert Lloyd, "Victor Fremont Lawson and His Newspapers, 1890–1900. A Study of the Chicago *Daily News* and the Chicago *Record*," Ph.D., Northwestern University, 1959.

Weaver, Philip Johnson, "The Gubernatorial Election of 1896 in North Carolina," M.A., University of North Carolina, 1937.

Wellborn, Fred Wilmot, "The Silver Republicans, 1890–1900," Ph.D., University of Wisconsin, 1926.

Wilcox, Benton Harris, "A Reconsideration of the Character and Economic Basis of Northwestern Radicalism," Ph.D., University of Wisconsin, 1933.

Woodard, Douglas Dutro, "The Presidential Election of 1896," M.A., Georgetown University, 1949.

PAMPHLETS, BOOKS, AND ARTICLES ON MONEY

Address to the Illinois Mine Workers and Others Who Toil for Wages. N.p., Illinois Republican Labor League Committee, 1896 (in Illinois State Historical Library).

Address of General A. J. Warner of Ohio, at the First Annual Meeting of the American Bimetallic League, Held at Washington, February 22, 23 and 24, 1893. Washington, D.C.: George R. Gray, 1893 (in University of Chicago).

American Bimetallic League. *Facts About Silver.* Washington, D.C.: Hartman & Cadick, 1895.

Andrews, Edward Benjamin. "Tariff Reform and Monetary Reform." *North American Review,* 158 (April, 1894), 464–76.

Atkinson, Edward. *The Cost of Bad Money.* Philadelphia: Sound Money League of Pennsylvania, [1895].

Barcus, James S. *The Boomerang or Bryan's Speech With the Wind Knocked Out.* New York: J. S. Barcus & Co., 1896.

Barley, Cotton M. [pseud.]. *The Financial School at Farmerville.* Chicago: Currency Publishing House, 1895.

Bell, Henry Allen. *Voters' Guide* [revised]. *Points on Coinage of Money and Standard of Money Account.* Springfield, Ill.: State Register Printing House, 1896.

Bland, Richard P. "The Future of Silver." *North American Review,* 160 (March, 1895), 345–51.

———. "The Hopes of Free Silver." *North American Review,* 158 (May, 1894), 554–62.

Bliss, H. L. *Coin's Financial Fraud. A Complete and Comprehensive Treatise on the Currency Question, And an Answer to and Complete Refutation of the Advocates of the Free Coinage of Silver.* Chicago: Donohue, Henneberry & Co., 1895.

Bryan, William Jennings. "Has the Election Settled the Money Question?" *North American Review,* 163 (December, 1896), 703–10.

Dawes, Charles G. *The Banking System of the United States And its Relation to the Money and Business of the Country.* Chicago: Rand, McNally & Co., 1894.

Del Mar, Alex. *Story of the Gold Conspiracy as Told at the Memphis Convention.* Chicago: Charles H. Kerr & Co., 1895.

Donnelly, Ignatius. *The American People's Money.* Chicago: Laird & Lee, 1895.

Fisher, Willard. " 'Coin' and His Critics." *Quarterly Journal of Economics,* X (January, 1896), 187–208.

Fisher, Willard. "Recent Books on Money." *Quarterly Journal of Economics,* X (April, 1896), 324–36.

Harvey, W[illiam] H. *Coin's Financial Series. The Crime of 1873 and the Harvey-Laughlin Joint Debate.* Chicago: Coin Publishing Co., 1895.

————. *Coin's Financial School.* Chicago: Coin Publishing Co., 1894.

————. " 'Coin's Financial School' and its Censors." *North American Review,* 161 (July, 1895), 71–9.

————. *Coin's Financial School Up to Date.* Chicago: Coin Publishing Co., 1895.

Helena [Montana] Bimetallic Club. *Prosperity, How to Restore It. Are You For England or America? An Address to Eastern Business Men By Their Western Patrons.* Helena, Montana: Helena Bimetallic Club, 1896 (in Newberry Library).

Horr, Roswell G. and William H. Harvey. *The Great Debate on the Financial Question.* Chicago: Debate Publishing Co., 1895.

Laughlin, J[ames] Laurence. *Facts About Money.* Chicago: E. A. Weeks & Co., 1895.

Lewelling, L. D. "Problems Before the Western Farmer." *North American Review,* 160 (January, 1895), 16–20.

Lexis, Dr. W. "The Present Monetary Situation." *Economic Studies,* I (October, 1896), 217–81.

Miller, Henry G. *Chapters on Silver as Published in the Chicago Times in the Summer of 1894.* Chicago: Coin Publishing Co., [1894?].

Norton, Seymour F. *Ten Men of Money Island.* Chicago: Chicago Sentinel Publishing Co., 1891.

Opening Address of General A. J. Warner, President of the American Bimetallic League, Delivered Before the Silver Convention at Chicago, August 1, 1893. Adopted as the Address of the Convention to the People. Washington, D.C.: George R. Gray, 1893.

Proceedings of the Bimetallic Conference Held at Washington, D.C., January 22 and 23, 1896. Including Resolutions and Address to the People of the U.S. Chicago, Illinois: American Bimetallic Union, 1896.

Proceedings of the First National Silver Convention Held at St. Louis, November 26, 27, and 28, 1889. St. Louis: Buxton & Skinner Stationery Co., 1889.

Pyle, J. G. *Cheap Money, Experiments in Money Making. The Farmer and the Cheap Dollar. Facts About Free Silver Coinage.* St. Paul, Minn.: no publisher, 1894 (in Knute Nelson papers, Minnesota Historical Society).

Chicago *Record. Free Silver Coinage Debate.* Chicago: Chicago *Record,* 1896. A compilation of articles on all sides of the silver question which appeared in Chicago *Record* during the campaign of 1896.

Roberts, Isaac. *Wages, Fixed Incomes and the Free Coinage of Silver or the Danger Involved in the Free Coinage of Silver at the Ratio of 16 to 1....* Philadelphia: John Highlands, 1896.

Taubeneck, H[erman] E. *The Condition of the American Farmer.* Chicago: Schulte Publishing Co., 1896.

Taussig, F. W. *The Silver Situation in the United States.* New York: G. P. Putnam's Sons, 1896.

Teller, James H. *The Battle of the Standards.* Chicago: Schulte Publishing Co., 1896.

C[harles] S. Thomas. "The Silver Side of the Question." *Century Magazine,* 47 (January, 1894), 473–6.

Tourgee, Albion W. *The War of the Standards. Coin and Credit versus Coin Without Credit.* New York and London: G. P. Putnam's Sons, 1896.

Tuttle, Charles R. *The New Democracy and Its Prophet.* Chicago: Charles H. Kerr & Co., 1896.

Waite, Davis H. "Are the Silver States Ruined?" *North American Review,* 158 (January, 1894), 24–9.

Walker, Francis A. "The Relation of Changes in the Volume of the Currency to Prosperity." *Economic Studies,* I (April, 1896), 23–45.

Warner, Adoniram Judson. *The Appreciation of Money: Its Effects on Debts, Industry, and National Wealth....* Philadelphia: Henry Carey Baird & Co., 1877.

———. *The Monetary Conference of 1881. The Effect of a Bi-Metallic Union on the Currencies of the Different Countries.* Marietta, Ohio: Times Steam Printing Establishment, n.d.

———. *Relation of Money to Bank Credits.* Washington, D.C.: George R. Gray, 1891.

———. *The Source of Value in Money, and the Proper Regulation of the Volume of Currency....* Philadelphia: Henry Carey Baird & Co., 1882.

Wells, David A. "The Downfall of Certain Financial Fallacies." *Forum,* XVI (October, 1893), 131–49.

White, Horace. "Coin's Financial Fool." *Sound Currency,* II (May 1, 1895), 1–20.

———. *Money and Banking.* Boston and London: Ginn & Co., 1895.

Index

419